Orientalism and Religion

'Drawing on a host of contemporary social and critical theorists, Richard King has written an impressive and truly cross-disciplinary study that tackles head-on some of the field's most deeply ingrained yet troublesome presumptions. *Orientalism and Religion* is therefore a crash course in intellectual self-defence, a primer for those who have long suspected that there is a powerful yet largely undetected politics moving within rhetorics concerning such "things" as unmediated experiences of the real. In recommending that religion be understood as an aspect of culture and, moreover, that the academic study of religion be redescribed along the lines of cultural studies, King joins a growing number of intellectuals who have stepped forward to accept the challenge of modernist roots. Accordingly, *Orientalism and Religion* promises to help set the terms for future debates on the status, methods, and theories of the study of religion.'

Russell T. McCutcheon, Southwest Missouri State University

'Richard King's *Orientalism and Religion* provides an insightful and provocative contribution to a recent series of studies that can be best characterized as "colonial discourse analysis". It is not so much about India and Europe as it is about Western "fantasies" and "constructions" about "India" and "Europe". The book rightly calls for a new critical "self-reflexivity" and a much more sophisticated "new comparativism".'

Gerald J. Larson, Indiana University

'This is an important book. The main theme, the "othering" of the East, is highly significant and original, painstakingly documented, and with major implications for western scholarship.'

Grace Jantzen, University of Manchester

Richard King is Reader in Religious Studies at the University of Stirling. He is the author of *Early Advaita Vedānta and Buddhism* and *Indian Philosophy: An Introduction to Hindu and Buddhist Thought*.

Orientalism and Religion

Postcolonial theory, India and 'the mystic East'

Richard King

London and New York

First published 1999 by Routledge
11 New Fetter Lane, London EC4P 4EE

Simultaneously published in the USA and Canada
by Routledge
29 West 35th Street, New York, NY 10001

Routledge is an imprint of the Taylor & Francis Group

Typeset in Times by Routledge
Printed and bound in Great Britain by MPG Books Ltd, Bodmin

British Library Cataloguing in Publication Data
A catalogue record for this book is available from the British Library

Library of Congress Cataloging-in-Publication Data
King, Richard
Orientalism and religion : post-colonial theory, India and the mystic
East / Richard King.
p. cm.
Includes bibliographical references and index.
1. India–Religion–Study and teaching. 2. Religions–Study and
teaching. 3. Philosophy, Indic–Study and teaching. I. Title.
BL2203.K56   1999   98-46343
200'.7–dc21   CIP

ISBN 0–415–20257–4 (hbk)
ISBN 0–415–20258–2 (pbk)

For Juli, my very own 'Fire CF'

Contents

Acknowledgements   ix

Introduction: changing the subject   **1**

1 The power of definitions: a genealogy of the idea of 'the mystical'   **7**
*The problem with definitions – Origins of the term 'mysticism' –
Medieval notions of the mystical – Modern definitions of
mysticism – The 'mystical' versus the 'rational' – 'Mysticism'
and the construction of modern philosophy – Silencing the
Orient: the absence of 'the mystical' in histories of
philosophy*

2 Disciplining religion   **35**
*Christian theology and the category of 'religion' – Secularism
and the 'iatrogenic' effect of studying religion – The
Enlightenment roots of religious studies – Modelling
religious studies: theology or 'cultural studies'*

3 Sacred texts, hermeneutics and world religions   **62**
*Textualism and the modern concept of 'world religions' –
Gadamer and hermeneutics: exploding the myth of
objectivity – Hermeneutics and cultural isolationism – Self-
reflexivity and ideology*

4 Orientalism and Indian religions   **82**
*Orientalism and the quest for a postcolonial discourse –
Orientalism and Indology – The inevitability of
'Orientalism'?*

5 **The modern myth of 'Hinduism'**   96
   The myth of homogeneity and the modern myth of 'Hinduism' –
   Christianity, textualism and the construction of 'Hinduism' –
   The status of the term 'Hinduism' – The relevance of
   feminism to the Orientalist debate

6 **'Mystic Hinduism': Vedānta and the politics of representation**   118
   The 'discovery' of Vedānta as the central theology of Hinduism
   – Romanticism and the debate about pantheism – Orientalist
   interest in Vedānta – Neo-Vedānta and the perennial
   philosophy

7 **Orientalism and the discovery of 'Buddhism'**   143
   The European discovery of 'Buddhism' – Intercultural mimesis
   and the local production of meaning

8 **The politics of privatization: Indian religion and the study of**
   mysticism   161
   The comparative study of mysticism – The constructivist
   response to perennialism – The social location of social
   constructivism – Indian constructivisms: the epistemology of
   enlightenment

9 **Beyond Orientalism? Religion and comparativism in a**
   postcolonial era   187
   Postcolonialism and the 'Subaltern Studies' project – Mimesis,
   hybridity and the ambivalence of colonial discourse – The
   mutual imbrication of religion, culture and power

   Notes   219
   Bibliography   259
   Index   277

Acknowledgements

I am indebted to the University of Stirling for two periods of sabbatical leave, in Spring 1994 and Autumn 1997 and to the British Academy for financing an additional period of research leave in Spring 1998 which allowed me to complete this work. I would particularly like to thank my colleagues in the Department of Religious Studies at the University of Stirling in Scotland, for taking on my administrative and teaching responsibilities during this time, especially captain at the helm Keith Whitelam for 'making it so'.

I would like to express my gratitude to Grace Jantzen for her constructive comments and criticism of the work as a whole, John Hinnells for his ongoing encouragement and support of my work and Adrian Driscoll, Anna Gerber and the rest of the team at Routledge for the efficiency and care taken in all stages in the production of this monograph. Mention should also be made of my sister Mary, who, along with Ber, Cat (Tinie) and Steph, provided a safe haven from my work in Den Haag. Thanks also to my friend, colleague and neighbour Jeremy Carrette for many enjoyable hours of intellectual (and not so intellectual) discussion, but most of all for his friendship. I am most indebted, however, to Juli, my partner, best friend and (now) Acupuncturist, for her love, understanding and general joie de vivre.

Chapters 4 and 5 contain material that also appears in *Numen* (1999) as 'Orientalism and the modern myth of Hinduism'. A work such as this inevitably reflects a multitude of intellectual influences. I trust that these are mostly self-evident from the text itself. It has become a standard academic convention to attribute the positive aspects of one's work (or as Buddhists might put it, to 'transfer one's merit') to others and to proclaim all errors as one's own. I will not differ in this respect.

Acknowledgements

Introduction
Changing the subject

This work can be located within the history of ideas and is an examination of a constellation of categories surrounding the cultural symbolic of the 'mystic East' in modern Western consciousness. The history of ideas is often distinguished from philosophy on the grounds that the latter involves an engagement and evaluation of ideas rather than a non-committal examination of concepts within their own cultural and historical context. However, I wish to argue that both philosophy and the history of ideas should take more seriously not only the social location of the concepts under examination but also their involvement in a wider cultural field of power relations, or what has become known as 'the politics of knowledge'. In particular, I wish to argue for an awareness of the mutual imbrication of religion, culture and power as categories. This is not to say that religion and culture can be reduced to a set of power relations but rather that religion and culture are the field in which power relations operate. Materialist and cultural analyses are not mutually exclusive, 'either/or' explanations. Power is not mere material conditions without cultural trace since there is no power in the abstract – power, indeed, is constituted in particular cultural forms. Equally, cultural forms are embedded in a field of power relations. What is required, therefore, is an approach that avoids materialist reductionism (which denies culture) or culturalist reductionism (which denies power) with a renewed emphasis upon the mutual imbrication of the two. My stance, therefore, is rather close to that of Nicholas Dirks in attempting to reintroduce 'power, hegemony and history into studies of culturally-constructed structures of thought' without falling into the opposite extreme of reducing everything to a discussion of power relations. The mistake is in separating the two in the first place.

> The form and relations of power in southern India efface social scientific distinctions of materialist etics from culturalist emics, for even an analysis of ritual action and language suggests the complex and conjectural foundations of hierarchical relations.[1]

Overall, my interest within this work has been to explore the interface between postcolonial theory and the comparative study of religion. Such a task is overwhelming in its enormity and work within this area has hardly begun. To focus my analysis I have concentrated upon the notion of 'the Mystic East' as a prevalent theme within Western understandings of India as 'the Other', particularly in relation to scholarly approaches to the study of religion and mysticism.

Chapter 1 provides the beginnings of a genealogy of 'the mystical' and attempts to demonstrate that a category that is often conceived to be pre-eminently 'otherworldly', private and apolitical is in fact implicated in a network of power relations in the contexts in which it has been employed. In order to understand the cultural presuppositions underlying the modern location of 'the mystical' it is necessary to consider the history of such claims. To achieve this end we must briefly consider the roots of modern Western thought in the philosophical and social revolution known as 'the Enlightenment'. Chapter 2 therefore provides a brief schematic overview of some of the cultural presuppositions of modern Western society in so far as they directly impinge upon the academic study of mysticism and religion. We shall also have cause to examine some of the broad strategies, orienta-tions and trends in contemporary feminist thought when we come to consider the implications of a postcolonial agenda for the study of mysti-cism and Indian religion. Chapters 2 and 3, however, are intended to be neither definitive nor comprehensive in their analysis of the contemporary study of religion (a task that would require a major monograph in itself). Nevertheless, the account contained therein is intended to furnish the reader with a broad, if somewhat selective, sketch of some of the cultural, philo-sophical and methodological factors that form the tapestry upon which scholarly approaches to the mystical have been painted. It will also provide an opportunity to discuss some of the underlying trends that directly impinge upon the search for a postcolonial approach to the comparative study of mysticism and religion. Chapters 2 and 3, therefore, analyse the concept of 'religion' and consider the Christian theological and Enlightenment roots of 'religious studies'. Chapter 2 discusses the relation-ship of the discipline to other academic fields (such as sociology and theology), and offers some reflections about the future of the study of reli-gion after the 'postcolonial turn'. Here I argue that religious studies as a discipline might better conceive of itself as a form of 'cultural studies', rather than as an offshoot of theology. In this way, the study of religion can bring an interest in cross-cultural engagement and the role of religion within culture to an emerging discipline that has generally been characterised by its secularist agenda and the Eurocentricity of its approach.

In Chapter 3 the hermeneutical philosophy of Hans Georg Gadamer is explored with regard to the question of the limits of cross-cultural under-standing and the textualist bias of modern concepts of religion. It is argued here that emphasis upon a number of 'world religions' as the subject matter of religious studies is highly problematic. Moreover, the internal dynamism and heterogeneity of 'cultures' and the *fact* (rather than the *problem*) of their interaction renders cultural isolationism an inadequate response to the supposed 'quagmire of cultural relativism'. Emphasis upon the diversity, fluidity and complexity *within* as well as *between* cultures precludes a reification of their differences and allows one to avoid the kind of monadic essentialism that renders cross-cultural engagement an a priori impossibility from the outset.

In later chapters we shall examine the implications of the realization that ideology plays an integral part in the very act of understanding, interpreting or studying anything. In particular we shall focus our attention upon the colonial elements within Western discourses about Indian culture and religion and the ways in which these aspects have constructed the object that they purport to explain. Before considering these issues, however, Chapter 3 will discuss the textualist bias that operates in the comparative study of religion and the role played by the academic emphasis upon 'sacred texts' in the construction of the various 'world religions'.

In Chapter 4 the reader is introduced to the terms of the 'Orientalist debate' as established by Edward Said and explores responses to Said's work, with particular reference to South Asia and developments within the field of Indology. The next three chapters provide specific case studies for the exploration of these issues with an examination of the development of the notion of 'Hinduism' as a world religion, the impact of colonialism upon the study of Buddhism and the role played by Western Orientalists and Indian intellectuals in the construction of an image of 'Hinduism' as a type of mysticism centred upon the philosophy of the Vedānta.

Orientalist essentialism has resulted in stereotypes about the West as well as the East. There are a multiplicity of 'Wests' hidden behind the veil of a homogenizing and ahistorical essentialism (occluded by myths of cultural/national homogeneity). According to the 'psychoanalytically nuanced' account of Ashis Nandy, the construction of an 'Orient' that functions as an inversion of 'the West' represents the projection of the' shadow' side of Western culture. The triumph of Western colonialism, he argues, was that:

> It *did* make Western man definitionally non-Eastern and handed him a self-image and a world-view which were basically responses to the needs of colonialism ... The 'discovery' of the Orient ... was designed to expel the other Orient which had once been a part of the medieval European consciousness as an archetype and a potentiality.[2]

Since the Enlightenment, it would seem, dominant representations of Western culture have tended to subordinate what one might call the 'Dionysian' (as opposed to the Apollonian) aspects of its own culture and traditions (that is, those trends that have been conceived as 'poetic', 'mystical', irrational, uncivilized and feminine). These characteristics represent precisely those qualities that have been 'discovered' in the imaginary realm of 'the Orient'. Of course, this is a grand narrative about a highly complex and contradictory set of cultural processes, but it involves the ascendancy of secular rationality as an ideal within Western intellectual thought, a concomitant marginalization of 'the mystical' and the projection of qualities associated with this concept onto a colonized and essentialized India.

Critics of Edward Said and 'the Orientalist' agenda have sometimes argued that too much emphasis is placed upon the earliest generations of Orientalist scholarship where complicity with colonial aspirations was more generally accepted and that modern scholarship should not be 'tarred with the same brush'. Of what relevance, one might ask, are outdated conceptions of Hinduism as 'mystical' or 'footnotes to Vedānta' in the modern era? The post-Enlightenment myth of the autonomous individual and the fetishistic obsession with innovation within the market-place of contemporary academic scholarship often occludes the role of tradition and continuity in the production of scholarly knowledge. In Chapter 8, analysis turns to contemporary debates within the comparative study of mysticism to demonstrate the continuation of ethnocentric presuppositions in the construction of the 'mystic East' as well as the ongoing 'epistemic violence' involved in contemporary appraisals of 'Asian mysticism'. Within this chapter the post-Kantian nature of contemporary debates about 'mystical experience' is problematized and it is suggested that the study of Asian cultures requires a much greater sensitivity and engagement with indigenous forms of knowledge if one is to avoid 'doing violence' to the object of one's analysis. Finally, the chapter questions the modern privatization of 'the mystical', particularly in so far as it renders traditional Asian religiosity amenable to a postmodern market-place characterized by a kind of post-Christian secularism.

The final chapter of this work provides a broad discussion of contemporary postcolonial theory, particularly with reference to the study of Indian history and culture. This provides an opportunity for locating the study within the wider debate about the future of scholarship in a postcolonial age. The chapter explores the work of a number of theorists, notably the Subaltern Studies Collective, Gayatri Spivak, Homi Bhabha and Gyan Prakash, and considers the relationship between post-structuralist, postcolonial and feminist theory. Finally, some reflections are offered concerning the role of the scholar in the light of the politics of knowledge and the mutual imbrication of religion, culture and power.

There are a number of ways in which one might wish to question the stereotype of Indian religion as examples of the 'mystic East'. One strategy would be to demonstrate that there are in fact a number of heterogeneous facets to Indian religions and that not all of these are what we might call 'mystical'. This, for instance, may involve moving away from an exclusively textual approach to the study of religion and the emphasis which has so often been placed upon the so-called 'otherworldly' renunciate philosophies of India. This is one way of *changing the subject*, but does not involve questioning the basic assumptions underlying the description of these movements as mystical.

I am largely taking for granted the approach that I have just outlined – that Indian religion is diverse and therefore not exclusively, or even essentially, mystical. There are innumerable scholars working on those aspects of these traditions that are not easily classifiable as mystical, both through textual studies and through sociological and anthropological study of Indian religion. My interest is in those traditions, doctrines and classical texts of Indian religion that are most liable to be described as 'mystical' – that is, Advaita Vedānta, the Yoga traditions, the Madhyamaka and Yogācāra schools of Mahāyāna Buddhism. It is these traditions that are so often focused upon and used as evidence to support the stereotype of the 'mystic East'.

Such a project might be described as an exercise in anthropological self-reflexivity, along the lines recently outlined by the Foucauldian scholar Paul Rabinow, who argues that:

> We need to anthropologize the West: show how exotic its constitution of reality has been; emphasize those domains most taken for granted as universal (this includes epistemology and economics); make them seem as historically peculiar as possible; show how their claims to truth are linked to social practices and have hence become effective forces in the social world ... We must pluralize and diversify our approaches: a basic move against either economic or philosophic hegemony is to diversify centers of resistance; avoid the error of reverse essentializing; Occidentalism is not a remedy for Orientalism.[3]

I am aware that some will read this work as implying a rejection of literary approaches to the study of religion and thereby see this as further evidence of a shift towards anthropological models of religion. It should be made clear, however, that in turning the Western anthropological gaze back upon itself the discipline of anthropology is itself called into question.

> Analytically, the desire of every 'rational practice' is to cultivate and make reference to its reason for existence ... Anthropology as a contemporary discursive practice having a disciplinary identity has become institutionalized ... [A]s such it is an institution fundamentally involved in the reproduction of Western society.[4]

The critique of the 'textualist bias' within Western approaches to religion, and Indian religion in particular, should not be seen, therefore, as a call to abandon textual analysis altogether. I firmly believe that there is a place for textual analysis within the study of Indian religion and philosophy, albeit resulting in less spectacular claims than has sometimes been the case in previous generations of scholarship. Gone are the days when one can study Śaṅkara's commentary on the *Brahma Sūtra* and claim to be providing an account of 'Hindu Theology' or 'the Hindu Mind' in general. As Julius Lipner remarks:

> Many Westerners believe – alas, this is true for too many of the modern Indian intelligentsia as well – that the great Advaitin Śamkara is representative of Hindu religious thinkers. Now this belief too strikes me as manifestly indefensible. No doubt Śamkara is central for our appreciation of the religious teaching and theological development of Vedanta, and indeed for Hinduism's self-understanding today, but he is hardly representative of Hindu theologians or even of Vedantins.[5]

Nevertheless, the analysis and interpretation of religious texts remains an important tool within the study of religion. The history of religious ideas, which I suppose is a good way of characterizing my own particular approach and interests, will always hold a special reverence for textual materials, if only because of the impossibility of doing fieldwork in the distant past. My suggestion, then, is not that historians of ideas and textual specialists should give up what they do and become anthropologists, but rather that much greater attention be paid to the power relations involved in the history of ideas, both as a subject matter of analysis and as a disciplinary regime of institutionalized knowledge.

The approach of this study, then, is to look at the categories of mysticism and religion, some of the presuppositions involved in the disciplines of religious studies and Indology, and the ways in which Indian religion became located within contemporary notions of 'the mystical'. My aim, therefore, is to *change the subject* (that is, mysticism and the comparative study of Indian religion), not by changing what we talk about (that is, by looking at something else) but rather by suggesting ways in which one might redirect the intellectual trajectory of comparative study in the light of postcolonial and post-structuralist theories. This requires an examination of the ways in which mysticism as a category has been constructed in the West, and the ways in which this notion has been projected onto Indian religious culture as a way of controlling, manipulating and managing the Orient. However, in order to carry out this project, one first needs to know something about the way in which the category of 'the mystical' has been defined in Western culture, and this will be the topic of Chapter 1.

1 The power of definitions

A genealogy of the idea of 'the mystical'

Other regions give us back what our culture has excluded from its discourse.
(Michel de Certeau)[1]

The modern academic study of mysticism began in earnest towards the end of the nineteenth century.[2] The term 'mysticism' derives from the same time period and, as Michel de Certeau demonstrates, is an offspring of '*la mystique*', a term that first comes to the fore in early seventeenth-century France.[3] 'Mysticism', of course, was initially coined by Western intellectuals to refer to that phenomenon or aspect of the Christian tradition that was understood to emphasize religious knowledge gained by means of an extraordinary experience or revelation of the divine. This has remained a constant theme in the academic study of the subject. For instance, Margaret Smith describes mysticism as 'the most vital element in all true religions, rising up in revolt against cold formality and religious torpor ... The aim of the mystics,' she says, 'is to establish a conscious relation with the Absolute, in which they find the personal object of love.'[4] Again, Evelyn Underhill, an important early figure in the study of mysticism, argues that the one essential feature of mysticism is 'union between God and the soul'. Going further than this, Underhill suggests that 'The mystic way is best understood as a process of sublimation, which carries the correspondences of the self with the Universe up to *higher levels than those on which our normal consciousness works*.'[5] For Underhill, the experience of the mystic is 'communion with a living Reality, an object of Love capable of response'. This language, of course, is uncompromisingly Western and Christian, but is applied by Underhill to all forms of mysticism throughout the different world-religious traditions. Thus, she argues that 'Even where it conflicts with the mystic's philosophy – as in Hinduism and Neoplatonism – it is still present.'[6]

This is an astonishing statement to make – that the notions of God, communion, the soul and themes of a loving relationship between the two can be found in (actually imposed upon) all non-Christian religious experience. Underhill and Smith, of course, are not alone in this regard. It has been a presupposition of a great deal of scholarship in the study of mysticism that one can apply Christian categories (including the category of mysticism itself) to religions, cultures and experiences beyond their original context.

I would like to draw attention at this point to two important features of such a theological approach to the comparative study of mysticism. First, there is the implicit monotheism of such definitions. As any student of religion will know, belief in God is by no means exhaustive of the religious possibilities available to humankind. Buddhism, as is often stated, is a non-theistic religion in so far as it does not posit a transcendent Creator beyond the wheel of rebirths (*saṃsāra*). As the study of mysticism has developed along the lines of the comparative study of religion, theistic definitions have become increasingly problematic. Indeed, mysticism suffers from the same problems of definition as does the equally problematic term 'religion', not least because of constant attempts by scholars to delineate the precise nature or 'essence' of the phenomena under consideration. Second, one should note the experiential emphasis in most contemporary characterizations of mysticism. As Grace Jantzen points out,[7] this reflects the influence of post-Kantian epistemology and the seminal work of the philosopher, psychologist and early scholar of 'the mystical', William James. While the limitations of narrowly theistic characterizations of the subject matter have been widely acknowledged by scholars as inappropriate, few voices have been heard that question the validity of the experientialist dimension of contemporary definitions.

It is clear, then, that before one can examine contemporary Western characterizations of Indian mysticism one first needs to understand something about the history of the term 'mystical' and the sociocultural transformations that have led to its particular connotations and denotations in modern Western culture. What is required, therefore, is a genealogy of 'the mystical' – that is, a history of the idea that pays specific attention to the power dynamic involved in the way in which it has been defined in various historical circumstances. What often happens at this point is that a definition of the subject matter is given, providing the basis for the ensuing discussion. However, it seems appropriate to make a few general remarks about the exercise of defining a subject matter such as 'mysticism' or 'religion'.

The problem with definitions

What is mysticism? A direct and unmediated experience of the divine? Is there something we can meaningfully refer to as 'the mystical' in the various world religious traditions? Is the mystical the central core of religion or a marginal and peripheral aspect of it? Could mysticism even be the common core underlying the world's religious traditions? Is mysticism the experiential dimension of religion, that is religion at its most private, subjective and intense?

In beginning studies such as this it has often been seen as necessary to define the subject matter under consideration. In our case this would involve examining the question of the meaning and denotation of terms like 'mysticism' and 'mystical'. Clearly, delimiting the scope of this term has proved a particularly pithy problem for contemporary scholars for a number of reasons. Before proceeding any further it would be useful to make a few points about defining the subject matter of mysticism.[8] Virtually all contemporary studies of mysticism fail to appreciate the sense in which notions of 'the mystical' (including those that are adopted in the studies themselves) are cultural and linguistic constructions dependent upon a web of interlocking definitions, attitudes and discursive processes, which themselves are tied to particular forms of life and historically specific practices. Not only are contemporary notions of the 'mystical' subject to the cultural presuppositions of the day, they are also informed by and overlap with a long history of discursive processes, continuities and discontinuities and shifts in both meaning and denotation. Just as these various meanings and applications of 'the mystical' have changed over time, so too have the variety of attitudes towards them and evaluations of their importance differed according to circumstance. Defining the mystical then is never a 'purely academic' activity (in the sense in which one means 'of no real consequence'), nor can it ever be completely divorced from the historical remains of past definitions of the term. In her excellent work *Power, Gender and Christian Mysticism*, Grace Jantzen argues:

> that the idea of 'mysticism' is a social construction and that it has been constructed in different ways at different times. Although ... medieval mystics and ecclesiastics did not work with a concept of 'mysticism', they did have strong views about who should count as a mystic, views which changed over the course of time ... The current philosophical construction of mysticism is therefore only one in a series of social constructions of mysticism; and, like the others, is implicitly bound up with issues of authority and gender.[9]

I agree with Jantzen, not only in acknowledging the sense in which the category of 'the mystical' is socially constructed, but also in recognizing that as a consequence 'the mystical' also represents the conceptual site of a historical struggle for power and authority. If we look at the questions surrounding the definition of mysticism again in the light of this realization, a new set of questions begin to present themselves. In any given sociohistorical context, what is the agenda of power underlying a particular characterization of mysticism? What evaluative judgements are being made in the decision to include or exclude certain phenomena from the category? What is at stake in giving a particular definition of the subject matter?

As Jantzen aptly demonstrates, the way one defines 'the mystical' relates to ways of establishing and defining authority. This is obvious in the pre-modern context since anyone claiming direct experiential knowledge of God or the ultimate reality is in effect claiming unmediated authority to speak the truth. In a traditional Christian context, for instance, such a claim might be seen as undermining the claim of the Church to mediate between humanity and the divine. Defining mysticism then is a way of defining power. One's answers to the questions 'What is mysticism?' and 'Who counts as a mystic?' reflect issues of authority. But, one might ask, of what relevance is mysticism to power and authority in the modern Western context? Surely the way we define mysticism today has nothing to do with social or political authority. Yet this can be seen to be a misguided (if understandable) objection, if we only pause to look below the surface. The very fact that 'the mystical' is seen as irrelevant to issues of social and political authority itself reflects contemporary, secularized notions of and attitudes towards power. The separation of the mystical from the political is itself a political decision!

Definitions shift over time, of course, and modern notions of mysticism differ significantly from early and medieval Christian understandings of 'the mystical' (in so far as they had one!). On this issue I have to agree with Talal Asad when he suggests that 'there cannot be a universal definition of religion' – or of mysticism, for that matter – 'not only because its constituent elements and relationships are historically specific, but because that definition is itself the historical product of discursive processes'.[10]

One can use working definitions in a heuristic and provisional manner but these remain the historical product of culturally specific and politically implicated discursive processes. Such definitions, however, will never be universally applicable when one addresses different cultural milieux or historical periods. An awareness of shifting cultural, political and semantic patterns throughout history means that the abstract search for an 'essence' of mysticism is fundamentally misconceived. The idea of 'the mystical' has gone through a number of significant changes in meaning and denotation and, as Jantzen notes, 'what counts as mysticism will reflect (and also help to constitute) the institutions of power in which it occurs'.[11] It would be useful, therefore, to consider some of the ways in which 'the mystical' has been characterized and defined by examining contemporary attitudes towards mysticism and religion.

As we shall see in the next chapter, the notion of 'religion' has also been subject to divergent representations, forged in a crucible of disputed power relations and discursive practices. The category of religion, in fact, is simply the production of the cognitive 'filtering out' or abstraction of certain aspects of a much broader cultural dynamic. This process of abstraction is founded upon the presuppositions of the Enlightenment. Other cultures and pre-Enlightenment Western culture did not view the human social world in this manner – they simply did not carve up the world in the way that we do. Religious phenomena were always seen as part and parcel of political, social and other cultural forms. The separation of religion from these is founded on a secular Enlightenment approach.

The search for the 'essence' of religion or the various religions, or of 'mysticism', is misguided since it is operating under the aegis of the essentialist fallacy that the phenomena included in the category of religion (for instance) must have something universally in common to be meaningfully classified as religious. The claim, frequently made from the methodological stance of the phenomenology of religion, that religion is *sui generis* – that it is a fundamental category of its own, is often put forward as a defence of the autonomy and irreducibility of religious phenomena in the overwhelmingly secular institution of the modern university.[12] The problem with this approach is that it can sometimes lead to a reification of religion. Such a claim, of course, also functions to validate the professional autonomy of scholars within the relatively new discipline of religious studies. This is acknowledged to some degree in the discipline with the widely accepted view that to do justice to the phenomena of religion requires the adoption of a multidisciplinary approach, since religions cannot really be abstracted from the cultural dynamic in which they exist, except in our minds and in our publications! Indeed, the modern category of 'religion' itself is a Western construction that owes a considerable debt to Enlightenment presuppositions. The term exists as an explanatory concept for classifying certain aspects of human cultural activity. As Jonathan Z. Smith argues:

> If we have understood the archaeological and textual record correctly, man has had his entire history in which to imagine deities and modes of interaction with them. But man, more precisely western man, has had only the last few centuries in which to imagine religion. It is this act of second order, reflective imagination which must be the central preoccupation of any student of religion ... Religion is solely the creation of the scholar's study. It is created for the scholar's analytic purposes by his imaginative acts of comparison and generalization. Religion has no independent existence apart from the academy. For this reason, the student of religion ... must be relentlessly self-conscious. Indeed, this self-consciousness constitutes his primary expertise, his foremost object of study.[13]

However, the Enlightenment preoccupation with defining the 'essence' of phenomena such as 'religion' or 'mysticism' serves precisely to exclude such phenomena from the realms of politics, law and science, etc. – that is, from the spheres of power and authority in modern Western societies. Privatized religion becomes both clearly defined and securely contained by excluding it from the public realm of politics. In other words, attempts to preserve the autonomy of religion can also lead to the marginalization of religion since it becomes separated from these other realms. In fact, if we look more closely at the concept of 'religion' itself we see that like the 'mystical' the term is an explanatory construct, which, while useful for focusing upon certain aspects of cultural activity, tends to marginalize that which it purports to explain if the term is reified and segregated from the wider cultural dynamic in which it occurs. This point is well made by Talal Asad:

> the insistence that religion has an autonomous essence ... invites us to define religion (like any essence) as a transhistorical and transcultural phenomenon. It may be a happy accident that this effort of defining religion converges with the liberal demand in our time that it be kept quite separate from politics, law and science – spaces in which varieties of power and reason articulate our distinctively modern life. This definition is at once part of a strategy (for secular liberals) of the confinement, and (for liberal Christians) of the defense of religion.[14]

One aspect of the modern construction of the categories of 'religion' and 'mysticism' that requires our immediate consideration is the location of the two concepts in terms of the post-Enlightenment dichotomy between the public and private realms. Modern science is generally considered to be part of the public sphere of human activity since it is seen as universally relevant and applicable to all. It is also public in the sense that it is seen as accessible, repeatable, quantifiable and empirical in orientation, and progressive by its very nature. Philosophers also claim the realm of the public as their own in so far as philosophy is said to be the quest for universal and objective truths (as opposed to subjective and individual opinions). Both philosopher and scientist utilize the language and rhetoric of objectivity to support their claims to public authority. The primary example of the public, however, is the realm of politics, the sphere of human activity relating to governing of the state in particular and to power in general.

In contrast to this, religion and mysticism (which has come to be seen as a specific sub-category of religion) have been firmly placed within the realm of the private since the Enlightenment. The view that religion is largely a matter of personal belief rather than of communal involvement is a prominent feature of modern Western religious consciousness. The extreme example of this is the phenomenon that Robert Bellah labels 'Sheilaism' – named after a respondent he met by the name of Sheila who claimed to have her own personal religion. Sheilaism, then, is the modern belief that one can have one's own religion. The modern privatization of religion is in fact enshrined in the Constitution of the most powerful nation on earth, the United States of America, with the explicit separation of Church and State and the freedom of the individual to practise the religion of his or her choice. Notice how the language of consumerism and choice has now entered the realm of religion. Religion becomes a phenomenon associated with the private realm and involves issues of individual choice rather than social or political authority. As Bryan Wilson has noted, in our modern era:

> Religion becomes privatized. In a consumer society it becomes just another consumer good, a leisure-time commodity no longer affecting

the centres of power or the operation of the system – even at the level of social control, socialization, and the organization of the emotions and of motivations. Religion becomes a matter of choice, but whatever religion is chosen is of no consequence to the operation of the social system.[15]

In fact if one examines the dichotomies of Enlightenment thought (and hence of modern Western society), one can see the following oppositional model at work:

Public	*Private*
Society	Individual
Science	Religion
Institutional Religion	Personal Religion (Mysticism?)
Secular	Sacred
Rational	Irrational/Non-rational
Male	Female

The secularization process that has occurred in modern Western societies since the Enlightenment has not led to the inevitable decline of religion, as some sociologists had prophesied, but rather to the erosion of the authority of institutional religions in the modern era. In this context the consequences of the Enlightenment dichotomy between public and private has been not only the delegitimization of institutional religion (i.e. religion as a social and political phenomenon) but also the increasing tendency to locate religion within the private sphere, thereby separating or excluding it from the realm of politics and power. Thus, while it is not true to say that religion is dying out in the Western world, it is certainly true to say that religion has been increasingly located at the margins of society, that is, away from the major centres of power and authority.

One consequence of the modern distinction between the spheres of religion and politics has been to foster a suspicion among Westerners that any linkage of the two realms is an example of a 'merely rhetorical' use of religious discourse to mask some underlying political, ideological or 'worldly' intention. This is a form of simplistic reductionism. Such a hermeneutic of suspicion is exemplified, for instance, in the Marxian-inspired claim that the Hindu doctrine of karma is promulgated by élite brahmins in order to justify caste divisions, control the masses and thus maintain their own authority. This approach presupposes that religion and politics can, and indeed should, be distinguished and that the political dimension is the more fundamental of the two. The political meta-discourse is thus given ultimate explanatory status, explaining what has been occluded by religious discourse.

One could just as easily reduce the other way around (though this rarely happens in the modern secular Academy). Nevertheless, a strategy similar to this can be found in the claim that political movements and ideologies, such as Marxism, nationalism, etc., are actually modern forms of religion.[16] Here is the academic site of a power struggle – namely, the justification of the autonomy of religion and of religious studies as a viable and important discipline within the modern secular University. The claim that the defining feature of humans is that they are *homo religiosus* (Mircea Eliade) should also be seen in this context – that is, as a response to an intellectual environment in which religion has often been marginalized and 'explained away' in terms of a higher-order meta-discourse.

However, I am not advocating reductionism in either direction. I am simply wanting to acknowledge the sense in which the 'religious' and the 'political' are not separate realms in reality. The separation of the two is an Enlightenment assumption that I do not accept. Seeing religion and definitions as conceptual sites for struggles for power is *not* a form of political reductionism. I am not saying that religious questions and issues should be reduced to their sociological or their political dimensions, rather I wish to reject the Enlightenment paradigm that cognitively separates these realms in the first place. Once this move is made, examples of religious and political association are no longer automatically seen as the inappropriate grouping of two separate spheres of human cultural existence. This, for instance, is the primary problem with Western attitudes to religious nationalism. Once the secular–religious divide is accepted as the normative paradigm, examples of politically active and religious authority become predisposed to the image of the manipulative and opportunistic ideologue. Those who accept the secular authority of such a figure thus become represented as subject to mass religious indoctrination. One does not have to look far to find contemporary examples of such a paradigm at work in Western representations of religions in the various mass media.

Origins of the term 'mysticism'

How does all of this relate to the category of mysticism? Well, the idea of 'mysticism', like its sibling 'religion', is a social construction and the way in which the subject matter has been defined represents both a cognitive site and a process of struggle over meaning and authority. Let me attempt to demonstrate this through a brief outline of the ways in which 'the mystical' has been constructed in the West.

The term 'mystical' has come to be used in a rather woolly and ill-defined manner in everyday language. The adjective is commonly used to describe any object, person, event or belief that has a vaguely mysterious aspect to it, to religious experiences, to the supernatural, to the magical and the occult. The term itself derives from the Greek adjective *mūstikos*, and is said to originate from the various mystery cults prevalent in the Roman Empire of the early Christian period. As a number of scholars have suggested, *mūstikos* derives from a Greek root *mūo*, meaning 'to close'. Many mystery cults of the Graeco-Roman world were esoteric movements and the term is usually taken to denote the practice of either closing one's eyes or of closing one's lips (that is, remaining silent). Both renditions can be seen in the way in which 'mysticism' is understood in contemporary academic usage. On the one hand the mystical is often understood to denote an experience that goes beyond the range and scope of everyday sensory experiences (such as visions) – an experience that transcends the sensory realm and perhaps even mental images as well. This approach, however, is not without its critics.[17] On the other hand, mysticism is often associated with the ineffable, that about which one should not, and indeed cannot, speak. This association is also prevalent in academic literature on the subject and constitutes a peculiarly modern preoccupation of studies of mysticism.

The best general account of the origins of the term in the Christian tradition is probably that offered by Louis Bouyer.[18] Bouyer argues that there are three dimensions to the early Christian concept of *mūstikos* – all of which very soon become intertwined as the tradition develops. These elements are: (1) biblical, (2) liturgical and (3) spiritual or contemplative. The first denotes the idea of a mystical hermeneutic of scripture – that is, an understanding of the biblical message rooted in allegorical interpretation. *Mūstikos* is also used to describe the liturgical mystery of the Eucharist – the timeless communion with the divine. Finally, the term is also used to denote a contemplative or experiential knowledge of God. For the Hellenized Church Fathers all three aspects were inextricably interwoven.[19]

Medieval notions of the mystical

In the medieval period, the 'mystical' continues to be used in this threefold manner. More specifically, 'mystical theology' (under the influence of Pseudo-Dionysius) came to denote the science of investigating the allegorical significance of biblical truth – that is, the discerning of the cryptic and hidden meaning of scripture. A distinction (perhaps first drawn clearly by Augustine)[20] was made between linguistic allegory (*allegoria in verbis*), when linguistic signs are used to refer to something other than their usual referents, and historical allegory (*allegoria in factis*), which denoted the hidden and subtle meanings underlying the objects, persons and events of history as created by God. One of the traditional functions of theology, then, was to examine God's rhetoric – as manifested in the unfolding pattern of historical events – and thus intuit the mystical meaning of history. This, no doubt, is something of the meaning behind the phrase, 'God moves in mysterious ways'. An early example of the adoption of a mystical hermeneutics to discern the divine plan for creation can be seen in the following extract from Justin Martyr (died 165CE). Justin points to the significance of the symbolism of the Cross as a clue to the divine plan and mystical truth of Christianity.

For look closely at all the things in the cosmos, and see whether they are administered or can be connected without this shape [of the Cross]. For the sea cannot be cut through unless this trophy which is called a sail remains intact in the ship; the earth is not plowed without it; diggers do not perform their work, nor artisans likewise, except with this shape. Human shape differs from that of irrational animals in nothing except this, and it both is upright and can have hands extended, and it bears on its face lined up from the forehead what is called a nose, through which both there is breath for the living being, and also none other than the shape of the cross is displayed.[21]

When we come to the Protestant Reformation, however, we find Martin Luther as the arch-critic of mystical or allegorical hermeneutics. Luther argued that:

The Holy Spirit is the simplest writer and speaker in heaven and earth. This is why His words can have no more than the one simplest meaning which we call the written one, or the literal meaning of the tongue.[22]

Luther dismisses the 'twaddle' (*merissimae nugae*) of a mystical theology, which he condemns as being more Platonic than Christian.[23] This relates to Luther's emphasis upon the transparency of the Bible's meaning and the importance of individuals having access to and being able to read the Bible for themselves. Thus, in the post-Reformation period the mystical/allegorical approach to biblical exegesis came increasingly under fire as we see the gradual decline in the status of the mystical within Western Christendom.

From the seventeenth century onwards we see the gradual secularization of 'the mystical'. The category now becomes closely associated with the metaphors and mysteries of poetry and 'literature' – cultural forms that became defined during this period in strict opposition to the alleged transparency of meaning to be found in prose and scientific writing. Thus, in the seventeenth century, so Certeau argues, Western science established its own distinctiveness – its cultural and political identity, through the exclusion of more expressive modes of thought and the construction of a category known as 'literature'. In this way, oppositions were set up between the opacity of rhetoric and allegory and the plain transparency of prose. Fiction becomes opposed to factual writing, subjectivity to objectivity, the metaphorical (allegorical) is contrasted with the literal, and the multivocality of 'literature' was seen as distinguishing it from the univocality of science.[24]

One consequence of the secularization of the mystical, so Certeau argues, is that the distinction between the two types of allegory becomes blurred. Thus, the divine allegory of historical events becomes subsumed by the general category of linguistic allegory and we see the confutation of 'mystical hermeneutics' (as provider of evidence of the mysteries of the divine in action through history) with the human use of linguistic allegory (*allegoria in verbis*). Mystical hermeneutics no longer refers specifically to the intuition of the timeless divine truth of scripture, but rather comes to denote merely a particular mode of speaking, a specific literary genre – the 'mystical text'. In this context is born a new *Corpus Mysticum* – a body of identifiable texts that come to represent 'mystical literature'.[25] This constituted a major shift in the understanding of texts. The modern tendency to associate the 'literal' meaning of a text with the original intentions of its author(s) reflects the influence of Romanticist approaches to hermeneutics. The narrowing of the 'literal' to denote human authorial intention coincided with Nietzsche's proclamation of the 'death of God' heralding with it a secularized 'birth of the author'. Thus, as Sandra Schneiders notes:

> For the ancient exegete the literal sense was the letter or 'body' of the text as opposed to its religious meaning or 'spirit,' whether or not the latter was intended or even known by the biblical writer. Thus, for example, if this theory were applied to the New Testament, the literal meaning of the account of the crucifixion of Jesus would be restricted to the physical and political facts of the story. Its salvific significance (which is obviously the primary meaning the evangelists wanted to convey) would belong to the spiritual meaning. In contrast, for the modern exegete the literal sense is the meaning intended by the human author ... the ancient exegete saw it primarily as a door (albeit an important and usually indispensable one) to the true meaning of the text whereas the modern exegete, persuaded that the true meaning of the text is determined by the author, would consider the literal meaning to be identical with the true meaning.[26]

'*La mystique*', therefore, came to represent an important aspect of the seventeenth-century construction of the distinction between science and literature (and therefore between 'the sciences' and 'the humanities'). By the middle of the seventeenth century, 'the mystical' is increasingly applied to the religious realm alone, and the term disappears from the emerging scientific literature of the day. Before this period, of course, the term had been used to denote the hidden meaning of God's universe and 'natural philosophy' (the natural sciences) was seen as one way of uncovering this hidden meaning. Such usage of 'the mystical' in scientific works, however, died out as the gradual secularization of the natural sciences displaced the mystical – locating it firmly within the (now separate) realm of the religious. In other words, the association of 'the mystical' exclusively with a realm denoted by the term 'religion' is a product of the process of secularization, which 'filters out' the religious dimension from other aspects of human cultural activity.

In the modern era, Certeau suggests, the traditional hagiographies and writings of the saints become adapted and designated 'mystical'. Thus one finds the invention of a Christian mystical tradition. Emphasis shifts from a focus upon the virtues and miracles of the saints to an interest in extraordinary experiences and states of mind. It is at this point in European history, Certeau argues, that 'already existing writings were termed "mystic" and a mystic tradition was fabricated'.[27]

Why did this happen? Seventeenth-century usage of the term 'mystical' appears to have become increasingly pejorative. Critics attacked the apparent novelty of the mystic – having a history, they argued, that spanned barely three or four centuries and usually said to originate with figures such as Meister Eckhart and John of the Cross. Apologists for the mystical responded to this critique in two ways. First, they claimed to reveal only what was already present in Holy Scripture. However, the claim to access the 'secret' meaning of scripture was always likely to be seen as a threat to the Church's institutionalization of biblical meaning if made by those outside its auspices. So, we find the predominance of a second strategy, namely the invention of an ancient mystical tradition within the orthodox walls of Christianity. This involved a selective colonization of classical Christian authors – in particular the early church fathers and a variety of medieval Christian writers and saintly figures. The consequence of this second strategy, of course, was that it tied the newly sanctified mystic and their apologists to the established tradition of exegesis and the overarching authority of the Church, as well as binding them to a canon of acceptable and orthodox ecclesiastical literature. So it would seem then that the birth of a 'Christian mystical tradition' also coincided with its domestication by the ecclesiastical authorities.

However, I do not want to give the impression that there was (or indeed could be) a uniformity to representations of the mystical in this period (or at any other time for that matter). 'The mystical', however one characterizes it, always represents a site of struggle, a conflict for recognition and authority. A number of contemporary writers, for instance, have argued that Christian mysticism represented a source of power and inspiration to a significant number of medieval women. The French feminist Irigaray has suggested that, in the medieval period, mysticism 'is the only place in the history of the West in which a woman speaks and acts so publicly'.[28] Aligning with this position, Elizabeth Petroff argues that:

> Visions led women to the acquisition of power in the world while affirming their knowledge of themselves as women. Visions were a socially sanctioned activity that freed a woman from conventional female roles by identifying her as a genuine religious figure. They brought her to the attention of others, giving her a public language she could use to teach and learn.[29]

While there is undoubtedly some truth in these claims, we should be wary of idealizing and appropriating the lives of such women as if they were all proto-feminists devoid of internalized misogyny and patriarchal conditioning. Male and female mystics within Christianity (as in other religious traditions) display a variety of attitudes towards sexuality and gender relations. It would be a mistake to think of female mystics as some sisterhood of proto-feminists working on behalf of their collective womanhood. Julian of Norwich, for instance, writes about her visions and the authority that she derives from them as being *in spite of* her female nature.[30] Hildegard of Bingen believed that women were unsuitable for the priesthood since they were clearly inferior to men.[31]

Scripturally sanctioned by 1 Timothy 2.12, women were (and indeed continue) to be systematically excluded from public teaching by male ecclesiastical authority. Despite this caveat however, there were a significant number of publicly active female visionaries and teachers in the medieval period. If we look at some of the literature of this period we can see further evidence of the fact that the defining of 'the mystical' is the site of a power struggle with clear gender implications.

It has been suggested by a number of scholars that there is a greater tendency for female mystics to somatize their religious experiences – that is, to experience and/or express them in terms of strong bodily sensations, often associated with bleeding, lactating and giving birth. It is certainly true, for instance, that a number of female mystics seem to explicitly associate with Christ's passion, with the brokenness of the bleeding and wounded Jesus on the Cross, rather than with Christ the virile hero – the invulnerable saviour of all. Such generalized gender differences clearly reflect prevailing beliefs in the greater carnality and emotionalism of women. One significant factor, however, in this situation is that most women were denied the privilege of a scholastic education (especially in Latin and Greek). Being excluded from theological colleges, we find that, in the main, the abstract and complex metaphysics of apophatic or negative theology deriving from Pseudo-Dionysius was overwhelmingly the domain of male intellectuals within the Church. This point should not be overstated since there are notable exceptions,[32] but it is clear that for many female mystics the primary means of experiencing the divine was through intensely somatic visionary experiences.

The medieval tension between the visionary and the apophatic dimensions of Christian mysticism reflects a power struggle over the definition of the authentically mystical. The anonymous fourteenth-century English author of *The Cloud of Unknowing* explicitly rejects the authority of visionary experiences in comparison to the path of negation, which rises above the discursive intellect and rejects all images of God. For the author, those who give authority to visions:

> twist their heads quaintly on one side, and stick their chins up. Mouth agape, they give the impression that they would hear with their mouths, and not with their ears! Some when they speak add emphasis by pointing with their fingers ... Some can neither sit still, stand still nor lie still, without waggling their feet or fidgeting with their hands ... Some

are everlastingly giggling and laughing at every word they speak, as though they were giddy women or common clowns who did not know how to behave.[33]

As Grace Jantzen has suggested, the sexist jibe at the end of this quote is probably no coincidence.[34] Here we have a textual reference to a conflict for the true voice of authority within the Church. Who counts as a mystic? Who has the most authentic experience of the divine and therefore the authority to speak about God? For the author of *The Cloud of Unknowing*, as indeed for John of the Cross,[35] Pseudo-Dionysius[36] (and, one should note, the occasional female mystic), visionary experiences are valid but only at a lower level. Such visions can be sources of attachment and intellectual narrowness, since they involve the visual (or aural) embodiment of God. However, as the transcendent Creator, God can never be encapsulated by the limitations of the human sense organs!

The two positions do not have to be polarized, however, and it seems to me that Teresa of Avila is a good example of a mystic who manages to emphasize the importance of visions while giving greater final authority to non-sensory experiences of the divine. For Teresa, in fact, the somatic quality of visionary experiences are not to be denigrated since they are God-given (though she still seems to place them below non-sensory experiences in terms of the degree of intimacy and knowledge of God that they provide!):

God gave us our faculties to use; each has its own proper reward. So let's not try to charm them to sleep but give them freedom to do their work until God calls them to higher things.[37]

Modern definitions of mysticism

The same issue comes up in deciding how *we* should define mysticism. Who are we choosing to include and who are we excluding? Definitions that focus on highly rarefied and non-sensory experiences of union with the Divine – that is, definitions that exclude visions – also, it seems to me, exclude a large number of female mystics from the category. For example, Ninian Smart considers: 'mysticism as primarily consisting in an interior or introvertive quest, culminating in certain interior experiences which are not described in terms of sense experiences or of mental images, etc.'[38]

Smart further characterizes mystical experiences as monistic or unitive in nature and explicitly distinguishes mysticism from 'prophetism, devotionalism and sacramentalism' (though he does acknowledge that these forms are often interwoven with each other). Smart's definition of mysticism is representative of a great deal of literature on the subject in the emphasis placed upon non-sensory and apparently ineffable experiences, said to be devoid of a subject–object distinction. This approach shifts the focus of the study of mysticism towards the textual and renunciate forms of Indian religion (such as Buddhism, Advaita Vedānta, Yoga), and fits well with the abstract and apophatic theologies of Meister Eckhart, John of the Cross and *The Cloud of Unknowing*, providing an overwhelmingly male object of study. In this sense, Smart is merely following in the apophatic tradition of *The Cloud of Unknowing*. In an interesting and perceptive article in which she criticizes the implicit association of mysticism with monism, Grace Jantzen makes the following observation:

> when philosophers and theologians make reference to mysticism as monism they also frequently refer to the sexual imagery used by mystics to describe the union of God and the soul; and take this sexual imagery to imply the complete loss of self, the submergence of the soul in God ... When this interpretation ... is coupled with the fact that the soul is always spoken of as feminine and God as masculine, it is hard to resist the idea that theologians and philosophers, predominantly male, have seen sexuality precisely in terms of the submergence of the female, her loss of name and self and any power of her own as a consequence of her union with the male. Is it possible that the consistent identification of mysticism with monism, and the persistent failure to read the mystics properly, is because taking them seriously would radically undermine patriarchal ideas of sexuality and power?[39]

One might argue that visions are sometimes included within scholarly definitions of the mystical, but of course 'the mystical' has become a marginal category in modern, Western society, and it is now safe to include women within the category since it no longer serves to give them power. This is a point that Jantzen makes in her recent feminist critique of the study of Christian mysticism. The privatization of mysticism – that is, the increasing tendency to locate the mystical in the psychological realm of personal experiences – serves to exclude it from political issues such as social justice. Mysticism thus becomes seen as a personal matter of cultivating inner states of tranquillity and equanimity, which, rather than seeking to transform the world, serve to accommodate the individual to the status quo through the alleviation of anxiety and stress. In this way, mysticism becomes thoroughly domesticated.[40]

Modern conceptions of the mystical have increasingly become divorced both from the originally Christian context of the term and from the scriptural and liturgical dimensions that the notion implied in ancient and medieval Christianity. The mystical becomes overwhelmingly experiential in the discourses of modernity. As a result, the contemporary study of mysticism, operating within a post-Enlightenment context, provides an overwhelmingly psychological construction of the subject area.[41] An excellent example of this is the seminal work of William James, *The Varieties of Religious Experience* (his 1901 Gifford Lectures). For James, 'organized' or institutional religion was 'second-hand' religion. True religion was to be found in the private, religious and mystical experiences of individuals.[42] This has almost become received wisdom in the modern era, representing as it does a trajectory that leads straight to what Robert Bellah calls Sheilaism, or the belief that one can have one's own personal religion. In criticizing this psychologized orientation, Grace Jantzen points out that:

> philosophers writing about mysticism after James regularly cite and accept his description of mysticism as a basis for their evaluation of it; but do not notice its provenance. Perhaps because of the empiricist strand in James' writing, and his liberal citation of sources, subsequent philosophers too readily take for granted that his description of mysticism is reliable, and, contrary to the spirit of James, do not investigate actual mystics for themselves.[43]

As the subject area of religious studies developed in the nineteenth century, it was influenced, and to some degree absorbed, by the emerging psychological discourse that was developing at that time.[44] William James's own approach to the study of mysticism was heavily influenced by Schleiermacher and the Romantic reaction to Kantian philosophy. One dominant trajectory in the contemporary study of mysticism since James has been the study of 'altered states of consciousness' and the phenomena connected with their attainment. James suggests that although such states are inaccessible to the ordinary rational mind (as it is often called), such experiences may impart exceptional meaning and truth-giving quality to the agent. Thus 'our normal waking consciousness, rational consciousness as we call it, is but one special type of consciousness, whilst all about it, parted from it by the filmiest of screens, there lie potential forms of consciousness entirely different'.[45]

The point is, of course, that contemporary Westerners do not normally take these states as 'normative' if they consider them at all. When such experiential states are discussed they are usually rejected as delusory, subjective and hallucinatory, or are described as 'altered' states of consciousness – a phrase that presupposes the normative nature of so-called 'everyday' experiences. In some religious traditions, however (especially in Buddhism and classical Yoga), such 'altered' states are sometimes taken to be the normative and 'natural' state of mind, and it is the everyday states of waking and dreaming, etc., that are somehow an 'alteration' of or an aberration from that norm. Thus in the *Yoga Sūtras* of Patañjali, yoga is defined as 'the cessation of the fluctuations of the mind' (*citta-vṛtti-nirodha*, YS I.2). The 'normal' status of the seer is to abide in its own form (*svarūpa*), as pure consciousness (Puruṣa, YS 1.3).

William James was, of course, a man of his time. The exclusively experiential emphasis reflects not only the emerging discipline of Psychology, of which James himself was an important figure, but also general features of modern Western culture, such as a clearly defined distinction between the public and the private realms, the rise of anti-clericalism and modern political and philosophical trends such as liberalism, democracy and the notion of the 'individual'. All of these factors have contributed to the marginalization of religion and classification of mystical and religious experience firmly within the realm of the private (and the individual) as opposed to the public (and the social) domain. The dichotomy between public and private spheres and the post-Reformation distinction between institutional/organized religion and private religion have had a large part to play in the psychologization of mysticism.[46]

Nevertheless, the modern preoccupation with 'extraordinary experiences' or altered states of consciousness does not accurately represent mystics and mystical traditions both in the pre-modern era and in non-Western cultures, though it does dovetail rather well with many contemporary forms of New Age religiosity that are developing in the West. As Bouyer's study of the use of the term *mūstikos* in early Christianity demonstrates, 'the mystical' initially denoted the mystery of the divine. It is the key for early Christian theologians like Origen which unlocks the allegorical meaning of scripture – that is, it denotes the way of interpreting the Bible that does not focus upon historical particularity, but rather unfolds a timeless and eternal message that remains relevant for the whole of Creation. In this sense, for Origen the mystical exemplifies that which is pre-eminently universal and is to be contrasted with the particularity of the historical and psychic dimensions of scriptural exegesis.

Again, the communal rather than the individualistic dimension of *mūstikos* is seen in the description of Christian liturgical practices, such as the Eucharist, as mystical. The mystical is that which transforms a mundane activity (consuming bread and wine) and sacramentalizes it, i.e. transforms it into an event of cosmic and eternal significance. It is through the Eucharistic celebration that the Christian may enter into communion with the timeless realm of God. As Bouyer's work suggests, there is a place in the early Christian tradition for an understanding of the mystical as a form of contemplative experience (the direct apprehension of the divine), but this is not to be divorced from the scriptural and liturgical dimensions of the mystical. This much is clear from Origen himself, for whom the allegorical interpretation of scripture and participation in Christian liturgical practices is not to be divorced from the inspiration of the mystical experience of the divine.

The separation of these various aspects of the mystical and the elevation of one aspect, the experiential, above all others is a product of the modern era. It is important to bear in mind, therefore, the extent to which the contemporary study of mysticism is carried out in the main by scholars wearing psychologically tinted lenses.

There is, of course, a clear experiential dimension to be found in most of the traditions and individuals usually described as 'mystical'. Teresa of Avila, Julian of Norwich, Meister Eckhart, Marguerite Porete, Śaṅkara, Buddhaghosa, etc., all show a great deal of interest in the experiential dimension of the religious life. It is for this reason that they have become of such great interest to modern psychologists of religion from James onwards. However, to study pre-modern mystics (whether Buddhist, medieval Christian or Hindu) without reflecting upon the experiential bias of modern accounts of mysticism will result in an inevitable distortion of the material. The narrowly experiential approach occludes or suppresses other aspects of the phenomenon of the mystical that tend to be more important for these figures and the traditions to which they belong – for example, the ethical dimension of the mystical, the link between mysticism and the struggle for authority, or the extent to which the statements and activities of mystics may relate to issues of politics and social justice. The privatized and narrowly experiential conception of the mystical results in a peculiar preoccupation in academic literature on the subject with indescribable and largely inaccessible experiences of an extraordinary nature. Mysticism at once become decontextualized (and thus amenable to simplistic comparative analysis), élitist (since only certain people can experience it), antisocial (since it is inaccessible to the public realm – to the rest of society), otherworldly (since it is about cultivating private experiences and not engaging with the world) and domesticated (since it is concerned primarily with the cultivation of inner states of tranquillity and the alleviation of anxiety). This formulation of the mystical makes it difficult to reconcile with the goal of political and social transformation. The mystic, it would seem, can only be a revolutionary in spite of, and not because of, her mystical qualities!

The 'mystical' versus the 'rational'

In a recent article in the *Times Higher Education Supplement* (20 August 1993), the question was asked 'Does it make sense to study mysticism in an academic setting?' This is a particularly difficult problem for the academic to answer, particularly if one insists upon a narrowly experiential definition of mysticism. The problem is further compounded if one also puts forward the frequent claim that mystical experiences are 'intuitive', ineffable and beyond the rational. In such circumstances, what hope can one have that academic study of such a topic will furnish fruitful results? Dr Peter Clarke of the Centre for New Religious Movements at King's College, London, is quoted in the article above describing mysticism as:

> an experiential subject ... It is emotional rather than academic or formal or even intellectual. The rise of mysticism is an attempt to get away from the formal outlook ... People want more than consumerism. They are searching for some deeper meaning by turning inwards for access to spiritual power.

Such a characterization of mysticism, while fairly widespread, remains deeply problematic when it is read back into pre-modern cultures (Western and non-Western). As we have seen, the focus upon certain out-of-the-ordinary experiences as constitutive of the mystical is by no means an uncontroversial approach. Such an orientation, while understandable given the modern emphasis on religion as essentially private and the predominance of 'the psychological turn' in the discipline of religious studies, needs to be seen as only one way in which the subject matter might be defined and approached.

The suggestion that 'mysticism' is somehow antithetical to rationality, academia and that it is emotional in contrast to a detached and dispassionate intellectual sphere remain to be argued for and cannot be uncontroversially assumed. Theologian Paul Tillich argues, for instance, that 'Mysticism is not irrational. Some of the greatest mystics in Europe and Asia were, at the same time, some of the greatest philosophers, outstanding in clarity, consistency and rationality.'[47] None the less, Tillich continues to characterize mysticism as a category primarily concerned with ineffable, ecstatic experiences. This caveat aside, Tillich's point is a valid one. Many of those figures who are frequently described as mystics, such as Plotinus, Augustine, Meister Eckhart, Nāgārjuna and Śaṅkara have produced intellectual systems and literary works of a highly sophisticated and erudite nature. Although such historically influential works may not figure prominently in university courses these days, the intellectual integrity and cultural importance of such figures and traditions can hardly be questioned.

In order to properly assess the claim that mysticism, mystics or the mystical is essentially irrational (or perhaps, as Rudolph Otto would have preferred, non-rational) it is important to highlight a number of relevant issues. First, one would have to determine precisely what 'rationality' actually is. Why is mysticism devalued by the adjective 'irrational' (or perhaps even 'non-rational', though here clearly to a lesser degree)? Why is rationality considered so important in modern society? Is rationality foundational (i.e. *sui generis*) or is each culture's ascription of what is rational merely an embodiment of its own social values, presuppositions and forms of life? In order to understand the cultural presuppositions underlying the contemporary claim that mysticism is antithetical to rationality it is necessary to consider the origin of such claims.

Why is mysticism so frequently claimed to be irrational and subjective in modern Western culture? There are a number of reasons for this, most notably the rise of secular rationalism and the location of religion and mysticism firmly within the private (as opposed to the public) sphere. In fact, 'the mystical' has tended to be defined in post-Kantian thought in direct opposition to the 'rational'. Mysticism comes to represent the pre-eminently private, the non-rational and the quietistic. As such it represents the suppressed Other that contributes to the establishment of and high status of those spheres of human activity that are defined as public, rational and socially oriented in the modern Academy.

The denial of rationality to the Other has been a common strategy in subordinating the Other throughout human history and is by no stretch of the imagination simply a Western phenomenon. Ancient Greek accounts of so-called barbarian states (for example, Herodotus on the Persians) have often portrayed such communities as somehow deficient in their thinking. Within Hindu Brahmanical texts we find a similar tendency to construct a largely undifferentiated category to represent foreign 'barbarians' (*mleccha*). Having constructed a largely homogeneous category based upon exclusion and deficiency ('they are not civilized like us', or 'they lack knowledge of the Dharma') it becomes a comparatively simple move to portray such groups as inferior and lacking in the essential qualities characterized by one's own particular community. Attribution of irrationality is thus one of a number of oppressive strategies adopted by the xenophobe throughout history and has also proven a useful weapon in the subordination of women in a variety of cultures.

Indeed, if we are looking for evidence of cross-cultural commonalities, as many contemporary scholars of mysticism seem to be, we ought also to consider the perennial occurrence of the forces of exclusion and subordination and the diverse strategies adopted in those attempting to maintain superiority and authority over others. In this respect, a rather ironic response to the romantic search for a *perennial philosophy* in mystical figures and texts would be to highlight the perennial process of *alterization* at work in the diverse cultures and religious systems of the world. In their avid enthusiasm to discern universalist, tolerant and all-embracing attitudes within mystical literature, proponents of the perennial philosophy tend to ignore the power dynamics and exclusionary strategies adopted by these same texts. If one wishes to emphasize cross-cultural similarities, it seems inappropriate to ignore constantly recurring themes such as oppression and ideology which are also representative of religious and mystical traditions and literature. Indeed in the attempt to construct a universalist perspective from these religions, proponents of the perennial philosophy are, in effect, ignoring some very important (if somewhat unsavoury) ingredients.

'Mysticism' and the construction of modern philosophy

'[T]he "retreat of the mystics" coincides with the dawning of the century of the Enlightenment.'

(Michel de Certeau)[48]

Since the seventeenth century those elements of Western culture that have been classified as 'mystical' have generally been marginalized or suppressed in mainstream intellectual thought, despite a resurgence in Romanticism and a comparable resurgence with the rise of a variety of New Age philosophies in the late twentieth century. In both Romanticism and the New Age, however, the anti-mystical presuppositions of secular rationalism are often inverted rather than rejected, with the revalorization of those factors that are (still) deemed to be irrational or non-rational. In these cases, therefore, the fundamental paradigm that dichotomizes the rational and the mystical has remained largely unquestioned.

One of the most important constitutive factors in determining the way in which the category of 'Mysticism' has come to be understood in modern Western culture is the contemporaneous category of 'Philosophy'. In a number of significant respects 'the mystical' has come to represent the nemesis or antithesis of 'the philosophical'. The polarization of the two is clearly demonstrated in William James' work, *The Varieties of Religious Experience*. Having discussed the (experiential) nature of mysticism in the previous lectures, James immediately turns his attention to the subject of philosophy. For James the juxtaposition of these two categories reflects their antithetical nature. He begins his lecture on Philosophy thus:

> The Subject of Saintliness left us face to face with the question, Is the sense of divine presence a sense of anything objectively true? We turned first to mysticism for an answer, and found that although mysticism is entirely willing to corroborate religion, it is too private (and also too various) in its utterances to be able to claim a universal authority. But philosophy publishes results which claim to be universally valid if they are valid at all, so we now turn with our question to philosophy. Can philosophy stamp a warrant of veracity upon the religious man's sense of the divine?[49]

James, following his own pragmatist line, questions the role of philosophy as a neutral arbiter of public truth, but maintains a significant role for philosophy as the principle of reasoned reflection necessary for making sense of mystical experience. Here a clear dichotomy is set up between reason (philosophy/theology) and a peculiar type of feeling (mysticism). For James, like Schleiermacher, 'feeling is the deepest source of religion' and 'philosophical and theological formulas are secondary products, like translations of a text into another tongue'.[50]

James' polarization of philosophy (rational reflection) and mysticism is highly representative of the relationship between these two spheres in post-Kantian intellectual culture. Philosophy is frequently characterized as the pursuit of rationality in contradistinction to the mystical, which is now seen as the pre-eminent example of the irrational (or non-rational). The philosopher is said to pursue truth using logic and pure argumentation. In contrast the mystic rejects or (more positively represented) transcends rational argumentation. The philosopher works in the public realm to demonstrate the truth through clearly discernible procedures that can (theoretically) be

followed by anyone; thus eschewing the trappings of dogmatism and esoteri-
cism. 'Mysticism', in contrast, refers to that which is esoteric and ill-defined;
the mystic remains interested in rarefied religious experiences available only
to a select few and frequently remains bound to a particular religious world-
view that those experiences merely confirm. This understanding of
'mysticism', of course, has led many in the modern West to suspect that
claims to mystical revelation and authority are dogmatic – since they are
immune to both empirical falsification and rational criticism. Thus mysticism as a manifestation of dogmatism may also be associated with the
phenomenon of religious fanaticism.

It is worth bearing in mind, of course, that the 'discourse on the mystical'
in the contemporary world is by no means homogeneous. The stereotype of
the irrational, dogmatic and private mystic has been questioned no doubt
ever since the term 'mystic' came into common parlance. This reflects the
point made in the introduction to this work, namely that the definition of
'the mystical' remains the cognitive site of a struggle for authority and
power. Thus, one will always find resistance to the dominant paradigm with
representations of mystics as rational, open-minded and socially oriented
figures. Indeed, many sympathetic studies of mystics seem to be motivated
by an attempt to overthrow the predominating stereotype of the world-
denying religious dogmatist. The problem with such approaches, however, is
that in the long run they invariably invert the dominant paradigm rather
than transcend it. Such studies, I would suggest, inevitably end up 'running
against the stream' because they do not pay attention to the broader historical, cultural and political factors that have constructed the modern category
of mysticism in the first place. It is important, therefore, that contemporary
characterizations of the mystical come under close scrutiny if we are to gain
some insight into the way in which the subject matter of 'the mystical' has
come to be represented in modern Western culture.

Silencing the Orient: the absence of 'the mystical' in histories of philosophy

It has become commonplace in the modern era to consider mystics, their
writings and the phenomenon of mysticism in general as being in some sense
antithetical to rationality. Specifically the characterization of Indian religions such as Hinduism and Buddhism as mystical has also tended to
support the exclusion of Hindus and Buddhists from the realm of rationality. I have argued elsewhere that Western philosophers (especially in the
Anglo-American analytic tradition) have tended to construct a secularized
image of their discipline as the exercise of 'pure rationality'. In contrast,
Indian forms of 'systematic thought' have usually been excluded from the
realm of philosophical debate on the grounds that they are tainted with
'theological' assumptions that are culture-specific (as if this were not the
case in the West).[50] Indian philosophy, we are frequently told, tends towards

the mystical and the otherworldly and thus does not maintain the high standards expected of Western philosophy as the pursuit of truth through the exercise of pure rationality. One hardly need point to the political consequences of such attitudes towards non-Western philosophies and cultures.

Postcolonial critics have pointed to the ethnocentricity of much Orientalist historiography. The most influential example being James Mill's *A History of British India* with its periodization of Indian history culminating in the 'liberating arrival' of the British. Eurocentric bias, however, is also apparent in the various histories of philosophy that continue to be produced, with their pointed exclusion of any intellectual thought from non-Western cultures. Such works are generally characterized by a questionable appropriation of ancient Greek culture under the exclusive rubric of the 'West' and the limited (if any) discussion of the importance of African and Islamic thought in the development of European philosophy and science. This point is well made by African philosopher Innocent Onyewuenyi who points out that the great Neoplatonic philosopher Plotinus, who made a number of trips to India and Persia in order to study Oriental thought, was an African – a native of Egypt – as was Hypatia, often acknowledged as the first (known) woman philosopher.

> Names like St Augustine, Origen, Cyril and Tertullian are not unfamiliar: they are black Africans. More pertinent to our subject is the fact that what today we call Greek or Western philosophy is copied from indigenous African philosophy of the 'Mystery System'. All the values of the mystery system were adopted by the Greeks and Ionians who came to Egypt to study, or studied elsewhere under Egyptian-trained teachers. These included Herodotus, Socrates, Hypocrates, Anaxagoras, Plato, Aristotle and others. Are we not taught that Socrates is the first man to say 'Man know thyself?' Yet this expression was found commonly inscribed on Egyptian temple doors centuries before Socrates was born.[51]

Histories of Western philosophy invariably begin with the Greeks and avoid the issue of African and Oriental influences upon ancient Greek thought. What is of particular interest is the absence of reference to the role played by Egyptian and Oriental 'mystery traditions' in the formulation of Greek philosophical ideas and approaches. The significance of these 'mystical' influences upon important early figures in Greek thought such as Plato and Pythagoras has been largely suppressed by modern historians of philosophy, who have remained intent upon drawing a sharp distinction between philosophy (the rational) and mysticism (the irrational). Indeed, since Kant one way in which 'mysticism' as a category has been defined is as the antithesis of rational investigation. 'Philosophy' has tended to include those (mostly male) figures whose writings have proven most amenable to 'secular rationalization'. As Kevin Hart notes:

[T]he ways in which Kant frames mysticism have been decisive, in the post-Kantian reception of mysticism and in the determination of 'philosophy'. From the institution of philosophy as an autonomous academic subject in the Enlightenment to the latter half of the twentieth century, philosophers have shown little interest in the problems generated by the claims of mystics. It was common enough before Kant for philosophy to define itself against poetry or theology; but it is Kant who, more vividly than any before him, introduces mysticism to this role: 'supernatural communication' and 'mystical illumination' become, for Kant, 'the death of philosophy'.[52]

This attitude has become firmly entrenched in the subsequent works of Western philosophers and is something of an a priori assumption in historiographies of philosophy. Descriptions of mysticism as irrational (or, more sympathetically following Rudolf Otto – the non-rational) reflect the construction of 'the mystical' as the excluded 'other' or shadow-side of 'the philosophical'. The force (literally, the *violence*) of such histories of philosophy is precisely in what they exclude from the discussion.

In a spirit of reconciliation between continental and analytic traditions of Western philosophy, Jorge Gracia has recently argued that there have been three strands to the Western philosophical tradition: the mainstream, the poetic and the critical. The mainstream tradition, Gracia suggests, has 'the largest number of adherents as well as the most influential philosophers in the history of Western philosophy until Kant'.[53] No evidence is given for the statistical claim that the mainstream tradition has actually contained the largest number of adherents, nor that members of this approach have been the most influential, but then this is not surprising since it is clear that the category is largely contrived by the author in terms of an a priori preconception of what constitutes (and thus who is to be included in) both 'mainstream' and 'philosophy'. According to Gracia, members of the mainstream tradition are Parmenides, Plato, Aristotle, Augustine, Averroës, Aquinas, Suárez, Descartes, Leibniz and Locke and are to be identified by their trust in our natural faculties of knowledge and 'a mode of philosophical discourse in which argumentation played an essential part'.[54] The poetic tradition includes Pythagoras, Plotinus, Pseudo-Dionysius, Tertullian, Meister Eckhart and Bruno. This tradition is characterized by a distrust of the natural faculties of the senses and reason, claiming that a true grasp of reality can only be gained 'through a mystical or quasi-mystical experience in which our inner self somehow is given direct access to it'.[55] Gracia describes this as a 'non-cognitive' approach, which is dependent upon metaphor and 'mystical insight' with 'little or no argumentation'.[56] Such an approach is said to be profoundly esoteric in the sense that adherents propound 'a private view that can be understood only by those who have had similar experiences'.[57]

> Philosophical discourse in this context becomes primarily expressive
> and directive ... Logical categories and pigeonholes, like contradiction,
> are dismissed because they apply to the realm of reason, not to what is
> beyond reason, with the consequence that supporters of the poetic
> tradition believe that no effective criticisms based upon logical cate-
> gories or empirical evidence can be brought against their point of
> view.[58]

Gracia's third category, the critical tradition, is largely a reaction to the
poetic approach and includes Protagoras, a variety of sceptics and posi-
tivists like Francis Bacon. This tradition eschews metaphysics in favour of
empirical knowledge of the material world and emphasizes 'the use of clear
and objective language in philosophical discourse'.[59]

Gracia's analysis is broader than most philosophical historiographies in
the acknowledgement of a 'poetic' or 'mystical' tradition of philosophy in
the pre-Kantian era. However, one can question not only the placement of
individual philosophers (Parmenides, for instance, would seem to fit equally
as well into the poetic tradition, and while Plato rejects the poetic form in
favour of prose writing, the 'mystical' elements of Platonic thought are
largely ignored by contemporary philosophers), but also the nature of the
typology itself. Who decides what is to count as 'mainstream philosophy'?
Gracia projects the post-Enlightenment construction of the mystical as
esoteric, non-rational, uninterested in argumentation and essentially
concerned with private experiences onto pre-modern materials where such
descriptions are anachronistically inappropriate.

In post-Enlightenment Europe the rise of nation-states and the distinction between public and private on which they were premised allowed for
religion and the mystical to be confined to the private realm (thereby
marginalizing both by depriving them of social and political status). What
sense does it make to talk of mysticism in such terms in a pre-
Enlightenment context? Gracia's association of Anglo-American Analytic
philosophy with the critical tradition and Continental (European) philosophy with the poetic is also somewhat simplistic, even if motivated by a
genuine interest in reconciling the two strands and by an awareness of the
broad differences between the Analytic and Continental approaches to and
definitions of the nature of philosophy.

Characterizations of 'philosophy', of course, require a category of 'non-
philosophical' by which they can be contrasted and defined. Just as the West
has tended to construct images of India as its 'other', modern Western
philosophy (upheld as the ideal of universal and objective rationality based
upon pure argumentation) has constructed a reverse image of 'mysticism' as
its shadow-side. Thus it is precisely the mystical and religious aspects of
Western intellectual thought that have been most systematically ignored by
philosophers and academics since the seventeenth century. It is important to
bear this in mind, not only in contextualizing debates about the nature of

'mysticism' but also in examining the peculiarly secular nature of much of modern Western philosophy. Given the relative lack of antagonism between 'philosophy' and 'religion' in non-Western contexts, the exclusion of apparently religious or mystical thought from the realm of philosophy provides one of the most obdurate obstacles to a postcolonial and cross-cultural dialogue between Western and non-Western cultural traditions. It is in this context that we should understand the claim that it is only the West that possesses philosophy (secular rationality), while the Orient is characteristically mystical (religious irrationality). Both claims are untrue in so far as they attempt to provide an essentialist and homogeneous picture of both Western and Asian cultures.

Associated with this differentiation, of course, are a variety of attendant dichotomies. Thus the West is liberal, egalitarian, secular and modern, whereas Indian culture is authoritarian, hierarchical, religious and traditional. In all cases the West has tended to portray itself as superior in its possession of the former qualities while Indian culture has been seen as inferior in so far as it exhibits the latter. Equally relevant here, of course, is the association of India with the female (and thus the West with the male), and the suggestion that Indian culture in so far as it is mystically inclined, is quietistic, otherworldly and lacking a social orientation.

The roots of the association between the mystical and the irrational (or non-rational) are quite ancient, but the explicit polarization of rationality and mysticism takes on a particularly potent influence in the modern era, particularly given the sheer authority that is now invested in secular and instrumental forms of rationality. 'The mystical' becomes constructed as that which is directly opposed to rational thought. In fact, as we have seen, for Kant 'the mystical' is the death of philosophy.

A more recent incarnation of this attitude can be found in the philosopher Bertrand Russell's article *Mysticism and Logic* (1914). Russell explicitly contrasts the mystical impulse with the scientific impulse and argues that the former has four basic traits: (1) valuing insight (intuition) over discursive analytical knowledge (reason), (2) belief in unity (i.e. a monistic inclination), (3) a denial of the reality of time and an assertion of the timeless (following on from 2), and finally (4) a belief that all evil is mere appearance (again derived from 2 and 3).

Despite an initial questioning of the Enlightenment opposition between intuition and reason, Russell retains the dichotomy by suggesting that creative intuition is what first leads to beliefs, which are then either confirmed or refuted by reason. In other words, rationality is superior to intuition (contrary to the first characteristic of 'the mystical impulse'). For Russell, the incipient monism of the mystical impulse involves an abandonment of logic in favour of unitive experience. 'The supposed insight of the mystic emotion,' Russell suggests, is 'malicious in regard to the world of science and common sense.'[60] Again, reason must prevail. The third aspect of Russell's 'mystical impulse' is the denial of time. For Russell this is simply false. On Russell's account the mystic has had three strikes and should be out of the game. However, Russell does find a place for the mystical feeling, albeit a severely curtailed one, which he suggests does not tell us anything about the world or the nature of reality, but is rather a reflection of our own emotional state of being. Here the mystical impulse has become completely psychologized and, like James before him, can only provide authoritative insights for the individual having the experience. Russell expresses his admiration for the mystical aspiration to universal love, which he sees as both noble and uplifting.

Interestingly enough, despite the tendency to define mysticism in terms of certain extraordinary, non-rational and highly emotional experiences, Russell does find a place for the mystical impulse as promoting an ethical awareness of a higher good. Nevertheless, as a source of authoritative insights into the nature of reality, mysticism fails on all four counts according to Russell, remaining decidedly inferior to the rational and empirical disciplines of philosophy and science. Of course, we have a clear example here of an author setting up a 'straw man' to attack, all the more successful because of the absence of specific examples. The abstract and non-specific nature of 'the mystical impulse' that Russell discerns in human nature is itself a transparently clear example of the construction of a category of mysticism that can then be refuted and/or assigned a relatively marginal role in human affairs.

In expunging or exorcizing the 'mystical' aspects of Western culture, post-Enlightenment thought has also tended to project these same characteristics onto the 'mystic East', which has thus played a significant role in defining the contours of Western cultural identity and thought. In this sense, as post-colonial critics from Edward Said onwards have acknowledged, Orientalism is as concerned with the Occident and the preservation of Western cultural identity through the projection of an Oriental Other as it has been with the manipulation of the East. It is interesting to note in this context that the association of religions such as Hinduism and Buddhism with mysticism and the stereotype of the navel-gazing, antisocial and otherworldly mystic has come to function as one of the most prevailing cultural representations of Indian religion and culture in the last few centuries.

The privatization of mysticism, when coupled with the post-Enlightenment association of the mystical with the non-rational or the irrational, has also led to a characterization of 'mystics' as largely uninterested in or antithetical to social, ecclesiastical and political authority. From within this interpretative paradigm one becomes predisposed to interpreting mystical doctrines, texts, traditions and authors in a manner that makes them appear peculiarly antisocial and otherworldly in orientation. Consequently mysticism becomes a marginal social phenomenon, irrelevant to issues of social justice. The mystical becomes an aspect of religion that is pre-eminently individualistic and private in nature. This characterization is of course a stereotype. Mystics are not necessarily quietistic, antisocial hermits, nor have they always been unconcerned with issues of social justice, poverty, sexual inequality, and so on. However, once this is acknowledged one must be wary of adopting the other extreme of representing mystics as social and political revolutionaries. This, of course, is little more than a reversal of the original stereotype. One suspects that the truth lies somewhere between (or beyond?) the two sides of the dichotomy. Nevertheless, it is important to note that the prevailing attitudes and presuppositions we have about mysticism are culturally specific and ultimately derive from the philosophical presuppositions of Western thought since the Enlightenment. One should therefore be wary of accepting such characterizations of the subject matter as an unproblematic representation of the phenomenon of mysticism, particularly when examining traditions in the pre-Enlightenment era and from non-Western cultures. Such a characterization too easily becomes the perfect model for modern privatized forms of spirituality, which shun engagement with the social, ethical and political issues of the day.

2   Disciplining religion

That there exist in the world such entities as 'the religions' is an uncontroversial claim. ... The concepts 'religion' and 'the religions', as we presently understand them, emerged quite late in Western thought, during the Enlightenment ... Whereas in the Middle Ages the concern of the Christian West had been with faith – a 'dynamic of the heart' – in the seventeenth century attention shifted to the impersonal and objective 'religion'. Increasingly this term came to be an outsider's description of a dubious theological enterprise. Along with 'religion' came the plural 'religions' – 'the Protestant Religion', 'the Catholic Religion', 'Mahometanism', 'heathen Religion', and so on.[1]

Christian theology and the category of 'religion'

I would like to begin this chapter by making a few remarks about the category of 'religion'. The term clearly has a history that is bound up with the cultural and intellectual history of the West and deserves some attention in any discussion on the nature of 'religious studies' as a discipline. I will draw attention, in a fairly rudimentary manner, to some trends in the use of this term and will eventually develop some conclusions of my own about the way the study of 'religion' might most fruitfully approach its own subject matter. In so doing I will also spend some time reviewing some recent attempts to discuss the relationship between religious studies and secularism (including the relationship between religious studies and the secular social sciences) on the one hand and various approaches to the question of the relationship between religious studies and theology on the other.

The term 'religion', of course, derives from the Latin *religio*. In the pre-Christian era Cicero provides an etymology of the term relating it to *relegere* – to re-trace or re-read. Thus, *religio* involves the retracing of 'the lore of the ritual' of one's ancestors.[2] This understanding of the term seems to have gained provenance in the 'pagan' Roman empire and made *religio* virtually synonymous with *traditio*. As such it represented the teachings of one's ancestors and was essentially not open to question. Primarily *religio* involved performing ancient ritual practices and paying homage to the gods.

This explains why the early Christians were frequently described by Romans as atheists precisely because they did not acknowledge the gods of others (including those of the Romans). Indeed, a clear feature of Roman *religio* seems to have been its general tolerance of different traditions (crucially, so long as this did not impinge upon acceptance of civic responsibilities). And why not? If *religio* is primarily about continuing the tradition of one's ancestors, the term clearly denotes an inherently pluralistic context. There can never be one *religio* since there are a variety of different social and ethnic groups with traditions and histories of their own. As Balagangadhara notes:

> When you look at religion as tradition, that is, as a set of practices transmitted over generations, then the term appears as a minor variation of our intuitive notion of culture: to have religion is to have culture. ... Tolerance of different traditions, 'respect' for tradition demonstrated actually by practising the tradition of the other where and when necessary, appear to characterize the Roman religio.[3]

The problem for Christians and Jews within ancient Roman society, therefore, was that they did not consider themselves to be *religiones*, i.e. traditions in this sense, and thus refused to acknowledge the validity of the traditions of other groups. Jews, of course, could argue that they had a recognizable group identity and an ethnic history – a *traditio* of sorts, to which they could appeal. For the early Christians, however, they seem to have been labelled atheists precisely in so far as they could not be seen as belonging to a recognizable *traditio*, having no common ethnic identity (a feature they shared to some extent with the Romans) and, having rejected Mosaic law, no clearly established body of traditional practices. It became increasingly important within early Christian discourses to drive a wedge between the traditional association of *religio* with *traditio*. This occurred through a transformation of the notion of *religio*. Thus, in the third century CE we find the Christian writer Lactantius explicitly rejecting Cicero's etymology, arguing instead that *religio* derives from *re-ligare*, meaning to bind together or link. Thus, for Lactantius, *religio* 'is a worship of the true; superstition of the false. And it is important, really, why you worship, not how you worship, or what you pray for ... They are superstitious who worship many and false gods; but we, who supplicate the one true God, are religious.'[4]

Religio, thus denotes 'the bond of piety', the Covenant between the one true God and man. To see this scholarly debate about the etymological origins of a word as merely academic is to ignore the sense in which debates about the meanings of key terms such as '*religio*' and '*mūstikos*' reflect underlying struggles for authority between rival power groups.

The Christian transformation of *religio* functioned not only to capture authority for Christians in Roman society but also to exclude certain groups from equal consideration. Those who did not bow down to the Almighty and Supreme Deity, worshipping other gods, were now 'alterized' as pagan (*paganus*: 'village idiot') and superstitious. The redefining of *religio* also served to establish the monotheistic exclusivism of Christianity as the normative paradigm for understanding what a religion is.

We cannot attribute the Christian transformation of the term to Lactantius alone, since his etymology (like all etymologies) is merely an attempt to justify current usage according to long-established linguistic convention. Thus, we should acknowledge that Lactantius constructs the etymological foundations of *religio* somewhat *after the fact* (as indeed did Cicero before him), since his writing is little more than an imaginative attempt to codify and legitimate Christian usage and practice with an authority based upon supposedly ancient etymological origins. Nevertheless, as a result of the new Christian theological rendering of *religio*, the ancient-ness of the Christian religion became exemplified fundamentally by the age of its doctrine. Early Christian apologists like Justin Martyr argued that Socrates and Moses were 'Christians before Christ', enlightened by the *logos spermatikos*. The light of the gospel message could be perceived in the scrip-tures of the Hebrew Bible (called the Old Testament by Christians) and in a more limited capacity in the works of Greek and Roman authors like Plato and Virgil.

The shift in the meaning of the term *religio* in a Hellenistic Christian context remains highly significant in our attempt to understand the way in which the concept of 'religion' is understood in modern Western culture. Modern discussions of the meaning and denotation of the term *religio* tend to follow Lactantius' etymology, thereby constructing a Christianized model of religion that strongly emphasizes *theistic belief* (whether mono-, poly-, heno- or pan-theistic in nature), exclusivity and a fundamental dualism between the human world and the transcendent world of the divine to which one 'binds' (*religare*) oneself. Even when Lactantius is not appealed to directly, 'religion' in a Christian (and post-Christian) context now becomes a matter of adherence to particular doctrines or beliefs rather than allegiance to ancient ritual practices.

The semantic shift, represented by Lactantius' discussion, transforms one's entire conception of the nature of religion. In the early Christian context, one consequence of this shift, of course, was the construction of a plethora of heretical movements inculcating what could now be seen as various forms of heterodox belief systems. We should bear in mind that, in a 'pagan' context, questions of truth and falsity were simply not applicable to *religio*. How could traditions and practices be described as either true or false? They were simply the ancestral practices of particular communities. As such, *religiones* were not the kinds of beast that could be approached or questioned in this regard. Note here the implicit pluralism of the Ciceronian understanding of *religio* and *traditio*. One could ask if one was faithfully adhering to a particular ancestral practice but one could not discuss its truth or falsity without funda-mentally misunderstanding the nature of *religio* and *traditio*. The terms were primarily descriptive rather than prescriptive (though Cicero places his own limitations on *religio* in terms of practice!). A modern equivalent of asking if this or that religion were true or false would be to ask if Spanish or Indian or Russian culture were true or false. I shall return to these points later when discussing ways to approach the study of 'religion'.

With a shift towards doctrine as constitutive of the essence of religion, the Christian appropriation of *religio* also represented a new emphasis upon the importance of the written word and its correct interpretation. Religion becomes primarily concerned with doctrine; 'true religion' becomes a matter of orthodoxy; and religion becomes a tradition precisely in so far as it can justify itself in terms of these ancient truths.

> To the pagans, by contrast, *religio* had to do with following ancient practices. The philosophers and the philosophical schools disputed about all kinds of doctrines, including the existence and nonexistence of gods and so forth. Irrespective of such disputations (or even because of them), one continued the traditional practices because they were those of one's forefathers. Variations in such ancestral customs among nations were not only recognized but were also seen as inevitable, because they were human products.[5]

Not surprisingly, contemporaneous pagans found the Christian under-standing of *religio* rather confusing. Why did this new religious movement not acknowledge the gods and traditions of other movements, sometimes even to the point of death (martyrdom)? Why were Christian writings so concerned with matters of belief (orthodoxy) rather than faithful adherence to ancestral practices (orthopraxy)? In the works of the early Christian Fathers we find a preoccupation not only with Hellenistic philosophy but also with a reconstruction of heretical systems of thought. The varieties of pagan movements that existed alongside Christianity in its formative centuries seem to have shown much less concern with the development of systematic theolo-gies. One consequence of this was that the Church Fathers had to turn to the work of Greek philosophers like Plato in order to construct and locate their own theological positions within Graeco-Roman culture.

As we noted in Chapter 1, the roots of the term 'mystical' predate Christian constructions of the term and seemed to have been first used by the various mystery religions of the Roman Empire. In this context 'the mystical', like the term *religio*, seems primarily to have been concerned with the secrecy of ritual practices performed by initiates of these movements. It is in a Christian context that the term comes to denote a spiritual (*pneu-matikos*) hermeneutic of scripture and eventually (in the works of Pseudo-Dionysius) a way of 'speaking about God' – that is, a type of theology. Thus, pagan constructions of 'the mystical' become transformed once they are passed through the theological prism of Christianity.

In the contemporary era we can see a great deal of continuity between modern conceptions of religion and the Christian understanding of *religio*.

Both tend to place a great deal of emphasis upon a faithful (*sic*) adherence to doctrine as indicative of religious allegiance, upon sacred texts as of central importance to religious communities and to questions of truth and falsity as of paramount importance to the religious adherent or 'believer'. The Christian interest in the truth and falsity of religion is distinctive in this aspect and the emphasis it places upon the importance of the historicity of the gospel story and the falsity of pagan mythologies. This is in sharp contrast to the pagan Roman approach, which does not project a dichotomy between myth and history onto the category of *religio*. It would seem that this characteristically Christian approach to religion is also a source of perplexity for those who remain culturally uninfluenced by it. German writer Bichsel relates the following conversation between himself and a young Balinese Hindu:

> A young Balinese became my primary teacher. One day I asked him if he believed that the history of Prince Rama – one of the holy books of the Hindus – is true.
> Without hesitation, he answered it with 'Yes'.
> 'So you believe that the Prince Rama lived somewhere and some-when?'
> 'I do not know if he lived', he said.
> 'Then it is a story?'
> 'Yes, it is a story.'
> 'Then someone wrote this story – I mean: a human being wrote it?'
> 'Certainly some human being wrote it', he said.
> 'Then some human being could have also invented it,' I answered and felt triumphant, when I thought I had convinced him.
> But he said: 'It is quite possible that somebody invented this story. But true it is, in any case.'
> 'Then it is the case that Prince Rama did not live on this earth?'
> 'What is it that you want to know?' he asked. 'Do you want to know whether the story is true, or merely whether it occurred?'
> 'The Christians believe that their God Jesus Christ was also on earth,' I said, 'in the New Testament, it has been described by human beings. But the Christians believe that this is a description of the reality. Their God was also really on Earth.'
> My Balinese friend thought this over and said: 'I had been already so informed. I do not understand why it is important that your God was on earth, but it does strike me that the Europeans are not pious. Is that correct?'
> 'Yes, it is,' I said.[6]

The above discussion is interesting precisely because it represents a dialogue between two different cultures. Both speakers have different conceptions of what it means to say that their religion is 'true'. The German interviewer understands truth in terms of historical actuality. For a story to be true it must have actually happened. His Indonesian teacher, however, seems to conceive of truth more in terms of whether or not the story has truthful insights within it. Questions of historical authenticity in this sense are irrelevant to the question of truth. Indeed the final question of the Balinese teacher suggests that for him the truth of a story is something to do with the practical question of the ethical behaviour of those who believe in it. A true story it would seem is one which promotes an authentic and ethical lifestyle. This approach seems to have much more in common with the Roman uses of *religio* and *traditio* and suggests that the Christian understanding of these terms is a peculiar feature that is perhaps only to be found in the Judaeo-Christian and Islamic traditions.[7] Such an approach also allows for a plurality of 'true' accounts (more than one mythological account can contain the truth within it, even if it does not relate to actual historical events).

There are of course modern exceptions to this rule. Twentieth-century forms of Hindu revivalism, as exemplified by movements such as the Vishwa Hindu Parishad (the Pan-Hindu-Movement), place a great deal of emphasis upon the historicity of figures such as Rāma and Kṛṣṇa as proof of the veridicality of Hinduism. This, however, clearly represents the sense in which modern Hindu movements have been influenced by Christian theological presuppositions as a result of Western colonial supremacy.

We should be aware, therefore, that the central explanatory category of religious studies, namely the notion of 'religion' itself, is a Christian theological category. Like the terms 'mystical' and 'mysticism', 'religion' is a culturally specific social construction with a particular genealogy of its own. In applying this category to the study of non-Western cultures, one should be aware of the theological origins of the term. Indeed for scholars like Balagangadhara its is highly questionable to even assume that there are such things as 'religions' outside a Christian-influenced context.

The concept of 'religion' is the product of the culturally specific discursive processes of Christian history in the West and has been forged in the crucible of inter-religious conflict and interaction. The term thus implies a pluralistic context. As Balagangadhara points out, Christianity has generally served as the prototypical example of a religion and thus as the fundamental yardstick or paradigm-case for the study of 'other religions'.[8] This being the case, one should acknowledge that the comparative study of religion remains founded upon a conceptual framework that is unmistakably theological and Christian in orientation.[9] One of the central tasks for the scholar of non-Christian religions is precisely to work towards untangling some of the Christian presuppositions that have framed the discussion so far.

One problem in discussions about the meaning, denotation and usefulness of the term 'religion' in a cross-cultural context is that the category itself is a privileged one. Balagangadhara makes this point by suggesting that 'religion' is a pre-theoretical category. The a priori (and therefore largely uncontested) status of the category 'religion' is reflected in the fact that in the West it is thought to be *simply common sense* that all cultures have religions and that those religions have been important constitutive factors in the development of those cultures. Debates about the precise denotation of the term 'religion', whether there is an 'essence' to religion or whether it is a polythetic concept, do not question the fundamental assumption that there are things called 'religions' that are easily identifiable and classified in terms of specific names such as Christianity, Islam, Judaism, Hinduism, Buddhism, Jainism, Taoism, etc.[10]

The precise nature of 'religion' and 'the religions' is still an issue that is frequently debated (even if the fundamental category itself is rarely questioned). As such, 'religion' remains a topic that is still subject to ongoing discursive processes. Like the category of 'the mystical', defining the nature of 'religion' remains a political exercise, even in a modern secular academic context. For example, the claim that Marxism, capitalism, nationalism or psychoanalysis might be classified as modern religions often reflects attempts by scholars of religion to establish greater authority for themselves in a context where 'religion' and religious questions have increasingly become marginalized concerns in modern Western society. In an age where the academic pursuit of knowledge has come under increasing pressure to justify itself to others, why invest finances and resources to study ancient religious traditions that no longer exist? Why bother to study new religious movements that are located on the fringe of modern society? However, if Marxism and nationalism can be understood as modern forms of religion then there remains a potentially important role for the scholar of religion in an apparently secularized society.

Secularism and the 'iatrogenic' effect of studying religion

The roots of contemporary academia, institutionalized in the modern, Western university system, are established in the soil of the Enlightenment. Religious studies, of course, is a relatively modern academic discipline that has tended to have a particularly uneasy relationship with its older sibling, theology. The distinction often made between the two runs along the following lines: theology is the traditional study of the Judaeo-Christian religions, usually with some presumption of Christian allegiance. Religious studies, on the other hand, is a secular discipline that neither presumes nor precludes allegiance to any particular religious system or world-view. In the modern era, religious studies has also taken on board a particularly pluralistic emphasis, extending the scope of its scholarly analysis to a wide range of religions other than Christianity. I shall label this model 'the separatist paradigm'. In many senses the separatist paradigm reflects the political dissociation of Church and State that characterizes many modern Western nations. I do not think that the political dimensions of this point should be underestimated. Within a secular academic institution the conception of religious studies as an avowedly non-confessional, secular and 'open-ended'

academic discipline has clear advantages in terms of the politics of the institution and prevailing attitudes towards the academic work of that
department. It also has implications for the perception of religious studies in
the wider academic and non-academic communities in which scholars live
and work. Depending upon the nature of those communities this model may
be advantageous or it may not. Putting aside the political dimension of the
debate for the moment (though I do not think we can afford to ignore that
dimension in the final analysis), I would like to spend some time examining
the supposedly 'secular' nature of 'religious studies'.

There are, of course, a number of ways in which one might wish to
approach the issue of the relationship between the study of religions and
more traditional academic interests in Christian theology. One might wish to
argue that religious studies is a secular and non-confessional discipline and
is not in fact confined by the presuppositions of Christian theology. This is a
dangerously naïve stance to take. The modern study of religion is not unaffected by the Christian heritage of Western culture and by the development
of theology as an academic discipline in the West, nor is the apparently
secular nature of religious studies a 'position from nowhere'. Indeed, as
scholars such as John Milbank have argued, humanistic and atheistic forms
of secularism in the post-Enlightenment West continue to define themselves
in opposition to the Christian theological categories that they claim to have
superseded. Just as atheism in the Roman Empire was defined as that which
opposed Roman conceptions of *religio* (and thus included Christianity),
atheism in the modern era has come to denote belief in the non-existence of
the Christian God. The post-Christian nature of contemporary Western
secularism has inevitable implications for the secular (and *apparently* non-
theological) stance of many contemporary scholars of religion. One of the
central methodological concerns of the study of religions is the issue of
those Christian and post-Christian presuppositions that continue to condition the discipline and limit our understanding of non-Christian cultures in
their own terms. It is easy to see why scholars of 'religious studies' have
attempted to legitimate their work within the intellectual framework of the
modern secular Academy by claiming to operate from a non-confessional
and 'neutral' stance, which they have described as secular. This, however,
should not prevent us from questioning the nature of that secularism and its
role in informing the discipline within which we work.

We should be aware of the sense in which the study of religion can have
iatrogenic consequences for the purported object of its study. *Iatrogenesis* is
a medical term referring to the damage or ill health that is sometimes caused
by the administering of medical treatment. Here I am using the term
metaphorically to highlight the sense in which religious studies as a cognitive
discipline may actually distort or reduce that which it is claiming to investi-
gate and explain. As an example of this we shall consider the possibility that
the secular framework upon which the modern discipline of religious studies
is founded may actually subordinate religious phenomena and emic explana-

tions of it to a secular meta-discourse. In other words, to what extent does the secular study of religion subvert or devalue religious beliefs and explanations of the world?

There are, of course, a number of theoretical presuppositions that condition the manner in which religions come to be understood by the modern Western academic. These reflect certain aspects of Western culture that have informed the development and orientation of the various cognitive disciplines. The most relevant factors involved in the (mis?)representation of religion in religious studies are:

(a) Literary bias. The two interrelated factors of the Protestant Reformation and the mass production and distribution of printed texts in Europe since the eighteenth century have both contributed to a high degree of literacy in the West. The Reformation promoted an individualistic approach to religion and the ideal that all Christians should be able to read the Bible for themselves. Combined with the growing availability of the printed word, we find a strong academic emphasis upon the text as the locus of religion.

(b) The success and development of the natural sciences and the rise of scientific rationalism as a potent world-view in the modern Western world. As we have seen, this has resulted in attempts to model all cognitive disciplines on the methodologies of the natural sciences. Thus, scholars of religion attempt to legitimate their work by the establishment of methodologies that claim to follow objective and neutral methods based upon rational analysis and sound empirical investigation in an attempt to avoid subjective prejudices and the favouring of predictable phenomena (e.g. rituals), which can be repeated, analysed and classified.

(c) The rise of secular humanism and the notion of a secular reason disembodied from tradition, which provides the foundation for the modern Western university system. This Enlightenment ideal resulted in the development of religious studies as a separate, secular discipline, distinguishable from theology. In the modern era, we have also seen the professionalization of academia along secular lines.

(d) Eurocentrism. Somewhat inevitably, given the culturally pluralistic nature of the subject matter of religious studies, Western scholars have often been guilty of contributing to the colonial process of the non-Western world in their analysis of other cultures.

Recently, all four trends have come under attack by scholars. The literary bias within academia and religious studies has been addressed by the work of Jack Goody, Walter Ong and Gregory Schopen. The belief that the 'interpretive' human disciplines should follow the lead of the natural sciences has been criticized from a number of quarters, but perhaps most effectively by the hermeneutics of Hans Georg Gadamer. The secular presuppositions of

religious studies has been subject to trenchant criticism by scholars such as
Robert Bellah and John Milbank. Finally, the pitfalls of Eurocentrism and
the propagation of Orientalist discourses have been critically analysed by
scholars such as Edward Said and Ronald Inden.

The Enlightenment roots of religious studies

Religious studies as an academic discipline developed from the seeds sown
during the Enlightenment. What is generally referred to as 'the
Enlightenment' is a particular period or movement within European intellectual history that had far-reaching sociopolitical and cultural
consequences for the modern Western world (and inevitably, given the hegemony of the Western world, of the entire globe). While 'the Enlightenment'
is not a homogeneous movement or process within eighteenth-century
European society,[11] there are a number of generally predominating factors
to be found in the intellectual thought of this period. A useful list is given by
Peter Hamilton in his attempt to outline the basic 'paradigm' of
Enlightenment thought.[12] The ten factors he lists are:

1   The primacy of reason and rationality as means for understanding and
    organising knowledge about the human and natural worlds.
2   Empiricism – the philosophical doctrine that all human knowledge
    about the world is ultimately derived from empirical evidence accessible
    through the sense organs.
3   The rise of science as an important cultural and intellectual factor in
    contemporary society. This was the result of rapid technological
    advancement within the natural sciences resulting in an increasing capa-
    bility for controlling and manipulating the natural world as well as a
    mood of growing anti-clericalism within European society.
4   Universalism, i.e. the belief that the principles of reason and science
    could be applied outside of the European context, and that there were
    certain rational procedures, logical rules and scientific laws that were
    applicable to all human societies, and perhaps even to the entire universe.
    It would seem that a major goal of 'the Enlightenment project' (if one
    can use such a phrase without necessarily implying a univocal and homo-
    geneous agenda) was the search for universal and unifying foundations
    such as the principle of rationality, a common human nature underlying
    cultural diversity and the development of a neutral or objective frame-
    work and methodology for discerning such universal principles.
5   A progressive view of history, whereby contemporary society is seen as
    the ever-developing pinnacle of previous historical epochs. Human
    history on this view progresses on a developmental path from ignorance
    (as seen in the description of the previous era as 'the Dark Ages') to
    enlightenment, from intolerance to tolerance, from social restriction to
    social liberation and freedom, from the dogmatic shackles of tradition-

alism to the liberalism and open-mindedness of free thought; all factors contributing to the continual increase in humankind's control of its own destiny and of the natural world and of increasing social amelioration.

6   Individualism – the notion that the individual is the most basic constituent of human society and history. Associated with this is, of course:

7   The promotion of the value of tolerance of others. The upholding of toleration as a cardinal virtue and the rise of individualism in the West have manifested themselves in the increasing emphasis upon the notion of fundamental human rights (as enshrined in the French Revolution's Declaration of the Rights of Man and of the Citizen and the Declaration of Independence and the Bill of Rights of the United States of America), the development of democratic political systems and the gradual abolition of slavery in the Western world.

8   A powerful rhetoric of Freedom – the censure and eventual abolition of traditional and feudal restrictions to trade, belief, social interaction, sexuality and ownership of property. Of course, one can hardly suggest that this rhetoric has been matched in practical terms, particularly for instance with regard to the status of women in society.

9   The uniformity of human nature – the fundamental belief that human beings have a common human nature (usually involving the cardinal faculty of rationality), which unites them across social, historical and cultural boundaries.

10   Secularism – the rejection of religious explanations of the world as ultimate. In the context of eighteenth- and nineteenth-century Europe, secularism was often incarnated as a particularly belligerent form of anti-clericalism, involving both a social critique of the authoritarian hegemony of the Church within European society and a rejection of Christian dogma based upon a variety of humanistic, philosophical and scientific grounds.

Clearly this outline is by no means comprehensive, nor is it so intended. Nevertheless, there are some important factors from the Enlightenment period of European history that are omitted by Hamilton and that have influenced modern Western perceptions of the world and therefore remain relevant to our discussion. In particular it is important to be aware of the rise of nationalist discourses. The dividing up of humanity into certain geocultural groupings called 'nations' is a relatively modern development. The roots of nationalism derive from social, economic and political changes in Europe from the sixteenth century onwards, but the notion of a national identity as a consciously unifying factor of people cannot be said to have been an influential social construct in Europe until the eighteenth century (and in some cases much later).

A second feature relevant to a discussion of the factors that have impinged upon the discipline of religious studies in a modern, Western

academic environment is naturalism – that is, the belief that the fundamental paradigm for acquiring knowledge of reality is to be found in the
methodology of the natural sciences. In its more aggressive forms, naturalism manifests as scientism – a full-frontal assault on any claim to
authority that is not mediated by (what is claimed to be) the experimental
methods of the natural sciences. Science, of course, does not necessarily
contradict the insights and claims to knowledge of religion, but scientism
clearly does. While there is no sense in which one could classify all
Enlightenment thought as scientistic, it is clear that the primacy with which
the natural sciences were held in the Enlightenment (and for that matter in
the modern era) when conjoined with anti-traditionalist, anti-clerical and,
broadly speaking, secularist trends within European society, have
contributed to the growth of scientism as a powerful world-view in the
modern Western world.

In a more covert form, scientism can be discerned in the hegemony of the
natural sciences in the field of modern academic disciplines of knowledge.
In this sense the natural sciences, due to their apparent record of success and
rapid advancement, the claimed verifiability of hypotheses within a neutral
or 'objective' framework and their resultant position of prestige within
contemporary society (all of which can and have been questioned by
philosophers), have been influential in the development of epistemic
methodologies beyond those involved in the analysis of the natural world.
As specialist discourses have developed with their own terminology and
object of study, various cognitive disciplines have arisen in an increasingly
compartmentalized and professionalized environment in the various
academic institutions in the modern, Western world. In such a context, the
cognitive discipline known as religious studies has developed and the various
methodologies of this subject area have been influenced by the prestige and
hegemony of the natural sciences. The consequence of this is that the natural
sciences have come to be seen by many as the paradigmatic model for the
pursuit of all forms of knowledge including, what is sometimes explicitly
called the 'scientific study of religion'. It is important to bear this, and the
scientistic presuppositions underlying it, in mind when considering current
methodologies for the study of mysticism and indeed of religion as a whole.

As we have seen, the roots of contemporary academia, institutionalized
in the modern, Western university system, are established in the soil of the
Enlightenment. The term 'Enlightenment' suggests a differential and negative appraisal of the previous era (the 'Dark Ages'). This reflects two aspects
of the Enlightenment enterprise: (1) the modern myth of progress, and (2)
modernity's self-conscious rupture with what preceded it, sometimes polarized as 'traditional versus modern'. While the first feature is often
questioned and condemned in what are usually labelled 'postmodern' writings, such works often display the second characteristic, emphasizing the
irruptive and novel situation created by the 'postmodern condition'.

It is not difficult to discern the roots of the schism between theology and religious studies in the ethos of the Enlightenment. The institutional usurpation of theology as 'queen of the disciplines' in the medieval university structure in favour of a more modern, secular framework for the pursuit and promulgation of knowledge in the academic institutions of the West has led to the development of a secularized approach to the study of religion. This has involved utilizing methodologies from a variety of other cognate disciplines (such as sociology, anthropology, history, and the phenomenological movement in European philosophy).

Scholars in the area of religious studies have often made the claim that the methodologies used in this discipline are objective and neutral in that they neither presuppose nor preclude any particular religious commitment. This claim, however, will only stand if it can be shown that studying religion from within a secular framework is objective and neutral and that such an orientation does not distort or misrepresent the object of study. As Walter Capps has argued, religious studies was constructed upon a foundation of readily identifiable Enlightenment convictions including the belief that:

1   objects of investigation have essences, which are discrete and unchangeable;
2   religion can be routinely investigated by the scientific method;
3   an agreed upon sense of 'objectivity' makes truth publicly or commonly accessible, regardless of what the subject is;
4   analysis can be separated from attitude; and
5   dispassionateness is a fit mode of scholarly enquiry, most able to make truth accessible. All of these assumptions presume the cardinal one, which is that clarity appears through the process of breaking things down into smaller and smaller pieces, so as to be able to discover the irreducible core.

These theoretical and methodological presuppositions have contributed to what I have called the iatrogenic effect of religious studies.

> The Enlightenment made the subject manageable, but Enlightenment-influenced approaches deal only with religious studies' manageable aspects ... Religion has been translated into religious studies so that a certain kind of mapwork might be invoked. In being translated, the subject has also been pared.[13]

Robert Bellah has also drawn attention to the Enlightenment heritage of modern academia in his critique of the secularist perspective of religious studies. According to Bellah:

> If one believes that the critical theories with which one explains religion are truer than the religious beliefs themselves, then one is opting for an ultimate stance which is at least quasi-religious. In this sense, what is

really being taught in religious studies is often positivism or relativism or historicism. These are powerful modern ideologies with spiritual, ethical and political implications. They may accord so closely with the majority ethos, or, if not the majority ethos, the influential ethos of the cognitive elite, what I have called 'enlightenment fundamentalism,' that they seem to be simply true rather than only one possible position among others. In the guise of teaching 'about' religion, very powerful beliefs, even dogmas, are being conveyed.[14]

Sociologist Peter Berger outlines a position that he labels 'methodological atheism'.[15] This approach reflects the social constructivism prevalent to varying degrees in modern sociology of religion, a position outlined in Berger and Luckmann's aptly named work, *The Social Construction of Reality*. Berger's position derives from the 'realization' that all religious phenomena (including all beliefs) are socially constructed, and therefore causally dependent upon social, historical and cultural factors for their existence. Berger's account, while it postures as an heuristic methodology rather than an outright dogmatic argument for the falsity of religion, nevertheless does exhibit the secularist and atheistic presuppositions of much contemporary sociological accounts of religion.[16] Sociologist Christina Larner, a proponent of this stance, even goes so far as to argue in the published edition of her 1982 Gifford Lectures that, 'In methodological atheism, religion is to be viewed as a human projection.'[17]

In response to this position, Robert Bellah has suggested that scholars should avoid the intellectual hubris of the social sciences, which he believes is present in all reductionist accounts of religious phenomena. According to Bellah, the relativism and historicism of social-scientific perspectives reduce religious experiences, beliefs and practices to cultural, sociohistorical and political factors, which are then seen as their primary causes and determinants. Such an approach subordinates the religious view to the higher-order analysis of the secular scholar, and results in the 'museumification of religion', where religions become little more than a series of quaint artefacts, like 'butterflies pinned to a wall'.[18] To prevent religious studies as a discipline from functioning as little more than a priesthood for militant secularism, Bellah emphasizes the importance of a non-reductionist approach to the study of religion, a methodology he labels 'symbolic realism'. Bellah's approach attempts to incorporate the critical and analytical perspectives and tools of the social sciences, which he acknowledges do furnish fruitful insights into the nature of religious phenomena. However, Bellah rejects any attempt to establish the secular and historicist presuppositions of these cognitive disciplines as superior to religious explanations themselves.

[A]s Durkheim said of society, religion is a reality *sui generis*. To put it bluntly religion is true. This is not to say that every religious symbol is equally valid any more than every scientific theory is equally valid. But it does mean that since religious symbolization and religious experience are inherent in the structure of human existence all reductionism must be abandoned. Symbolic realism is the only adequate basis for the social scientific study of religion.[19]

In contrast to Peter Berger's approach, which appears to represent the mainstream sociological position, one might call Bellah's approach a form of 'methodological agnosticism',[20] in so far as it allows for further analysis and dialogue between the specialist and the religious tradition he or she is studying.[21] Bellah, following the work of Paul Ricoeur, suggests a methodological stance of 'secondary naïveté'.[22] Primary naïveté reflects an uncritical and unreflective approach to religion. Contemporary academic scholarship combats this with the use of critical and analytical techniques. However, Bellah suggests that if this is the final word the religious subject matter under examination becomes belittled by the critical spectacles through which it is viewed. Thus, one should return to the religious symbol itself, not by abandoning criticism, but by allowing the object under investigation to speak in the light of such critical analysis. Talal Asad has also criticized 'the sociologism according to which religious ideologies are said to get their real meaning from the political or economic structure, and the self-confirming methodology according to which this reductive semantic principle is evident to the (authoritative) anthropologist and not to the people being written about.'[23]

I find both Asad's and Bellah's arguments in this regard quite challenging, and the movement towards a more dialogical relationship with the religious phenomena under examination is, in my view, to be encouraged. The circular nature of Bellah's three-stage methodology (i.e. the religious perspective, the critical analysis thereof, followed by a consideration of the religious response to such analysis), provides a built-in methodological corrective to the irreligious dogmatism of secular reductionism.[24] This approach, while undoubtedly rather vague and schematic, is at the same time flexible enough to provide a broad guideline for study, and will inform much of the analysis and discussion to be found in this book.

One criticism of 'methodological agnosticism', however, might be that it is also a posture, or a 'public relations' exercise, since it is in practice impossible to maintain a position of hermeneutical 'agnosticism', free from prejudice (a criticism that some might lay at the feet of phenomenological approaches to the study of religion).[25] It is indeed a fallacy to believe that any sophisticated methodology can be adhered to at all times. As a fallibilist, I think that we should acknowledge that the scholar as a human being is unable to aspire to the heights of complete 'objectivity'. We should look upon methodologies not as cast-iron structures, within which we can established fixed and definitive positions, but rather as praxis-ideals that one should at least attempt to aspire to. One may never actually attain an idealized realm of complete neutrality or objectivity, but this should not preclude attempts to aspire in the direction of a greater understanding of the phenomena under discussion.

Recently, the secularist presuppositions of the social sciences (particularly the sociology of religion) have been attacked by John Milbank in his book *Theology and Social Theory: Beyond Secular Reason*. He argues that:

> all the most important governing assumptions of such [secular social] theory are bound up with the modification or the rejection of orthodox Christian positions. These fundamental intellectual shifts are, ... no more rationally 'justifiable' than the Christian positions themselves.[26]

According to Milbank, modern theology has been 'emasculated' by the hegemony of secular reason in contemporary intellectual circles. The historicism of social theories has made theology aware of the contingency of all movements, beliefs and ideas, including itself. Milbank, however, sees this position as self-defeating, opening up the possibility for a postmodern response to secularism.

> [T]he question has now arisen for social theory as to whether Nietzschean suspicion is the final and truly non-metaphysical mode of secular reason, or else itself embodies an ontology of power and conflict which is simply another mythos, a kind of re-invented paganism. To pass critically beyond Nietzsche is to pass into a recognition of the necessity and yet the ungrounded character of some sort of meta-narrative, some privileged transcendent factor, even when it comes disguised as the constant element in an immanent process.[27]

Thus, according to Milbank, postmodern social theory 'increasingly finds secularization paradoxical, and implies that the mythic-religious can never be left behind'.[28] For Milbank and the 'Radical Orthodoxy', however, this heralds the establishment of an enclave for the preservation of Christian belief and practice, now safely reinforced from secular criticism by the end of all master narratives. This rendering of the 'postmodern' situation, however, takes no account of the pluralistic context of contemporary Western culture, nor does it unmask the colonial dimensions of the continued 'will-to-power' involved in the promotion of Christian evangelism and theology, whether traditional or 'radical' in nature.

One should note, however, that the notion of 'secularism' under attack here is itself not without ambiguity. The 'militant secularism' that Bellah and Milbank are attacking in their critique of the disciplines of sociology and religious studies seems to amount to an irreligious rejection of religious points of view. Both scholars argue that this is itself a 'religious' (or ultimate) stance in direct competition with other religious points of view. However, it is also possible to understand secularism in a manner that is not directly antagonistic to religious perspectives in general, though remaining reluctant to endorse any particular religious world-view as definitive. This model of secularism, taken from contemporary Indian politics and influenced by Indian reformers such as Mohandas Gandhi and Swāmi Vivekānanda, bases itself upon the principle of *Sarva Dharma Sambhava* (often loosely translated as 'let all religions prosper'), entailing a kind of 'non-specific religiosity'. This position amounts to a refusal to endorse any particular religious perspective, while leaving open the very real possibility of the truth of any (or all) of them. As such it appears to be compatible with Bellah's symbolic realism, which he explicitly describes as a perspective that acknowledges the truth claims of religion without necessarily endorsing every religious symbol as equally valid.[29]

The problem with the first form of secularism (which I have labelled 'militant secularism'), as repudiated by Bellah and Milbank, is that it manifests a strongly anti-religious bias (being antithetical to religion, or, more specifically given its Enlightenment origins, to Christianity – hence Milbank's description of this position as 'neo-paganism'). Militant secularism, therefore, tends towards a positivistic attitude towards other perspectives. Indian secularism, however (at least that version of it that I am here outlining), while avoiding the aggressive and anti-religious hubris of militant secularism, attempts to sit on the fence. This, of course, has led to problems in modern Indian politics. Some have argued that it is precisely the 'slippery' pragmatism of Indian politics that has fuelled communal unrest in contemporary India, as well as a widespread feeling that politicians are opportunistic chameleons, changing their colours to suit the particular voting community to whom they are appealing for support.[30] In a similar vein, Bryan Turner has accused Bellah's 'symbolic realism' of avoiding the issue of truth claims, arguing that such an approach tends to undermine the particularity of religious truth claims (in its attempt to avoid assessing the truth claims of all religions) and that it dovetails too easily with modern American secularism and notions of a non-specific civil religion.[31] Turner, in fact, has defended causal accounts of religion on the grounds that they do not in and of themselves have a bearing upon the truth or falsity of religious beliefs.[32] Turner is correct to distinguish explaining religion in social terms from 'explaining away' religion, but I would want to stress the necessity of resisting sociological causal theories as *definitive* accounts of such beliefs. It seems to me that to accept the sociological explanation as a sufficiently adequate account is precisely to erase the religious or 'revelatory' dimension of religious phenomena.

Another problem with the non-specificity of this second form of 'secularism' is that it can also function as a means to hide the particular prejudices and stance of the scholar of religion. One does not know from what position the scholar is speaking and what prejudices might be at work in the ensuing analysis. For some this might be seen as a good thing, since personal preferences might be seen as having no legitimate role to play in the academic study of religion. However, others might want to argue that positionality is inevitable and that as a methodological position within religious studies such 'open-ended secularism' may frequently function precisely to cloak the implicit prejudices of the scholar. My own methodological preference is to favour this second form of secularism ('methodological agnosticism'), so long as it is combined with an attempt by the scholars concerned to highlight their own 'pre-judgements' and stance when approaching the material. Stating one's own view may not always be appropriate and indeed may get in the way of providing an account of the material one is discussing, but in general I am an advocate of the importance of self-reflexivity on the part of the academic practitioner. In my own approach to teaching and writing about religion, I find a form of 'methodological agnosticism' to be a more fruitful way forward in attempts to understand the religious phenomena than 'methodological atheism', which, in so far as it takes reductionist accounts more seriously than religious accounts of the same phenomena, amounts to the promulgation of a non-religious world-view as ultimate. This is not to endorse a particular religious perspective but rather to acknowledge the sense in which the academic study of religion and scholars working in that area cannot claim ultimate jurisdiction in these matters. To avoid what I believe are the very real concerns highlighted by Bellah and Milbank's analyses of this latter form of secularism in the study of religion, one must be prepared to confront the secularist context of religious studies head on and come to terms with the provisionality and fallibility of one's own findings.

I have spent some time discussing the relationship between religious studies and the secular study of religious phenomena. It would be worth while at this juncture to consider more closely the relationship between religious studies and the particular religious perspectives, traditions and movements that it purports to examine. It seems to me that religious studies occupies a contested space in Western academic circles and in that respect can also function as a mediator between two types of competing meta-discourses – the secular and the religious. This is the problematic within which much of the work of scholars of religion can be located. In so far as academics maintain the right of freedom of expression, the scholar of religion should be able to express alternate opinions and challenge perspectives offered by the religious traditions themselves. However, on the other hand it is also the case that scholars of religion, in so far as they are claiming authority to speak about the various religions, have a certain responsibility to provide a balanced and fair portrayal of that in which they are claiming expertise. All scholars of religion are caught in this tension and different academics will locate themselves at different places on the continuum in order to deal with that tension with regard to their own specialisms. Sometimes it is tempting to opt for either the rock or the hard place just to get some shade, though I would like to argue that the effectiveness of scholars of religion resides precisely in their *unwillingness* to resolve this tension with any degree of finality. As intellectuals, scholars of religion both live and work in that unresolved tension.

Modelling religious studies: theology or 'cultural studies'?

I shall frame this section of the debate in terms of the relationship between religious studies and its older sibling 'theology', but wish to suggest that 'religious studies' might avoid some of the problems traditionally associated with its methodology by redefining itself as a specific form of 'cultural studies'. Such an approach constitutes, I would argue, a reconceptualization of the notion of 'religion' in such a way that it no longer remains bound to the peculiar orientations of Christian theological speculation. Such a reconstruction of the fundamental category of analysis, of course, resonates much more closely with the pre-Christian understandings of *religio*, just as it has more in common with the approach of our Balinese friend mentioned earlier, for whom a religion could be 'true' (that is, symbolically valid) even if it did not correspond to historical fact.

Although in the British context with which I am most familiar, 'theology' generally refers to Christianity, one could also conceive of this debate in terms of the relationship between religious studies and Islam, or religious studies and Buddhist doctrine, etc. Most of the remarks that follow will refer to the cultural context in which most Western scholars of religion find themselves, and this will inevitably mean reference to the Christian theological context. However, the issues that arise are also relevant to the question of confessional stances or 'insider perspectives' in other traditions as well. Consider, then, the following three models of the relationship between religious studies and theology (there may well be others):

Model 1: 'The separatist paradigm'

This model conceives of theology as a way of studying religion which can be clearly differentiated from the secular, pluralistic and non-confessional stance of religious studies.

Model 2: Religious studies as a 'broad church' (pun intended!)

On this view the theological approach is merely one of a number of methodologies for studying religion. This approach establishes a place for theology *within* religious studies, though, of course, problems remain in reconciling theological and secular presuppositions within the discipline.

Model 3: Theology as a 'broad church'

The third approach is to place religious studies within the larger framework of 'theology'. From this perspective the entire endeavour of studying religion – even from an avowedly secular and pluralistic perspective – functions within the wider sphere of theology as a whole.

Approaches that emphasize the distinctiveness of the secular study of religion from theology (variants of Model 1) are usually motivated by concerns that taking an insider's stance from a particular religious tradition undermines critical reflection and the acknowledgement of alternative perspectives. Ninian Smart, for instance, has frequently argued that the best person to teach a course on Buddhism is someone who is *not* a Buddhist, since they are more likely to be able to maintain some sense of critical distance and detachment from the material they are examining and thereby avoid the dangers of promulgating their own version of Buddhism (proselytization). The advantage of an outsider's perspective can also be seen in the readiness of such a scholar/teacher to entertain positions and explanations that might be seen as antithetical to the truth claims of the particular religious perspective under consideration. Some of the problems and issues of taking an 'outsider's' approach to the study of religion have been mentioned earlier in the discussion of the views of Robert Bellah and John Milbank. Interestingly, Ninian Smart has revised his earlier position and now argues that the best person to teach a course on Buddhism is someone who was a Buddhist in a past life!

Model 2 acknowledges the polyvocality and multidisciplinarity of religious studies. Scholars within religious studies utilize a variety of methodological approaches, including anthropology, history, sociology, literary studies, philosophy, psychology *and* theology. There are of course a number of tensions or problems involved in this attempt to establish some commonality between religious studies and theology. In particular, how does one reconcile the generally secular approaches of anthropology, sociology and philosophy, etc., with the theological association with a particular religious tradition and/or perspective? One way of doing this is to emphasize the importance of interdisciplinarity rather than multidisciplinarity. If religious studies is an interdisciplinary exercise then no particular methodological approach should be seen as immune from critical examination and interaction with the perspectives and approaches of other methodologies. Thus, philosophical approaches should remain mindful of and subject to the insights of anthropological, sociological, psychological and theological approaches to the material; theological approaches remain subject to philosophical, sociological, and anthropological analysis, anthropology requires engagement with the philosophical debates that impinge upon its study, and so on.

An advocate of Model 1 (separatist paradigm) might criticise Model 2 on the grounds that there is no place for the *practice* of theology within religious studies, though there is clearly a place for the examination of theological works and perspectives. On this view the religious studies scholar is more of a historian of religious ideas (who thus studies theology as an object of investigation) rather than a *practising* theologian.

Model 3 (theology as the umbrella for religious studies) places the latter within the wider circle of theology as a discipline. On the face of it this might be thought to be the implicit position of the variety of theology and religious studies departments in existence throughout the various UK universities, for instance, though in reality this would be too simplistic an analysis, as different departments and scholars within those departments clearly take a variety of stances on this issue. Model 3 is historically grounded in the antiquity of theology as opposed to religious studies as a traditional academic subject in European universities. What has tended to happen in recent decades is that traditional theology departments or faculties have expanded to include religious studies – largely in response to changes in the religious and social profile of the contemporary North-Western world. There are a variety of reasons why particular scholars might advocate some version of this model. For instance one might wish to argue that religious studies is itself merely another (modern) type of theology. Perhaps the study of religion in the West remains so inextricably bound up with the explanatory categories of Western intellectual history that it remains fundamentally Christian and theological in nature. Of course this might turn out to be the case. The question remains then, should religious studies continue to be located within (and subsumed by?) departments or faculties of theology?

Perhaps of the three models I have outlined it is the distinction between Model 1 and the other two that is most striking. Some scholars, particularly those influenced by contemporary postmodernist trends, might want to argue that, in so far as there is no such thing as a neutral 'view from nowhere', all stances, whether explicitly theological or secular and non-religious, remain bound up with particular personal preferences. Prima facie, this approach seems to undermine the foundations on which the separatist model is built. If the no-man's-land that the separatist paradigm maintains between theology and a non-confessional approach to the study of religion disappears, theological and secular perspectives remain competing perspectives in an arena with no neutral ground.

However, problems remain with this stance. If the secular (non-religious?) study of religion is merely one of a number of competing stances along with the Christian study of religion, the Buddhist study of religion, the Islamic study of religion, the Rastafarian study of religion, where is one to draw the line between the competing confessional perspectives? Are scholars of religion to allow Hindu, Muslim, Christian and atheistic approaches to religion but disregard Scientology, Unificationism, and Baha'ism, presumably on the grounds that they do not have enough advocates in their own particular neck of the woods to warrant legitimacy? If one acknowledges that 'everyone has a position' where does one draw the line between what is acceptable and what is not?

Perhaps the answer lies somewhere in the acceptance of the principle of diversity – i.e. the explicit acknowledgement of the importance of multiperspectival approaches and the pluralism engendered by the study of a variety of religious traditions. Good scholarship in whatever academic discipline has always been based upon the examination of a variety of perspectives. Variety after all, we are told, is the spice of life. The multidisciplinary (perhaps interdisciplinary) and multireligious focus of religious studies places it in a much stronger position than most academic disciplines (including 'theology' as traditional conceived) in the open-ended examination of alternative perspectives and world-views. Perhaps what is distinctive about religious studies (as opposed to say theology or sociology) is that it explicitly refuses to advocate a particular position (whether that be Christianity, Buddhism, atheism or whatever) as final or ultimate. Individual scholars may have their own belief stances, but this in itself does not prevent them from examining and entertaining a variety of positions in their academic work – both in research and in teaching. Perhaps it is precisely the provisionality, polyvocality and multiperspectival approach of religious studies (so often cited as evidence of the relativistic and 'muddled' nature of the area) that establishes its viability, integrity and strength as an academic subject. *Vive la différence*?

These competing visions of the study of religion, of course, are adopted by a variety of scholars at different times and for different political purposes. If one believes, as I do, that the study of religions should strive towards the development of conceptual frameworks that are not constrained by Christian theological categories (in order to do justice to non-Christian religiosity), Western scholars of non-Christian 'religions' should actively work to extricate their studies from the theological presuppositions of their own Christian heritage. This requires a much more critical and self-reflexive stance with regard to those approaches, presuppositions and categories than has generally been accepted as unproblematic. This would even include problematizing the category of 'religion' itself, which in its modern form displays the imprints of the discursive processes of a particular cultural phenomenon, namely Christianity.

In this context, something like Bellah's symbolic realism or some form of 'methodological agnosticism' is, in my opinion, a useful starting point so long as it is thoroughly grounded in an acknowledgement of the importance of diversity and a variety of disciplinary approaches. Such an orientation will ensure a broad and enriched conception of the subject matter. In so far as methodological agnosticism takes something of a middle position between militant (non-religious) secularism and specific religious confessionalism, it avoids the issues associated with secular reductionism on the one hand and the problems involved in taking a particular confessional stance in the study of religions (emphasis being placed here upon the variety of religions). One might argue that avoiding these problems is not good enough and that one has to come down off the fence at sometime and declare which side one is on. My point is that this is not always a good thing to do – particularly if one is not convinced by the alternatives. Indeed, in the rejection of the role of an arbiter of ultimate truth claims and the explicit acknowledgement of the validity and plurality of religions, the position I have taken resonates more closely with pre-Christian, Roman conceptions of *religiones* as *traditiones* than with Christian and post-Christian definitions of religion in terms of historical truth (as opposed to *mythos*) and exclusivity (as opposed to an acceptance of pluralism). In this sense one might argue that the conception of 'religion' most appropriate to the modern study of religions resonates with traditions of usage that predate the rise of (Christian) 'theology', particularly in its acknowledgement of the impor-tance of studying a variety of religions and in its *unwillingness* to become embroiled in debates about historical truth claims. As the Balinese Hindu in my earlier example stated with reference to his own belief in Rāma: 'It is quite possible that somebody invented this story. But true it is, in any case.'

If we approach the study of religions (religious studies) as one would approach the study of cultures (cultural studies) rather than as an investiga-tion of divergent truth claims (the 'theology of religions') one need not become especially concerned with the question of which religion, if any, has cornered the market on truth. We do not ask if Russian or Spanish culture is true or false, nor do we need to in order to gain some understanding of them. Cultures are not the sort of things that are usually thought of as true or false. Perhaps it is also important to acknowledge in religious studies that the academic pursuit of knowledge has its limitations – that these are not the sorts of questions that the academic study of religion can (or possibly should) attempt to answer. I have no illusions that this approach is free of tensions or problems of its own. Indeed, to some extent, 'methodological agnosticism' continually balances on a tightrope between the secular on the one hand and the various religious traditions under examination on the other. However, the tension on the tightrope is precisely what makes the study of religion such a fascinating and worthwhile exercise.

Bellah's symbolic realism of course dovetails rather well with a kind of 'non-specific religiosity' and a civic religion of modern liberalism. His approach, as with phenomenologists such as Mircea Eliade, however, seems to be based upon a privileging of the category of 'religion' as *sui generis*. However, reconstructing the study of religion in the manner suggested by Tim Fitzgerald (see below) and Russell McCutcheon, as non-essentialist and avowedly interdisciplinary, avoids the pitfalls of phenomenological reduc-tionism, or 'the religionist perspective' as it is sometimes described. There is a need also to resist the 'turn to naturalism' if by this one means the secu-larist erasure of the emic perspectives of those under examination. This is not to claim some *sui generis* status for the category of religion but rather to acknowledge that modern social scientific perspectives do not close our account on reality. As Asad notes, 'There is no single, privileged narrative of the modern world.'[33] For Russell McCutcheon, therefore, this allows for the possibility of a more open-ended and interdisciplinary approach for devel-oping naturalistic theories of religion grounded in the realization of the historical embeddedness of scholarly knowledge and practice.

Given the role played by postmodern and social constructionist critiques in situating scientific discourses within their own historical and discursive contexts, a naturalistic approach to the study of religion can no longer claim to produce a final theory, just as the study of religion can no longer find its justification in absolute autonomy – be that the autonomy of the discourse on *sui generis* religion or the absolute objectivity of the science of religion.[34]

Nevertheless, it is important to note that the contemporary debate today is not between secularism and religion. Rather it is between secularism, Christianity, Buddhism, Hinduism, Islam, Rastafarianism, etc. Since the Enlightenment the discipline of 'theology' has tended to conceive of itself as involved in a debate between Christianity and atheistic humanism. Modern theologians such as Gavin D'Costa are acknowledging that the situation has changed and that the debate is now between Christianity and a variety of religious and non-religious beliefs and lifestyles. D'Costa has recently called for an end to 'systematic theology' as we know it and the reconstitution of (Christian) 'theology' in a way that engages much more explicitly with the various religions of the world. In institutional terms, he relates this explicitly to the importance of having a 'religious studies' adjunct to traditional departments of 'theology'.

If systematic theology required the teaching of Western philosophy within faculties of theology alongside biblical studies, patristics, church history and so on, then theology faculties, if they are to produce modern theologians (rather than historians of theology), must also provide teaching of the world religions in some measure. This in itself will not require a change in the way world religions are taught in religious study faculties but will require Christian theologians to interact in a systematic fashion with these traditions. Succinctly put: departments of theology must become departments of theology and religious studies, if they are properly to remain departments of theology! This is required if theology is to retain its integrity in the modern world, which is intellectually inhabited by many worlds, both religious and non-religious, all of which are relevant to the proclamation and articulation of Christianity.[35]

This is likely to be an increasing trend in theology circles as the religious profile of Europe and North America continues to develop in diverse and highly eclectic ways. However, what is problematic about D'Costa's account and necessitates the continued existence of religious studies as an *autonomous* discipline is that it does not conceive of itself as *'Christian theology' engaging with 'other religions'*. In theology circles the centre is inhabited by Christianity and the circumference is crowded by alternatives to the hegemonic position (as D'Costa's writing demonstrates). In religious studies circles the centre is inherently diverse and does not presume any particular position, whether religious or not, as the dominant discourse. In its breadth and open-endedness religious studies is, to paraphrase the Hermetic tradition, a circle whose centre is everywhere and its circumference nowhere! Regardless of one's own religious (or non-religious) preferences, religious studies requires an acknowledgement of diversity – both in terms of the variety of religions under examination and in terms of the variety of methodological orientations necessary to provide a rounded account of the subject matter.

Where then should the 'study of religion' be carried out in the twenty-first century university? My first answer is that it should continue to be practised in a variety of disciplinary environments, since this will continue to enrich the variety of approaches and perspectives on offer. As McCutcheon argues, the role for the scholar of religion in this context involves giving up the claim that 'religion' has an autonomous essence and 'developing interdisciplinary connections with their colleagues in the social sciences, investigating the theoretical basis for their scholarly interests, and communicating to their undergraduate and graduate students the situated, polymethodic, and polytheoretical nature of scholarly discourses'.[36]

Religious studies, however, should continue to maintain some sense of autonomy as an institutional site, though I agree with McCutcheon that this should not be based upon privileging 'religion' as a *sui generis* category or discourse. Acknowledging that religions, like politics, literature and the natural sciences are implicated in a wider field of cultural practices and power relations does not in and of itself require us to erase the emic perspectives of those one is attempting to understand.

> The study of religion conceived as a theoretically grounded interdisciplinary exercise is no different from any other scholarly pursuit within the university because politics, economics, physics, biology, geography, and so on, are all equally analytic, strategic conceptual categories formed by assorted discourses ... Only if one presumes, for example, that zoology or sociology has a one-to-one fit with reality or that the idea type known as *Homo economicus* is an accurate description of how actual human beings behave, would one believe that the study of religion, conceived as an interdisciplinary endeavor, would be somehow less than other scholarly fields.[37]

I have also suggested that 'religious studies' as an academic discipline might look towards reconceiving itself as a type of 'cultural studies' rather than as an offspring of theology. In a similar fashion Timothy Fitzgerald has recently argued that we should 'reconceptualise Religious Studies as the study of institutionalised values, and the relation between values and the legitimation of power in a specific society'. Indeed, he continues:

the only thing the continued use of the word religion does in a scholarly context is damage, since it creates the illusion that something substantive is being picked out and analysed. What is actually happening, in my view, is that analysis is frequently being impoverished by being cut off at the wrong places under the distorting influence of a partly unconscious idea. What I want is for the study of institutionalised values and their relation to power to be clearly and consciously separated from disguised theology in the field which is now covered by 'religion'.[38]

Such a move distances the study of religion from Christian theological categories and opens up spaces for alternative conceptions of religion to emerge (and in some cases re-emerge) from the silence imposed by the dominance of Christian and secular approaches to the subject matter. The danger of such a proposal is that 'religion' might become subsumed within 'culture' as a category, thus causing the study of religions to conform to the secularist ideology that characterizes much of the work within 'Cultural Studies'. It is important, therefore, to maintain a commitment to cross-cultural and comparative analysis as well as a refusal to be limited by secular and Eurocentric categories. Moreover, a recognition of the mutual imbrication of religion, culture and power requires a dogged refusal to slip into simplistic reductionisms that collapse categories into a single mode of analysis. A useful distinction here is made by Russell McCutcheon between the heuristic use of the category of 'religion' as a way of demarcating a certain aspect of human cultural activity for the purposes of analysis and the positing of a distinct ontological reality to the category of 'religion' as a signifier of something that transcends cultural, economic and political considerations.[39] In problematizing the Christian theological roots of modern conceptions of religion I am not necessarily advocating abandoning the term. My concern is that the way the term has been employed results in the privileging of certain features of Christian and post-Christian Western culture and locates 'other cultures' within an implicitly theological framework that transforms them as much as it attempts to make sense of them. Ivan Strenski has recently lamented the academic loss of faith in the category of religion: 'further breast-beating over how the modern concept of "religion" threatens to dominate the Other enjoys a rather limited scope of application. It is time to stop whining and time to move on.'[40] One must question, however, the extent to which the category does justice to the diversity of indigenous practices and forms of life to which it has been applied. The task of creating a space for and recovering indigenous perspectives and practices in a postcolonial age has barely begun. Problematizing the ethnocentric presuppositions of taken-for-granted categories such as 'mysticism' and 'religion' is an important first step in that process and is not to be dismissed so lightly.

In this chapter I have attempted to look both ways before crossing the road, that is to look back at the concept of 'religion' before it was transformed by the Christian theological prism, and to look forward to the future of the academic study of religion. I do not 'look back' motivated by some nostalgia for lost origins, nor in some forlorn hope to find some 'true' or 'original' meaning of the term 'religion', to which we might all safely return. Such a project is as misguided as it is problematic. Rather, the genealogical approach I have adopted is a tentative step in throwing light upon the power relations involved in attempts to define and explain the nature of 'religion'.

Secular theory in the social sciences has tended to take it own presuppositions about the non-religious nature of reality more seriously than the phenomena under consideration, veering towards materialist or naturalist forms of reductionism. Nevertheless, the advantage of such analysis is that it locates human practices in material and social realities. On the other hand, traditional phenomenological or 'religionist' approaches have tended to rest upon a claim for the *sui generis* nature of religion and thereby divorced 'religion' from wider sociocultural and political factors. Religion becomes ahistorical, dislocated from the cultural realities in which it occurs, and separated from the wider material and political fabric of human life. This is itself a form of 'culturalist' reductionism, but is at least grounded in a commitment to preserve indigenous, emic perspectives from what Asad describes as 'the sociologism' of Western secular accounts. What is required, however, is an approach to the study of religions that takes seriously both the material and the political on the one hand and the cultural and the religious on the other as mutually imbricated dimensions of human existence. In the longer term this may involve abandoning concepts such as 'religion', but at the very least it will require their transformation. What must not be lost, however, in the call to abandon categories such as 'religion' and the autonomy and distinctiveness of 'religious studies' as a discipline is the pluralistic and multidisciplinary focus that prevents the erasure of indigenous perspectives and contests the hegemony of secularism in the Western Academy. Whatever form the comparative study of religion takes in a post-colonial and post-theological era, it has an important role to perform as a 'foreign body', an alien presence, challenging the secularist and Eurocentric foundations on which the Western Academy has been established.

3   Sacred texts, hermeneutics and world religions

In the West we inevitably take as models, in courses on comparative religion for example, those that have written texts on myth, doctrine and ritual. These are the world religions, sometimes called the ethical religions.[1]

There is a clear literary bias within modern Western conceptions of religion. The Protestant Reformation in Europe placed a great deal of emphasis upon the importance of the written word of scripture as the key to the understanding of Christianity as well as a stress upon the individual's relationship to God. When this was conjoined with mass production and distribution of printed texts and increased literacy rates, the possibility of reading the Bible for themselves became a viable option for a substantial minority of the population. This process has, of course, continued unabated since the eighteenth century onwards and has led to the creation of a highly literate culture in the so-called 'developed' nations. Such historical circumstances have resulted in a particularly 'text-oriented' approach to knowledge in the modern West.

It has been estimated that of the thousands of languages that have been spoken by humans throughout history only some 106 have ever produced anything that might be described as literature.[2] Equally, the vast majority of humans throughout history have participated in an oral as opposed to a literate culture. This point perhaps needs to be underlined, for it means that the vast majority of religious expression throughout history has been of a non-literate nature, taking the form of speech, song, performance or iconography. Bearing this in mind we should note that the literary bias in Western notions of religion does not accurately reflect the diversity of human experience. In terms of our own interest in the way the categories of religion and the 'Mystic East' have developed, it has been suggested, for instance, that 'Our knowledge of mysticism is based on the study of texts ... The study of mysticism is primarily, if not exclusively, a philological and exegetical enterprise.'[3]

Within academia the bias towards writing of course reflects the fact that the whole notion of 'studying' is dependent upon the development of writing. As Walter Ong notes:

All thought, including that in primary oral cultures, is to some degree analytic; it breaks its materials into various components. But abstractly sequential, classificatory, explanatory examination of phenomena or of stated truths is impossible without writing and reading. Human beings in primary oral cultures ... learn a great deal and possess and practice great wisdom, but they do not 'study'. They learn by apprenticeship, ... by discipleship ... by listening, by repeating ... by assimilating ... by participating.[4]

Writing speech down transforms it. In speech, once the words are spoken there is nothing left of them to work over. However, if speech is 'translated' into a written form it immediately becomes accessible to study, a greater degree of analysis, and to recontextualization and reinterpretation. If one combines this with the wider audience one might hope to reach in a literate community one can see the 'universalizing' tendency of writing, a tendency that seems to work against the immediacy and particularity of the oral event. This creates a problem for the modern, highly literate student of religion, for, as Ong notes, writing is ' a particularly pre-emptive and imperialist activity that tends to assimilate other things to itself'. Consequently, a literate person cannot hope to recover the sense of the spoken word as it occurs in a purely oral culture.[5]

The primacy of non-literate[6] or oral expression in the religious expression of humankind produces its own problems for the transmission of traditional wisdom. To promulgate knowledge in an oral context it is necessary to have interlocutors and lineages structured in such a way as to preserve such insights. Memorization techniques, such as the use of mnemonic patterns, rhetorical formulae, and stylistic repetitions, are frequently adopted to aid the transmission of knowledge from generation to generation. This inevitably causes tensions when such originally oral material is 'translated' and studied in a written format by the modern scholar. The rhythmic and redundant nature of oral expressions is likely to strike the literate reader as overly laborious and repetitive.

Classical Sanskrit, in common with Rabbinic Hebrew, scholastic Latin, classical Arabic and classical Chinese, functioned mainly (though not exclusively) as a literary language – that is, a language that is not spoken as a mother tongue (in the literal sense of not being passed on from mother to child, as with colloquial or 'first' languages). Consequently, all of these languages were controlled mainly through the medium of writing, were on the whole spoken by males exclusively and were generally spoken only by those who had mastered the language in a literary form.[7] Despite this, it is clear that there remains a strong residue of orality within many Indian religious and philosophical texts.

The English word 'text' appears to derive from a root meaning 'to weave'. Interestingly enough this approximates to the Sanskrit term '*sūtra*', denoting a 'thread', in this case the basic thread of teachings. The repetition and redundancy of many oral compositions is perhaps most readily apparent in the vast canon of Buddhist sūtras, much of which, as one can see from the regularity of such mnemonic devices, appears to have originated in an oral context.

On the other hand, some Indian sūtras (e.g. the *Brahma Sūtra*, the *Yoga Sūtra*) are characterized not by redundancy but by extreme brevity of expression. In this sense only the most basic 'thread' of teaching is given, making the composition amenable to mnemonic memorisation, but also requiring commentarial exposition for meaning to become clear. The emphasis placed upon chanting and communal recitation (*saṅgāyanā*) is further evidence of the importance of orality in traditional Indian culture (and elsewhere). It is clear that many of the religious 'texts' that are studied by scholars were originally chanted rather than read. However, if viewed as a written work the repetitious nature of some religious compositions appears peculiarly redundant, while on the other hand the extreme brevity of others can be frustrating to a literate person looking for explicit and elaborate expression.

The residue of orality, of course, is never totally absent, particularly when one is examining 'texts' that were composed before the European printing revolution. The rhetorical structure of oral expression is still present in many Indian philosophical works where theories are outlined in the context of a debate between an objector (*pūrvapakṣin*, or 'first position') and the author, in the dialogical format of Plato's major works and in the *Summa Theologiae* of Thomas Aquinas, to name but a few instances. However, one should bear in mind the dangers of distortion involved in treating an originally oral composition as a written text. Frequently, the textual 'version' is likely to have been subjected to a number of levels of editing and what literary-minded scholars call 'interpolations'. In oral cultures the transmission of teachings can be adapted, revised and elaborated according to particular context, and from generation to generation. In studying these compositions in the form of printed texts one inevitably imposes a degree of uniformity, consistency and univocal stability that may not have been present in the plastic and dynamic transmission of the teachings in their original, oral context.[8] Without questioning the way in which we approach such material we are likely to continue viewing the 'object' of our study through tinted lenses.

Textualism and the modern concept of 'world religions'

The development of writing and, even more, of widely available printed texts has contributed to a number of significant trends within the modern, literate, Western world. Both reading and writing are now generally understood to be essentially solitary and silent activities. This is a comparatively modern development.[9] Until fairly recently, reading was primarily, though not exclusively,[10] a verbalized and communal activity. In his *Confessions*

(VI.3), Augustine expresses his amazement at the sight of Bishop Ambrose reading silently to himself. In medieval Europe, reading continued to be both an oral and a communal event. The development of print allowed for the production of small and portable books, contributing to the privatization of reading, and the eventual adoption of silent reading as the primary manner in which to read texts.

Other factors inevitably develop as a result of the print revolution:

> Print created a new sense of the private ownership of words ... With writing, resentment at plagiarism begins to develop ... The old, communal oral world had split up into privately claimed freeholdings. The drift in human consciousness towards greater individualism had been served well by print.[11]

As Ong points out, print facilitated the 'quantification of knowledge', eventually (though not initially) reduced the appeal of iconography and encouraged the 'sense of closure' – that is, the sense that the content of the text was final and complete.[12] This sense of finality, enshrined within the written text, was further encouraged by the uniformity of printed editions. Editorial privilege, which allows for the practice of what Goody calls 'backward scanning',[13] enables the author to present a work of much greater uniformity than before and create the impression of a univocal, fixed and consistent point of view throughout his or her composition.

The possibility of an ongoing revision and editing of texts, a practice that is, of course, impossible during speech, combined with the sense of finality of the printed word, has no doubt contributed to the claim that one can give an objective and definitive account of that which one is studying. Printed texts become disembodied and decontextualized in so far as they can now be separated from their original contexts. The written text lacks the contextual richness of the oral composition for it cannot convey intonation, bodily gesticulation, emphasis or dialect to the same degree. Certain features of speech can be represented in script, such as italics or an exclamation mark for emphasis, but the effect is minimal in comparison to that of the oral. Indeed, as Ong notes, written texts reflect the supreme example of decontextualization, since they even become independent of their authors, most of whom are now dead.[14]

The decontextualized nature of the written text, often labelled 'intertextuality' by contemporary literary theorists, has no doubt contributed to the greater universalizing power of the written word. The ideas and ideals conveyed within a written text can no longer be firmly tied to their authorial context since, as Roland Barthes has shown, the meaning that one finds in a text is also a product of the reader and the interpretations he or she places upon it. The universalizing aspects of literacy therefore provide a means of idealizing religion and locating it within the abstract world of the text. It is in this sense that we can understand Ong's reference to the 'imperialist' tendency

of writing. Goody argues that it is the development of literature that effectively allows certain religious world-views to spread beyond their particular
and local context and become 'world religions'.[15] In general agreement with
this position, Walter Ong has argued that writing, through its separation of
the knower and the known, has contributed to an 'increasingly articulate
introspectivity', and therefore made possible the introspective religious traditions of Buddhism, Judaism, Christianity, Islam, etc.[16]

Literature retains an ahistorical quality in so far as it persists outside of
its own context. Such a situation clearly cannot prevail in the dynamic and
impermanent moment of oral expression. The literary bias within Christian
and post-Christian conceptions of 'religion' has also contributed to a
homogenization of other cultures and the way in which they are represented.
When studying Sanskrit and Pāli texts for the sources of Hindu and
Buddhist religious expression we are, of course, focusing on the literary
expressions of an élite.[17] Neither Sanskrit nor Pāli are vernacular languages,
thus they cannot reflect the religious opinions of the non-literate masses in
anything other than an indirect manner. S.J. Tambiah, for instance, in a
study of Buddhism in a Thai village, notes that:

> Few village monks are versed in Pali and therefore this specialized
> learning is infrequent. It is for this reason that I have argued that the
> majority of village monks or novices are largely ignorant of Pali (or at
> least have a shaky knowledge) and therefore of the content of Pali
> chants and Pali doctrinal texts. While the latter are accessible in local
> script, the chants cannot be reduced into the words of the local
> language for then they would lose their sacredness and their efficacy.[18]

Thus, in a village context even the majority of religious specialists (the
monks or *bhikkhus*) do not understand their own scriptures in the original,
but rather rely on translation.[19] Nor, given a context where the monk has a
number of social duties and functions to perform, can it be argued that the
monks have much time or inclination to become great scholars of their own
tradition. Focusing upon the globalizing and text-based 'world-religions'
(what Robert Redfield called the 'great traditions' within any given culture),
inevitably marginalizes more localized religious forms (i.e. the 'little traditions'). Clearly the literate religions have not fully reflected the religious
expression of humankind.

The 'world-religions' approach to the study of religion, which focuses
upon a few globalized religious entities as expressive of the religious experience of humankind, shows clear evidence of this textualist bias. The work of
Jack Goody, for instance, has focused upon the universalizing tendencies of
the literate (i.e. 'world') religious traditions. He suggests that:

> it may be significant that it was only with alphabetic writing that some
> religions decisively broke through their national frontiers to become reli-

gions of conversion ... at one level, written religions are clearly working on a more explicitly abstract (or generalized) base than those of purely oral societies ... Ideals embodied in a text rather than a context are no longer attached to present concerns in the same tight way.[20]

In effect, an exclusive focus upon the so-called 'world religions' concentrates attention upon those religious ideologies that remain directly comparable with the universalistic and proselytizing elements of Christian theology, with its emphasis upon universal human salvation. In this context, as Timothy Fitzgerald has suggested, it is the presuppositions of Christian theology that have predominated in the construction of discourses about the 'Other' (in this case the other 'world religions').[21] Within an overarching Christian paradigm, complete with its textualist, salvationist and universalistic presuppositions, all other forms of religious expression are discussed (one might even say 'constructed') in terms of the prevailing theological paradigm. Thus, Fitzgerald suggests that:

> This idea of a World Religion is, in some important respects, a theological concept, but it has become incorporated as a basic category of Religious Education. The universalistic pretensions of some theologies have passed over into a belief among scholars about the kind of things that exist in the world. It is possible that the prototype World Religion derives from evangelical Christianity of the capitalist west, which in the 19th century proclaimed a message of salvation equally valid to individuals everywhere, regardless of class, race and colour.[22]

Let me make it clear at this point precisely what I am suggesting. I am not claiming that nineteenth-century Western Christianity is the only example of a universalizing religious ideology, or of a 'world religion'. Far from it. Rather, my suggestion is merely that more attention should be paid to the theoretical and methodological assumptions of the world-religions approach to the study of religion. In particular, modern Western presuppositions about the nature of religion need to be examined critically if one is to avoid textualizing, Westernizing and, to some degree, Christianizing 'other' cultures. Besides the Westernizing dimension of the world-religions approach, one should also be aware of the narrowness of such an orientation. In choosing to concentrate on the universalistic religions, one focuses attention upon the globalizing ideologies of a literary (and largely male) élite. Such ideologies might fit in well with the modern Western (and capitalistic) emphasis upon internationalism and a globalized interaction in the economic, cultural and political spheres, but it is important to realize that the 'world religions' as they are usually portrayed are idealized and largely theoretical constructs that bear some relationship to, but are by no means identical with, the actual religious expression of humankind, especially in the pre-modern era. One should also note that such 'universal' faiths are simultaneously the homogenizing and imperialistic ideologies of a religious world. In effect by focusing upon the brahmanical strands of Indian religion, the theological treatises of Catholicism, or the scholarly Qu'ranic commentaries of Islam, one inevitably marginalizes a significant proportion of human religious experience and expression.

Religious Studies is, of course, a particular academic discipline, which has developed in a post-Enlightenment, capitalistic and Christian or post-Christian society. In this sense we would do well to note Michel Foucault's insights into 'disciplines' as regimes of power:

> disciplines are techniques for assuring the ordering of multiplicities ... The disciplines use procedures of partitioning and verticality ... they define compact hierarchical networks ... the disciplines have to bring into play the power relations, not above but inside the very texture of the multiplicity.[23]

It is the very nature of all cognitive disciplines, therefore, that they order multiplicities, make conceptual distinctions and extrapolate universal abstractions from the heterogeneity and fluidity of what they purport to explain. Accepting, for the moment at least, the view that there is something out there that is being misrepresented (a position that Foucault might find problematic), representation is always likely to distort or transform what is being represented, if only for the trivial reason that it is a representation and not the thing itself. Nevertheless, even if one argues that there are only representations and that discourses construct what they purport to explain, one can still criticize the homogenized result of the world-religions approach on the grounds that it marginalizes and suppresses the heterogeneity of religious expression.

Emphasis upon the apparently globalized 'world' religions thus tends to promote a simplistic, essentialist and overly homogeneous account of human religiosity. The set of issues surrounding the textual and world-religions approach also highlights the question of the true locus of religion. Is the 'religious' to be found in the corpus of canonical texts studied by academics or in the beliefs and practices of actual adherents of the religion under consideration? Goody unintentionally points to the narrowness of the textualist/world-religions approach to the study of religion when he suggests that the literate religions, by virtue of their universality and tendency towards abstraction, take on an existence distinguishable from actual social and historical contexts. Thus:

> For example, while Hindus may recognize spirit cults, Hinduism does not. Christianity more deliberately excludes magic, but to many Christians alternative beliefs in astrology have been as much a part of their world-view as alternative medicine to many a hospital patient.[24]

Whose religion do idealized doctrinal systems, labelled 'Hinduism' and 'Christianity', represent if they can be said to exist in separation from and, in some instances, in direct opposition to what actual Hindus and Christians believe? What sense does it make to refer to the actual beliefs and practices of certain religious people as 'Hindu' or 'Christian' if these phenomena bear little relationship to the doctrines and practices of Hinduism and Christianity?

According to Goody, religions such as Christianity, Buddhism and Hinduism are abstract, ahistorical and universal entities that transcend any and all particular historical instances of them. The whole, if you like, is greater than the sum of its parts. The essentialism endemic in such an approach involves the construction of abstract notions of 'religion' that can then be extrapolated from their local, cultural context. In this sense, religions become divorced from their actual historical circumstances and manifestations.

The reification of religion prevalent in the textualist and world-religions approaches to the study of religion are further supported by those religious ideologies that conceive of themselves in such terms. Many forms of Christianity uphold an essentialistic and universalizing self-image, grounded in a firm belief in the transcendental and ahistorical nature of the Christian message. Augustine's distinction between the historical Church and the timeless, 'true' Church in *The City of God* is perhaps the best example of this. In an Asian context, the Western-influenced neo-Vedānta of Indians such as Rammohan Roy, Mahātma Gandhi, Vivekānanda, Aurobindo and Radhakrishnan has played a seminal role in the construction of contemporary notions of Hinduism as a universal world religion. This influence is so prevalent that today what most Religious Education courses mean by 'Hinduism' is a colonially filtered and retrospective Vedānticization of Indian religion.

The universalistic claims of such ideologies as neo-Vedānta occlude the cultural and historical particularity of such movements. In other words, such claims suppress the fact that they derive from a particular community with a particular agenda at a particular time in a particular cultural space. In the case of neo-Vedānta, for instance, we find a largely middle-class, Western-educated élite responding to European colonial hegemony in a manner that reflects the influences of a Christian and nationalistic agenda. To accept the universalistic claims of such groups to represent all Hindus *in toto* is to fail to grasp the heterogeneous nature of Indian (and indeed human) religiosity in general, and to ignore the historical particularity and 'group-tied' nature of such ideologies.[25]

French Catholic scholar Gabriel Le Bras has argued, for instance, that it makes no sense to talk of Christianity as the religion of pre-Revolutionary France other than in the limited sense of being so deemed by the monarchial constitution. Christianity was the state religion, but can it be said unproblematically to be the religion of the people? Le Roy Ladurie has also called such views into question with his analysis of the enduring Catharism of villages such as Montaillou in Southern Languedoc.[26] Equally, what sense does it make to say that Christianity became the religion of the Roman Empire after Constantine? Humbert of Romans (1200–77) wrote that the poor rarely attended church or listened to sermons and that consequently, 'they know little of what pertains to their salvation'.[27] Mircea Eliade, in discussing the beliefs and practices of the European peasant, suggests that:

> It is true that most of these rural European populations have been Christianized for over a thousand years. But they succeeded in incorporating into their Christianity a considerable part of their pre-Christian religious heritage, which was of immemorial antiquity. It would be wrong to suppose that for this reason European peasants are not Christians. But we must recognize that their religion *is not confined to the historical forms of Christianity* ... becoming Christian, the European cultivators incorporated into their new faith the cosmic religion that they had preserved from prehistoric times.[28] [my italics]

Eliade's essentialist position gives primacy to an 'idealized' and textual Christianity, which he describes as 'historical' despite its radically ahistorical nature. Consequently, the religion of the European peasants is subordinated to an abstract form of Christianity that bears limited resemblance to actual historical forms of Christianity. In the 'discourse of religion' it would seem that religion often has little to do with what people actually believe and practise and more to do with what can be found in the canonical texts of that religious tradition.

Recently, the literary bias within the more specific field of Buddhist Studies has come under criticism. Martin Southwold argues that:

> We think that Buddhism must be essentially and criterially the teaching of its alleged founder, because that is how we think of Christianity; and we think that the Buddhist scriptures must be the key to Buddhism because that is how we think, under the influence of Protestantism, of the place of the Christian scriptures in our own religion ... The fundamental error in the study of Buddhism has been to approach it from the side of belief, doctrine rather than of practice.[29]

The discrepancy between 'textual Buddhism' and 'actual Buddhism' has long been noted by scholars.[30] With regard to the Buddhist doctrine of no-abiding-self (*anattā*), for instance, it had been noted as early as the nineteenth century that:

> The difficulties attendant upon this peculiar dogma may be seen in the fact that it is almost universally repudiated. Even the sramana priests, at one time, denied it; but when passages teaching it were pointed out to

them in their own sacred books, they were obliged to acknowledge that it is a tenet of their religion.[31]

More recently, Richard Gombrich has admitted that the *anattā* doctrine is little understood by all but the most scholarly inclined Buddhists in Sri Lanka and that 'belief in personal survival after death is a fundamental feature of Sinhalese Buddhism in practice'.[32] Using epigraphical evidence, Gregory Schopen has also cast considerable doubt upon the actual acceptance of such 'cardinal' Buddhist beliefs as the inexorable nature of the law of karma and the prohibition of monastic ownership of property and money on an individual basis. Such dichotomies between textual or 'canonical' Buddhism and 'living Buddhism' are dealt with by scholars in a number of different ways. Heinz Bechert, for instance, draws a distinction between religious ideology (as manifest in the canonical texts) and religious practice (as found among everyday Buddhists); in a comparable manner Richard Gombrich distinguishes between 'cognitive' and 'affective' religion. Thus Gombrich notes that while many Buddhists adhere to the canonical Buddhist position with regard to doctrines such as *anattā* and the transcendent nature of the Buddha on a cognitive or intellectual level, many of their actions suggest belief in personal survival after death and in the efficacy of worshipping the Buddha on an affective level.

However, we should not dismiss the 'textual Buddhism' of the classical Indologist as an 'abstract fiction' functioning purely on an ideological or ideal level. While scholars should certainly be aware of the distorting lenses of literacy and the 'textualist' presuppositions of religious studies, these findings should not deter philologically and philosophically inclined scholars from studying religious texts. It is clear that such texts can never be totally divorced from the historical reality in which they are produced, and they do, in fact, provide important insights into the nature of the religion under consideration. To argue that 'textual Buddhism', for instance, bears no relation to actual Buddhist religious belief and practice is to overstep the mark wildly. There is much of practical significance that can be gleaned from religious texts as one of many potential source materials for the study of religion. Attempts to establish a polarized opposition between 'ideal' religious texts and 'actual' religious beliefs drive a false wedge between two facets of the total religious phenomena, which, in practice, interact with one another in a dynamic fashion. One cannot claim to provide a fully comprehensive account of a religion if one focuses only upon the scriptures of that tradition, but equally one cannot hope to understand the actual religious beliefs and practices of the so-called world religions without a grounding in the literature of those traditions.[33] As Goody notes:

for the study of institutions which have been profoundly influenced by writing (and of these religion is perhaps the most important), the village community is a legitimate isolate only in a limited sense. To suppose that one can study Burmese Buddhism in the same framework as one studies Australian totemism is to commit an intellectual solecism.[34]

An additional factor, which should encourage the textualist to continue his or her work, is the contemporary context. In a situation of increasing global literacy, more and more people are discovering, being influenced by, and participating in the literary expressions of human religiosity. In that sense, the study of religious texts has never been so relevant to the religious experience of humankind as it is becoming today. Nevertheless, it needs to be emphasized that the literary bias within religious studies (as within academia in general) can lead to a serious misrepresentation of the nature of religion if left unchecked. In this sense, religious studies needs to develop a much greater awareness of itself as a 'multimedia' discipline involving the study of the diversity of religious expressions *in toto*, using a variety of techniques, methodologies and 'lenses' in order to counteract the dangers of academic myopia. It also remains vitally important that scholars of religion consider and confront the implications of the secular presuppositions of their discipline, as well as the subtle ways in which epistemological and methodological paradigms within religious studies remain conditioned by modernist, Western and Christian presuppositions about the nature of religion.

Gadamer and hermeneutics: exploding the myth of objectivity

A further element in the Enlightenment heritage of religious studies is the hegemony of the natural science paradigm of knowledge and the related notions of the detached, dispassionate researcher working towards a neutral and objective knowledge of the subject matter. With the advent of postmodern scepticism about the viability of the scientistic paradigm, the notion of objective and value-free knowledge is coming under increasingly critical scrutiny. Particularly relevant to such discussions is the hermeneutic philosophy of Hans Georg Gadamer, as expounded in his 1960 work *Wahrheit und Methode* (1975 English translation: *Truth and Method*). Gadamer, taking his lead from Heidegger's phenomenological emphasis upon *Dasein* (being-in-the-world), posits understanding (the hermeneutic situation) as the ontological starting point of all human action and thought, significantly broadening the traditional conception of hermeneutics as the methodology of biblical exegesis or of philological and textual analysis in general.[35] Earlier I suggested that it is important to bear in mind the literary bias of academia in general but also within religious studies in particular and the ways in which such an approach tends to distort the subject matter under consideration. One problem with the hermeneutical approach is that it also tends to reduce the scope of religion to that of a text or text analogue.[36] Nevertheless, the philosophy of Hans Georg Gadamer remains relevant to our discussion as his work has clear implications for the study of religion and mysticism (and indeed for the 'human sciences' in general).

According to Gadamer, hermeneutics is not a methodology but a question of the nature of existence itself. One cannot avoid being involved in interpretation by virtue of one's historical situatedness – that is, the facticity of one's being-in-the-world. Thus, Gadamer has consistently argued that his philosophical works are primarily ontological and not methodological treatises.

Critics and supporters alike have focused upon Gadamer's rejection of the claim that we can aspire to an 'objective' knowledge of that which we study. Gadamer argues that the roots of such positivistic hubris derive from the attempt to establish the methodology of the natural sciences within the so-called human and social sciences. Gadamer clearly locates this tendency in the growth of positivism and scientific rationalism since the eighteenth century. Gadamer's work, then, is often seen as a reaction to the values of the Enlightenment, though as Georgia Warnke has argued, his relationship with the Enlightenment is by no means so straightforwardly antagonistic.[37]

According to Gadamer, Enlightenment thought and its modern successors display a 'prejudice against prejudice'. The Enlightenment ideal of objective knowledge involved the notion of eradicating all subjective prejudgements in favour of a 'neutral' and 'objective' approach, detached from emotional, affective and personal biases, through the skilful use of the faculty of reason and a sound methodology. Gadamer argues that such a conception of knowledge is itself prejudicial in so far as it is the historically conditioned result of sociocultural factors relating to the rise of Enlightenment thought. Specifically, Enlightenment thought placed the faculty of reason in opposition to tradition and prejudice, and glorified the former to the detriment of the latter. In contrast to this, Gadamer's work is clearly an attempt to reassess the importance of both tradition and prejudice in the act of understanding. Gadamer argues that both tradition and prejudice are inevitable features of any act of interpretation since they reflect the historical and cultural situatedness of human beings. Thus, understanding is conditioned by the past (our 'tradition') as well as by our own present circumstances and agendas (our prejudices). The particularity of our situation makes any notion of an objective and value-free interpretation inherently problematic.

The inevitability of prejudice in any interpretation, however, is not seen in pessimistic terms by Gadamer. On the contrary, he argues that it is the prejudices deriving from our 'effective history' – that is, our historical situatedness – that provide the basic framework that facilitates understanding. One cannot understand anything without relating it to one's own 'being-in-the-world'. There is no possibility of a universally applicable meta-narrative or bird's-eye view of reality. One of the purposes of Gadamerian hermeneutics, therefore, is to overcome 'the phantom of a truth severed from the standpoint of the knower'.[38] Somewhat reminiscent of Roland Barthes' rejection of authorial privilege in interpreting literary works, Gadamer argues that:

> The real meaning of a text, the way in which it speaks to the interpreter does not depend on contingencies that the author and his original public represent. At least, it is not exhausted by them. It is also always codetermined by the historical situation of the interpreter. The meaning of a text goes beyond its author not only occasionally but always.[39]

For Gadamer, then, there can be no possibility of a definitive or objective reading of a text for at least two reasons. First, one cannot hope to place oneself in the position of the text's original author in order to discern its 'original meaning'. Thus, as Andrew Tuck has suggested, 'for an interpreter to believe that he can accurately reconstruct the intentions and beliefs of the original author without betraying his presence is nothing less than belief in his own scholarly omnipotence'.[40] Also, even if one could somehow discern the intentions of the author that in itself would not exhaust the possible and valid interpretations of the text. Understanding is not 'a mysterious communion of souls in which the interpreter grasps the subjective meaning of the text. Rather, it is a fusion of horizons; the interpreter's horizon is fused with the horizon of the author.'[41] This is inevitable since the implications, meanings and importance of statements made within the text will be different according to the historical circumstances of interpreters of the text. Thus, for Gadamer, the meaning is not so much to be *found in* the text, as *negotiated between* the text and the interpreter. Understanding is an event in which both interpreter and text mutually determine one another.

Some have interpreted Gadamer's work in a subjectivist and highly relativistic manner, particularly, one might note, Gadamer's sternest critics.[42] One of the ironies of Gadamer's analysis, of course, is that one cannot make definitive claims about the meaning of his work from a Gadamerian perspective because of the rejection of such attempts to find a definitive, objective and univocal interpretation of any text (or text analogue). Because of this, or perhaps even despite it, Gadamer's work need not be interpreted in a radically subjectivist manner. Indeed, Gadamer appears to place a great deal of emphasis upon the importance of tradition as a conditioning factor that provides a clear limit upon the ways in which one may interpret a text. As Warnke suggests, for Gadamer, our historical situatedness:

> means that the issues we bring to the process of interpretation are not our preoccupations alone but rather refer to issues and concerns that have developed within the historical tradition to which we belong ... [O]ur understanding stems from the way in which the event or work has previously been understood and is thus rooted in the growth of a historical and interpretive tradition ... These prejudices are not our personal property alone.[43]

Thus tradition safeguards against idiosyncratic interpretations. Much of Gadamer's argumentation suggests that we are incapable of escaping the boundaries of our respective tradition(s). Thus, even in disagreeing with the tradition, or in establishing a 'new' point of view, one is making a conscious effort to distance oneself from the tradition, and therefore one remains inextricably bound up with it. Thus, as far as Gadamer is concerned, one cannot escape from tradition since disagreeing with it amounts to an agreement to disagree! It would seem then that whatever one does, 'tradition' remains the normative paradigm. Such an orientation, of course, sounds like cultural isolationism and, from within the perspective of such an approach, our bond to tradition (whether through agreement or opposition) becomes an a priori inevitability and the notion of *fundamental* paradigm shifts remains inherently problematic. Such cultural relativism has dire consequences for those who wish to study and understand cultures other than their own. We shall discuss some of the problems related to cultural isolationism/relativism a little later.

Gadamer avoids the charge of endorsing any and every interpretation as equally valid, however arbitrary, by shifting the focus of attention and 'subjectivity' from the individual interpreter to the tradition to which he or she belongs. Nevertheless, what prevents the tradition itself from being arbitrary? Gadamer argues that his position is not a form of simple relativism,[44] and points to the individual circumstances and experiences of the interpreter as a further factor that continually modifies tradition.

In fact, tradition is not the only wedge that Gadamer uses to forestall a subjectivist interpretation of his position. To safeguard a distinction between valid and invalid interpretations of a text, Gadamer also appeals to the notion of interpretation as a dialogue between interpreter and text. Although one inevitably projects one's own interests onto the text one studies, arbitrariness can be safeguarded by fostering an attitude of agnosticism and humility towards the text itself, as well as an appreciation of one's own fallibility, that is an 'openness to experiences' (a form of methodological agnosticism, perhaps). Gadamer wants us to ask of the text what it can teach us, and to be open to the possibility of the 'completeness' or truth of the text. Clearly, when dealing with a literary work, the notion of a dialogue seems somewhat inappropriate given the fact that the text cannot actually talk back, but in the hermeneutical sense that Gadamer means by the term 'dialogue' the text can respond, but only if we remain hermeneutically open to its response.

> Whoever wants to understand a text is rather prepared to let it say something to him. Hence a hermeneutically schooled consciousness must be sensitive to the otherness of the text from the beginning.[45]

The process of interpreting a text, then, according to Gadamer, inevitably involves the projection of one's own values, interest and agenda onto the text. It is easy to see this in the works of one's predecessors, but not so easy to see it in ourselves. Nevertheless, Gadamer argues, such prejudice is always present and establishes the boundaries of possibility for all understanding. Our prejudices, however, are never purely individual since they remain constrained by the past interpretations of our tradition. This, Gadamer suggests, is the hermeneutical situation with which we always find ourselves and that constitutes the very nature of our existence (hence the claim that his work is primarily ontological and not methodological). The individual circumstances and experiences of the interpreter modify the tradition and allow for its continued development. A good interpretation, Gadamer suggests, is one that incorporates a 'fusion of horizons' – in other words, one that proceeds in a dialogical fashion aiming at some level of agreement between the horizon of meaning provided by the text (as provided by the circumstances under which the text was produced) and that provided by the interpreter. Thus, arbitrariness is avoided because of the historical situatedness of both the interpreter and the text. Interpreting texts, then, is an ongoing process that occurs within the context of a particular community and tradition and is perhaps more appropriately to be modelled on the act of negotiation between two parties than on the Enlightenment paradigm of the scientist as a detached observer, dissecting and analysing the 'objective' contents of the specimen under consideration, free from personal or political motivations.

Gadamer denies that his conception of understanding is a licence to propound any and all readings of a text, however idiosyncratic and subjective. Nevertheless, he maintains that all readings are isogetical in so far as they involve an unconscious 'reading into' the text. Thus for Gadamer all readings are creative renderings. Nevertheless, consensus can be reached about interpretations and 'truth' can be attained. However, from a Gadamerian perspective this 'truth' will never be final, definitive or objective because of its historical situatedness; for, as long as history continues, further development and insight can be acquired. Thus, for Gadamer, those within the humanities and the 'social sciences' (including philosophers) should reject the positivistic hegemony of the paradigm of 'objective' knowledge and ahistorical truth furnished from the natural sciences and focus instead upon the historical givenness and particularity of our being-in-the-world.

Hermeneutics and cultural isolationism

In the light of Gadamer's insights into the interpretive nature of all acts of understanding, it would seem that the scholar has to give up the claim to a neutral, value-free and 'objective' interpretation of the text(s) under consideration. Interpretation of any text inevitably involves a degree of isogesis (or 'reading into') and a highlighting or 'prejudicing' of aspects of the text, if only to make the text amenable, relevant and understandable to the modern, Western interpreter and his or her readership. However, this is not the devastating bombshell that some have taken it to be. Value distinctions can (and indeed must) be made between rival interpretations, in terms of their appropriateness, the level of 'hermeneutical openness' to the text, and the degree of depth and contextualized knowledge displayed by the interpreter. In this sense, it seem appropriate to utilize the notion of a 'thick description', a term coined initially by the philosopher Gilbert Ryle, but subsequently elaborated by the anthropologist Clifford Geertz.[46] Basically, a 'thick description' is one that contains a high degree of contextual richness – that is, an attention to the sociocultural and historical circumstances which contribute to the meaning of the event. Consider a simple example recently offered by Friedhelm Hardy. In the modern West shaking one's head from side to side is a commonly understood way of expressing disagreement or a negative response to a question. Thus, if I am asked if I have a knowledge of Swahili I might elicit a negative reply by shaking my head. However, in India shaking one's head from side to side is often an expression of emphasis. In this context, shaking one's head might imply the opposite, that I do indeed possess a knowledge of Swahili. Of course, in many instances potential misunderstandings resulting from such cultural differences are overcome by a variety of other clues that point to the meaning of the action. Perhaps at the same time as shaking her head, the Indian would say yes and proceed to demonstrate a mastery of the language.

The point of a 'thick description', then, is that it successfully articulates the significance of an action, feeling or statement by paying close attention to the contextual richness of the situation. In giving up the ideal of complete objectivity, one does not have to relinquish the distinction between superficial and in-depth interpretations. In fact, as Charles Taylor has argued, the attention to context and the cultural significance of events that one aims for in a 'thick description' is precisely what the more positivistic methodologies modelled on the natural sciences attempt to avoid.[47]

Gadamer, in his emphasis upon the normative power of tradition, seems to imply on occasions that attempts to understand texts that belong to a different culture (and hence a different 'tradition') are deeply problematic.

> Although in the meantime the research in Eastern philosophy has made further advances, we believe today that we are further removed from its philosophical understanding. The sharpening of our historical awareness has rendered the translations or adaptations of the texts ... fundamentally problematic ... We cannot speak of an appropriation of these things by the Occidental philosophy. What can be considered established is only the negative insight that our own basic concepts, which were coined by the Greeks, alter the essence of what is foreign.[48]

The Eurocentricity and cultural isolationism exemplified by such statements have recently been criticized by Wilhelm Halbfass on the grounds that the European tradition is itself a fusion of diverse cultural sources, and that there is no reason to assume that the problem of understanding between cultures is drastically different from that of understanding within cultures. Referring to Gadamer's philosophical approach, Wilhelm Halbfass suggests that:

> There is ... no compelling reason why its hermeneutical concepts and perspectives should not be applicable in a wider, trans-cultural context. Indeed, we belong to the European tradition which has its origins in Greece. But this tradition has its own modes of openness and self-transcendence. Within the European tradition itself, there has been a 'fusion' of different cultural horizons, Greek, Roman, Hebrew, etc. That we relate to other traditions does not imply that we are estranged from 'our own' tradition. The phenomena of understanding and misunderstanding, which occur 'within' a particular tradition, need not be fundamentally different from those which we encounter when we try to approach other traditions. We have no reason to assume more than a difference in degree, which may, however, be very significant.[49]

The problem with the particular form of cultural relativism that I have labelled 'cultural isolationism' is that it presupposes an absolutistic and monolithic conception of cultures, strongly based upon the 'nationalist' model. The English term 'culture' is generally used in two senses. First there is what is known as the *belles lettres* sense of the term, which distinguishes between 'high' and 'low' (or 'popular') culture, and second there is 'culture' in the sense of the particular customs, mores, and world-view of a particular community of people. The interesting feature about this latter sense (which is most relevant to our current discussion) is that 'cultures' are usually classified along geopolitical, continental and nationalistic lines. The dividing up of humanity into certain geocultural groupings called 'nations' is a relatively modern development. The roots of nationalism derive from social, economic and political changes in Europe from the sixteenth century onwards, but the notion of a national identity as a consciously unifying factor of people cannot be said to have been an influential social construct in Europe until the eighteenth century (and in some cases much later). Indeed, upon analysis it would seem that 'national identity' is not nearly so static and immutable as is sometimes thought.[50] For instance, in the twentieth century the British have often been described as exhibiting a 'stiff upper lip'. In contrast one often finds the Spanish and the Italians represented as 'fiery, passionate and hot-blooded Latins'. Yet, in the eighteenth century the British were stereotyped throughout Europe as highly emotional! The construction of nationality and national identity since the eighteenth century clearly involves a 'reading back' into history of categories and cultural groupings that would have made little sense in the past. Nationalism is fundamentally based upon an imaginative geography and history that projects anachronistic symbols and meanings into history, resulting in a myth of 'national' homogeneity.

The problem with cultural isolationism, therefore, is that it has taken the classification of humankind into 'cultures' or 'nations' as constitutive of the way things are rather than simply as the way the world has been divided up since the eighteenth century by Europeans (and, through European hege- mony, the rest of the world). So powerful is the hold of the 'nationalist' model in our highly geopolitical, modern consciousness that it is easy to forget the relatively recent, historically contingent and European origins of this way of classifying the people of the world. In contrast to this, I would like to suggest that the rigid and absolutist distinctions of cultural isola- tionism actively misrepresent the fluid and dynamic qualities implied by the term 'culture'. Cultures are not homogeneous and static entities or essences (as summed up in such phrases as 'the Indian mentality', or the 'Western world-view', etc.); rather they are historically evolving processes, which are distorted if they are reified. In so far as a culture persists, it is constantly subject to revisions, reinterpretations and transformations of one kind or another.[51]

> The foundations of [mainstream] cultural critique – a dialogic relation with an 'other' culture that yields a critical viewpoint on 'our own culture' – assumes an already-existing world of many different, distinct 'cultures,' and an unproblematic distinction between 'our own society' and an 'other' society.[52]

However, once one rejects the isolated and monolithic conception of culture, the question of the incommensurability of cultures does not disappear. Yet neither can one reject authentic cross-cultural fertilization as an a priori impossibility. If the cultural isolationist were right, new cultural forms could never arise or be transformed as a result of interaction between cultures, since, on isolationist presuppositions, such interaction is impossible. As Anthony Giddens has suggested, 'the dialogue which is established when two cultures meet is not different in quality from that which is implied within any vital tradition or "form of life", which is constantly "tran- scending itself"'.[53]

Just as cultures are constantly evolving, so, of course, are scholarly tradi- tions of interpretation, which remain manifestations of such cultural development. We may have to give up our long cherished but ultimately illu- sory goal of total 'objectivity' in the interpretation of a text, but should this really be seen as a source of despair? As Gadamer has argued, rejecting the ideal of neutral and ahistorical objectivity does not necessarily lead to an anarchistic acceptance of any and all interpretations, however idiosyncratic, as equally valid. Interpretations occur within the context of a particular hermeneutical tradition and history and analyses continue to be produced that improve upon their predecessors; new and interesting insights can be found in the text, and new approaches can contribute to a greater apprecia- tion of its context.

Thus, in the sense in which I am interpreting Gadamer's insights (which differs, for instance, from the radical appropriation of his work by Richard Rorty)[54], one does not have to give up the claim of making progress in the interpretation of a text, nor does this require us to adopt a cultural isolationism that militates against any form of meaningful cross-cultural dialogue or comparison.

Self-reflexivity and ideology

Critics such as Jürgen Habermas[55] and Karl Otto Apel[56] have argued that Gadamer's hermeneutics remains politically conservative and naïve since he does not question the ideological elements of tradition. Gadamer, of course, refutes this charge and claims that the hermeneutical act of understanding involves critical reflection upon the sociopolitical issues related to the ideology of the text and the tradition to which one belongs.[57] Nevertheless, the emphasis Gadamer places upon the normative authority of tradition on the one hand and on the necessity of an 'openness to the truth of the text' on the other seems to restrict the possibility of social and political criticism. To counteract this it is necessary to combine Gadamer's insights into the 'historical situatedness' of the interpreter with an awareness of the ideological elements at play in both text and interpreter. Gadamer's redemption of prejudice suggests that the interpreter, rather than suppressing his or her biases and agenda in the pursuit of scholarly neutrality, should, on the contrary, bring such prejudices to the fore. Such an approach involves an attitude of critical reflexivity towards one's own work.

What I envisage here is a methodological programme that involves two types of 'thick description'. The first, in the original sense of the phrase as used by Ryle and Geertz, is an immersion in the contextual complexity and richness of the phenomenon under consideration. This, it seems to me, has always been the aim of classical scholarship, to provide a good contextual grounding in the sociocultural environment of the text. Under the aegis of naturalism (the natural science paradigm for all cognitive disciplines), classical philologists in religious studies and Indology tended to believe that a rigorous and detailed knowledge of the culture, language and tradition under consideration would yield the true import of the text. In the light of Gadamer's work, this can be seen to be hermeneutically naïve. Sound philology needs to be aligned with good interpretative and philosophical skills if it is to produce an insightful understanding of the text under consideration. However, to provide a balanced interpretation, it is also necessary to incorporate a self-reflexive examination of the cultural context and prejudices of the interpreter. This is the second type of 'thick description', which attempts precisely to clarify those factors present in the approach of the interpreter that directly impinge upon his or her conception of the subject matter. From this perspective, the best hermeneutical works are those that manifest an awareness and appreciation of the context of both the text and the interpreter. One can be critical of Western scholars who end up appropriating and interpreting the religious phenomena under discussion in terms of Western categories. Gadamer's message, however, is that such appropriation is an inevitability, and thus one should attempt to bring these prejudices to the fore, to positively highlight them in one's analysis. This does not necessarily entail a strong form of cultural relativism, merely a continuum where the final end of objectivity is always out of reach. One cannot reach the end of an infinite series, but that does not prevent one from moving backwards or forwards within the finite range of possibilities open to us as contingent and historically situated human beings.

For hermeneutic understanding it follows that we are not limited to the premises of our tradition but rather continually revise them in the encounters with and discussions we have of them. In confronting other cultures, other prejudices and, indeed, the implications that others draw from our own traditions we learn to reflect on both our assumptions and our ideas of reason and to amend them in the direction of a *better* interpretation.[58]

Given the inevitability of prejudice on the part of the investigator, it is important to consider the conditioning factors that provide the boundaries of possibility for understanding. It is for this reason that we have been considering some of the cultural and historical factors that have influenced the development of the various cognitive disciplines in modern academia in order to see some of the ways in which these factors have impinged upon the modern, Western, understanding of religious phenomena. In the next chapter, we shall examine the implications of the realization that ideology plays an integral part in the very act of understanding, interpreting or studying anything. In particular we shall focus our attention upon the colonial elements within Western discourses about Indian culture, philosophy and religion and the ways in which these aspects have constructed the object that they purport to explain.

4   Orientalism and Indian religions

Orientalism and the quest for a postcolonial discourse

> [A]nthropologists who would study, say, Muslim beliefs and practices will
> need some understanding of how 'religion' has come to be formed as concept
> and practice in the modern West. For while religion is integral to modern
> Western history, there are dangers in employing such a normalizing concept
> when translating Islamic traditions.[1]

This statement by Talal Asad can be equally well applied to the study of
Asian culture in general. In recent years scholars involved in such study have
become increasingly aware of the extent to which Western discourses about
Asia reflect power relations between Western and Asian societies. In the
postcolonial era, it has become imperative, therefore, to examine this relationship with critical acumen. In 1978 Edward Said published his
groundbreaking work, *Orientalism: Western Conceptions of the Orient*.[2] In
this book, Said launched a stinging critique of Western notions of the East
and the ways in which 'Orientalist discourse' has legitimated the colonial
aggression and political supremacy of the Western world. In the previous
chapter, we have seen how the academic discipline of religious studies has
contributed to the construction of the object of its analysis, creating a textualized, homogeneous and limited group of world religions largely
constructed in its own (modern, Western) image.[3] In this process it is not the
totality of religious phenomena that is focused upon, but rather those
aspects of the religious dynamic that remain amenable to management and
classification from within the parameters of modern academic discourse.
Equally, Orientalism refers to those particular discourses that, in conceptu-
alizing the Orient, render it susceptible to control and management.

According to Said, 'Orientalism' refers to three interrelated phenomena.
First, an 'Orientalist' is 'anyone who teaches, writes about, or researches the
Orient – and this applies whether the person is an anthropologist, sociologist,
historian or philologist' – in other words, anyone claiming to have expert
knowledge or understanding of oriental cultures. Second, 'Orientalism is a

style of thought based upon an ontological and epistemological distinction made between "the Orient" and (most of the time) "the Occident." ' This is a large and fairly amorphous category that would include the thoughts and writings of anyone who effectively divided the world up in this bipolar manner. Third, and perhaps most significantly for Said:

> Orientalism can be discussed and analyzed as the corporate institution for dealing with the Orient – dealing with it by making statements about it, authorizing views of it, describing it, by teaching it, settling it, ruling over it: in short, Orientalism as a Western style for dominating, restructuring and having authority over the Orient.[4]

For Said, all three elements in the Orientialist equation are interrelated, though he never really clarifies the nature of their relationship. Thus his work points to the complicity between Western academic accounts of the nature of 'the Orient' and the hegemonic political agenda of Western imperialism. Indeed such has been the influence of Said's work in this area that the term 'Orientalism' is often now used as a pejorative term denoting the colonial manipulation of the Orient in general.

Nevertheless there are certain ambiguities and limitations to Said's work, despite its wide-ranging significance. While he is deeply indebted to the thought of Michel Foucault, it is not clear to what extent Said is prepared to follow a completely Foucauldian line in his analysis of Orientalism.[5] At times Said appears to endorse an anti-representational view, akin to Foucault's own position, whereby there is no authentic 'Orient' to be found, only representations of it. Thus, Said says:

> the real issue is whether indeed there can be a true representation of anything, or whether any and all representations, because they are representations, are embedded first in the language and then in the culture, institutions, and political ambience of the representer. If the latter alternative is the correct one ... then we must be prepared to accept the fact that a representation is *eo ipso* implicated, intertwined, embedded, interwoven with a great many other things besides the 'truth', which is itself a representation.[6]

Said, however, acknowledges elsewhere that there is an authentic 'Orient' out there that is actively being misrepresented. 'It would be wrong,' Said suggests, 'to conclude that the Orient was essentially an idea, or a creation with no corresponding reality.'[7] James Clifford has noticed this ambiguity in Said's three definitions of 'Orientalism':

> [I]n the first and third of Said's 'meanings' Orientalism exists merely as the construct of a questionable mental operation. This ambivalence, which sometimes becomes a confusion, informs much of Said's

arguments. Frequently he suggests that a text or tradition distorts, dominates or ignores some real or authentic feature of the Orient. Elsewhere, however, he denies the existence of any 'real Orient', and in this he is more rigorously faithful to Foucault and the other radical critics of representation whom he cites.[8]

Indeed, as a number of Said's critics have argued, his work displays a somewhat ambivalent oscillation between a radical and Foucauldian critique of representation and a humanistic stance that appears profoundly incompatible with Foucault's own work[9] and with the relativistic anti-representationalism with which Said seems to flirt.[10] But it is important to note, as Bruce Robbins has suggested, that 'if *everything* is representation, then representation is not a scandal. Or if *all* representation is a scandal, then no particular representation is especially scandalous.'[11] Said's problem, then, is that, in so far as he wishes to plead the case for those dispossessed by such colonialist discourses on humanistic grounds, he believes that he must endorse such grounds as fundamental, thereby rejecting a relativistic conception of all Orientalist discourses (humanistically inspired ones being superior). Foucault's repudiation of the Enlightenment goal of a foundational knowledge of objective truths precludes the possibility of a universal discourse or strategy for overturning oppressive regimes of thought. Consequently, Said balks at a complete endorsement of the Foucauldian position. Indeed, in an interview in 1986, Said remarks that:

> *Orientalism* is theoretically inconsistent, and I designed it that way: I didn't want Foucault's method, or anybody's method, to override what I was trying to put forward. The notion of a non-coercive knowledge, which I come to at the end of the book, was deliberately anti-Foucault.[12]

However, the claim that one requires absolute and universally applicable knowledge as a foundation for political action is precisely one of the modernist presuppositions that Foucault wishes to challenge. Despite Foucault's position as an 'anti-strategist', he leaves open the possibility of participating in 'local resistance' to particular hegemonic constellations of power and knowledge.[13] Indeed, given Foucault's rejection of the universalist enterprise, this is the only position available to the cultural and political critic. Thus Foucault's vision of the 'specific intellectual' is of a subversive who 'questions over and over again what is postulated as self-evident ... to dissipate what is familiar and accepted'[14] as opposed to the Enlightenment notion of the 'legislative intellectual' who determines the nature of truth through his position of authority. However, who is to say that Said's own orientation is not also an imperialistic projection of the humanistic values of Enlightenment Europe onto the material under consideration? Thus, Clifford argues:

the privilege of standing above cultural particularism, of aspiring to the universalist power that speaks for humanity, for the universal experiences of love, work, death and so on, is a privilege invented by a totalizing Western liberalism. This benevolent comprehension of the visions produced by mere 'local anecdotal circumstances' is an authority that escapes Said's criticism.[15]

Said avoids problems related to his own position by refusing to outline an alternative conception of the Orient, yet it is clear from his own humanistic and cosmopolitan value system that he does have a position. In this sense critics such as Aijaz Ahmed have argued that Said's half-hearted Foucauldian analysis is destructive of old regimes rather than constructive of new ones.[16] The ambivalences within Said's work, however, have been embraced by some post-structuralist reviewers of *Orientalism* as a catechrestic move that destabilizes the cognitive and disciplinary boundaries set up by colonial and neo-colonial regimes of knowledge.[17]

Said's work, of course, is also notable for a number of obvious omissions. His analysis of French, British and, to a limited degree, American Orientalism does not touch upon the strong tradition of Orientalist scholarship in Germany, where it was not accompanied by a colonial empire in the East. In fact, Sheldon Pollock has shown how German Orientalist analysis of Indian Vedic lore profoundly affected Germany by furnishing a racially based Indo-European myth of the pure Aryan race, which could subsequently be used to distinguish the Semites as 'non-Aryan'.[18] Thus, not only has Said's work ignored important currents within European Orientalist discourse, it has also tended to ignore the ways in which such discourses affect the colonizer as well as the colonized.[19] Indeed, the examples of German Orientalists, on the one hand, and Japan, on the other, cast doubt upon Said's thesis that Orientalist discourse is always associated with an imperial agenda, since Germany had no Eastern empire to manipulate and control, and Japan was subjected to Orientalist discourses without ever being colonized by the West.[20]

Sheldon Pollock's discussion of German Orientalism suggests that the authoritative power of such discourses could equally be applied at home to create a powerful 'internal narrative', in this case instrumental in the construction of a German national consciousness, and ultimately in the hands of the National Socialists in 'the colonization and domination of Europe itself'. Jayant Lele has argued that as well as its obvious consequences for Asia, Orientalism also functions to insulate the Occident from the self-analysis that would be involved in a proper engagement with the cultures and perspectives of the non-Western world. He further suggests that Orientalist discourses censure attempts to analyse the West in a self-critical and comparative manner, by misrepresenting both Asian and Western culture. Thus, 'through a culturally imposed stupefaction of the people', both Western and non-Western people are manipulated and subjugated through the 'same project of control and exploitation'.[21] This is a point rarely noticed by critics of Orientalism: namely, that in representing the Orient as the essentialized and stereotypical 'Other' of the West, the heterogeneity and complexity of both Oriental and Occidental remain silenced.[22]

Critics of Said's work have suggested that he places too much emphasis on the passivity of the native,[23] and that he does not really discuss, nor even allow for, the ways in which indigenous peoples of the East have used, manipulated and constructed their own positive responses to colonialism using Orientalist conceptions. Homi Bhabha's notion of 'hybridity', for instance, reflects an awareness that colonial discourses are deeply ambivalent and not susceptible to the constraints of a single, monolithic agenda. For Bhabha the master discourse is appropriated by the native whose agency reflects cultural resistance in the form of the mimicry and parody of colonial authority.[24] In similar fashion, Richard G. Fox has pointed to the ways in which Sikh reformers in the 1920s accepted Orientalist stereotypes of the Sikh, and yet used them to create a mass movement in opposition to British colonialism.[25] The same transformation can be seen in the Hindu context, where Orientalist presuppositions about the 'spirituality' of India, etc., were used by reformers such as Rammohun Roy, Dayānanda Saraswati, Swāmi Vivekānanda and Mohandas K. Gandhi in the development of an anti-colonial Hindu nationalism. This no doubt reflects not only the level of permeation of Orientalist ideas amongst the native (and colonially educated) intelligentsia of India, but also the fact that such discourses do not proceed in an orderly and straightforward fashion, being in fact adapted and applied in ways unforeseen by those who initiated them. Thus, Orientalist discourses soon became appropriated by Indian intellectuals in the nineteenth century and applied in such a way as to undercut the colonialist agenda, which, Said suggests, is usually implicated in such discourses.

We have already seen that Said's own negative appraisal of Orientalism does not appear to leave room for indigenous appropriations of Orientalist discourses for positive, anti-colonial goals. Equally, his work places little emphasis upon what Clifford calls a 'sympathetic, nonreductive Orientalist tradition'.[26] Richard Fox refers to this strand as 'affirmative Orientalism', and has in mind such Western apologists for Indian culture as the Theosophist Annie Besant, Hindu convert Sister Nivedita, and apostle of non-violence Leo Tolstoy.[27] In this context, one should examine what is probably the most scathing critique of Said to date. David Kopf attacks Said for 'dropping names, dates and anecdotes' and for adopting a method that is 'profoundly structural and synchronic' and thus 'diametrically opposed to history'.[28] While Kopf sees a great deal of merit in Said's work, he decries the use of the term 'Orientalism' to 'represent a sewer category for all the intellectual rubbish Westerners have exercised in the global marketplace of ideas'.[29] Kopf, in fact, believes that Said has provided an overly negative and one-sided analysis, which fails to take into account the positive elements within Orientalist discourses. He suggests that modern Orientalism was born in Calcutta in 1784 with the establishment of the Asiatic Society of Bengal and that, as such, British Orientalism can be said to have given birth to the Bengal Renaissance since it 'helped Indians to find an indigenous identity in the modern world'.[30] Kopf suggests that these Orientalists 'were men of social action, working to modernize Hindu culture from within'.[31] These are to be contrasted, Kopf argues, with the anti-Orientalist Westernizers, as represented by the staunch Anglicist Thomas B. Macauley, for whom 'a single shelf of a good European library was worth the whole native literature of India and Arabia'.[32] Kopf comments, 'It is curious to me that Said completely ignores this very group of proto-imperialists who were anti-Orientalist. It is their ideology and not that of the Orientalists which Said reviews in his work.'[33]

If we examine Kopf's position more closely we can see the source of dispute and confusion between him and Said. Kopf praises the modernizing efforts of the Orientalists who:

> ... served as avenues linking the regional élite with the dynamic civilization of contemporary Europe. They contributed to the formation of a new Indian middle class and assisted in the professionalization of the Bengali intelligentsia. They started schools, systematized languages, brought printing and publishing to India, and encouraged the proliferation of books, journals, newspapers, and other media of communication. Their output was urban and secular. They built the first modern scientific laboratories in India and taught European medicine. They were neither static classicists nor averse to the idea of progress, and they historicized the Indian past and stimulated consciousness of history in the Indian intellectual.[34]

What is striking about this description of the activities of British Orientalists in India is that Kopf praises it so unequivocally, while critics such as Said (and I would include myself here) find such activities deeply problematic. Kopf's dispute with Said is really a debate about the extent to which one can differentiate modernization from Westernization. Kopf's view is that the two can be easily differentiated and that the Orientalists were solely in favour of modernization, while Anglicists like Macauley were fervently in favour of both.[35] Thus, according to Kopf, 'nineteenth century Europe was not so much the source of modernity as it was the setting for modernizing processes that were themselves transforming Western cultures', and that, for the Orientalist, 'the important thing was to set into motion the process of modernization through which Indians might change themselves according to their own value system'.[36]

However, it seems at best naïvely simplistic, and at worst downright false, to suggest that we can drive a firm wedge between Westernization and modernization. As we have seen in the previous chapter, 'modernity' is intrinsically bound up with the European Enlightenment project. Thus, despite the claimed cultural and political neutrality of the language of 'modernization', and their dispute with the Anglicists, Kopf's (affirmative) Orientalists were still involved in the Europeanization of the Orient, and, even when they appeared to be promoting the vernacular and the indigenous, their methods, goals and underlying values presupposed the supremacy of European culture. That this is so can be seen even by an examination of the quotations that Kopf elicits as evidence of the Orientalist's opposition to Westernization. Thus he quotes H.H. Wilson, whom he describes as 'one of the greatest Orientalists' as promoting the cultivation of Sanskrit so that native dialects may 'embody European learning and science'.[37] Again, W.H. MacNaughten is quoted as attacking the Westernizer's position on the grounds that 'if we wish to enlighten the great mass of the people in India we must use as our instruments the Languages of India ... [O]ur object is to impart ideas, not words.'[38] Thus, despite Kopf's protestation to the contrary, the Orientalists were also acting in complicity with European imperial aspirations even if their rhetoric was less confrontational, aggressive and condescending. The complexity of the issues surrounding the Anglicist versus the Orientalists in the postcolonial era is reflected, for instance, in Gayatri Spivak's refusal to endorse a blanket return to 'native' languages in India. It is perhaps important to note that English has become increasingly 'nativized' in colonial and postcolonial India, and still represents a much greater potential for international interaction (albeit due to British imperial hegemony) than the 'native' languages. Nevertheless, Spivak suggests an 'inter-literary' approach, arguing that 'the teaching of English literature can become critical only if it is intimately yoked to the teaching of the literary or cultural production in the mother tongue'.[39]

As Gyan Prakash has noted, what is at issue in the criticism of Said's analysis by scholars such as Kopf is the question of the relationship between politics and knowledge.

> The claim that many scholars and several strains within the Orientalist tradition escaped its pernicious prejudices and politics ... is not principally about the differing assessment of the scholarship of particular individuals, but about the relationship between political authority and authoritative discourse ... Implicit in this formulation is the assumption that cultural frameworks and political interests distort truth: they do not form the basis of its enunciation. The authority of Orientalist knowledge, from this point of view, depends on the claim that its complicity with Western domination was peripheral and episodic, not integral and enduring.[40]

In a manner reminiscent of Kopf, O.P. Kejariwal eulogizes William Jones as 'the first scholar from the West to look at the East without a Western bias'.[41] The colonial context of such 'eminent scholars' of the Orient as William Jones and James Mill (father of John Stuart Mill), however, is evident throughout their work. William Jones, for instance, was instrumental in introducing a 'textualized' India to Europeans.

> The most significant nodes of William Jones' work are (a) the need for translation by the European, since the natives are unreliable interpreters of their own laws and culture; (b) the desire to be a law-giver, to give the Indians their 'own' laws; and (c) the desire to 'purify' Indian culture and speak on its behalf ... In Jones' construction of the 'Hindus', they appear as a submissive, indolent nation unable to appreciate the fruits of freedom, desirous of being ruled by absolute power, and sunk deeply in the mythology of an ancient religion.[42]

As Tejaswini Niranjana suggests, 'This Romantic Orientalist project slides almost imperceptibly into the Utilitarian, Victorian enterprise of 'improving' the natives through English education.'[43] James Mill's three-volumed *History of British India* (1817) continues to be influential in its monolithic approach to Indian culture, its homogenizing references to 'Hinduism', and its highly questionable periodization of Indian history.[44]

It is naïve of Kopf to believe that all Orientalists were opponents of Westernization. He fails to see both the polyphonic nature and multiple layers of colonial discourse and the broader political context in which Orientalist writings were enunciated. Viewing Said's 'Orientalist problematic' as an attempt to look beyond the veil of rhetorical subterfuge in order to intuit the underlying imperialistic motivations of Orientalists, Kopf fails to appreciate the implications of scholarly knowledge within a wider field of power relations that cannot be reduced to the level of individual intentions.[45] Said, however, complicates the debate by making his own appeal to voluntarism, allowing his critics to respond that some Orientalists had good intentions. This is not what an analysis of Orientalism as a discourse is fundamentally concerned with, highlighting as it does the wider structural and political context in which the work of Orientalists occurs. Assessment of individual scholars, then, is not primarily concerned with intentions but with the broader (perhaps in many cases unconscious) implications of their work. Kopf misses this point and so argues that:

> Orientalism was the polar opposite of Eurocentric imperialism as viewed by the Asians themselves ... If Orientalism was merely the equivalent of imperialism, then how do we account for the increasingly nostalgic view of Orientalists nurtured by later generations of Hindu intelligentsia?[46]

Our answer to this question has already been put forward in the recognition that the 'Hindu intelligentsia' were themselves influenced by the West's stereotypical portrayal of India. The extent to which the Anglicist Macauley was successful in his aim 'to form a class who may be interpreters between us and the millions whom we govern: a class of persons, Indian in blood and colour, but English in taste, in opinions, in morals, and in intellect'[47] will become readily apparent later when we consider the development in the eighteenth and nineteenth centuries of the notion of a single religious entity known as 'Hinduism'. The notion of a Hindu religion, I wish to suggest, was initially invented by Western Orientalists basing their observations upon a Judaeo-Christian understanding of religion. The specific nature of this 'Hinduism', however, was the product of an interaction between the Western Orientalist and the brahmanical pundit. This construct, of course, was subsequently adopted (and adapted) by Hindu nationalists in their quest for home rule (*swaraj*) and in response to British imperial hegemony. Nevertheless, as Subaltern historian Ranajit Guha notes:

> The historiography of Indian nationalism has for a long time been dominated by elitism – colonialist elitism and bourgeois-nationalist elitism … Both these varieties of elitism share the prejudice that the making of the Indian nation and the development of the consciousness – nationalism – which informed this process were exclusively or predominantly elite achievements.[48]

Orientalism and Indology

Edward Said's examples are mainly taken from the 'Middle-Eastern' context, no doubt a reflection of his own Palestinian origins, and it has been left to others to explore the implications of his work further afield. In recent years, with the publication of Wilhelm Halbfass's work, *India and Europe: An Essay in Understanding* (1988), and Ronald Inden's study, *Imagining India* (1990), the Orientalist problematic has been discussed in relation to the study of Indian religion and philosophy. Inden, for instance, suggests that Indological analysis functions to portray Indian thoughts, institutions and practices as aberrations or distortions of normative (i.e. Western) patterns of behaviour.[49] According to Inden, Indological discourse transforms Indians into subjugated objects of a superior (i.e. higher-order) knowledge, which remains in the possession of the Western Indological expert. This is because Indological works do not provide merely descriptive accounts of what they study, but also provide commentaries that claim to represent the thoughts and actions of the Indian subject in such a manner as to communicate their general nature or 'essence' to the Western reader. Inden is also critical of 'hegemonic' accounts that provide reductionist and causal explanations for the 'irrational' behaviour of Indians (irrational in the sense that it requires explanation to the rational Westerner). Such reductionist accounts suggest that:

> Indian civilization is thus, unlike the West, fundamentally a product of its environment, and a defective product at that. European civilization is

the product of rational human action. Especially since the so-called Enlightenment the West has been guided by scientific reason in shaping its institutions and beliefs ... Modern science has acquired privileged knowledge of the natural world. It has made a 'copy' of that external reality unprecedented in its accuracy. The institutions of the West have therefore come more closely to conform to what is, in this discourse, 'natural'. Traditional and non-Western societies have, because of their inaccurate or false copies of external reality, made relatively ineffective adaptations to their environments. They have not evolved as fast as the modern West.[50]

Within this account one can see some of the important features of post-Enlightenment thought that we have already considered: for example, that the importance of scientific rationalism is underpinned by a Eurocentric conception of history and a firm belief in the progressive evolution of Western society. Inden, however, often overstates his case. I do not accept that all explanations of Indian thought and behaviour imply the irrationality of Indians. Explanations are necessary because Indian culture is different from Western culture in many respects; rejecting Orientalist projections of an 'Other' will not smooth over these differences. Providing an insightful account of Indian thought for the Western reader, while it may involve some distortion of the material under consideration, is necessary for this reason and not because Europeans are superior or more rational than Indians. Equally, reductionist accounts can be, and increasingly are being, applied to Western history and culture itself. In fact, one might argue that the current wave of postmodern anxiety about the foundations of Western civilization is partly a consequence of historicist and reductionist analysis being applied reflexively to the West itself.

Inden thus provides us with a highly polemical and generally negative account of Indological scholarship.[51] His analysis, however, is insightful on innumerable occasions and contains a number of salient points. He suggests that Indological scholarship in the past has been dominated by the privi-leged voice of the 'positivist' and the 'empirical realist'.[52] Inden, at times reminiscent of the neo-pragmatism of Richard Rorty and the epistemolog-ical anarchism of Paul Feyerband, rejects what he describes as the 'positivist' claim that there is 'a single, determinate reality' and that the tools of Western science have privileged access to that reality through forms of knowledge that directly correspond or 'mirror' it.

I reject the duality of knower and known presupposed by this episteme. It is my position that knowledge both participates in the construction of reality and is itself not simply natural (in the sense of necessary and given), but, in large part, constructed.[53]

Inden also suggests that the essentialism inherent in most Orientalist discourses should be comprehensively refuted. This is the tendency within most Indological accounts to claim to have uncovered the 'essence' of the object under consideration, through careful scholarly analysis. Thus works that purport to explain the 'Oriental mind-set' or the 'Indian mentality', etc., presuppose that there is a homogeneous, and almost Platonic 'essence' or 'nature' that can be directly intuited by the Indological expert. Inden is correct, in my view, to attack such essentialism, not just because it misrepresents the heterogeneity of the subject matter, but also because of the way in which such essentialism results in the construction of a cultural stereotype that may then be used to subordinate, classify and dominate the non-Western world. One of the problems with Inden's radical rendering of post-structuralist constructivism, however, is that he does not take seriously enough the material 'realities' underlying the imaginary constructions of 'India'.[54]

Inden's work, however, is interesting for his critical analysis of 'affirmative Orientalism'. This strand of Orientalist discourse, labelled 'romantic' by Inden because of its indebtedness to European Romanticism, is generally motivated by an admiration for, and sometimes by a firm belief in the superiority of, Eastern cultures. The romantic image of India portrays Indian culture as profoundly spiritual, idealistic and mystical. Thus, as Peter Marshall points out:

> As Europeans have always tended to do, they created Hinduism in their own image. Their study of Hinduism confirmed their beliefs and Hindus emerged from their work as adhering to something akin to undogmatic Protestantism. Later generations of Europeans, interested themselves in mysticism, were able to portray the Hindus as mystics.[55]

We shall have reason to discuss some of the implications of the characterization of Indian religion as 'mystical' in later chapters. At present, however, we would do well to note the reason why Inden criticizes the romanticist conception of India as the 'Loyal Opposition'. This reflects the fact that 'romantic Orientalism' agrees with the prevailing view that India is the mirror-opposite of Europe; it continues to postulate cultural 'essences' and thus perpetuates the same (or at least similar) cultural stereotypes about the East. The romanticist view of the Orient, then, is still a distortion, even if motivated at times by a respect for the Orient. As such, it participates in the projection of stereotypical forms that allows for a domestication and control of the East.

What is interesting about the 'mystical' or 'spiritual' emphasis that predominates in the romanticist conception of India is not just that it has become a prevalent theme in contemporary Western images of India, but also that it has exerted a great deal of influence upon the self-awareness of the very Indians that it purports to describe. Some might argue, as David Kopf clearly does, that such endorsement by Indians themselves suggests the anti-imperial nature of such discourses, yet one cannot ignore the sense in which British colonial ideology, through the various media of communication, education and institutional control, has made a substantial contribution to the construction of modern identity and self-awareness among contemporary Indians.

> European translations of Indian texts prepared for a western audience provided to the 'educated' Indian a whole range of Orientalist images. Even when the anglicised Indian spoke a language other than English, 'he' would have preferred, because of the symbolic power attached to English, to gain access to his own past through the translations and histories circulating through colonial discourse. English education also familiarised the Indian with ways of seeing, techniques of translation, or modes of representation that came to be accepted as 'natural.'[56]

Perhaps the primary examples of this are the figures of Vivekānanda and Mohandas K. Gandhi.[57] Vivekānanda (1863–1902), founder of the Ramakrishna Mission, an organization devoted to the promotion of a contemporary form of Advaita Vedānta (non-dualism), placed particular emphasis upon the spirituality of Indian culture as a curative for the nihilism and materialism of modern Western culture. In Vivekānanda's hands, Orientalist notions of India as 'other worldly' and 'mystical' were embraced and praised as India's special gift to humankind. Thus the very discourse that succeeded in alienating, subordinating and controlling India was used by Vivekānanda as a religious clarion call for the Indian people to unite under the banner of a universalistic and all-embracing Hinduism.

> Up India, and conquer the world with your spirituality ... Ours is a religion of which Buddhism, with all its greatness is a rebel child and of which Christianity is a very patchy imitation.

> The salvation of Europe depends on a rationalistic religion, and Advaita – non-duality, the Oneness, the idea of the Impersonal God, – is the only religion that can have any hold on any intellectual people.[58]

Colonial stereotypes thereby became transformed and used in the fight against colonialism. Despite this, stereotypes they remain. Vivekānanda's importance, however, goes far beyond his involvement with the Ramakrishna Mission. He attended (without invitation) the First World Parliament of Religions in Chicago in 1893, delivering a lecture on Hinduism (or at least on his own conception of the nature of Hinduism and its relationship with the other 'world religions'). Vivekānanda was a great success and initiated a number of successful tours of the United States and Europe. In the West he was influential in the reinforcement of the romanticist emphasis upon Indian spirituality, and in India Vivekānanda became the focus of a renascent intellectual movement, which might more accurately be labelled 'neo-Hinduism' or 'neo-Vedānta' rather than 'Hinduism'. In the next chapter we shall examine the way in which 'Hinduism' has been constructed in the modern era and the crucial role played by Western Orientalists in the construction process.

The inevitability of 'Orientalism'?

In common with Said, Inden and the post-structuralist agenda in general, I believe that it is important to look beyond images of homogeneity and univocality in the study of humankind in whatever field of study. This, indeed, has been my primary motivation in calling into question the textualist, essentialist and 'world-religions' approaches within religious studies. Such simplistic representations only serve to foster stereotypical and ahistorical forms that palpably fail to represent accurately the heterogeneity of human experience. Not only that, as we have seen, such images frequently serve not only to distort the complexity of the subject matter but also remain in complicity with particular ideological agendas.

However, in the light of Gadamer's rejection of the positivistic myth of scholarly objectivity and neutrality, as well as the work of Foucault and Said, which highlight the intimate relationship between knowledge and power, it would seem that it is impossible for any narrative or discourse to be free from some form of ideological conditioning. From this perspective it would seem to be impossible to avoid the act of 'plundering' or 'colonization', which Said labels 'Orientalism', when studying Indian religious and philosophical material. Prima facie, this approach seems to create a curiously self-defeating logic whereby everyone (including Said, Inden and the critics of Orientalism in general) ends up appropriating 'the Orient' for his or her own political and 'personal' agenda. Thus, as Bruce Robbins has suggested, Said's thesis that the profession of Orientalism ('explaining the Orient') promotes the privileged status of the Orientalist over and above those for whom he or she claims to be speaking can also be applied to Said and other critics of 'Orientalism'.

> Said and others like him can be charged ... with keeping the unrepresented from representing themselves, substituting their own élite intellectual work for the voices of the oppressed even as they claim to represent those voices.[59]

Said of course wishes to avoid this position, as well as the suggestion that only Orientals can legitimately speak of the Orient (a position that mistakenly presumes that the Oriental is also free from an agenda), and he does so by refusing to associate with a strong form of relativistic anti-representationalism (*à la* Foucault), whereby everyone is involved in constructing imaginary conceptions of 'the Orient' that have no identifiable referent in extra-linguistic reality. Others, such as David Ludden and perhaps Ronald Inden, have ventured further in this direction. As we have seen, however, Said's final position accepts the theoretical *possibility* of a legitimate representation of the Orient and is grounded in a universal humanism, despite Said's own equivocations about the means for determining such legitimacy in practice.

Nevertheless, the general tenor of the arguments furnished by Foucault, Said and Gadamer, despite their many differences, does seem to imply that the very act of interpretation by Western Orientalists when approaching the Orient inevitably involves an appropriation and 'colonialization' of the material under consideration. Indeed, this is not only an issue for the Orientalist, or even for the Westerner, but for everyone involved in the hermeneutical moment. As Gadamer argues, understanding something implicitly involves the prejudices of one's own 'historical situatedness'; one simply cannot avoid having an agenda or a perspective upon things by virtue of one's cultural and historical particularity.

Those who remain under the spell of a positivistic conception of objectivity and the ideal of absolute neutrality might despair at this point, but one does not have to follow Donald Davidson in the view that to understand something is merely to understand (i.e. appropriate) it in terms of one's own world-view. This argument suggests that world-views are fixed and closed. If one rejects the isolationist premises that underpin the Orientalist's absolute distinction between East and West, the possibility of interaction, dialogue and a 'fusion of horizons' remains so long as we remain 'hermeneutically open-minded'.

5   The modern myth of 'Hinduism'

[I]t would appear that there is an intrinsic connection between the
'Hinduism' that is being constructed in the political arena and the
'Hinduism' of academic study.[1]

Of the many enduring images of 'the Orient' that have captured the imagination of Westerners over the centuries, it is the characterization of Eastern
culture, and Indian religions in particular, as 'mystical' that is most relevant
to our current discussion. As European culture became increasingly
intrigued by the cultural mysteries and economic resources of foreign lands
in an age of colonial expansion, it was inevitable that a developing awareness of the diversity of cultures and religions would require some
characterization of these 'alternative perspectives' in a way that displayed
their *alterity* when compared to the normative European (Christian)
perspective.

As we have seen from the work of Michel de Certeau, the imaginative
construction of a 'mystical' tradition within Western Christianity seems to
have gained increasing credence in the seventeenth and eighteenth centuries.
With a greater awareness of the plurality of religious perspectives
throughout the world furnished by colonial encounters abroad it became
inevitable that comparisons with Christianity would come to the fore. It is
perhaps no coincidence, then, to find the Protestant presuppositions of
many Europeans (especially in the growing scholarly fields of German and
English Orientalism) being reflected in their characterization of non-
Christian religion. Given Protestant distrust of the 'mystical' elements of
Catholicism, it is also of little surprise to find a tendency to disentangle the
'mystical' from its particular Christian application and to reapply this characterization in a pluralistic religious context.

Once the term 'mystical' became detached from the specificity of its originally Christian context and became applied to the 'strange and mysterious
Orient', the association of the East with 'mysticism' became well and truly
entrenched in the collective cultural imagination of the West. Note, however,
that the association of Indian religion with the 'mystical' was by no means

always intended as a critique. Indeed the Romantic movement in Europe represents a good counterexample of a positive attempt to valorize 'the mystical East'. One should be wary, therefore, of assuming that colonial discourses are unidirectional and that enthusiastic portrayals of the East somehow remain untainted by the colonial enterprise.

Equally, it is worth noting that the characterization of the Orient as 'mystical' in the colonial period is not *just* about the classification and control of foreign lands and peoples; it also carries with it the weight of another burden – the implicit (and sometimes explicit) criticism of contemporary elements of the Orientalist's own culture. For scholars such as Peter Harrison, this reflects the fact that:

> The whole comparative approach to religion was directly related to confessional disputes within Christianity ... Accordingly, the 'religions' of the 'Orient', of the Pacific and the Americas, of ancient Greece and Rome were pressed into the service of the religious interests of the West. They became heresies which were formally equivalent to some undesirable version of Christianity, be it papism, Calvinism, Arminianism, or any other of the myriads of Protestant sects.[2]

Thus, for some, describing religions of the East as 'mystical' is a way of differentiating the essential historical truth of Christianity from its inferior rivals – and implicitly to attack those within Western Christianity who might want to focus upon the 'mystical' dimensions of their own tradition. However, for many of the Romantics 'the mystic East' represented the spirituality that much of contemporary Christian religion seemed to lack. Thus, as the term 'mystical' became divorced from a Christian context and was applied to other religions by Western theologians and Orientalists, it continued to function at home as the site of a power struggle in the battle to define European and Christian cultural identity.

Today, there are perhaps two powerful images in contemporary Western characterizations of Eastern religiosity. One is the continually enduring notion of the 'mystical East' that we have been discussing – a powerful image precisely because for some it represents what is most disturbing and outdated about Eastern culture, while for others it represents the magic, the mystery and the sense of the spiritual that they perceive to be lacking in modern Western culture. The depravity and backwardness of the Orient thus appears to sit side by side with its blossoming spirituality and cultural richness. Both of these motifs have a long historical pedigree, deriving from the hopes and fears of the European imagination and its perennial fascination with the East.

The second image of Eastern religion – one indeed that is increasingly coming to the fore in Western circles, is that of the 'militant fanatic'. Such a characterization also has a considerable ancestry, being a contemporary manifestation of older colonial myths about Oriental despotism and the irrationality of the colonial subject. The particular nature of this construct is, of course, heavily influenced by the secularist perspective of much of modern Western culture. The image of the militant fanatic or religious 'fundamentalist', while frequently interwoven with 'the mystical' characterization (particularly in the emphasis that Western commentators place upon the 'religious' dimension of conflicts such as Ayodhyā in India), is rarely explicitly associated with the notion of 'the mystical East' precisely because modern Western understandings of 'the mystical' tend to preclude the possibility of an authentic mystical involvement in political struggle. The otherworldly Eastern mystic cannot be involved in a this-worldly political struggle without calling into question the strong cultural opposition between the mystical and the public realms. The discontinuity between these two cultural representations of the East has frequently created problems for Western and Western-influenced observers who find it difficult to reconcile notions of spiritual detachment with political (and sometimes violent) social activism.[3]

Thus in the modern era we find Hinduism being represented both as a globalized and all-embracing world religion and as an intolerant and virulent form of religious nationalism. Despite the apparent incongruity of these two representations, I will argue in this chapter that one feature that both characterizations share in common is the debt they owe to Western Orientalism. My argument does not entail that the modern concept of 'Hinduism' is *merely* the product of Western Orientalism. Western influence was a necessary but not a sufficient causal factor in the rise of this particular social construction. To argue otherwise would be to ignore the crucial role played by indigenous brahmanical ideology in the formation of early Orientalist representations of Hindu religiosity.

The myth of homogeneity and the modern myth of 'Hinduism'

As we saw in Chapter 3, scepticism about the applicability of globalized, highly abstract and univocal systems of thought onto the religious experience of humankind (as manifested in the concept of 'world religions') has been expressed by scholars like Wilfred Cantwell Smith on the grounds that such an approach provides us with an overly homogenized picture of human cultural diversity.[4] We can see the implications of this more clearly if we consider the claim, supported by such figures as Gandhi, Sarvepalli Radhakrishnan and Vivekānanda, that there is a single religion called 'Hinduism', which can be meaningfully referred to as the religion of the Hindu people.

The notion of 'Hinduism' is itself a Western-inspired abstraction, which until the nineteenth century bore little or no resemblance to the diversity of Indian religious belief and practice. The term 'Hindoo' is the Persian variant of the Sanskrit *sindhu*, referring to the Indus river, and as such was used by the Persians to denote the people of that region.[5] Al-Hind, therefore, is a term denoting the people of a particular geographical area. Although indigenous use of the term by Hindus themselves can be found as early as the fifteenth and sixteenth centuries, its usage was derivative of Persian Muslim influences and did not represent anything more than a distinction between 'indigenous' or 'native' and foreign (*mleccha*).[6] For instance, when Belgian Thierry Verhelst interviewed an Indian intellectual from Tamil Nadu he recorded the following interchange:

Q: Are you a Hindu?
A: No, I grew critical of it because of casteism ... Actually, you should not ask people if they are Hindu. This does not mean much. If you ask them what their religion is, they will say, 'I belong to this caste.'[7]

Indeed, it is clear that the term 'Hindu', even when used by the indigenous Indian, did not have the specifically religious connotations that it subsequently developed under Orientalist influences until the nineteenth century.[8] Thus eighteenth-century references to 'Hindoo' Christians or 'Hindoo' Muslims were not uncommon.[9] As Romila Thapar points out in her discussion of the reception of Muslims into India:

The people of India do not seem to have perceived the new arrivals as a unified body of Muslims. The name 'Muslim' does not occur in the records of the early contacts. The term used was either ethnic, *turuṣka*, referring to the Turks, or geographical, Yavana, or cultural, *mleccha*.[10]

One should also note the distinctively negative nature of the term, the primary function of which is to provide a catch-all designation for the 'Other', whether negatively contrasted with the ancient Persians, with their Muslim descendants, or with the later European Orientalists who eventually adopted the term. Indeed the same is apparent from an examination of modern Indian law. For example the 1955 Hindu Marriage Act, section 2(1) defines a 'Hindu' as a category including not only all Buddhists, Jains and Sikhs but also anyone who is not a Muslim, a Christian, a Parsee or a Jew. Thus even in the contemporary context the terms 'Hindu' and 'Hinduism' are essentially negative appellations, functioning as an all-inclusive rubric for the non-Judaeo-Christian 'Other'.[11]

'Hindu' in fact only came into provenance amongst Westerners in the eighteenth century. Previously, the predominant Christian perspective amongst the Europeans classified Indian religion under the all-inclusive rubric of Heathenism. On this view there were four major religious groups, Jews, Christians, Mahometans (i.e. Muslims) and Heathens. Members of the last category were widely considered to be children of the Devil, and the Indian Heathens were but one particular sect alongside the Africans and the Americans (who even today are referred to as American 'Indians' in an attempt to draw a parallel between the indigenous populations of India and the precolonial population of the Americas). Other designations used to refer to the Indians were 'Banians', a term which derives from the merchant populations of Northern India, and 'Gentoos', which functioned as an alternative to 'Heathen'. Nevertheless, as Western knowledge and interest in India increased, the term 'Hindu' eventually gained greater prominence as a culturally and geographically more specific term.

The term 'Hinduism', which of course derives from the frequency with which 'Hindu' came to be used, is a Western explanatory construct. As such it reflects the colonial and Judaeo-Christian presuppositions of the Western Orientalists who first coined the term. David Kopf praises this 'gift' from the Orientalists seemingly unaware of the Eurocentric agenda underlying it and the extent to which the superimposition of the monolithic entity of 'Hinduism' upon Indian religious material has distorted and perhaps irretrievably transformed Indian religiosity in a Westernized direction. Thus he states that:

> The work of integrating a vast collection of myths, beliefs, rituals, and laws into a coherent religion, and of shaping an amorphous heritage into a rational faith known now as "Hinduism" were endeavors initiated by Orientalists.[12]

The term 'Hinduism' seems first to have made an appearance in the early nineteenth century, and gradually gained provenance in the decades thereafter. Eighteenth-century references to the 'religion of the Gentoos' (e.g. Nathaniel Brassey Halhead (1776), *A Code of Gentoo Laws*) were gradually supplanted in the nineteenth century by references to 'the religion of the Hindoos' – a preference for the Persian as opposed to the Portuguese designation of the Indian people. However, it is not until the nineteenth century proper that the term 'Hinduism' became used as a signifier of a unified, all-embracing and independent religious entity in both Western and Indian circles. The *Oxford English Dictionary* traces 'Hindooism' to an 1829 reference in the *Bengalee* (Volume 45), and also refers to an 1858 usage by the German Indologist Max Müller.[13] Dermot Killingley, however, cites a reference to 'Hindooism' by Rammohun Roy in 1816. As Killingley suggests, 'Rammohun was probably the first Hindu to use the word Hinduism.'[14] One hardly need mention the extent to which Roy's conception of the 'Hindu' religion was conditioned by European, Muslim and Unitarian theological influences. Ironically there is considerable reason, therefore, for the frequency with which Western scholars have described Roy as 'the father of modern India'.

Western Orientalist discourses, by virtue of their privileged political status within 'British' India, have contributed greatly to the modern construction of 'Hinduism' as a single world religion. This was somewhat inevitable given British control over the political, educational and media institutions of India. If we note, for instance, the extent to which the British

established an education system that promoted the study of European literature, history and science, and the study of Indian culture through the
medium of English or vernacular translations of the work of Western
Orientalists, if we also acknowledge the fact that all of India's universities
were established by the British, and according to British educational criteria,
we can see the extent to which Macauley's hope of an élite class of
Anglicized Indians was put into practice.

Christianity, textualism and the construction of 'Hinduism'

European colonial influence upon Indian religion and culture has
profoundly altered its nature in the modern era. In particular I would like to
highlight two ways in which Western colonization has contributed to the
modern construction of 'Hinduism' – first by locating the core of Indian
religiosity in certain Sanskrit texts (the textualization of Indian religion),
and second by an implicit (and sometimes explicit) tendency to define
Indian religion in terms of a normative paradigm of religion based upon
contemporary Western understandings of the Judaeo-Christian traditions.
These two processes are clearly interwoven in a highly complex fashion and
one might even wish to argue that they are, in fact, merely two aspects of a
single phenomenon – namely the Westernization of Indian religion.
Nevertheless, they require some attention if we are to grasp the sense in
which the modern conception of Hinduism is indeed a *modern* development.

Western literary bias has contributed to a textualization of Indian religion.[15] This is not to deny that Indian culture has its own literary traditions,
rather it is to emphasize the sense in which Western presuppositions about
the role of sacred texts in 'religion' predisposed Orientalists towards
focusing upon such texts as the essential foundation for understanding the
Hindu people as a whole. Protestant emphasis upon the text as the locus of
religion placed a particular emphasis upon the literary aspects of Indian
culture in the work of Orientalists. Academics and highly educated Western
administrators are already inclined towards literary forms of expression
because of their training, and so it is not all that surprising to find
Orientalists (both old and new) being drawn towards Indian literary materials as sources for understanding Indian culture. Many of the early
European translators of Indian texts were also Christian missionaries, who,
in their translations and critical editions of Indian works, effectively
constructed uniform texts and a homogenized written canon through the
imposition of Western philological standards and presuppositions onto
Indian materials.[16] Thus the oral and 'popular' aspect of Indian religious
tradition was either ignored or decried as evidence of the degradation of
contemporary Hindu religion into superstitious practices that bore little or
no relation to 'their own' texts. This attitude was easily assimilated with the
Pūraṇically inspired, brahminical belief in the current deterioration of civilization in the age of *kaliyuga*.

The textualist bias of Western Orientalists has had far reaching consequences in the increasingly literate India of the modern era. As Rosalind O'Hanlon writes:

> [T]he privileging of scribal communities and authoritative interpreters of 'tradition' provided, on the one hand, an essential requirement of practical administration. On the other, it formed a crucial component in colonialism's larger project itself for the textualization of cultures, for the construction of authoritative bodies of knowledge about Hindu communities as the means of securing 'freedom' to follow their own customs.[17]

William Jones for example, in his role as Supreme Court Judge in India, initiated a project to translate the *Dharmaśāstras* in the misguided belief that this represented the law of the Hindus, in order to circumvent what he saw as the 'culpable bias' of the native pundits. In taking the *Dharmaśāstras* as a binding law-book, Jones manifests the Judaeo-Christian paradigm within which he conceived of religion, and the attempt to apply such a book universally reflects Jones' 'textual imperialism'.[18] The problem with taking the *Dharmaśāstras* as pan-Indian in application is that the texts themselves were representative of a priestly élite (the *brāhmaṇa* castes), and not of Hindus *in toto*. Thus, even within these texts, there was no notion of a unified Hindu community, but rather an acknowledgement of a plurality of local, occupational and caste contexts in which different customs or rules applied.[19] It was thus in this manner that:

> society was made to conform to ancient *dharmaśāstras* texts, in spite of those texts' insistence that they were overridden by local and group custom. It eventually allowed Anglicist administrators to *manipulate the porous boundary between religion as defined by texts* and customs they wished to ban.[20] [my italics]

There is, of course, a danger that in critically focusing upon Orientalist discourses one might ignore the importance of native actors and circumstances in the construction of Western conceptions of India. Here perhaps we should note the sense in which certain élitist communities within India (notably the scholarly *brāhmaṇa* castes) exerted a certain degree of influence upon the Western Orientalists, thereby contributing to the construction of the modern, Western conception of 'Hinduism'. The high social, economic and, to some degree, political status of the *brāhmaṇa* castes has, no doubt, contributed to the elision between brahmanical forms of religion and 'Hinduism'. This is most notable, for instance, in the tendency to emphasize Vedic and brahmanical texts and beliefs as central and foundational to the 'essence' of Hinduism, and in the modern association of 'Hindu doctrine' with the various brahmanical schools of the Vedānta (in particular, Advaita

Vedānta, the subject of Chapter 6). Indeed, neo-Vedāntic rhetoric about the underlying unity of Indian religion has tended:

> to support the Westerners' preconceived notion that it was one religion they were dealing with. Since they were used to the Christian tradition of an absolute claim for only one truth, of a powerful church domi-nating society, and consequently of fierce religious and social confrontation with members of other creeds, they were unable even to conceive of such religious liberality as would give members of the same society the freedom, by individual choice, to practice the religion they liked.
>
> As a result, western students saw Hinduism as a unity. The Indians had no reason to contradict this; to them the religious and cultural unity discovered by western scholars was highly welcome in their search for national identity in the period of struggle for national union.[21]

C.A. Bayly notes, for instance, the extent to which the administrative and academic demand for the literary and ritual expertise of the brahmins placed them in a position of direct contact and involvement with their impe-rial rulers, a factor that should not go unnoticed in attempting to explain why Western Orientalists tended to associate brahmanical literature and ideology with Hindu religion *in toto*.[22] It is clear that, in this regard at least, Western Orientalists, working under the aegis of a Judaeo-Christian reli-gious paradigm, looked for and found an ecclesiastical authority akin to Western models of an ecclesiastical hierarchy. In the case of the brahmanical 'priests' and pundits, already convinced of the degradation of contemporary Indian civilization in the present era of *kaliyuga*, these scholars generally found a receptive and willing religious élite, who, for that very reason remained amenable to the rhetoric of reform.

The brahmanical religions, of course, had already been active in their own appropriation of non-brahmanical forms of Indian religion long before the Muslim and European invasions. Brahmanization – the process whereby the Sanskritic, 'high' culture of the brahmins absorbed non-brahmanical (some-times called 'popular' or even 'tribal') religious forms – was an effective means of assimilating diverse cultural strands within one's locality, and of maintaining social and political authority.[23] The process works both ways, of course, and many of the features of Sanskritic religion initially derived from a particular, localized context.[24] Nevertheless, in the case of the educated *brāhmaṇa* castes, the British found a loosely defined cultural élite that proved amenable to an ideology that placed them at the apex of a single world-reli-gious tradition.[25] If one asks who would most have benefited from the modern construction of a unified Hindu community focusing upon the Sanskritic and brahmanical forms of Indian religion, the answer would, of course, be those highly educated members of the higher *brāhmaṇa* castes, for whom modern 'Hinduism' represents the triumph of universalized, brahmanical forms of religion over the 'tribal' and the 'local'. Statistically, for example, it would seem that in post-Independence India the brahmin castes have become the dominant social group, filling 36 to 63 per cent of all government jobs, despite representing only 3.5 per cent of the Indian population.[26] As Frykenberg points out:

> Brahmins have always controlled information. That was their boast. It was they who had provided information on indigenous institutions [for Western Orientalists]. It was they who provided this on a scale so unprecedented that, at least at the level of All-India consciousness, a new religion emerged the likes of which India had perhaps never known before.[27]

The Sanskritic 'brahmanization' of Hindu religion (itself representing one stage in the textualization process) was filtered through colonial discourses, thereby furnishing a new holistic and unified conception of the multiplicity of Indian religious phenomena throughout history. Such an approach remains profoundly anti-historical in its postulation of an ahistorical 'essence' to which all forms of 'Hinduism' are said to relate. As Said has suggested, such an abstract and synchronic approach is one way in which Orientalist discourses fundamentally distinguish the passive and ahistorical Orient from the active and historically changing Occident. In this manner, Orientals are effectively dehumanized (since denied an active role in the processes of history), and thus made more amenable to colonial manipulation. As Romila Thapar suggests, this new Hinduism, furnished with a brahmanical base, was merged with elements of 'upper caste belief and ritual with one eye on the Christian and Islamic models', and was thoroughly infused with a political and nationalistic emphasis. Thapar describes this contemporary development as 'syndicated Hinduism', and notes that it is 'being pushed forward as the sole claimant of the inheritance of indigenous Indian religion'.[28]

This reflects the tendency, during and after European colonialism, for Indian religion to be conceived by Westerners and Indians themselves in a manner conducive to Judaeo-Christian conceptions of the nature of religion, a process that Veena Das has described as the 'semitification' of Hinduism in the modern era. Thus, since the nineteenth century, 'Hinduism' has developed, and is notable for, a number of new characteristics, which seem to have arisen in response to Judaeo-Christian presuppositions about the nature of religion. This new form of organized or 'syndicated Hinduism':

> seeks historicity for the incarnations of its deities, encourages the idea of a centrally sacred book, claims monotheism as significant to the worship of deity, acknowledges the authority of the ecclesiastical organization of certain sects as prevailing over all and has supported

large-scale missionary work and conversion. These changes allow it to transcend caste identities and reach out to larger numbers.[29]

In the contemporary era, then, 'Hinduism' is characterized by both an emerging 'universalistic' strand that focuses upon proselytization (for example, neo-Vedānta, Sathya Sai Baba, Bhagwan Shree Rajneesh, transcendental meditation) as well as so-called 'fundamentalist', 'revivalist' and 'nationalist' strands that focus upon the historicity of human incarnations of Viṣṇu, such as Rāma and Kṛṣṇa, the sacrality of their purported birthplaces, and an antagonistic attitude towards non-Hindu religions (notably the Indian Muslims).[30] One hardly need point to the sense in which these developments mimic traits usually associated in the West with the Judaeo-Christian traditions.[31]

Indeed, it would seem that the key to the West's initial postulation of the unity of 'Hinduism' derives from the Judaeo-Christian presuppositions of the Orientalists and missionaries. Convinced as they were that distinctive religions could not coexist without frequent antagonism, the doctrinal liberality of Indian religions remained a mystery without the postulation of an overarching religious framework that could unite the Indians under the flag of a single religious tradition. How else can the relatively peaceful coexistence of the various Hindu movements be explained without some sense of religious unity? Why else would Hindus of differing sectarian affiliations accept the existence of rival gods unless they belonged to the same religious tradition? Failure to transcend a model of religion premised on the monotheistic exclusivism of Western Christianity thereby resulted in the imaginative construction of a single religion called 'Hinduism'. Of course, being able to classify Hindus under a single religious rubric also made colonial control and manipulation easier. The fact that the semblance of unity within India owed considerable debt to imperial rule seems to have been forgotten. The lack of an orthodoxy, of an ecclesiastical structure, or indeed of any distinctive feature that might point to the postulation of a single Hindu religion, was dismissed, and one consequence of this was the tendency to portray 'Hinduism' as a contradictory religion, which required some form of organization along ecclesiastical and doctrinal lines and a purging of 'superstitious' elements incompatible with the 'high' culture of 'Hinduism'.

This new *epistēme*[32] created a conceptual space in the form of a rising perception that 'Hinduism' had become a corrupt shadow of its former self (which was now located in certain key sacred texts such as the Vedas, the *Upaniṣads* and the *Bhagavad Gītā* – all taken to provide an unproblematic account of ancient Hindu religiosity). The perceived shortcomings of contemporary 'Hinduism' in comparison to the ideal form, as represented in the text, thus created the belief (among both Westerners and Indians) that Hindu religion had stagnated over the centuries and was therefore in need of reformation. The gap between original (ideal) 'Hinduism' and the contemporary beliefs and practices of Hindus was soon filled, of course, by the rise of what have become known as 'Hindu reform movements' in the nineteenth century – groups such as the Brahmo Samaj, the Ārya Samaj and the Rāmakṛṣṇa Mission. Virtually all textbooks on Hinduism describe these groups as 'reform' movements. This representation, however, falls into the trap of seeing precolonial Hindu religion(s) through colonial spectacles. When combined with a highly questionable periodization of Hindu religious history (which ultimately derives from James Mill's *A History of British India*), the impression is given (1) that Hinduism is a single religion with its origins in the Vedas, (2) that from the 'medieval' period onwards (*c.* tenth century onwards) Hinduism stagnated and lost its potential for renewal, and (3) that, with the arrival of the West, Hindus became inspired to reform their now decadent religion to something approaching its former glory. This picture of Indian history, as problematic as it is prevalent, reflects a Victorian and post-Enlightenment faith in the progressive nature of history. Thus Hinduism in the twentieth century is allowed to enter the privileged arena of the 'world religions', having finally come of age in a global context and satisfying the criteria of membership established by Western scholars of religion!

To illustrate the arbitrariness involved in the homogenization of Indian religions under the rubric of 'Hinduism', let us briefly consider what happens if one applies the same a priori assumption of religious unity to Judaism, Christianity and Islam. As von Stietencron argues, if one takes these three 'religions' to be sects or denominations of a single religion one can point to a common geographical origin in the Near East, a common ancestry (Abrahamic tradition), a common monotheism, a common prophetism, all three accept a linear and eschatological conception of history, uphold similar (though varying) religious ethics, work within a broadly similar theological framework with regard to their notions of a single God, the devil, paradise, creation, the status of humankind within the workings of history, as well as, of course, revering the Hebrew Bible (to varying degrees). On the other hand, however, there is no common founder of the three movements, probably no doctrine that is valid for all adherents, no uniform religious ritual or ecclesiastical organization, and it is not immediately clear that the adherents of these three movements believe in the same God.[33] If we then consider the diversity of religious movements usually subsumed under the label 'Hinduism', we shall find a similar picture. Perhaps the difference lies in the fact that nineteenth- and twentieth-century 'Hindus' have generally not objected to the postulation of a single religious tradition as a way of understanding their beliefs and practices, whereas Jews, Christians and Muslims generally remain very protective of their own group identities. This Hindu attitude does not merely reflect the colonization of their thought-processes by the Orientalists. Postulation of Hindu unity was to be encouraged in the development of Indian autonomy from British rule. *Swaraj* (home rule) was seen to be inconceivable without the unification of

India along nationalistic and cultural lines. Not only that, although sectarian clashes have always occurred, in general Indian religious groups appear to have been able to live together in a manner unprecedented in the history of the Judaeo-Christian religions in the West.

Consequently, it remains an anachronism to project the notion of 'Hinduism' as it is commonly understood into precolonial Indian history. Before the unification begun under imperial rule and consolidated by the Independence of 1947, it makes no sense to talk of an Indian 'nation', nor of a religion called 'Hinduism' that might be taken to represent the belief system of the Hindu people. Today, of course, the situation differs in so far as one can now point to a loosely defined cultural entity that might be labelled 'Hinduism' or, as some prefer, 'neo-Hinduism' (though this latter term implies that there was a unified cultural entity known as 'Hinduism' that can be pinpointed in the precolonial era). The presuppositions of the Orientalists cannot be underestimated in the process whereby nineteenth- and twentieth-century Indians have come to perceive their own identity and culture through colonially crafted lenses. It is clear, then, that from the nineteenth century onwards Indian self-awareness has resulted in the development of an intellectual and textually based 'Hinduism', which is then 'read back' (if you pardon the 'textual' pun) into India's religious history. Indeed:

> The construction of a unified Hindu identity is of utmost importance for Hindus who live outside India. They need a Hinduism that can be explained to outsiders as a respectable religion, that can be taught to their children in religious education, and that can form the basis for collective action ... In an ironic twist of history, orientalism is now brought by Indians to Indians living in the West.[34]

As mentioned earlier, the invention of 'Hinduism' as a single 'world religion' was also accompanied by the rise of a nationalist consciousness in India since the nineteenth century.[35] The modern nation-state, of course, is a product of European sociopolitical and economic developments from the sixteenth century onwards, and the introduction of the nationalist model into Asia is a further legacy of European imperialism in this area. It is somewhat ironic, therefore, to find that the very Hindu nationalists who fought so vehemently against British imperialist rule themselves accepted the homogenizing concepts of 'nationhood' and 'Hinduism', which ultimately derived from their imperial rulers.[36] To some extent it is difficult to see what alternative the opponents of colonialism had, since the nation-state provides the paradigmatic building block of all contemporary economic, political and cultural interaction. Thus, as David Ludden has suggested, the authority of Orientalist discourses initially derived from colonialism:

but it was reproduced by anti-imperial, national movements and reinvig-
orated by Partition, in 1947, and the reorganization of Indian states, in
1956; it thrives today on conflict expressed in religious and ethnic terms.
In its reification of tradition and of oppositions between East and West,
nationalized orientalism suffuses postcolonial political culture and
scholarship that claims to speak for India by defining India's identity in
a postcolonial world ... Having helped to make nations in South Asia
what they are, orientalism fuels fires that may consume them.[37]

Romila Thapar consolidates this position by pointing to the political consequences of the construction of a common Hindu identity. Thus she argues
that:

> Since it was easy to recognize other communities on the basis of reli-
> gion, such as Muslims and Christians, an effort was made to consolidate
> a parallel Hindu community ... In Gramsci's terms, the class which
> wishes to become hegemonic has to nationalize itself and the 'nation-
> alist' Hinduism comes from the middle class.[38]

The status of the term 'Hinduism'

Given the evidence that we have just considered, is it still possible to use the
term 'Hinduism' at all? One might wish to argue that the term 'Hinduism' is
a useful construct in so far as it refers to the general features of 'Indian
culture' rather than to a single religion. Julius Lipner has recently argued
that scholars should retain the term 'Hinduism' in so far as it is used in a
non-essentialist manner to refer to Hindu culture and not to the idea of a
single religion. Lipner suggests that the Western term 'Hinduism' when used
in this sense is effective so long as it represents the 'dynamic polycentrism' of
Hindutā (Hindu-ness).[39]

However, even Lipner's characterization of 'Hinduism' remains deeply
indebted to Sanskritic brahmanism. It is difficult to see, even on this view,
why Buddhism and Jainism are not themselves part of *Hindutā*. Despite
Lipner's explicit disavowal of an essentialist or reified rendering of the term,
his description of 'Hinduism' as 'macrocosmically one though microcosmi-
cally many, a polycentric phenomenon imbued with the same life-sap, the
boundaries and (micro)centres seeming to merge and overlap in a complexus
of oscillating tensions'[40] is likely to continue to cause misunderstanding, just
as it is also likely to be appropriated by the inclusivism of neo-Vedānta
(which attempts to subsume Buddhism (in particular) under the umbrella of
an absolutism of the Advaita Vedānta variety) and Hindu nationalist groups
alike. Although the modern Indian Constitution (article 25 (2)) classifies all
Buddhist, Jains and Sikhs as 'Hindu', this is unacceptable for a number of
reasons. First, it rides roughshod over religious diversity and established
group-affiliations. Second, such an approach ignores the non-brahmanical

and non-Vedic elements of these traditions. Fundamentally, such assimilation effectively subverts the authority of members of these traditions to
speak for themselves. In the last analysis, neo-Vedāntic inclusivism remains
inappropriate for the simple reason that Buddhists and Jains do not generally see themselves as followers of sectarian denominations of 'Hinduism'.

Lipner's appeal to 'polycentricism' and perspectivism as characteristic of
Hindu thought also fails to salvage a recognizable sense of Indian *religious*
unity, since it amounts to stating that the unity of 'Hinduism' (or *Hindutā*)
can be found in a relativistic recognition of perspective in a great deal of
Hindu doctrine and practice. This will hardly suffice if one wishes to use the
term 'Hinduism' in a way that is in any meaningful respect classifiable as a
'religion' in the modern Western sense of the term. One might wish to postulate 'Hinduism' as an underlying *cultural* unity, but this, too, is likely to
prove inadequate once one moves beyond generalized examination and
appeals to cultural homogeneity. Yet even if one accepts 'Hinduism' as a
cultural rather than as a specifically religious unity, one would then need to
acknowledge the sense in which it was no longer identifiable as an 'ism',
thereby rendering the term obsolete or at best downright misleading. To
continue to talk of 'Hinduism', even as a broad cultural phenomenon, is as
problematic as the postulation of a unified cultural tradition known as
'Westernism'. There are general features of both Indian and Western culture
that one can pinpoint and analyse to a certain degree, but neither term
should be reified.

Indologist Wilhelm Halbfass has attacked the claim that 'Hinduism' is an
Orientalist construction by appealing to the universality of the concept of
dharma in pre-modern Hindu thought:

> We cannot reduce the meanings of *dharma* to one general principle;
> nor is there one single translation that would cover all its usages.
> Nevertheless, there is coherence in this variety; it reflects the elusive,
> yet undeniable coherence of Hinduism itself, its peculiar unity-in-
> diversity.[41]

According to Halbfass, despite specific 'sectarian' allegiances (for example,
to Vaiṣṇavism or Śaivism) the theoreticians and literary representatives of
these traditions 'relate and refer to one another, juxtapose or coordinate
their teachings, and articulate their claims of mutual inclusion or transcendence' in a manner indicative of a wider sense of Hindu unity and identity.[42]
However, the 'elusive' glue which apparently holds together the diversity of
Indian religious traditions is not further elaborated upon by Halbfass, nor is
this 'unity-in-diversity' as 'undeniable' as he suggests. As we have seen, the
nineteenth-century Orientalists tended to postulate an underlying unity to
Hindu religious traditions because they tended to view Indian religion from
a Western Christian perspective. Halbfass at least is willing to admit that the
reality of 'Hinduism' is 'elusive' and that the use of the term 'religion' to

translate the concept of *dharma* is problematic.[43] Nevertheless, in my view he fails to appreciate the sense in which the postulation of a single, under-lying *religious* unity called 'Hinduism' requires a highly imaginative act of historical reconstruction. To appeal to the Indian concept of *dharma* as unifying the diversity of Hindu religious traditions is moot, since *dharma* is not a principle that is amenable to a single, universal interpretation, being in fact appropriated in diverse ways by a variety of Indian traditions (all of which tended to define the concept in terms of their own group-dynamic and identity). The appeal to *dharma* therefore is highly questionable in the same sense that an appeal to the notion of the Covenant would be in estab-lishing that Judaism, Christianity and Islam were actually sectarian offshoots of a single religious tradition.

Despite all of these problems, one might argue that there are a number of reasons why one should retain the term 'Hinduism'. First, the term remains useful on a general, superficial and introductory level. Second, it is clear that, since the nineteenth century, movements have arisen in India that roughly correspond to the term as it was understood by Orientalists. Indeed, as I have argued, Orientalist accounts have themselves had a significant role to play in the rise of such groups. Thus 'Hinduism' now exists in a sense in which it certainly did not before the nineteenth century. Third, one might wish to retain the term, as Lipner does, with the qualification that its radi-cally polythetic nature be understood. What I have in mind here is a non-essentialist approach that draws particular attention to the ruptures and discontinuities, the criss-crossing patterns and 'family resemblances' that are usually subsumed by unreflective and essentialist usage. Ferro-Luzzi, for instance, has suggested that the term 'Hinduism' should be understood to be a 'polythetic-prototypical' concept, polythetic because of its radically heterogeneous nature, and 'prototypical' in the sense that the term is frequently used by both Westerners and Indians to refer to a particular idealized construct. Prototypical features of Hinduism function as such either because of their high frequency among Hindus (for example, the worship of deities such as Śiva, Kṛṣṇa and Gaṇeśa, temple worship, and the practice of *pūja*), or because of their prestige among Hindus (such as the so-called 'high' culture of Hindus – that is, the brahmanical concepts of *dharma, saṃsāra, karma, advaita, viśiṣṭādvaita*, etc.), which remain impor-tant normative or prototypical paradigms for contemporary Hindu self-identity, although only actually believed in by a minority. With regard to this latter category, Ferro-Luzzi suggests that:

> Even though only a minority of Hindus believe in them or even know them they enjoy the greatest prestige both among educated Hindus and Westerners. Besides, their influence upon Hindus tends to increase now with the spread of education [and literacy in particular, one might add]. The prototype of a Hindu might be a person who worships the above deities, visits temples, goes on a pilgrimage and believes in the above

concepts. Undoubtedly, such persons exist but they are only a minority amongst Hindus.[44]

In my view, however, the problems deriving from the use of 'Hinduism' make it inappropriate as a term denoting the heterogeneity of 'Hindu' religiosity in the precolonial era. Nevertheless, whatever one's view on the appropriateness of the term 'Hinduism', the abandonment of essentialism, rather than facilitating vagueness and disorder, opens up the possibility of new directions in scholarship. Indeed, a proper acknowledgement of the heterogeneity of Indian religious phenomena, as outlined in a postcolonial critique of homogenizing and hegemonic discourses (whether Western or Indian), also allows for attempts to overcome the cultural and political élitism supported by them, and for the possibility of subaltern responses to dominant ideological constructs and the cultural and political élitism that they tend to support.

The relevance of feminism to the Orientalist debate

So far I have suggested that in the construction of 'Hinduism' as a single religion the Orientalist creates a homogeneous picture of the world constructed according to Enlightenment (and ultimately Judaeo-Christian) presuppositions about the nature of religion. Orientalist discourses, however, also tend to focus upon the radical 'otherness' of Indian religion as a way of contrasting the Indian with the normative (i.e. Western) paradigm. At first sight this might seem to entail a contradiction. How can Orientalist discourses conceive of Indian religion in their own image and at the same time conceive of that same phenomena as the mirror-opposite of that image? In fact it is precisely because 'Hinduism' is conceived of in terms of Western conceptions of religion that it can then be meaningfully contrasted with the normative paradigm itself. In this sense, Orientalist discourses on Indian religion often become confined within a self-contained process of identification and differentiation constructed according to a normative paradigm (frequently modern, Western Christianity but sometimes secular liberalism). In the context of such discourses, the Indian subject remains trapped within the self-perpetuating logic of identity and difference, and thus remains subordinate to the normative paradigm. The complicity of identity and difference is an important feature of such discourses. Thus 'Hinduism' was conceptualized by Western Orientalists according to their own Western presuppositions about the nature of religion. It was precisely this that enabled them to construct an image of India that was the inverse of that paradigm.

As Kalpana Ram has pointed out:

> The logic of comparison – which is, on the face of it, concerned with difference – functions rather as a logic of identity, in which the Indian

subject does not enjoy independent status, and is made intelligible only in opposition to the fundamental or privileged values of Western modernity ... In the hegemonic discourse of modernity and liberalism, the Western subject has been conceived as an individuated self-conscious authorial presence (the 'author' of his own activities) ... [T]he 'Indian' is not simply different from the 'Westerner', but is his exact inverse.[45]

This dilemma is reflected in the catch-22 situation in which the Indian colonial subject is placed. To agree with the colonial discourse is to accept one's subordination in terms of a hegemonic Western paradigm. However, in rejecting such discourses one often perpetuates the paradigm itself, even if the categories are now inverted, reversed or revalorized. This, for instance, is the situation with regard to Hindu nationalist movements of the late nineteenth and early twentieth centuries. In their quest for home rule (*swaraj*) and freedom from imperial control, Hindus tended to perpetuate the nationalistic, romantic and homogenizing presuppositions of their British rulers.

As we have already seen, the manner in which Indological discourse has constructed India as the 'Other' or the 'shadow' of the West is a feature that is stressed in a number of critical accounts of Indological orientalism, e.g. the work of Ronald Inden (1985, 1990) and Ashis Nandy (1983). A number of scholars have pointed to work such as Louis Dumont's classic sociological study of the Indian caste system, *Homo Hierarchicus* (1970), as clear examples of this tendency. The hierarchical 'Indian' represented in this work comes to represent the antithesis of the ideal 'Western Man', or *homo aequalis*.[46] The essentialism endemic within such approaches necessitates a stereotypical representation of the Westerner in order that the Indian might reflect his polar opposite. The Westerner, presupposed as the normative paradigm in such analysis, tends to be idealized as modern, egalitarian, civilized, secular, rational and male. In contrast, the Indian is often represented as tied to tradition, primitive, hierarchical, uncivilized, religious, irrational and effeminate.

Rosalind O'Hanlon argues that the complicity between patriarchal and colonialist discourses has gone largely unnoticed by Edward Said and many of his followers, though Said has been quick to respond to this charge.[47] O'Hanlon suggests that the use of gender classifications to represent cultural differences and thus to establish the inferiority of the Orient:

> ... seems to me to run right through what he [Said] defines as the central principles of oriental representation from the late eighteenth century, almost as their natural substratum: the persistent reference to the effeminate sensuality of Asiatic subjects, their inertia, their irrationality, their submissiveness to despotic authority, the hidden wiles and petty cunning of their political projects. Implied in this femininity of weakness is also its opposite: an open dynamism and self-mastered rationality in colonial

culture, what Said describes as 'the clarity, directness and nobility of the Anglo-Saxon race'.[48]

Similar criticisms have also been offered by Jane Miller and Reina Lewis.[49] Perhaps the most striking example of the feminization of Indians is to be found in British conceptions of the Bengali male as weak, docile and effeminate. Thus, in a work lucidly entitled *An Essay on the Best Means of Civilising the Subjects of the British Empire in India and of Diffusing the Light of the Christian Religion throughout the Eastern World* (1805), John Mitchell suggests that 'there seems to be a natural alliance betwixt the gentleness of the Hindoo, and the generosity of the Briton'.[50] Mitchell warns the reader, however, of the dangers of 'diluting' the manly virtues of the British by spending too long away from the homeland: 'there is danger lest the bold and somewhat rugged elements of our national spirit, should, instead of assimilating the Hindoo character to itself, be melted down into the softness of the country'.[51]

Mitchell's anxiety is grounded in a belief that national characteristics are at least partially a consequence of climatic conditions, and demonstrates British concerns about the threat of contamination by Indian sensibilities and characteristics as a result of one's isolation from the homeland. Similarly, Tejaswini Niranjana points out that British Orientalist William Jones usually represented the Hindus as:

a submissive, indolent nation unable to appreciate the fruits of freedom, desirous of being ruled by an absolute power, and sunk deeply in the mythology of an ancient religion ... The presentation of Indians as 'naturally' effeminate as well as deceitful often go hand in hand in Jones' work.[52]

The passive, feeble and generally 'unmanly' nature of the Indian is highlighted in the following turn-of-the-century account of the Bengali people, taken from John Strachey's *India* – a standard text for English trainees in the Indian Civil Service.

The physical organization of the Bengali is feeble even to effeminacy. He lives in a constant vapour bath. His pursuits are sedentary, his limbs delicate, his movements languid. During many ages he has been trampled upon by men of bolder and more hardy breeds ... His mind bears a singular analogy to his body: it is weak even to helplessness for purposes of manly resistance; but its suppleness and tact move the children of sterner climates to admiration not unmingled with contempt.[53]

It is here that we can see the ways in which notions of gender, race and nationality impinge upon each other in the colonial context. This is aptly demonstrated, for instance, in Mrinalini Sinha's analysis of the relationship between British 'colonial masculinity' and 'Bengali effeminacy'.[54] Such work opens up the possibility of a link between feminist critiques of Western patriarchal culture and postcolonial critiques of Western hegemony, since the colonial subjects of India and Africa have both been described in terms of the prevailing feminine stereotypes of the day. Indeed, one might even wish to argue, as Kalpana Ram, Veena Das and Rosalind O'Hanlon have, that the link between Western conceptions of India and of the female coincide to such a degree that:

> often, Indian male and female subjects are made to share a common subject position that is 'feminine' in relation to the Western model. The link explored here is not simply between Woman and Native, conceived in general terms, but between Western Woman (or Woman in Western discursive traditions) and the Indian Native. In Western discourses on modernity and subject-hood these terms have often been positioned in such a way that their attributes overlap and coincide.[55]

Just as the myth of India has been constructed as the 'Other' (i.e. as 'not-West') to the West's own self-image, women have been defined as 'not-male' or other in relation to normative patriarchal paradigms. The construction of images of the 'Other' has thus increasingly become a target of both the feminist critique of patriarchy,[56] and of postcolonial critiques of Orientalism. Indeed, it would seem that the patriarchal discourses that have excluded the 'feminine' and the female from the realms of rationality, subjectivity and authority have also been used to exclude the non-Western world from the same spheres of influence.

In this sense, one might wish to point out that colonialism, in the broadest sense of the term, is a problem for all women living in a patriarchal society, and not just for those living under the political domination of a foreign power. Thus French feminist Hélène Cixous's appeal to the body as a source of female awareness stems from the fact that women have been unable to conceptualize their own experience as females because their bodies have been colonized by patriarchal discourse.[57] The potential links between the feminist and 'Third World' agendas are noted by Veena Das, who argues that:

> Categories of nature and culture, emotion and reason, excess and balance were used to inferiorize not only women but also a whole culture. This means that if feminist scholarship is to claim for itself, as I believe it should, a potential for liberation … , that there is the possibility of a natural alliance between feminist scholarship and knowledge produced by (and not *of*) other cultures.[58]

Another parallel worth exploring, though beyond the scope of this work, is the exclusion of women and the 'Third World' from the privileged domain

of science and technology. The rhetoric of 'modernization' and 'development' theory, as enshrined, for instance, in the popular tripartite distinction
between First, Second and Third World nations, perpetuates the belief that
Western technological 'progress' is not only superior to that of the non-
West, but also that the manner in which it transforms societies is a politically
and culturally neutral process through which the non-Western world can
'catch up' with the West through modernization and development.[59]

The work of Claude Alvares provides a highly critical account of the
ways in which European powers either appropriated or marginalized the
indigenous agricultural, industrial and medical technologies of the Asian
world. Despite its polemical nature, his analysis provides a useful corrective
to the standard modernist historical accounts, which portray European technology as vastly superior to that of the East. Alvares argues that the
imitation (and appropriation) of Indian craftwork practices was essential to
the revolution of European textile industries, particularly from the sixteenth
century onwards.[60] He also points to the Indian origins of plastic surgery,
which, it is claimed, derives from the necessity to reconstruct noses as a
result of an Indian custom of amputating the nose of criminals as a punitive
practice, and to the effectiveness but eventual suppression of indigenous
brahmanical inoculations against smallpox.[61] I am reminded here of Francis
Bacon's famous remark that the three most important scientific discoveries
in the history of the world have been paper and printing, gunpowder and the
compass. These three discoveries have been instrumental in the development
of the mass media of communication, the arms race, merchandising and the
cultural interaction and exploration of the world. All three were, of course,
initially discovered in Asia by the Chinese and not, as might be thought, in
the West.

With regard to the status of women, feminists, from a number of
different perspectives, have long argued that a similar position holds with
regard to the subordination and exclusion of women from the realms of
science and technology. Susan Hekman in a recent review of contemporary
feminist theory writes:

> Because only subjects can constitute knowledge, the exclusion of
> women from the realm of the subject has been synonymous with their
> exclusion from the realm of rationality and hence, truth ... [B]ecause
> women are defined as incapable of producing knowledge, they are
> therefore defined as incapable of engaging in intellectual, and specifi-
> cally, scientific activities.[62]

In order to see the relevance of such statements to colonial discourses about
India, one need only replace the term 'Indians' for 'women' in the above
quote and then reread it. The context changes but the analysis of power
relations remains just as appropriate. Thus, just as women are denied subjectivity and agency in history, so too are Indians in colonial discourses. In this

sense both become dehumanized and silenced. Equally comparable is the association of the female with nature and the irrational in Western thought (themes taken up by ecofeminism and radical feminism), and the parallel equation of the colonized subject with the uncivilized and irrational savage. In this regard one is reminded of the time an English reporter asked Mahātma Gandhi what he thought of British civilization. Gandhi's reply – 'I think that it would be a good idea!' – provides a humorous example of the deliberate inversion of British colonial prejudices.

Conclusions

Let me sum up some of the strands of argument that I have been considering as they relate to the study of Hinduism in general. The study of Asian cultures in the West has generally been characterized by an essentialism that posits the existence of distinct properties, qualities or 'natures' which differentiate 'Indian' culture from the West. As Inden has shown, Western scholars have also tended to presuppose that such analysis was an accurate and unproblematic representation of that which it purported to explain, and that as educated Westerners they were better placed than the Indians themselves to understand, classify and describe Indian culture.

Simplistically speaking, we can speak of two forms of Orientalist discourse, the first, generally antagonistic and confident in European superiority, the second, generally affirmative, enthusiastic and suggestive of Indian superiority in certain key areas. Both forms of Orientalism, however, make essentialist judgements that foster an overly simplistic and homogenous conception of Indian culture.

However, Orientalist discourses are not univocal, nor can they be simplistically dismissed as mere tools of European imperialist ideology. Thus, the 'new' Indian intelligentsia, educated in colonially established institutions, and according to European cultural standards, appropriated the romanticist elements in Orientalist dialogues and promoted the idea of a spiritually advanced and ancient religious tradition called 'Hinduism', which was the religion of the Indian 'nation'. In this manner, Western-inspired Orientalist and nationalist discourses permeated indigenous self-awareness and were applied in anti-colonial discourses by Indians themselves. However, such indigenous discourses remain deeply indebted to Orientalist presuppositions and have generally failed to criticize the essentialist stereotypes embodied in such narratives. This rejection of British political hegemony, but from a standpoint that still accepts many of the European presuppositions about Indian culture, is what Ashis Nandy has called 'the second colonization' of India.

In this regard, the nature of Indian postcolonial self-identity provides support for Gadamer's suggestion that one cannot easily escape the normative authority of tradition, for, in opposing British colonial rule, Hindu nationalists did not fully transcend the presuppositions of the West, but rather legitimated Western Orientalist discourse by responding in a manner that did not fundamentally question the Orientalists' paradigm.

Through the colonially established apparatus of the political, economic and educational institutions of India, contemporary Indian self-awareness remains deeply influenced by Western presuppositions about the nature of Indian culture. The prime example of this is the development since the nineteenth century of an indigenous sense of Indian national identity and the construction of a single 'world religion' called 'Hinduism'. This religion is now the cognitive site of a power struggle between internationally orientated movements (such as ISKCON and the Rāmakrṣṇa Mission) and contemporary Hindu nationalist movements (such as the Vishwa Hindu Parishad and the Rashtriya Svayamsevak Sangh). The prize on offer is to be able to define the 'soul' or 'essence' of Hinduism. My thesis in this chapter has been that this 'essence' did not exist (at least in the sense in which Western Orientalists and contemporary Hindu movements have tended to represent it) until it was invented in the nineteenth century. In so far as such conceptions of Indian culture and history prevail and the myth of 'Hinduism' persists, contemporary Indian identities remain subject to the influence of a Westernizing and neo-colonial (as opposed to truly postcolonial) Orientalism.

6 'Mystic Hinduism'
Vedānta and the politics of representation

> They assert that the world is nothing but an illusion, a dream, a magic spell, and that the bodies, in order to be truly existent, have to cease existing in themselves, and to merge into nothingness, which due to its simplicity amounts to the perfection of all beings. They claim that saintliness consists in willing nothing, thinking nothing, feeling nothing ... This state is so much like a dream that it seems that a few grains of opium would sanctify a brahmin more surely than all his efforts.
>
> (Diderot)[1]

The 'discovery' of Vedānta as the central theology of Hinduism

One finds a considerable interest in the archaism of Indian culture among Orientalists and the Romantic movement of the eighteenth and nineteenth centuries. In 1808 Friedrich Schlegel, a central intellectual figure in the Romantic movement in Germany, wrote *On the Language and Wisdom of the Indians*, expressing the characteristically Romantic yearning for spiritual guidance from the East in the wake of the radical social and political transformations occurring as Europe entered the modern era. For many, most notably J.G. Herder (1744–1803), the archaic nature of the Hindu Vedas represented the origins of human civilization, the source of Indo-European mythology and language, and provided a window into the mysterious prehistory of humankind. India was the land of precious metals and stones mentioned by Moses and constituted the 'cradle of the human race'. Moreover, for the early Orientalists the ancient Vedic materials became the normative paradigm for the entire Hindu tradition – an ahistorical yardstick by which all subsequent forms of Hindu religiosity could be measured, assessed and evaluated. This nostalgia for origins, usually grounded in an evolutionary history of humankind, tended to conceive of India as a throwback to the 'childhood' of humankind. While Europe and the New World were undergoing enormous social and political changes, India seemed to have remained unchanged for thousands of years, representing a crucial example of static archaism with which the dynamic modernity of the West could be successfully contrasted.[2]

Locating the 'essence' of the Hindu tradition in origins (*archē*), in this case the ancient Vedas, however, was also prevalent among the nineteenth-century Hindu reformers as a nationalist and anti-colonial stratagem. For Dayānanda Saraswati and the Ārya Samaj, for instance, the Saṃhitas were the source of all legitimate manifestations of Hinduism and also provided evidence of the superiority of Hinduism over 'younger' religions such as Christianity. For Saraswati, Christianity was a poor imitation of the Hindu religion. Indeed, all knowledge, he believed, could be demonstrated to have originated in Mother India from time immemorial, including modern technologies such as aircraft, long-forgotten and now claimed to be the sole invention of the colonizing Westerners. Equally, since William Jones had established an Indo-European link between Sanskrit and the classical languages of European culture, interest in comparative linguistics had developed steadily among Orientalists and the search for a common Indo-European source most often turned its attentions eastwards. Saraswati explicitly identified this 'Ur-language' with Vedic Sanskrit, now conceived as the 'mother of all languages'. This approach, of course, intersected well with Romantic representations of India as the geographical point of origin of European civilization.

There is an increasing tendency, however, from the late eighteenth century onwards to emphasize the 'mystical' nature of Hindu religion by reference to the 'esoteric' literature known as the Vedānta, the end of the Vedas – namely the *Upaniṣads*. Western readers were first introduced to these works with the publication of the *Oupnek'hat* (a Latin translation of Dārā-Shukōh's Persian translation of parts of the Sanskrit *Upaniṣads*) in 1801–2 by Anquetil-Duperron. The *Oupnek'hat* became enormously influential as a sourcebook of ancient Hindu wisdom in the early nineteenth century, despite criticism from Orientalists for its reliance upon Persian translations of the Sanskrit texts and the idiosyncratic nature of the work.[3] Anquetil-Duperron appealed to Western intellectuals, in particular those engaged in the contemporary debate with Kant and German Idealism, to engage with the philosophical content of the *Upaniṣads*.[4]

> Anyone who carefully examines the lines of Immanuel Kant's thought, its principles as well as its results, will recognize that it does not deviate very far from the teachings of the Brahmins, which lead man back to himself and comprise and focus him within himself.[5]

This call was met most strikingly by the German idealist Schopenhauer, who remained deeply interested in Vedāntic and Buddhist philosophical ideas and indebted to Anquetil-Duperron's *Oupnek'hat* as the fundamental sourcebook for understanding the mystic wisdom of India. Indeed, Schopenhauer described Anquetil's work as 'the most rewarding and edifying reading (with the exception of the original text) that could be possible in the world; it has been the solace of my life and will be the solace of my death'.[6] For Anquetil, however, the *Upaniṣads* did not merely represent the central philosophy of the Hindus, it also provided evidence that the fundamental teachings of Christianity already existed in the ancient scriptures of the Hindu faith, albeit in a distorted and unclear fashion.

> The books of Solomon, the Sacred Canons of the Chinese, the Vedas of the Hindus and the Zend-Avesta of the Persians, all contained the same basic truth, and had one common parenthood in their origin. What one would find in the books of Solomon, one would find also in others, but with one single difference, namely, what the former would have clearly and lucidly, others would have blurred by false reasoning, as it were dusty and rusty. But a skilled artisan should know how to extract the gold alone, which lies mixed with mud and scoria.[7]

Thus, the initial reception of Vedānta in the West was framed by a perennialist agenda (note, however, that Anquetil's perennialism explicitly privileges Christianity), becoming the key Hindu example of the perennialist thesis that all religions, at a fundamental level, express the same basic truth.[8] This characterization, though subject to contestation by Orientalists from the outset, has continued to play a significant role in Western interpretations of the *Upaniṣads* on a more popular or 'culturally diffused' level. The influence of the works of the Theosophical Society in the early twentieth century and of New Age literature in the late twentieth century have contributed to this perennialization of Vedānta.

In many respects an early impetus was gained in the popularity of the perennialist position by the emphasis that early Orientalists placed upon the *Bhagavad Gītā*, a text that is really a part of a much longer Hindu Epic, the *Mahābhārata*. The *Gītā* was first translated into English in 1785 by Charles Wilkins, one of the small group of pioneering British Orientalists (such as William Jones and Henry Thomas Colebrooke) usually associated with the birth of modern Indological research. Wilkins suggests in his preface that:

> The Brahmans esteem this work to contain all the grand mysteries of their religion and so careful are they to conceal it from the knowledge of those of a different persuasion, and even the vulgar of their own, that the Translator might have fought in vain for assistance, had not the liberal treatment they have of late experienced from the mildness of our government, the tolerating principles of our faith, and, above all, the personal attention paid to the learned men of their order by him under whose auspicious administration they have so long enjoyed in the midst of surrounding troubles.[9]

From a subalternist perspective, Wilkins' remarks are suggestive of the complicity of interests between the brahmanical pandits and the 'liberal' British ruler in this enterprise, but what is interesting for our current concerns is the way in which the *Gītā* is seen by Wilkins and subsequent Orientalists as representative of the 'grand mysteries' of the Hindu religion as a whole. William Jones, for instance, recommends that those who wish 'to form a correct idea of Indian religion and literature' should 'begin by forgetting all that has been written on the subject, by ancients and moderns, before the publication of the *Gītā*.[10] The attention received by this text in the West and subsequently among the Bengali intelligentsia has led to references to the *Gītā* as 'the Hindu version of the Bible', a clear reference to the centrality of the text in the development of a unifying ideology of 'Hinduism,' constructed in the image of Christianity.[11]

The *Gītā* propounds its own type of inclusivism,[12] a feature that Wilkins saw as the central import of the text:

> It seems as if the principal design of these dialogues was to unite all the prevailing modes of worship of those days and, by setting up the doctrine of the unity of the Godhead, in opposition to idolatrous sacrifices, and the worship of images, to undermine the tenets inculcated by the Vēds, for although the author dared not make a direct attack ... his design was to bring about the downfall of Polytheism; or, at least, to induce men to believe God present in every image before which they bent, and the object of all their ceremonies and sacrifices.[13]

Despite Wilkins' reference to the Vedas in this passage he acknowledges that at the time of writing he had not yet read any of the Vedas,[14] though it is likely that he was aware of the spurious *Ezourvedam*, a Jesuit work purporting to be a French translation of a Hindu Veda. Although the fraudulent nature of the work was not demonstrated until 1782 by Pierre Sonnerat, such was the hyperbole surrounding this text (and Voltaire's vigorous promotion of it) that it seems unlikely to have escaped Wilkins' attention. The *Ezourvedam* offered a critique of the ritual practices and polytheism of the Hindu masses and propounded a monotheistic position that approximates closely to Wilkins' own rendering of the import of the *Gītā*. Indeed, Wilkins even goes as far as to describe the 'most learned Brāhmans' of his day as Unitarians and states that this is in accordance with the teachings of the *Gītā*. The Hindus, he points out, believe that they are bound to transmigration until 'all their sins are done away' and aspire to ' "Mooktee", eternal salvation, by which is understood a release from future transmigration, and an absorption in the nature of the Godhead, who is called Brähm'.[15]

For authoritative commentaries upon these texts, Orientalists soon turned to the exegetical literature of the various Vedānta traditions, especially those of Rāmānuja (Viśiṣṭādvaita) and Śaṅkara (Advaita), for whom the *Gītā* represented one of the three scriptural foundations (*prasthānatraya*), alongside the classical *Upaniṣads* and the *Brahma* or *Vedānta Sūtras*.

References to the *Upaniṣads* as 'mystical' and esoteric texts have generally appealed to a creative etymological rendering of '*upa-ni-ṣad*' as 'sitting at the feet of' – suggesting as it does the availability of such teachings to a select few.[16] The classical Upaniṣadic material was composed over a period of almost a thousand years,[17] and reflects, even in its earliest stages, a movement away from the ritualism of the Saṃhitās and Brāhmaṇas and the development of an increasingly allegorical interpretation of Vedic sacrificial practices. This allegorical approach is exemplified, for instance, in the opening passage of the *Bṛhadāraṇyaka Upaniṣad*:

> Truly, the dawn is the head of the sacrificial horse; the sun his eye; the wind his breath; the universal fire his open mouth. The year is the body (*ātman*) of the sacrificial horse; the sky his back; the atmosphere his stomach ... ; the stars his bones; the clouds his flesh ...

Here, ancient Vedic sacrificial practices are universalized in their meaning (*artha*) by the establishment of a series of homologies (*bandhu*) or 'correspondences' between the microcosm (the ritual event) and the macrocosm. Interestingly, this is reminiscent of the phenomenon of mystical hermeneutics within Christianity where similar allegorical interpretations of biblical events were seen as representative of the 'hidden' meaning of the divine plan. Perhaps the most characteristic example of this phenomenon within the *Upaniṣads* is *prāṇāgnihotra* – the transformation of the fire sacrifice (*agnihotra*) from an external, ritualized act into an interiorized yogic practice involving the control of one's breath/vital life-force (*prāṇa*).

The philosophical orientation of the *Upaniṣads* and the *Gītā* seems to have appealed to Westerners with a variety of interests and agendas. The texts appealed to the anti-clerical and anti-ritualistic sentiments of many Western intellectuals and proved amenable to abstraction from their own context via an emphasis upon interiority. The allegorization of Vedic ritual found in the *Upaniṣads* could be applied to all religious practices and institutions, proving amenable to the growing interest in non-institutionalized forms of 'spirituality'. On the other hand, for Christian missionaries the *Upaniṣads* could also be used as evidence of an incipient monotheism within the Hindu tradition. For the liberal Christian this provided a platform for inter-faith dialogue between Christianity and Hinduism and a recognition of some commonality between faiths. Max Müller, for instance, was interested in the comparability of Indian religion and his own liberal version of Christianity and became increasingly preoccupied by the possibilities of a 'Christian Vedānta' in his later years.[18]

For Christians with a more evangelical zeal, the *Upaniṣads* represented a way into the 'Hindu mind-set' which opened up the possibility of converting Hindus to Christianity. J.N. Farquhar, for instance, saw Vedānta as the apex of Indian religious thought and a precursor for the Christianization of India.

The Vedānta is not Christianity, and never will be – simply as the Vedānta; but it is a very definite preparation for it … It is our belief that the living Christ will sanctify and make complete the religious thought of India. For centuries … her saints have been longing for him, and her thinkers, not at least the thinkers of the Vedānta, have been thinking his thought.[19]

Furthermore, the allegorization of ritual in the *Upaniṣads* suited missionary critiques of Vedic ritualism as well as providing an indigenous source for the critique of Hindu polytheism and idolatry. Thus, under fervent pressure and criticism from Christian missionaries and increasing interest from Orientalists, one finds an emphasis among the various Hindu 'reform' movements on the repudiation of idolatry (particularly in the cases of Dayānanda Saraswati and Rammohun Roy). Both the Ārya Samaj and the Brahmo Samaj promulgated an uncompromising monotheism as the essence of the Hindu religion. Saraswati argued that this monotheism was present in the ancient Vedic *Saṃhitās* (despite their apparent dedication to a variety of deities) and Roy argued strongly for a monotheistic interpretation of the Vedānta. Both movements, of course, reflect the influence of Western constructions in their exposition of the core of Hinduism.

The *Upaniṣads* themselves represent the reflections of a (largely male) brahmanical élite increasingly influenced by *śrāmaṇa* (especially Buddhist) renunciate traditions.[20] Interest in these texts by Western and Hindu intellectuals alike also contributed to the development of an image of the heroic and noble ascetic as representative of the core values of Hinduism. As Indira Chowdury-Sengupta has recently argued, this image of the heroic *saṃnyasin* functioned in the 'Bengali Renaissance' of the nineteenth century as a direct repudiation of the missionary emphasis upon the renunciate as an unreliable and dangerous fakir, as well as providing a model of heroic and celibate masculinity to counteract Western discourses about the effeminacy of the Bengali male.[21] This was a particular feature, for instance, of the position taken by Swāmi Vivekānanda, who remained a staunch advocate of the cultivation of 'manly pursuits'. Indeed, Vivekānanda is even known to have remarked on one occasion that 'You will be nearer to God through football than through the *Bhagwad Gita*.'[22]

Thus we should note that the construction of 'Hindu mysticism' and the location of a 'spiritual' essence as central to the Hindu religion is bound up with the complexities of colonial and gender politics in nineteenth-century India. This is far from a simple story, as there have been a number of shifts in popular conceptions of the Mystic East. As Paul Wills points out:

Within [Western] popular culture there must have been numerous expressions of the sense of the East being different, mystical, and spiritual. How different was the general public's perception in the 1890s based on experiences like the carnival 'swami' or 'fakir' from that of the public in the 1960s when transcendental meditation cults, Nehru jackets and incense were part of the popular culture.[23]

Romanticism and the debate about pantheism

The Romantic interest in Indian culture frequently focused upon the question of its apparent pantheism. Herder was himself deeply involved in debates about the validity of Spinoza's philosophical system and saw a similar pantheistic monism at the core of Hindu thought.[24] Despite his highly idealized picture of India as the cradle of civilization, Herder remained convinced of the superiority of his own Christianity to anything Indian culture could offer. Similarly, Schlegel associated Hindu and Buddhist thought with pantheism. As Wilhelm Halbfass points out, Schlegel's early flirtation with pantheism is what first aroused his interest in the East, but in 1808, shortly after his conversion to Catholicism, Schlegel condemns the doctrine of pantheism as leading to moral indifference and a destruction of the imagination.[25] Such a shift precipitated responses from figures such as F.W.J. Schelling (1775–1854), who providing a spirited defence of pantheism and its implications for the moral life.[26] Although, Schelling's knowledge and involvement in the study of India was minimal, he often praises Indian culture and towards the end of his life became convinced that a noble form of pantheism was best exemplified in the philosophy of Vedānta (by which he meant of course Śaṅkara's Advaita system). Vedānta was 'nothing more than the most exalted idealism or spiritualism'.[27]

Brief mention should also be made at this point of G.W.F. Hegel (1770–1831) for whom the Indian 'could only attain a dream-world and the happiness of insanity through opium'.[28] Hegel remained interested in Asia throughout his life, though he tended to disparage the Romantic fascination with all things Oriental. Hegel's representation of India is bound up with his own conception of history as the unfolding of the world-spirit and of systematic philosophy as a movement towards a consciousness of freedom. Within this universal picture of world history, divided by Hegel into childhood, adolescence and maturity, India represented the first period in human history – the childhood of mankind. Thus India had nothing to contribute to modernity. Similarly, philosophy, in the specific sense of a 'consciousness of freedom', was a Greek innovation reaching its modern fruition in the Germanic nations where consciousness of human freedom had reached its apex.[29] Hegel remained indebted to the works of contemporary Indologists, especially H.T. Colebrooke, for his appreciation of Indian thought.[30] Through his reading of Colebrooke, Hegel was made aware of the diversity of Indian philosophical thought, but he remained firm in his association of Hindu thought with a Vedāntic type of monism.

In the massively wild religion of the Indians, which is totally devoted to fantasy, they distinguish indeed one thing as ultimate, namely Brahm or

Brahma, also called Brahman. This unity is regarded as the Supreme, and the characterization of man is to identify himself with this Brahm.[31]

Debates about the nature of Indian thought and culture at this time cannot be disentangled from the internal debates and critiques provided of each other by contemporary thinkers. Representations of India functioned as a screen on which European debates could be projected and played out. As Halbfass notes:

> Hegel's interest in India is inseparable from his anti-Romantic attitude and his criticism of the Romantic glorification of India … Furthermore, Schlegel's criticism of Hegel sometimes reminds us of, and even seems to echo, Hegel's own polemics against Schlegel. While Hegel finds 'infinite absolute negativity' in Schlegel's thought, Schlegel in turn finds 'the evil spirit of negation and contradiction' in Hegel; both accuse each other of abstractness … Schelling's philosophy, too, is included in Hegel's criticism of India … [K]ey terms of Hegel's interpretation of India, such as 'substantiality,' the abstract 'One,' the empty absolute, were first developed or employed in Hegel's critique of Schelling.[32]

Schopenhauer was also an influential figure in nineteenth-century European thought and inspired the interest of many in the 'spiritual' philosophies of India as well as contributing in his own way to the popularity of Anquetil's *Oupnek'hat*. In contrast to Schlegel and Christian missionary polemics, Schopenhauer argued that the moral life was itself grounded in a principle of universal identity. Indeed, Schopenhauer, perhaps influenced by Anquetil-Duperron here, propounds a form of perennialism when he notes that 'Buddha, Eckhardt, and I all teach essentially the same.'[33]

Schopenhauer's association of Buddhist and Vedāntic thought with the apophatic theology of Meister Eckhart has become a recurring theme in Western representations of 'the Mystic East' from the late nineteenth century onwards and continues to this day. From a scholastic point of view, probably the most influential example of the association of Vedānta with Christian mysticism is Rudolf Otto's *Mysticism East and West* (1932), now generally acknowledged to be a classic work in the comparative study of mysticism. Otto provides a comparative study of the theologies of Eckhart and Śaṅkara and provides an account that is not as dated as one might at first think. Otto avoids a simplistic perennialism that confutes the two thinkers, though this is not surprising since his work is a clear attempt to establish the superiority of the German mysticism of Eckhart over the Indian mysticism of Śaṅkara. Otto's own liberal Lutheranism prevented him from indulging either in statements of crass similarity between Eckhart and Advaita, but it also furnished him with an opportunity to defend the intellectually rigorous nature of Śaṅkara's system against less sympathetic critics of Indian religion.

However, it is clear that one of the central concerns of *Mysticism East and West* is to redeem the mysticism of Eckhart in the eyes of Otto's predominantly Protestant circle.

> The reproach is often made against Eckhart and against mysticism in general, that the full, vital, individual life of religion, of personal faith, love, confidence and fear and a richly colored emotional life and conscience, is finally submerged in pale abstractions, in the void and empty formula of systematized nonentities to become one with the One ... [S]uch reproaches are misunderstandings of the experiential content of Indian mysticism. But applied to Eckhart they are simply monstrous.[34]

This reflects what I consider to be an important feature in the Western 'discovery' of Vedānta as the central philosophy of the Hindus: namely, the projection of Christian theological debates and concerns about the nature and status of Christian mysticism onto an Indian canvas. In other words, we should bear in mind that when Christian missionaries, Western Orientalists and European intellectuals spend so much time discussing the non-dualistic philosophy of Vedānta, they are also involved in domestic debates and concerns that are being 'played out' abroad. As Ashis Nandy has suggested, all writing about India is in some sense autobiographical.

Otto's critique of Advaita Vedānta as detached, amoral and world-denying, therefore, allows him to displace contemporary Christian debates about the status and implications of Eckhart's mystical theology onto an Indian 'screen'. Through this process, Eckhart becomes redeemed or absolved of precisely those characteristics for which he has been so frequently criticized (particularly by the German Protestant theologians of Otto's time). Otto achieves this through a demonstration of Eckhart's Christian allegiance and superiority to the quietistic illusionism of Śaṅkara's Advaita. Eckhart's system is alive and dynamic, while Śaṅkara's tends towards abstractions,[35] Śaṅkara's goal is 'quietism, tyaga, a surrender of the will and of doing, an abandonment of good as of evil works',[36] while Eckhart's quietism is in reality an 'active creativity'.[37] Śaṅkara rationalizes the paradoxes of mystical language while Eckhart 'excites his listeners by unheard of expressions'.[38] Unlike Śaṅkara, Eckhart's theology 'demands humility'.[39] Śaṅkara's Brahman is a static and unchanging absolute, while Eckhart's is a God of 'numinous rapture'.[40] Towards the end of his study Otto places a great deal of emphasis upon what he sees as the antinomian implications of Śaṅkara's system. The charge of amoralism – of mystical antinomianism, is, along with pantheism, probably the most consistent criticism made of Eckhart's writings by subsequent Christian theologians. Indeed, the Papal condemnation of Eckhart's writings (*In Agro Dominico*) explicitly censures Eckhart for implying that the soul's emptying of self-will leads to a renunciation of works. Otto's concern, however, is to demonstrate that this representation of Eckhart is inaccurate and he arrives at this conclusion by contrasting Eckhart's 'dynamic vitalism' with what Otto sees as the amoral and static quietism of Śaṅkara.

> It is because the background of Sankara's teaching is not Palestine but India that his mysticism has no ethic. It is not immoral, it is a-moral. The Mukta, the redeemed, who has attained ekata or unity with the eternal Brahman, is removed from all works, whether good or evil ... With Eckhart it is entirely different. 'What we have gathered in contemplation we give out in love.'[41]

Otto's representation of Śaṅkara's Vedānta system, therefore, becomes a useful foil, a theological cleansing sponge if you like, which purifies Eckhart of heresy while at the same time absorbing these heretical defects into itself. That this is a major motivating force behind Otto's comparison can be seen by his frequent attempts to render Eckhart compatible with his own Lutheranism.[42] Otto never really questions the normative characterization of 'mysticism' as quietistic, amoral and experientialist. If anything, his work (especially *The Idea of the Holy*) actively reinforces such associations. However, what Otto attempts in *Mysticism East and West* is a displacement of the negative connotations of 'the mystical', which he relocates or projects onto a 'mystic East' exemplified by the Advaita Vedānta of Śaṅkara. Otto declares in the conclusion that 'Eckhart thus becomes necessarily what Sankara could never be'.[43] This remark is more accurate than Otto realizes, since it demonstrates the unassailable logic of his own methodology of comparison. Śaṅkara functions in Otto's study as a mirror to hold up to Eckhart, but one that thereby remains wholly inferior to that which it (only partially) reflects. The following table reflects the dichotomies set up by Otto's comparative analysis:

Eckhart	*Śaṅkara*
West	East
German	Indian
Supra-Theism grounded in Grace	Supra-Theism verging on Pantheism
Activist	Quietist
Moral	Amoral
Dynamic God	Static Brahman
Love	Cool detachment
World affirmed as God	World denied as illusion

Note that Otto's Orientalist dichotomy between the East and West allows him to associate characteristics on each side of the dichotomy with each other. Thus, the moral activism of Eckhart is bound up with his Germanic roots and the urge for righteousness derives from the Palestinian origins of Christianity.[44] Śaṅkara's amoral quietism is seen as a product of his Indian background. Otto's comparativism also highlights the politics of representation. The contrast between these two representatives (Śaṅkara and Eckhart) can be universalized to demonstrate the differences between East and West in general. This elision is subtle but effective. The universalization of a single representative of Indian religious thought creates a caricature of Indian culture that is then shown to be inferior to the normative standards of German/Lutheran and Christian examples.

Orientalist interest in Vedānta

Heavily influenced by German idealism (especially Kant and Schopenhauer) as well as Romanticism, early Orientalists such as H.T. Colebrooke, Max Müller and Paul Deussen tended to locate the central core of Hindu thought in the Vedas, the *Upaniṣads* and the traditions of exegesis that developed from them. Müller in fact was instrumental in fetishizing the Vedas, representing them as the authentic embodiment of Hindu religiosity that had been 'misunderstood and perverted' by the 'theological twaddle' of the later Brāhmaṇas.[45] For Deussen, an avid disciple of Schopenhauer, the Vedānta philosophy of Śaṅkara represented the culmination of Hindu thought, providing evidence that the idealisms that were in vogue in nineteenth-century European thought were already present at the 'core' of the Hindu religion. In particular one finds an increasing tendency within Western scholarship not only to identify 'Hinduism' with the Vedānta (thus establishing an archaic textual and canonical locus for the Hindu religion) but also a tendency to conflate Vedānta with Advaita Vedānta – the non-dualistic tradition of Śaṅkarācarya (c. eighth century CE). Advaita, with its monistic identification of Ātman and Brahman, thereby came to represent the paradigmatic example of the mystical nature of the Hindu religion.

This increasing emphasis upon the Vedāntic literature and reliance upon one particular strand of Vedānta as representative of Hindu culture require some attempt at an explanation. Although it is common to find Western scholars and Hindus arguing that Śaṅkarācarya was the most influential and important figure in the history of Hindu intellectual thought, this does not seem to be justified by the historical evidence. Until Vācaspati Miśra (tenth century CE), the works of Śaṅkara seems to have been overshadowed by his older contemporary Maṇḍana-Miśra. It is Maṇḍana who seems to have been considered in the centuries after Śaṅkara to have been the most important representative of the Advaita position.[46] Moreover, Śaṅkara's theology was ultra-conservative and highly polemical in nature and he shows little evidence of championing Hindu unity, as is often claimed by neo-Vedāntins. In fact, the polemical nature of Śaṅkara's work creates a significant obstacle to modern attempts to interpret him in an inclusivist fashion. Indian scholar and Advaitin T.M.P. Mahadevan, for instance, responds to this problem in the following fashion:

> The answer is very simple. When Śaṅkara points out the defects and inconsistencies in the various schools and cults, he does so not in the spirit of a partisan, but with a view to making them whole ... [P]artisanship is incompatible with Advaita. The function of criticism performed by Advaita teachers should be viewed, not as destructive, but as a constructive help.[47]

Presumably Mahadevan would also argue that Śaṅkara's ultra-conservative position, which allows only brahmins to take up the life of a *saṁnyāsin*,[48] is also grounded in a deeply rooted concern for the salvation of all Hindus regardless of their caste status. Contemporary Advaita teachers, of course, have been quick to accept the mantle of spokesmen for Hinduism as a whole and have demonstrated a great deal of interest in the presentation of Advaita doctrine as a unifying theology for all Hindus. None of these issues, of course, would have been central concerns for Śaṅkara, living as he did in an era when there was no conception of India as a unified nation, no developed sense of 'Hindu' identity, nor any likelihood of establishing a unifying world-view for all Hindus, given the diversity of philosophical positions available and the polemical tone of his own writings.

The Śaṅkarācārya *sampradāyas* in Śringeri, Kanchi, Dwaraka, Puri and Badrinath (established, according to Hacker,[49] not by Śaṅkara but by Vidyāraṇya in the fourteenth century) make great efforts to establish a secure historical lineage which can be traced back to Śaṅkara himself. This is less arduous in the case of the Śringeri *maṭha* since the other four centres adhere to the traditional dates of Śaṅkara, which place him in the fifth century BCE. Emphasis on the establishment of an uninterrupted apostolic lineage reflects not only sectarian struggles between different centres as the 'authentic representative' of the Śaṅkarite Advaita tradition, but also the increasing importance of Advaita as a cultural icon in India.

> The concern for historical affirmation, *especially in this century* among devotees, is fundamentally a concern for apostolic succession, so to speak, which is to say for a teaching tradition possessing personal and unbroken lineage.[50] [my italics]

Once Advaita was established by exponents of neo-Hinduism and Western Orientalists alike as the connecting theological thread that united Hinduism into a single religious tradition, a great deal of popular authority has become invested in the Śaṅkarācārya *sampradāyas* in modern India. This cultural power is not so much because modern Hindus see themselves as adherents of the Advaita position, but rather because, even at a popular level, Hindus have been educated to believe that Śaṅkara was a central figure

in their cultural and intellectual history. Thus, Advaita has gained a significant degree of generalized cultural power in modern India as an iconic
representation of Hindu religion and culture without necessarily being able
to depend upon widespread adoption of or adherence to its fundamental
belief system or traditions by Hindus.

Given the fact that most Hindus are not Advaitins, why was so much
emphasis placed upon Śaṅkara's version of Vedānta as the central philosophy of the Hindus? Niranjan Dhar in his 1977 work, *Vedānta and the
Bengal Renaissance*,[51] argues that Vedānta was first identified as 'the philosophy of the Hindus' by Henry Thomas Colebrooke (1765–1837).[52]
Colebrooke was head of the Department of Sanskrit at the College of Fort
William set up by Lord Wellesley in 1800, and argued that the early Vedic
scriptures postulated 'the unity of the Godhead'. Ironically, there were few
Vedāntic schools in Bengal and little evidence of the involvement of
Vedāntic pundits in the activities of the school.[53] Dhar argues that the
choice of a spiritualized, non-activist and conservative Vedānta as the
'central philosophy of the Hindus' was motivated by British concerns about
the wider political consequences of the French Revolution and the stability
of the British Empire. Wellesley was the brother of the future Duke of
Wellington (later to defeat Napoleon at Waterloo in 1815) and frequently
spoke out against the French Revolution in the years leading up to his establishment of the College of Fort William. As David Kopf notes, 'a root cause
of Wellesley's actions was, by his own admission, his fear and hatred of
France and the very real danger of French expansion into India'.[54]
Nevertheless, in a private letter to Wellesley, Henry Dundas, chairman of the
board of control for India from 1784 until 1801, expressed his doubts about
the establishment of the College at Fort William:

> [M]y chief objection to such an establishment arises from a considera-
> tion of the danger attending the collection of literary and philosophical
> men, which would naturally be collected together in consequence of
> such an institution. I would not be surprised if it should ultimately
> resolve itself into a school of Jacobinism, in place of a seminary for
> education. I hate Jacobinism everywhere, as I know you do, but in India
> I should consider it as the Devil itself, and to be guarded with equal
> assiduity.[55]

What these doubts demonstrate is the extent to which the British authorities
feared the spread of revolutionary tendencies in the aftermath of the French
Revolution. Wellesley in fact quickly moved to allay concerns about the
proposed college, replying to Dundas that the best policy would be 'an early
corrective' as 'the most effectual barrier' to the spread of Jacobinism in
India.[56] It was in this political context that the College at Fort William was
established. In his *Minute on the Foundation of a College* (10 July 1800),
Wellesley made it clear that an explicit aim of the College was 'to fix and

establish sound and correct principles of religion and government' as 'the best security which could be provided for the stability of British power in India'.[57] This process, of course, required the complicity of the Bengali landowners (*zamindars*) and intelligentsia, and Dhar argues that this resulted in the identification of a world-denying and ascetic spirituality (Vedānta) as the central teaching of Hinduism, thereby functioning as an effective and indigenous ideological bulwark against social activism, revolutionary tendencies and challenges to the status quo.

It is, of course, far too simplistic to claim that the choice of Vedānta as the representative philosophy of the Hindus was the result of a self-conscious conspiracy by a small (albeit influential) élite. Similarly, David Kopf interprets Ronald Inden's critique of British Orientalism as an account of 'hegemonic agents' involved in 'a huge conspiracy to deprive Asians of everything from their wealth and cultural origins to their innocence'.[58] Reading the Orientalist critique initiated by Said and Inden as a type of conspiracy theory effectively dislocates any insight to be gained from an analysis of the deeper, structural implications of the 'power–knowledge' relationship. The Orientalist critique is not primarily an analysis of the intentions of individual scholars but rather concerns the involvement of the Orientalist enterprise in a wider colonial dynamic. As we saw in Chapter 4, Edward Said himself muddies the waters of his own analysis by introducing the notion of intention into the Orientalist debate. However, as Jyotsna Singh points out:

> Overall, we cannot, with the hindsight of history, pre-judge the motives and intentions of men like Colebrooke and Jones. By all accounts, it would be fair to consider William Jones a liberal, and a humanist, albeit with an intensely romanticizing imagination ... Jones's interest in Indian culture was accompanied by an abiding concern for the Indian natives ... Yet these [characteristics] are countered by (and contained within) the pervasive ideological assumption about the British rulers' role as interpreters, translators, and mediators of Indian culture, language, and laws in the face of the Hindus' inability to carry out these tasks ... [T]he main aspects of Jones's well-intentioned efforts – aimed at the 'discovery' of Indian tradition and the reform of society – fed into a larger liberal, yet colonial, discourse of civilization and rescue that interpellated the Indian subject.[59]

Dhar also ignores earlier interest in the Vedas and Vedānta in the work of William Jones and the influence of Christian missionary work (especially Jesuit scholarship) that preceded the publication of Colebrooke's essays.[60] He also fails to acknowledge the existence of a divergent strand within Orientalist scholarship at the College of Fort William, located by Kopf in the works of H.H. Wilson, which focused upon so called 'medieval Hindu' traits.[61]

It seems more appropriate, therefore, to point to a *confluence of interests* which allowed the 'discovery' of Vedānta to come to the fore and remain largely uncontested until well into the twentieth century. Hindu reformers such as Rammohun Roy followed Orientalists such as Jones and Colebrooke in identifying Vedānta as the central philosophy of Hinduism, seeing this as an overarching theological framework for organizing the confusing diversity of Hindu religiosity.

> In the *Abridgement of the Vedant*, Rammohun argued that image worship as then practised in India was an aberration from the authentic monotheistic tradition, wherein worship of 'the true and eternal God' left no room for idolatry. Whether or not Rammohun was influenced by his knowledge of Islam, the fact is that already, in the manner of the Jones-Colebrooke Orientalists, he divided Indian history into a vedantic period that provided the authentic model for 'the whole history of the Hindoo theology, law and literature' and 'was highly revered by all the Hindoos,' and a later period of 'Hindu idolatry' with its innumerable gods, goddesses and temples' which have been destroying 'the texture of society.'[62]

This approach proved amenable to Christians wishing to criticize the 'idolatrous' practices of Hindu religion. On the other hand, the equation of Vedānta with the 'essence' of Hinduism provided an easy 'monistic' target for Christian missionaries wishing to engage the Hindu religion in debates about theology and ethics. By characterizing Hinduism as a monistic religion, Christian theologians and apologists were able to criticize the mystical monism of Hinduism, thereby highlighting the moral superiority of Christianity. As we have seen, this usually involved the projection of the antipathy felt towards the apparently monistic trends of Christian mysticism (such as Meister Eckhart) onto the Hindu tradition. In colonial terms, of course, the conflation of Advaita Vedānta and 'Hinduism' also provided a ready-made organizational framework within which the Western Orientalist and the colonial ruler could make sense of the fluid and diverse culture that it was their job to explain, classify, manage and control.

It is problematic to claim to be able to intuit the precise motivations of men such as Wellesley and Colebrooke, but Dhar is correct to draw attention to the political circumstances in which the College of Fort William was established and flourished. It would be preposterous to suggest that the pioneering work of British Orientalists such as Colebrooke and Wilkins remained unaffected by British fears about the wider impact of the French Revolution at home and abroad. The fear of Indian insurgency and the potential encroachment of France into British imperial territory must have played a significant role in focusing the minds of those early scholars attempting to make sense of and represent Indian culture to the wider community at large. Moreover, the Orientalists, supported by Warren

Hastings, were also embroiled in controversy with the Anglicists concerning the nature and future development of British rule in India. In this highly charged atmosphere of suspicion and anxiety about the stability of British governmentality both at home and abroad, it is inconceivable to suggest that late eighteenth- and early nineteenth-century representations of Indian religion remained unaffected by the wider sociopolitical issues of the day.

Nevertheless, in the emphasis placed upon Vedānta, neither Dhar nor the British Orientalists seem to have appreciated the sense in which the discovery of a 'central philosophy of the Hindus', however apparently ascetic and otherworldly in orientation, would provide solace for Hindus involved in an anti-colonial struggle for home rule (*swaraj*). The 'discovery' of Vedānta provided an opportunity for the construction of a nationalist ideology that could unite Hindus in their struggle against colonial oppression. The irony of the Orientalist emphasis upon the apparently quietistic and counterrevolutionary philosophy of Vedānta is that it further demonstrates the impossibility of controlling the polyvalent trajectories of Orientalist discourses once they have entered the public domain and become subject both to contestation and creative reinterpretation. This feature of discourses was perhaps first noted in the emphasis placed upon heteroglossia and the indeterminacy of language in the work of Mikhail Bakhtin:

> The word in language is half someone else's. It becomes 'one's own' only when the speaker populates it with his own intention, his own accent, when he appropriates the word, adapting it to his own semantic and expressive intention. Prior to this moment of appropriation, the word does not exist in a neutral and impersonal language (it is not, after all, out of a dictionary that the speaker gets his words!), but rather it exists in other people's mouths, in other people's contexts, serving other people's intentions: it is from there that one must take the word, and make it one's own.[63]

Just as the speaker or the author of a text is unable to control the meaning applied to the words which he or she uses once they enter the public domain, the colonial ruler is unable to control the meaning of the cultural symbolic that he constructs in interaction with the colonized subject. As Foucault reminds us, 'there is no binary and all-encompassing opposition between rulers and the ruled at the root of power relations'.[64] The conditions in which power operates 'is the moving substrate of force relations which, by virtue of their inequality, constantly engender states of power, but the latter are always local and unstable'.[65] Thus:

> Whereas Jones and Wilkins translated the Sanskrit classics into English for European readers, the college – perhaps unwittingly – encouraged translations into Indian vernaculars, thereby creating a body of printed

material which would eventually break the intellectual monopoly of the Brahmans.[66]

From the perspective of the Hindu intellectual, searching for a unifying banner in an anti-colonial struggle for home rule (*swaraj*), the discourse of Vedānta provided a centralizing ideology around which Hindus might rally as well as providing an established indigenous and highly intellectual Hindu theology which might aid, through a national system of education, in the promotion of a sense of a unified, national identity.

In this sense, for the Hindu intelligentsia of the nineteenth century, the philosophical traditions of Vedānta seemed to typify the ancient, noble and ascetic 'spirituality' of the Hindu people well. Rammohun Roy, Dayānanda Saraswati, Swāmi Vivekānanda and Sarvepalli Radhakrishnan were all unanimous in a rereading of Vedānta (however differently conceived) that rendered it compatible with social activism and worldly involvement. Perhaps the most poignant and ironic example of the inability of the British to control the implications and direction of their own colonial discourses is Gandhi's appropriation of the ideal of the otherworldly *saṁnyasin* in terms of social activism. Gandhi, quite self-consciously it would seem, inverted colonial presuppositions about Bengali effeminacy, otherworldly spirituality and the passivity of the ascetic ethics of non-violence (*ahiṃsā*) and reapplied these cultural symbols in terms of organized, non-violent, social protest. Unlike the emphasis placed by earlier Hindu thinkers on the 'manly spirituality' of Vedānta, Gandhi's injunctions to engage in passive resistance thereby 'feminized the usually masculinist struggle against the colonizer'.[67] Furthermore:

> Gandhi represented himself as 'female,' performing 'feminine' roles like spinning. His own feminization in this type of political iconography – the image of the 'Mahatma' sitting before the 'charkha' patiently spinning 'khadi' – was effective particularly in mobilizing women and men to satyagraha work.[68]

Quite remarkably therefore, Vedānta – the renunciate philosophy that exemplified for the British a passive and otherworldly quietism – became a vehicle for anti-colonial and revolutionary protest through the Gandhian principle of *satyagraha*. The extent to which Gandhi's approach constituted an authentic and effective means of subaltern resistance remains a subject of considerable debate.[69] Nevertheless, as Richard G. Fox notes:

> Gandhian cultural resistance depended on an Orientalist image of India as inherently spiritual, consensual and corporate ... Otherworldliness became spirituality ... Passiveness became at first passive resistance and later nonviolent resistance ... The backward and parochial village became the self-sufficient, consensual and harmonious center of decen-

tralized democracy ... Gandhian utopia reacts against negative
Orientalism by adopting and enhancing this positive image. It therefore
ends up with a new Orientalism, that is, a new stereotype, of India, but
an affirmative one, leading to effective resistance.[70]

It is clear then that the representations of the Advaita Vedānta of
Śaṅkarācarya as a powerful cultural symbolic provided the necessary material for the development of an inclusivistic and nationalist ideology for
uniting Hindus in their struggle for independence from British rule. It is to
the development of this 'neo-Vedānta', exemplified in the following discussion by the work of Vivekānanda, that I shall now turn in order to highlight
the influence that neo-Vedāntic representations of 'Hinduism' have had
upon the modern notions of the 'spiritual' or 'mystical' nature of the Hindu
religion.

Neo-Vedānta and the perennial philosophy

Advaita Vedānta in its modern form (often called neo-Hinduism, neo-
Vedānta or more accurately neo-Advaita) has become a dominant force in
Indian intellectual thought thanks particularly to the influence of Swāmi
Vivekānanda, renowned scholar and one-time President of India Sarvepalli
Radhakrishnan, and the Western Orientalist tendency to establish Advaita
as the 'central theology of Hinduism'. The influence of such thinkers has
also helped in the perpetuation of the view, both in India and abroad, that
Hindu thought is Vedānta and little else. In a popular and widely read work
entitled *The Hindu View of Life*, Radhakrishnan outlined this position in
unequivocal terms:

> All sects of Hinduism attempt to interpret the Vedānta texts in accor-
> dance with their own religious views. The Vedānta is not a religion, but
> religion itself in its most universal and deepest significance. Thus the
> different sects of Hinduism are reconciled by a common standard and
> are sometimes regarded as the distorted expressions of the one true
> canon.[71]

The problem with such an account, however, is that it relies heavily upon
earlier strands of Orientalist scholarship, which portrayed Hinduism as a
single 'world religion', centred upon a mystical theology, and inevitably
involved the denigration of heterogeneous Hindu beliefs and practices as
'distortions' of the basic teachings of Vedānta. Radhakrishnan was well
aware of the problems of reconciling the 'mystical core' of Vedāntic
Hinduism with the variegated realities of Hindu belief and practice, particularly at the 'popular' (or subaltern) level, and it is at this point that we see his
underlying concern to educate the masses in the philosophy of Vedānta as
part of a national programme of 'consciousness-raising' within India:

It is, however, unfortunately the case that the majority of the Hindus do not insist on this graduated scale but acquiesce in admitting unsatisfactory conceptions of God ... There has not been in recent times any serious and systematic endeavour to raise the mental level of the masses and place the whole Hindu population on a higher spiritual plane.[72]

The claim made by neo-Vedāntins such as Vivekānanda and Radhakrishnan that Hinduism was the only truly world religion – that is, the only religious tradition to acknowledge fully the importance of diversity and to preach tolerance, provided an effective means whereby the long-established Hindu inferiority complex could be overthrown and a considered response be made to centuries of Christian polemic. The advancement of this Hindu inclusivism provided the rhetoric of tolerance necessary to establish possession of the moral high ground. This was clearly a prevailing feature of Vivekānanda's writings and lectures and, as Radhakrishnan himself notes, provided inspiration to the young Hindu intellectual at the turn of the century, intent upon responding to the view that Indian culture was backward, superstitious and inferior to the West.

It is that kind of humanistic, man-making religion that gave us courage in the days when we were young. When I was a student in one of the classes, in the matriculation class or so, the letters of Swami Vivekananda used to be circulated in manuscript form among us all. The kind of thrill which we enjoyed, the kind of mesmeric touch that those writings gave us, the kind of reliance on our own culture that was being criticized all around – it is that kind of transformation which his writings effected in the young men in the early years of this century.[73]

The inclusivist appropriation of other traditions, so characteristic of neo-Vedānta ideology, occurs on three basic levels. First, it is apparent in the suggestion that the (Advaita) Vedānta philosophy of Śaṅkara (c. eighth century CE) constitutes the central philosophy of Hinduism. Second, in an Indian context, neo-Vedānta philosophy subsumes Buddhist philosophies in terms of its own Vedāntic ideology. The Buddha becomes a member of the Vedānta tradition, merely attempting to reform it from within. Finally, at a global level, neo-Vedānta colonizes the religious traditions of the world by arguing for the centrality of a non-dualistic position as the *philosophia perennis* underlying all cultural differences. These strategies gains further support from many modern Hindus concerned to represent their religious tradition to Westerners as one of overarching tolerance and acceptance, usually as a means of contrasting Hindu religiosity with the polemical dogmatism of the Judaeo-Christian–Islamic traditions.

It is true to say that the Indian traditions have rarely shown the same propensity towards the establishment of orthodoxies as can be found, for instance, in the history of Christianity, and, as Wilkins had noted in the case of the *Bhagavad Gītā*, there is evidence of inclusivism in the Vedāntic corpus of teachings. Indeed, if one examines the earliest clearly Advaitic text – the *Māṇḍūkya-Kārikā* of Gauḍapāda (*c.* sixth century CE) one finds evidence of a similarly inclined inclusivism at the roots of the Śaṅkarite tradition of Advaita.[74]

> The dualists are firmly convinced in the establishment of their own conclusions and contradict one another; but this [view] does not conflict with them. Non-duality is indeed the ultimate reality; duality is said to be a differentiation of it. For them [the dualists] there is duality both ways; therefore this [view] does not conflict [with theirs].
>
> Neither does an existent nor a non-existent originate in any manner [whatsoever]. Those dualists (*dvaya*), [through their] disputing, in fact reveal Non-origination. We approve of the Non-origination revealed by them; we do not dispute with them. Know how it is free from dispute (*avivāda*)![75]

The inclusivistic position of this early Advaita text, however, is not taken up or developed significantly by Śaṅkara, though it remains a recognisable strand within the Vedānta tradition.[76] In the modern era, however, the inclusivist move has emerged as the central platform in the neo-Vedāntic response to Western missionary activity and colonialism.

Contemporary neo-Vedāntins, further supported in the Vedānticization of other traditions by the perennialism of the Theosophical Society, argue for the unity of Hindu doctrine by suggesting that the six 'orthodox' (*āstika*) schools of 'Hindu' philosophy (*darśanas*) are in fact commensurable perspectives on a single truth. This strategy involves taking *darśana* to mean a 'point of view', and suggesting that the six '*darśanas*' are like six points on a compass – all equally valid and complementary 'perspectives' leading to the same fundamental truth. This final truth, however, seems to be best represented by the philosophy of Advaita Vedānta. In a lecture delivered to the Vedānta Society in New York in June 1900, Vivekānanda argues that:

> The different sectarian systems of India all radiate from one central idea of unity or dualism. They are all under Vedānta, all interpreted by it. Their final essence is the teaching of unity. This, which we see as many, is God. We perceive matter, the world, manifold sensation. Yet there is but one existence. These various names mark only differences of degree in the expression of that One.[77]

This position is also reflected in subsequent Western introductions to Indian thought. Note, for instance, the following from Theos Bernard's 1947 work *Hindu Philosophy*, published in the year of Indian Independence from British rule:

Together [the *darśanas*] form a graduated interpretation of the Ultimate Reality, so interrelated that the hypothesis and method of each is dependent upon the other. In no way are they contradictory or antagonistic to one another, for they all lead to the same practical end, knowledge of the Absolute and Liberation of the soul.[78]

It is important to point out that such a view of the Indian *darśanas* is historically inaccurate, as even a cursory examination of the philosophical texts of each school will demonstrate. Although inclusivist trends existed within a variety of Indian schools of thought, the traditional relationship between the *darśanas* was not nearly so cordial and straightforwardly 'graduated' as Bernard's analysis implies. Indian philosophical texts in fact are highly polemical in nature and remain firmly committed to the refutation of rival positions. Indeed classical Indian *darśanas* have tended to define themselves in opposition to the paradigmatic perspectives of their rivals, thriving upon debate, disputation and the defeat of rival philosophies.

Neo-Vedāntins such as Vivekānanda have also promulgated the view that Buddhism (particularly the Mahāyāna) is in fundamental agreement with their own belief in a non-dual Absolute supporting the world's appearance and, as such, represents a mere branch of the great Hindu banyan tree. Thus, in his 1893 lecture, 'Buddhism – the fulfilment of Hinduism', Vivekānanda states that:

I am not a Buddhist, as you have heard, and yet I am. If China, or Japan, or Ceylon follow the teaching of the Great Master, India worships him as God incarnate on earth. You have just now heard that I am going to criticise Buddhism, but by that I wish you to understand thus. Far be it from me to criticise him whom I worship as God incarnate on earth. But our views about Buddha are that he was not understood properly by his disciples.[79]

One should not confuse Buddhism and Vedānta, Vivekānanda warns elsewhere, as this would be like mistaking the Salvation Army for Christianity.[80] Vivekānanda says that he cannot accept the Buddhist rejection of a self, but, nevertheless, honours the Buddha's compassion and attitude toward others. One should note, however, that 'every one of Buddha's teachings is founded in the Vedantas'.[81] In fact as Vivekānanda says in 'India's Gift to the World', the teachings of Christ can themselves be traced back to the Buddha,[82] and since 'Buddhism is a rebel child of our religion, of which Christianity is a patchy imitation',[83] Christ is ultimately dependent upon Hindu Vedānta for his central teachings!

The Vedānticization of Buddhism is highly problematic as an examination of the sacred literature of the various Buddhist traditions will soon display. Buddhism is not a form of Vedānta and Vedānta is certainly not a form of crypto-Buddhism. Both traditions have structural similarities and some doctrinal commonalities, grounded in the case of Mahāyāna and Advaita in quite different types of non-dualism, but their world-views remain fundamentally incommensurable. The Madhyamaka school of Mahāyāna, for instance, explicitly rejects the postulation of an unchanging absolute (like the Vedāntic Brahman) in favour of the interdependence of evanescent *dharmas* (the dynamic, process philosophy of *pratītyasamutpāda*). Similarly, in the Yogācāra school there is no postulation of an unchanging principle of consciousness as there is in Advaita. The Yogācāra store-consciousness (*ālayavijñāna*) remains an entirely phenomenal repository of karmic seeds and, for Asaṅga and Vasubandhu at any rate, is to be relinquished upon the realization of enlightenment (*bodhi*).[84]

Nevertheless, if one examines Vivekānanda's works closely, it is clear that he has a shrewd grasp of the Buddhist orientation towards impermanence and no-abiding-self and is aware of the roots of the Buddhist–Vedantic debate over the issue of change and the necessity (or not) of positing an underlying substratum. Buddhist philosophies in India tended to deny the existence of an ontological substratum underlying the manifestation of the universe, leading Vivekānanda to note that 'This has been held as the central idea of most of the Buddhistic philosophies, that this world is itself all-sufficient; that you need not ask for any background at all; all that is, is this sense-universe … The idea of substance comes from the rapid interchange of qualities, not from something unchangeable which exists behind them.' However, he argues in characteristically Vedāntic fashion that, convincing though some of these arguments might seem, they fail to appreciate the point (made by both dualists and non-dualists) that the idea of change requires the postulation of an Unchangeable.

> All we see are waves, but those waves themselves are non-different from the mighty Ocean … There is, therefore, but one Atman, one Self, eternally pure, eternally perfect, unchangeable, unchanged; it has never changed; and all these various changes in the universe are but appearances in that one Self.[85]

Where Vivekānanda's subtlety emerges, however, is in his Advaitic appropriation and interpretation of the Buddha. The various Buddhist traditions, he argues, have in fact misunderstood what the Buddha was teaching and fail to appreciate his indebtedness to Vedāntic philosophy.

Neo-Vedānta theorists extend this inclusivism beyond India, providing their own colonization of other cultures in the form of an 'essentialist' view of the various 'world religions'. This approach, despite its universalistic pretensions, succeeds in locating Vedānta philosophy at the pinnacle of human religious expression. Thus Vivekānanda argues that 'The Vedānta includes all sects … We are all glad to remember that all roads lead to God.'[86] Both Vivekānanda and Radhakrishnan argue that all the major religions are essentially the same. Vivekānanda states, for instance, that 'I accept all religions that were in the past, and worship with them all; I worship God with every one of them, in whatever form they worship Him.'[87] This is what Vivekānanda describes as the Universal Religion that resides at the core of all religions, rendering them all complementary in their attempts to express the nature of the Absolute.

> I believe that they are not contradictory; they are supplementary. Each religion, as it were, takes up one part of the great universal truth, and spends its whole force in embodying and typifying that part of the great truth.[88]

However, closer examination of Vivekānanda's Universal Religion demonstrates that other religions tend to function as 'supplementary' truths to the higher-order truth of Advaita Vedānta. Although Vivekānanda strongly opposes homogenization, arguing that a diversity of religions is necessary to satisfy the diverse interests and characteristics of humanity, his own understanding of the universal principles underlying the various religions is, as we have seen, closest to Advaita Vedānta in its philosophical specificity, with a Buddhist-inspired emphasis upon compassion and a pinch of Christian social activism added for good measure.[89]

Such inclusivist approaches tend to underplay and devalue the diversity of the world's religious traditions and fail to take seriously the heterogeneity of Indian religion. Vivekānanda's theistic proclamation of tolerance, for instance, palpably ignores the non-theism of Buddhism, Jainism or Taoism in the Asian context, though it might satisfy theistic perennialists from Judaism, Islam and Christianity. The problem with the search for a universal *philosophia perennis* is that the wider the focus of the perspective the more diluted the commonality becomes. The essence towards which the perennialist points becomes so abstract, vacuous and culturally non-specific (in order to fit all examples) that it becomes unrecognisable to the adherents of the particular traditions themselves.

The 'reverse-colonialism' of the West at work in the essentialism of neo-Vedānta is clearly an attempt to establish a modern form of Advaita not only as the central philosophy of Hinduism but also as the primary candidate for the 'Universal Religion' of the future. For Vivekānanda, Hindu culture had been saved from the ravages of a pernicious and hedonistic materialism by the arrival of the Buddha. Over time, however, Buddhism degenerated, largely because it did not offer a belief in God, and 'materialism came to the fore' again.

> Then Shankaracarya arose and once more revivified the Vedanta philosophy. He made it a rationalistic philosophy ... By Buddha the moral side of the philosophy was laid stress upon, and by Shankaracarya, the intellectual side. He worked out, rationalised, and placed before men the wonderful coherent system of Advaita.[90]

This historical conflict between good (spirituality) and evil (materialism) continues to this day, Vivekānanda stressed throughout his lectures and writings, particularly when addressing Western audiences. It is the task of neo-Vedānta, therefore, to colonize a materialistic and depraved Europe with Hindu spirituality:

> The salvation of Europe depends on a rationalistic religion, and Advaita- non-duality, the Oneness, the idea of the Impersonal God, – is the only religion that can have any hold on any intellectual people. [91]

Buddhism, according to Vivekānanda, was the first missionary religion but did not attempt to convert by force. This establishes an important historical precedent for Vivekānanda for the missionary activity of Vedānta in the modern world. This relatively new and now exported form of Vedānta has over time become an internationally focused and decontextualized spirituality, thanks largely to the efforts of Vivekānanda and his Rāmakṛṣṇa Mission, the influence of the Theosophical Society (with its own peculiar mixture of occultism, spiritual evolutionism and pseudo-Vedāntic perennialism) and continued Western interest in the 'Mystic East'.

With the founding of the Vedānta Society in the United States by Vivekānanda in 1897, the twentieth century has seen the development of Vedānta in the West as an imported example of the 'mysticism' of the Hindu religion that has proved particularly amenable to modern Western interests in non-institutional and privatized forms of spirituality. Note, for instance, the following description of Vedānta taken from a popular introduction entitled *Vedānta, Heart of Hinduism*, written by Hans Torwesten in 1985:

> Vedanta is above all a spiritual outlook, an attitude of mind, and not so much a closed religion with well-defined doctrines. There is no ceremony by which one 'joins' Vedanta. It is true that adherents of Vedanta tend to share certain convictions. Most, for example, believe in reincarnation and the Law of Karma; devote themselves to meditation; believe in the innately divine nature of man, the Atman, and in a transcendent, supra-personal 'ground' behind Creation – the latter considered by most as mere *maya* (illusion).[92]

One wonders what relationship this 'universal religious system' [93] has with the more traditional concerns of the Śaṅkarācarya lineages (*saṃpradāya*) and monasteries (*maṭha*) of traditional and modern India. Torwesten's location and description of Vedānta (actually a form of neo-Advaita) is heavily skewed towards California rather than Śringeri or Kanchi. Indeed, the universalism of neo-Advaita (as initially expounded by Vivekānanda and subsequently by Sarvepalli Radhakrishnan) seems ultimately to transcend itself – becoming identical with the *philosophia perennis*. Thus Torwesten says:

Just as the radical Zen master goes beyond Zen, so the true Vedantin – the one who has arrived at the heart of Vedantic wisdom – in the end no longer knows what Vedanta is ... At the highest level all words and concepts disintegrate. In this 'poverty of the spirit' the Vedantic mystic finds himself eye to eye with a Meister Eckhart, a Johannes Tauler, a Zen monk chuckling to himself, a humble Sufi mystic, and probably also an ancient seer of the era of the Upanishads.[94]

The neo-Vedāntic conception of Hinduism (what has sometimes been called 'neo-Hinduism') has been a powerful influence in both modern Indian and modern Western conceptions of Hindu religion and culture. We can see how this emphasis upon the spirituality of India and the material superiority of the West allowed Hindus to turn Western colonial discourses to their own advantage. The West may have material prosperity and power, but it lacks the inner spiritual life that is present in Indian culture. Clearly this is a tactical response to the Western, colonially inspired sense of superiority (though without questioning whether such stereotypes of 'East' and 'West' are appropriate). In this sense at least, however, Swāmi Vivekānanda was a great visionary and prophet, for it is precisely the lure of the exotic and 'mystical' nature of the East and the belief that it can provide Westerners with some much-needed spirituality that underlies the contemporary interest of many Western new religious movements and New Age groups in the religions of the East. The rise of Hindu- and Buddhist-inspired groups throughout the West, much of contemporary New Age mythology as well as media advertising and popular culture in general, demonstrates the ongoing cultural significance of the idea of the 'Mystic East', and the continued involvement of the West in a romantic and exotic fantasy of Indian religions as deeply mystical, introspective and otherworldly in nature.

7 Orientalism and the discovery of 'Buddhism'

The European discovery of Buddhism

> Throughout the course of the 18th century three interconnected factors were gestating that would help give birth to what we know as 'Buddhism'. These were the emergence of the rationalist Enlightenment, the decline of religious authority and the consolidation of colonialism.[1]

The existence of a world religion known as 'Buddhism' has been a largely unquestioned assumption both in academic scholarship and in popular conceptions of 'religion'. Indeed, so convincing is the existence of such entities that for most people it is part of what one might call 'common sense' in the West. We have already seen how the notion of 'Hinduism' as a unified global religion has its roots in the interaction between brahmanical ideology and Western colonial representations of Hindu religions. Classifying 'Buddhism' as a 'world religion' might seem less problematic than Hinduism since one can at least point to a significant historical presence in a variety of cultural milieux (South-East Asia, Tibet, China, Japan, etc.).

In contrast to 'Hinduism', where one can find nothing resembling an ecclesiastical framework or centralized institutional focus, there is a well-established institutional framework in Buddhist countries, namely the community of ordained religious specialists (*bhikṣu/bhikṣuni*) known as the *Saṅgha*. 'Buddhism' also has a clear historical founder (Siddhārtha Gautama) at its reputed point of origin, and a body of teachings (the *Dharma*) that is associated with that founder and his subsequent followers. This provides some sense of religious identity and unity among Buddhists that was largely absent in the case of pre-colonial Hindus. Thus, as Donald Lopez Jr. notes, 'It would seem ... that Buddhism, as constructed and understood in Europe, must have some referent in Asia, that it must possess a more stable ontological status than Hinduism, for example.'[2]

Nevertheless, the term 'Buddhism' seems to have arisen at around the same time as its sibling 'Hinduism',[3] and it is by no means a straightforward task to find a meaningful version of the term (or indeed for the terms 'religion' or 'mysticism') in Asian languages. This is not, as has often been stated, merely a problem of translation but one of social identity. It is not clear that the Tibetans,[4] the Sinhalese[5] or the Chinese[6] conceived of themselves as 'Buddhists' before they were so labelled by Westerners. Thus Frits Staal argues that:

> The inapplicability of Western notions of religion to the traditions of Asia has not only led to piecemeal errors of labelling, identification and classification, to conceptual confusion and to some name-calling. It is also responsible for something more extraordinary: the creation of so-called religions.[7]

The study of Buddhism in the West came rather late on the scene in comparison to the study of other Indian religions.[8] Buddhology is an offshoot of Indology, Sinology and classical philology, and this is reflected both in the relative youth of 'Buddhist studies' as a distinctive discipline within the Academy and in the manner in which the discipline and its subject matter have been constructed. By the time India had become part of the British Empire the only remnants of Buddhism existing in the land of its origins were the fossilized remains that were now accessible only through the examination of archaeological artefacts and palm-leaf manuscripts.[9] One consequence of this was that early Western conceptions of 'Buddhism' failed to distinguish it from other religions. Influenced by the fashionable pursuit of comparative etymology, scholars identified the Buddha with a whole host of mythological and divine personages from Neptune and Wodan to Apollo and Śiva. Early theories that postulated two Buddhas (one a Hindu founder, the second a historical reformer) and speculations about the African origins of the Buddha were gradually superseded by the middle of the nineteenth century as scholarship firmly located the origins of Buddhism in India.[10]

Somewhat inevitably, Western Orientalists were also influenced by the ideological positioning of brahmanical pundits in India, particularly in the tendency to represent Buddhism as little more than a branch of the vast Hindu banyan tree. A clear example of this was the attention that Orientalists gave to the Hindu characterization of the Buddha as the ninth *avatāra* of the god Viṣṇu. This is an apt illustration of the existence of colonization, assimilation and the subordination of alternative perspectives and movements within India before the arrival of the Europeans. As we have seen, the brahmanization of Buddhism continues to this day in the works of those influenced by the neo-Vedānta of Sarvepalli Radhakrishnan and Swāmi Vivekānanda. Ironically, contemporary neo-Vedāntic thinkers tend to suppress the sense in which their own classical non-dualistic (*advaita*) philosophy is itself deeply indebted to Buddhist doctrine, particularly in the formative stages of its development.[11]

One trend within Western accounts of Buddhism worth noting was the tendency in the mid-nineteenth century to portray the Buddha as an Indian

version of Martin Luther. Extrapolating from their knowledge of the historical relationship between Protestantism and Catholicism in Western
Christianity, many Western scholars tended to represent Buddhism as a
form of Hindu Protestantism. Such an approach, of course, represents
precisely the phenomenon we have mentioned before in our analysis of
'Hinduism': namely, the tendency to represent 'Asian religions' in the image
of Western Christianity and to project domestic concerns and tensions onto
the colonies abroad. An early example of this can be found in Charles F.
Neumann's *Catechism of the Shamans* (1831). In this translation of a
Chinese Buddhist text on the ethical precepts, Neumann demonstrates the
tendency to project Christian sectarian conflicts onto the Asian religious
map. Buddhism is described as the Lutheranism of 'the Hindoo Church',
while Jinism (Jainism) is said to represent Hindu Calvinism with the Sikh
tradition of Guru Nanak being classifiable as a Hindu form of
Socinianism.[12]

Often associated with the Lutheran characterization of Gautama was a
romantic vision of the Buddha as a social and religious reformer, reacting
against the metaphysical, ritualistic and social excesses of the Hindu brahmanical priests and thereby initiating a return to the simple and pure origins
of Indian religion. This characterization of Gautama functioned in the
Victorian context as a useful foil for the critique of Hindu religion in general
and brahmanical priestcraft in particular. Thus the *Journal of Sacred
Literature* remarked in 1865 that:

> Gautama did for India what Luther and the Reformers did for
> Christendom; like Luther, he found religion in the hands of a Class of
> men who claimed a monopoly of it, and doled it out in what manner
> and what measure they chose; like Luther, he protested that religion is
> not the affair of the priest alone, but is the care and concern of every
> man who has a reasonable soul; both laboured to communicate to all
> the knowledge which had been exclusively reserved for the privileged
> class ... And as Europe bestirred itself at the voice of Luther, so India
> awakened heartily to the call of Gautama.[13]

However, by the late nineteenth century the characterization of the Buddha
as a social reformer became much less prevalent. One reason for this,
Almond suggests, was the fear that the apparent atheism of the Buddha
might be perceived as early evidence of precisely those forms of socialism
that were seen by many as a threat to the structure of English society from
the 1880s onwards.[14] Again, we see the sense in which representations of
Eastern religions remain implicated in the vagaries of Western political
concerns at home.

Perhaps the most significant feature in the Western construction of
'Buddhism' (as with Hinduism) was the tendency for Orientalists to reify the
object of their discourses and to locate that reified 'essence' (now labelled

'Buddhism') firmly within a clearly defined body of classical texts. There are, of course, a number of factors involved here that we have already had cause to mention, namely the post-Reformation location of religion in the printed word, the literary and philological roots of Orientalist scholarship, and Christian assumptions about the nature of religion and the importance of a canon of authoritative works.

> Buddha-Dharma first became Buddhism, and then Buddhism became a world religion. By the beginning of the twentieth century it had its own Bible, commandments, fundamental principles agreed to by all 'Buddhist' sects, and its international conferences. Concerned Westerners played a major part in initiating all of this activity. There is a marked difference between a religion that is imagined as being culturally and geographically localized, such as that of Australian Aborigines, and one imagined as being a world religion, such as Buddhism, Islam or Christianity ... Since the nineteenth century, Westerners have continually sought to grasp some essence of Buddhism, to systematize it, and to encode it.[15]

Utilizing the 147 Sanskrit manuscripts initially brought back from Nepal by Brian Hodgson in 1824, Eugene Burnouf wrote his monumental *Introduction à l'histoire du Buddhisme indien* in 1844, a near 600-page work of awesome depth and insight. Burnouf has rightly been seen as a founding father of the discipline of Buddhology in the West. His *magnum opus* is the first attempt in a Western treatise to construct a rational framework and organizational structure for the study of Buddhism. Burnouf's work provided a sourcebook for an entire generation of scholars and intellectuals looking to engage with the 'wisdom of the East' through the study of the sacred texts of Buddhism.

Locating the essence of 'Buddhism' in certain 'canonical' texts, of course, allows the Orientalist to maintain the authority to speak about the 'true' nature of Buddhism, abstractly conceived. Such ahistorical constructs can then be contrasted with the corrupt and decadent practices of contemporary Asian Buddhists by a normative appeal to the purity of the 'original texts'. As Almond notes:

> Buddhism had become by the middle of the nineteenth century a textual object based in Western institutions. Buddhism as it came to be ideally spoken of through editing, translating, and studying of its ancient texts could then be compared with its contemporary appearance in the Orient. And Buddhism, as could be seen in the East, compared unfavourably with its ideal textual exemplifications contained in the libraries, universities, colonial offices, and missionary societies of the West. It was possible then, as a result of this, to combine a positive eval-

uation of a Buddhism textually located in the West with a negative evaluation of its Eastern instances.[16]

Another feature of nineteenth-century interest in Buddhism that we have
encountered before is a nostalgia for origins. When Friedrich Schlegel
proclaimed that 'everything, yes, everything without exception has its origin
in India',[17] he was reiterating a prevalent theme in nineteenth-century
Romantic and Orientalist representations of India as the primeval 'cradle of
civilization'. As we have seen in the case of Hinduism, this nostalgia for lost
origins became an important strand in Western representations of the
'mystic East'. India and Tibet become geographical sites that are 'shrouded
in mystery' and 'deeply mystical' in nature. Such characterizations function
to define the essential modernity and rationality of Western culture through
a projection of contrary qualities onto the Oriental Other. In the specific
case of the role of Tibet and Tibetan Buddhism in the Western imagination,
Peter Bishop suggests that:

> Tibet's frontiers were equivalent to the boundary of a *temenos*, a sacred
> place. Within such a space, time and history are suspended. Again and
> again we read of Westerners commenting that Tibet was a society in
> deep freeze, left on the shelf, a museum. Rarely was any interest shown
> in Tibetan history, but mainly in its mythology, its reincarnations, its
> supposedly unchanging tradition. Such a static, fixed and isolated view
> of Tibet is a gross exaggeration. Tibet has a colourful history. Its institu-
> tions are not immemorial. It was the Western imagination which needed
> an unchanging Tibet outside time and history. How nicely this mystical
> fantasy dovetailed with imperial demands.[18]

Thus, for the West, India provided some, albeit limited, access to its own
past. The mystic East remains a timeless memorial to a bygone age – the
time of the ancients. This nostalgia for origins provided, on the one hand, a
much needed sense of continuity with archaic traditions and the natural
world and, on the other, a way of defining the West as quintessentially
'modern' in contrast to the 'primitive' or 'traditional' cultures of the East.
Asia in general and India in particular came to be seen as the West's gateway
to its own past – to the lost innocence and childhood of humanity.

Eugene Burnouf, in his inaugural lecture at the Collège de France in
1833, appeals explicitly to this well-established theme, justifying the study of
Buddhism in terms of an understanding of the ancient origins of our
common humanity:

> We should not close our eyes to the most brilliant light that may ever
> have come from the Orient, and we shall attempt to comprehend the
> grand spectacle offered to our gaze … It is more than India, gentleman,

it is a page from the origins of the world, of the primitive history of the human spirit, that we shall try to decipher together.[19]

Interest in the search for the historical (as opposed to the 'mythical') Buddha also parallels the nineteenth-century quest for the historical Jesus. Western scholars located 'Buddhism' in classical texts, which they then tended to accept uncritically as accurate *descriptions* of 'primitive Buddhism' rather than as *prescriptive* and ideological representations of Buddhist belief and practice. This provided a justification for those accounts that emphasized the apparent degradation and corruption of contemporary Buddhist religion and society. From such a perspective not only had India failed to appreciate the Buddhist contribution to its own culture but even contemporary forms of Asian Buddhism fail to pass muster when compared to the textual paradigm of 'pristine' or 'original' Buddhism. This radically ahistorical and textualized Buddhism, located in and administered from the libraries of Europe rather than in Asia, now provided the normative standard by which all particular examples of Buddhism could be both defined and (negatively) assessed.

> Thus, Buddhism could be construed as a transhistorical and self-identical essence that had benevolently descended on various cultures over the course of history, its instantiations, however, always imperfect ... This hypostatized object, called 'Buddhism,' because it had been created by Europe, could also be controlled by it, and it was against this Buddhism that all of the Buddhisms of the modern Orient were to be judged, and to be found lacking.[20]

Intercultural mimesis and the local production of meaning

One feature of nineteenth-century Buddhist scholarship that still remains prevalent today is the tendency to offer a prescriptive account of Buddhism and to associate 'authentic Buddhism' (whatever that might be) with the teachings of the founder, a trait that I have already described as a 'nostalgia for origins'. It should be noted, however, that this trait is not merely a Western post-Reformation interest. Throughout the history of Buddhism, movements have appealed to the example of the Buddha and his teachings as a source of authority for their own particular formulations of the *Dharma*. This is an important point to note and draws our attention again to what Charles Hallisey has called *intercultural mimesis* – a phrase denoting the cultural interchange that occurs between the native and the Orientalist in the construction of Western knowledge about 'the Orient'. Hallisey criticizes recent works such as Philip Almond's *The British Discovery of Buddhism* (1988), for placing too much emphasis upon the European role in the construction of 'Buddhism' in the modern era.

It is worth noting ... that while Almond refers to an image of the Orient, he makes no attempt to reconstruct Buddhist thought and practice in nineteenth-century Asia. Although this omission would seem to make good sense for a project concerned with 'the internal consistency of Orientalism and its ideas about the Orient' (Said, 1978: 5), it has the unintended consequences of once again hypostatizing and reifying an absolute divide between 'the West' and 'the Orient' – a basic premise of Orientalist constructions of knowledge (Said, *ibid.*: 2, 43) – by proceeding as if a genealogy of the West's account of Buddhism could be made without any reference to the people and places from which it is imagined to emanate. Moreover, this omission has the ironic effect of once more denying any voice to 'Orientals' in the Western apprehension of what they are about even as it makes us more aware of the historicity of our concepts of Buddhism.[21]

This is an important point to make. One of the weaknesses of many contemporary critiques of 'Orientalism' is precisely the sense in which the production of images of 'the Orient' is represented as an autonomous and exclusively Western phenomenon. As Said notes, one should avoid assuming that 'the Orient was *essentially* an idea, or a creation with no corresponding reality',[22] as such an approach effectively erases the Oriental subject from history.

In the discussion of the Orientalist construction of Hinduism in the nineteenth century in Chapter 5, I stressed the importance of acknowledging the role played by indigenous brahmanical pundits in the nineteenth-century construction of Hinduism as a bona fide 'world religion'. It is important to reiterate at this point the role played by Asian Buddhists and specific Buddhist texts in the modern construction of Buddhism. As should be clear from earlier discussions, I do not accept the extreme view that modern notions of Buddhism are *merely* imaginary projections or Western fantasies that bear no relationship to, or correspondence with, Buddhist texts or actual Buddhist practices. My point is rather that 'Buddhism' has been represented in the Western imagination in a manner that reflects specifically Western concerns, interests and agendas. Asian Buddhists and their sacred literature, however, have not been *wholeheartedly* silenced by the Orientalist gaze, though they have been manipulated, conceptually framed and thereby transformed by Western interests and aspirations. Nevertheless, we should acknowledge the ways in which Buddhists have responded to the Orientalist gaze and thereby contributed to Orientalist representations of 'Buddhism'.

It is in this sense that we should see the construction of Orientalist notions such as 'Buddhism' and 'Hinduism' as the product of a process of intercultural mimesis. As Hallisey suggests, such an approach explicitly problematizes those works that 'interpret Orientalist representations as being primarily embedded in European culture'. In contrast, emphasis upon the interaction between Western Orientalists and the Asian subjects they are purporting to study places the emphasis upon the local production of meaning rather than on the European role in the construction of knowledge about the Orient.[23] Note, for instance, the following remarks by Max Müller, which clearly demonstrate the crucial role played by native informants in the construction of Western knowledge of 'the Orient':

> These men, who formerly lived on the liberality of the Rajahs and on the superstition of the people, find it more and more difficult to make a living among their countrymen, and are glad to be employed by any civilian or office who takes an interest in their ancient lore. Though not scholars in our sense of the word, and therefore of little use as teachers of the language, they are extremely useful to more advanced students, who are able to set them to do that kind of work for which they are fit, and to check their labors by judicious supervision. All our great Sanskrit scholars, from Sir William Jones to H.H. Wilson, have fully acknowledged their obligation to their native assistants ... In fact, if it had not been for the assistance thus fully and freely rendered by native scholars, Sanskrit scholarship would never have made the rapid progress which, during less than a century, its has made, not only in India, but in almost every country in Europe.[24]

As Hallisey notes, the pioneering Western scholars of Buddhism relied in a routine manner upon vernacular commentarial materials and native reports (even if they were sometimes decried as unreliable!).[25] Nevertheless, the involvement of native informants was usually subordinated to the insights to be gained from a careful reading of the 'canonical' works of ancient Buddhists. This was seen as the most effective way to discern the true essence of Buddhism. The consequence of this trend was that 'pure' or 'authentic Buddhism' became located not in the experiences, lives or actions of living Buddhists in Asia but rather in the university libraries and archives of Europe – specifically in the edited manuscripts and translations carried out under the aegis of Western Orientalists. The authorial presence of the Western Orientalists in the construction of this textualized 'Buddhism' was safely hidden from view by a philological positivism which claimed to be revealing, through the medium of translation, nothing more than the meaning embodied in the original text itself.[26]

Again the contemporary trend of Buddhist revivalism in Sri Lanka that has been labelled 'Protestant Buddhism' by scholars such as Gananath Obeyesekere and Richard Gombrich is sometimes represented in scholarly writings as an example of the Westernization of Buddhism – that is, as a purely Western phenomenon. However, as Obeyesekere notes in his explanation of the term, the mimetic ambiguity of 'Protestant Buddhism' is captured well by the epithet itself.

> The term 'Protestant Buddhism' in my usage has two meanings. (a) As we have pointed out many of its norms and organisational forms are

historical derivatives from Protestant Christianity. (b) More impor-
tantly, from the contemporary point of view, it is a protest *against*
Christianity and its associated western political dominance prior to
independence.[27]

It is true, for instance, to say that the phenomenon of 'Protestant Buddhism'
reflects to a significant degree the internalization of Protestant Christian
attitudes and presuppositions by the new, Western-educated middle classes
of Sri Lanka. A clear example of this can be found in the critique provided
by figures such as Dharmapāla of the corruption or degradation of 'village
Buddhism'. This trend within certain Sinhalese circles represents not only
the influence of Western attempts to locate 'pure Buddhism' in certain
canonical texts but also the impact of a quasi-Christian construction of
'heresies', labelled as 'village' (literally 'pagan') and therefore classed as inferior to a literate, urbanized and textually derived Buddhism. Nevertheless,
Protestant Buddhism is not merely a regurgitation of the agenda and
discourses of the white colonial master as it represents an indigenous
Sinhalese protest against British colonial hegemony. Again we see how the
colonial discourse of the British became mimetically reproduced in an
indigenous and *anti*-colonial form.

Moreover, this process of intercultural mimesis can also be exemplified
by examining the relationship between the emerging 'protestant' trends in
Sinhalese Buddhism of the late nineteenth century and contemporaneous
debates in the West concerning the relationship between religion and science.
The entry of Buddhism into the Western imagination in the mid- to late
nineteenth century coincided with the publication in 1859 of Charles
Darwin's *Origin of the Species* and the ensuing controversies between the
evolutionists on the one hand and the creationists on the other. 'Buddhism'
arises in the Western consciousness at this time and is very soon 'located'
amidst the science versus religion dispute. One result of this has been the
enormous interest that has been shown in the question of the relationship
between Buddhism and modern science. How scientific is Buddhism? This
was initially a Western debate (no one seems to ask 'How Buddhist is
modern science?' since cultural power is overwhelmingly granted to the
natural sciences); Asian Buddhists, however, have been quick to seize upon
the opportunity to 'prove' that Buddhism is compatible with science and
therefore not only worthy of consideration but also superior to Christianity.
In the nineteenth and early twentieth centuries, Buddhist philosophy was
often appealed to as compatible with the physics of the day – at this time
overwhelmingly Newtonian in approach. The apparent repudiation of metaphysical speculation in the Buddha's teaching, the Abhidharma theory of
dharmas and atomic particles (*paramāṇu*) were seen as a prefiguring of
modern atomic theory. In the latter half of the twentieth century, of course,
physics has moved on from its Newtonian and Cartesian premises and,
correspondingly, so has the discourse about 'scientific Buddhism'. Today,

comparisons are made between quantum mechanics and the 'new physics' on the one hand with the non-substantialism and non-dualism of Mahāyāna Buddhist thought. Increasingly, one also finds a 'greening' of Buddhism with an ecological rendering of the Buddhist doctrine of interdependent origination (*pratītyasamutpāda*) as a realization of the interconnectedness of all things. Connections are also being made between transpersonal and depth psychologies and Buddhist meditative traditions (particularly the Abhidharma). However, as Bishop notes in his discussion of this cultural phenomenon:

> Only occasionally do we read of religion's different-but-equal claims to be of value in the modern world. The Buddhism of faith, and especially that of the imagination, seems to have been swamped in this continuing rush to give it a literal scientific and rational legitimation.[28]

'Protestant Buddhism' may be Western-inspired and constructed in response to Western interests but it has also come to reflect the innovations, tactics and ingenuities of colonial subjects. In this regard we should bear in mind the work of Michel de Certeau on the ingenious ways in which the relatively powerless resist, negotiate and transform the system and discourses of the relatively powerful. Supplementing, and to some degree revising, Foucault's analysis of power relations, Certeau questions Foucault's analysis of the 'microphysics of power' precisely because it 'privileges the productive apparatus (which produces the "discipline")'. Foucault's approach requires a supplemental analysis which uncovers:

> ... what popular procedures ... manipulate the mechanisms of discipline and conform to them only in order to evade them ... [T]he goal is not to make clearer how the violence of order is transmuted into a disciplinary technology, but rather to bring to light the clandestine forms taken by the dispersed, tactical, and makeshift creativity of groups or individuals already caught in the nets of 'discipline'.[29]

Certeau's interest in the tactics and *bricolage* of the relatively powerless, from the 'poaching reader' and 'graffiti on the underground' to the *apparent* Christianization of South American tribes, reflects his concern to acknowledge the ingenuity and agency of the 'ordinary man' (to whom his book *The Practice of Everyday Life* is dedicated). Certeau's emphasis, like Bhabha's notion of 'hybridity' and Hallisey's 'intercultural mimesis', underline the agency of those who are subjected to the disciplinary powers of the more powerful. Indeed, it would seem that some acknowledgement of the agency of the oppressed and the relatively powerless is central to any gender-critical, postcolonial or subaltern view of history. Thus, one cannot legitimately refer to cultural trends such as 'Protestant Buddhism' as examples of the Westernization of Buddhism since this does not take account of the role played by indigenous discourses, actions and inversions of the Western 'master discourse'. Nevertheless, this does not prevent us from highlighting the violence done to Asian cultures that remains even in the mimetic responses and strategies of the colonized respondent. This involves acknowledging that the cultural interchange between the European and the Asian has not occurred on a level playing field.

Donald Lopez has also questioned Said's elision of colonialism with Orientalism. He suggests that Buddhist studies, although clearly a form of Orientalism, developed in the late nineteenth century and does not appear to have been particularly interested in or implicated by the colonial endeavour.[30] However, the lack of a real imperial foothold in Buddhist regions of East Asia is clearly not due to a lack of colonial aspirations. If the existence of academic complicity with British imperial power and aspirations in Asia were in any doubt in such situations consider, for instance, the following account of the Chinese taken from the preface of Charles F. Neumann's 1831 study, *Catechism of the Shamans*:

> How delightful it is to find, so far from home, in the midst of the self-conceited and *semi-barbarous Chinese*, kindred feelings and pursuits! I say, semi-barbarous Chinese, for a nation which enjoys a regular government and a copious literature, should not be called an assemblage of barbarians. But, on the other hand, it may be said, that a nation which will never acknowledge the rights of any other independent people, – that a government who from principle, will never admit any alterations in its worn-out institutions, and precludes itself from all the advantages which foreign intercourse and foreign inventions offer – cannot be called, in the modern sense of the world, a civilized state. For what else is civilization than the progressive cultivation and development of our reasoning faculties? The Romans, as Montesquieu remarks, only became Romans through adopting foreign customs and institutions which were better than their own:– the Chinese, however, act quite contrary to this Roman policy; they have all the proud and disgusting ignorance of an over-polished and cowardly people. It seems, therefore, that we Europeans have a right to call China a half barbarous, or half civilized country. The time is perhaps not far distant, when some philosophic historian, in explaining the downfall of this ancient empire, may use the remarkable words of a highly gifted British statesman, – the words of the late Sir Thomas Munro, regarding the conquest of India by Great Britain: '*A civilized and war-like nation surrounded by half-civilized neighbours, must necessarily, in spite of itself, extend its empire over them.*'[31]
> [italics in original]

Despite the lack of a firm imperial foothold in China, Neumann here indulges in a fantasy of colonial domination in which the semi-barbarous Chinese are liberated from their own 'ancient empire' by the civilized British.

Clearly one does not need actual control of a territory in order to indulge in a colonialist fantasy. This caveat aside, however, Lopez is right to point out that 'Buddhism' came comparatively late onto the scene, being, in effect, one of the last 'world religions' to be 'discovered' (or perhaps invented) in the nineteenth century.

One response to my analysis might be to suggest that I have deliberately chosen examples from the *early* days of Orientalist scholarship to demonstrate an open complicity between Western colonial aspirations and the scholastic representation of Indian religions. One might also criticize my account for its apparent negativity and for the tendency to commit academic patricide. Let us not forget, my critic might suggest, the enormous contribution that such pioneering scholars have made to our understanding of Asian culture and religion. Equally, one should bear in mind the sense in which Orientalist accounts of India were frequently sympathetic and deeply appreciative of their chosen object of study. Consider, for instance, the attitude of Warren Hastings in his foreword to Wilkins' (1785) translation of the *Bhagavad Gītā*, where he expresses the hope that the reception of the text will convince his fellow English of the 'real character' of the Indian people.

> It is not very long since the inhabitants of India were considered by many, as creatures scarce elevated above the degree of savage life; nor, I fear, is that prejudice yet wholly eradicated, though surely abated. Every instance which brings their real character home to observation will impress us with a more generous sense of feeling for their natural rights, and teach us to estimate them by the measure of their own.[32]

I am in open admiration of the stance Hastings takes here and the noble motivations which his support for the publication of the *Gītā* seems to represent. Indeed Hastings had already implored the reader to exclude 'all rules drawn from the ancient or modern literature of Europe', since the *Gītā* was the product of 'a system of society with which we have been for ages unconnected, and of an antiquity, preceding even the efforts of civilization in our own quarter of the globe'. In this sense David Kopf is correct to point to the dispute between the Anglicists and the Orientalists as evidence of both positive and negative appraisals of Indian culture amongst the British.[33] Colebrooke is known to have ridiculed Hastings' indigenization policy and 'Sanskrit-mad' scholarship before later flourishing as an Orientalist himself in the atmosphere of Indophilia precipitated by Hastings' approach.[34] However, the postcolonial critique of the Orientalist enterprise is not based upon a simplistic evaluation of the personal motivations of Indologists towards Indian culture. Rather, it is grounded in an awareness of the complicity of Orientalist representations in the colonial enterprise and the maintenance of British hegemony over the Indian people. When Hastings suggests that the *Gītā* will elucidate the 'real character' of the Indian and that 'such instances can only be obtained in their writings', he is contributing to a type of essentialism and textualism that homogenizes Indian culture and renders it amenable to stereotypical representation and manipulation. It is for this reason that Ronald Inden refers to this form of 'positive Orientalism' as the Loyal Opposition. As Nicholas Dirks points out:

> Colonialism was neither monolithic nor unchanging through history. Any attempt to make a systematic statement about the colonial project runs the risk of denying the fundamental historicity of colonialism, as well as conflating cause with effect. It is tempting but wrong to ascribe either intentionality or systematicity to a congeries of activities and a conjunction of outcomes that, though related and at times coordinated, were usually diffuse, disorganized and even contradictory.[35]

Moreover, it is precisely the continued *influence* of the early Orientalists and their presuppositions about India that warrants further attention. The comparative study of religion, Indology, Asian studies and Buddhist studies, etc., are not ossified in an outdated (and largely discredited) colonialist agenda, but the practice of Orientalism remains as embedded in the wider context of power relations between the West and the rest in spite of the (apparent) end of the colonial era. Similarly, many of the presuppositions of the 'founding fathers' of these disciplines persist today in both intellectual and popularized conceptions of Asian religion and culture.

Orientalist discourses construct a conceptual space where the 'East' and the 'West' may meet, but only to be safely and carefully distinguished within that space. A consequence of this (usually unequal) meeting of the domestic and the foreign is that domestic narratives and debates from 'the homeland' are easily transposed onto the conceptual map of the 'foreign land'. We have already seen numerous examples of the projection of domestic concerns, tensions and power struggles onto the colonies abroad, but we should acknowledge the sense in which this interaction can also occur in the opposite direction. We noted in Chapter 4 that Orientalist discourses can also function as a form of 'internal colonialism' at home (for example, German Orientalism and the myth of the Aryans). Orientalism, despite its pretensions otherwise, is a phenomenon that is thoroughly embedded in Western concerns and power struggles and is concerned with the West as much as it is with the East.

Nevertheless, Charles Hallisey's point must be taken seriously. The enterprise of Orientalism, as represented by Said and Almond, is in danger of being seen as an exclusively Western phenomenon with little or no reference to the Orient itself. Ironically, the emphasis upon Western concerns has perpetuated the same tendency to divorce Orientalist discourse from any relationship to a real Orient outside of itself.[36] I have attempted to demonstrate in these last few chapters that Orientalist discourses are not merely Western projections onto an Oriental *tabula rasa*. Indigenous Indian agents and ideologies both influenced, informed and engaged with Orientalist positions in a variety of manners. The *polyphonic* trajectories that result from this interactive process manifest the diverse ways in which Orientalist discourses develop and become transformed over time by competing interest groups. 'Orientalism', therefore, can never be a unilinear projection of the Western imagination onto a colonized and passive Orient, since it always involves a degree of intercultural mimesis.

Critics of Orientalism from Said onwards have been quick to point to the lacunae in this process – namely the failure of the West to recognize its own reflection in the mirror being held out to it. Thus, in a discussion of modern constructions of Zen Buddhism, Robert Sharf notes that:

> The irony ... is that the 'Zen' that so captured the mind of the West was in fact a product of the New Buddhism of the Mejji. Moreover, those aspects of Zen most attractive to the Occident – the emphasis on spiritual experience and the devaluation of institutional forms – were derived in large part from Occidental sources. Like Narcissus, Western enthusiasts failed to recognize their own reflection in the mirror being held out to them. [37]

The decontextualized version of Zen that suited Japanese nationalist interests in the Mejji period is comparable to the construction of an internationally focused neo-Vedānta, most notably in the works of Vivekānanda and the Western Theosophists. Both neo-Vedānta and the new Zen provided a 'portable' and exportable version of indigenous Asian traditions in terms of a non-specific religiosity that explicitly eschewed institutional connections, ritualized forms and traditional religious affiliations. Thus, D.T. Suzuki's version of Zen and Vivekānanda's neo-Vedānta became ideal Asian exports to the disaffected but spiritually inclined Westerner searching for an exotic alternative to institutional Christianity in the religions of 'the Mystic East'. Indeed, Suzuki's abstract, universalized and non-institutionalized 'Zen', like the neo-Vedānta of Vivekānanda and Radhakrishnan, provided a classic example of the universality of 'mysticism', increasingly conceived as the experiential 'common core' of the various 'world religions'. Suzuki's Zen thus functioned as the archetypal Japanese example of the perennial philosophy for Theosophists and scholars of mysticism alike.

> The allure of Zen lay in the fact that it seemed to confirm the theories of mysticism propounded by Otto and his intellectual descendants, for here was an authentic mystical tradition of considerable antiquity that clearly articulated the crucial distinction between (1) unmediated religious experience per se and (2) the culturally determined symbols used to express it. The purported anti-intellectualism, antiritualism and icon-

oclasm of Zen were ample evidence that Zen had not lost touch with its mystical and experiential roots. [38]

The extent to which figures like Vivekānanda and Daisetz Suzuki were able to exploit the relative ignorance of Westerners about the traditions of the East can be seen by the uncritical manner in which their own idiosyncratic versions of Hinduism and Buddhism were adopted by Western scholars of religion, particularly in the emerging discipline of the comparative study of mysticism. Vivekānanda, for instance, was a crucial source for William James in his *Varieties of Religious Experience*,[39] and is praised as 'that paragon of Vedāntists'.[40]

Radhakrishnan, himself influenced by James' understanding of mysticism as the private and experiential core of religions,[41] argued in *An Idealist View of Life* that there are seven universal elements to the mystical experience: (1) it is self-authenticating; (2) it is an experience which involves the whole person; (3) it is intuitive and not intellectual; (4) it is self-satisfying; (5) it results in feelings of 'inwards peace, power and joy'; (6) it is ineffable; and (7) such experiences are non-dual.[42]

This is clearly Radhakrishnan's own revision of the four qualities of the mystical initially outlined by William James in his *Varieties of Religious Experience*. Elements 1 and 4 seem to correspond to James' noetic quality, and 6 is identical to the Jamesian emphasis upon ineffability. What is interesting about Radhakrishnan's account is the way in which it locates the core of mysticism in terms of a non-dual experience, while James' account remains much more resolutely pluralist in its acknowledgement of different types of mystical experience. Radhakrishnan is also keen to avoid the implications of James' suggestion that mystical experiences are transient – from a Vedāntic point of view the experience of Brahman (*brahmānubhava*) is a permanent realization and is not to be confused with transient states of mind. Equally, James' suggestion that mystical experiences are characterized by passivity is comprehensively repudiated by Radhakrishnan, concerned as he was to respond to Western criticisms of Advaita Vedānta as a quietistic and amoral religious system.

Suzuki, in similar fashion, offered Westerners an account of Zen Buddhism that emphasized its similarities with Christian mystics such as Meister Eckhart. In fact, Suzuki's discovery of the writings of Eckhart convinced him 'that the Christian experiences are not after all different from those of the Buddhist'.[43] One is tempted to describe Suzuki's rendering of Eckhart as a Buddhification of the Christian thinker, particularly since Suzuki consistently locates quotations from Eckhart's writings within an overarchingly Buddhistic framework. Thus 'Eckhart is in perfect accord with the Buddhist notion of *śunyatā*, when he advances the notion of Godhead as "pure nothingness" (*ein bloss niht*).'[44] However, Suzuki's own rendering of the Buddhist tradition is highly idiosyncratic, allowing him to 'translate' the Zen patriarch Bodhidharma's words into Eckhartian terminology:

> 'What is Reality? What is Godhead?'
> 'Vast Emptiness and no distinctions whatever (neither Father nor Son nor Holy Ghost).'[45]

For Suzuki, in fact, Buddhism postulates an unconditioned and permanent reality – an Absolute – underlying the transitory manifestations of the world.[46] This sounds rather closer to the substantive position of the Vedāntic tradition than the non-substantialist philosophies of Buddhism. Indeed, for Suzuki, the Buddhist and Vedāntic uses of the term '*ātman*' differ – the former being understood as an empirical and personal ego (*pudgala*) and the latter being understood as an 'abstract metaphysical substance'. Consequently, Suzuki was able to argue that the Buddhist and Vedānta traditions were essentially compatible with one other, as Asian examples of the perennial philosophy underlying all forms of mysticism.[47]

The problem with Suzuki's decontextualization (and to some extent Vedānticization) of Zen, however, was that neither Japanese nor Western enthusiasts were able to see the ideological motivations or multiple consequences of abstracting traditional Zen doctrines and practices from their local and institutional contexts. Thus, as Sharf notes:

> Asian apologists, convinced that Zen was making significant inroads in the West, failed to recognize the degree to which Zen was 'therapeutized' by European and American enthusiasts, rendering Zen, from a Buddhist point of view, part of the problem rather than the solution. And Western enthusiasts systematically failed to recognize the national ideology underlying modern Japanese constructions of Zen.[48]

Here again we see further evidence of the complex network of discursive and non-discursive processes in which discourses about the Orient both arise and exert influence. To ignore the role played by Asians themselves in the construction of Orientalist discourses results not only in the myth of the passive Oriental but also perpetuates precisely the East–West dichotomy that is such a feature of Orientalist discourses. On the other hand, by paying attention to the convoluted and multiple trajectories and processes involved in the construction and appropriation of Orientalist discourses by different groups (both for colonial and anti-colonial ends), one can move beyond the simplistic association of Orientalist discourses with Western colonial aspirations. Equally, by focusing upon the ways in which Western Orientalist discourses remain deeply informed by already existing and indigenous forms of colonization (such as the brahmanization of Indian religions in the precolonial era), one avoids the tendency to deny agency to the colonial subject, as well as the tendency to see colonialism as a peculiarly Western disease (a view that is itself a form of Occidentalism).

In Chapter 5 we noted that the modern construction of 'Hinduism', while largely inspired by the Judaeo-Christian presuppositions of the nineteenth-century Orientalists, was also built upon a much older legacy of brahmanization – that is, a process of assimilation and colonization of non-brahmanical forms of Indian religion. The form that the newly homogenized Hinduism took was also further consolidated by the search for a sense of national identity by Hindus looking beyond British imperial control of India. The indigenous Indian examples of brahmanization and the Hindu search for *swaraj* (home rule) are important for a number of reasons. First, they demonstrate that native Indians were not passive recipients of Western Orientalist discourses but in fact were actively involved in the discursive and non-discursive processes that led to the rise of 'Hinduism' as a dominant ideological and explanatory construct. Second, such examples also illustrate the sense in which totalizing discourses and the impulse towards universalization are by no means exclusively Western ideological trends. Indeed, it would seem that what we now call the 'world religions' are precisely those universalizing ideologies, filtered through a Western Christian theological prism.

One feature that has become clear from our analysis of the construction of Western images of 'Hinduism' and 'Buddhism' is not only the crucial role played by Western Orientalists in this process, but also the cultural power invested in selected individuals, who are imbued with the authority to speak on behalf of the diverse traditions, cultures and groups which they claim to represent. As Paul J. Will notes:

> Throughout the history of the contact between East and West, the perception of each respective culture is dependent on who is the spokesperson for that culture. The fact that early Western scholars of Buddhism were in contact with Theravada Buddhism has meant that a particular view of Buddhism as a whole became accepted. Even today, the idea that Theravada Buddhism is closer to the Buddha's original teaching, and is thus purer, persists much to the dismay of other Buddhists. Because D.T. Suzuki became the major spokesperson for Zen Buddhism in the West, Rinzai Zen, which he championed although it was the minor Zen sect in Japan, became representative of Zen in general. In the West the Vedanta school of Hindu thought has dominated early Western explanations of Hinduism.[49]

Will, however, does not ask why and how certain figures become so authorized to speak for the majority, nor does he question the representative nature of the images that they offer. The neo-Vedāntic representation of Advaita as the spiritual essence of Hinduism is deeply problematic given the heterogeneity of 'Hindu' religiosity. Equally, the work of Robert Sharf and others has conclusively demonstrated that D.T. Suzuki's version of Zen is itself a modern construction implicated in Japanese nationalist discourse of the Mejji period.[50]

Representations of the 'mystic East' are constructed in a contested space set up, but by no means completely controlled, by Western Orientalists. The response to these representations by certain spokesmen (and they were overwhelmingly *men*) for the traditions under discussion was to appropriate these representations and reinterpret them. What is lost in this mimetic process, however, is a critique of the politics of representation as a whole. More specifically, what is lost is any truly subaltern response to the struggle to represent India. This is an issue to which we shall return in the final chapter.

8   The politics of privatization
Indian religion and the study of mysticism

In Chapter 1 we noted that a peculiar feature of modern conceptions of mysticism is the emphasis that has been placed upon an experiential definition of the subject matter. The dominant trajectory within the contemporary study of mysticism, following William James, has conceived of its subject matter as the study of 'mystical experiences' or 'altered states of consciousness' and the phenomena connected with their attainment. However, exclusive emphasis upon the experiential dimension of 'the mystical' ignores the wider social, ethical and political dimensions of the subject matter and also misrepresents pre-modern usage of the term within the Christian tradition.

As we have seen, in early and medieval Christianity the mystical denoted the mystery of the divine. For Origen the mystical represented the key for unlocking the hidden meaning of scripture. Christian liturgical practices such as the Eucharist were also described as mystical, being that which transforms a mundane activity (taking bread and wine) into a religious sacrament of cosmic and eternal significance. Although there was a place within the Christian tradition for an understanding of the mystical in terms of religious experience (that is, as the direct apprehension of the divine), this was not divorced from the other dimensions of the term. Thus, for Origen, the mystical interpretation of scripture and participation in the Eucharist cannot be divorced from a mystical experience of the divine. The separation of these various aspects of the mystical and the elevation of one aspect – the experiential – above all others is a product of the modern era and the post-Enlightenment dichotomy between public and private realms.

The comparative study of 'mysticism' has also tended to focus upon the textualized 'world religions' as representative of the 'religious experience of humankind'. Having examined the construction of 'Hinduism' and 'Buddhism' within Western culture and the association of India with the cultural symbolic of the 'mystic East', it is worth while exploring the ways in which Indian religions, as Asian representatives of 'the global phenomenon of mysticism', have been interpreted and located within the modernist and experientialist framework of modern approaches to the study of mysticism. In this chapter, therefore, we shall examine the enduring legacy of

Orientalist tropes about the 'mystical' nature of Indian religion within contemporary scholarship. I also wish to call into question the experientialist paradigm that has so narrowly framed the terms of contemporary debate about the 'nature' of mysticism.

The comparative study of mysticism

A prevalent, one might even say perennial, theme within modern writings on mysticism is a theological position known as perennialism. According to this doctrine there is an essential commonality between philosophical and religious traditions from widely disparate cultures. As we have seen, this essentialist position is a dominant theme in neo-Vedānta and is especially to be found in the works of Sarvepalli Radhakrishnan and Swāmi Vivekānanda. The notion of a *philosophia perennis* that runs through the philosophical and religious traditions of the world is also a major theme in the works of René Guénon, the Theosophical Society, and undergirds much of the New Age appropriation of 'Eastern religions' within contemporary Western culture. In a world increasingly influenced by processes of globalization and cultural homogenization, the belief that the different religious traditions share some fundamental message or 'common core' is often expressed by those with an interest in religion but with no specific religious affiliation. What is interesting about the essentialist or perennialist claim from the perspective of our current discussion is that this perceived commonality is often given what its proponents have described as a 'mystical' content. In a popular and widely read work on mysticism by F.C. Happold, the author suggests that:

> Not only have mystics been found in all ages, in all parts of the world and in all religious systems, but also mysticism has manifested itself in similar or identical forms wherever the mystical consciousness has been present. Because of this it has sometimes been called the Perennial Philosophy.[1]

In terms of the modern study of mysticism the most influential work of this genre is clearly *The Perennial Philosophy* by Aldous Huxley (1944). The book itself is an anthology of excerpts (in English translation) from a variety of religious and philosophical texts from around the world, with a great deal of emphasis placed upon Plotinus, Meister Eckhart, Advaita Vedānta, and a Vedānticized Buddhism. Huxley's technique is to juxtapose excerpts from different religious and cultural traditions so as to make explicit their underlying doctrinal commonality. To consolidate the point further, Huxley also provides a series of editorial comments of his own liberally sprinkled throughout the anthology, weaving an evocative and often compelling tapestry of quotations from the literature of the so-called 'world religions'. The problems with such an approach are, of course, manifold. For example, the very fact that all of the excerpts occur in a single linguistic medium, namely the English language, has already significantly transformed and homogenized the selections to begin with. Without recourse to the originals from which such translations were made, Huxley's perennialist thesis remains unsubstantiated and problematic. Equally, to suggest that one can lift out sections of a text (which have already been transformed by English translation) and recontextualize them without significantly changing the meaning and interpretive tone of such excerpts is to display considerable hermeneutical naïvety. Quotations are provided but there is no attempt to provide a sense of the social, historical or cultural location of these religious expressions. This is perhaps no surprise since the perennialist position tends to underplay the significance of sociohistorical context. It is precisely the particularity of human religious expression that we must look beyond if we are to see the 'common core' or *philosophia perennis* underlying apparent differences.

Huxley describes the *philosophia perennis* as:

> the metaphysic which recognises a divine Reality substantial to the world of things and lives and minds; the psychology that finds in the soul something similar to, or even identical with, divine Reality; the ethic that places man's final end in the knowledge of the immanent and transcendent Ground of all being.[2]

For Huxley, this perennial philosophy exists in all human cultures throughout history and remains the focal point or essence of the world's religious expression. In 1954 Aldous Huxley published *The Doors of Perception*, an account of his experiences as a result of taking the drug mescaline. The result of this was a mystical experience of the 'unfathomable mystery of pure being', where visual sensation became greatly enhanced and Huxley experienced 'being my Not-Self in the Not-Self which was the chair'.[3] Huxley compared this to the mystical experiences of the various world religions:

> Words like Grace and Transfiguration came to my mind, and this, of course, was what, among other things they stood for ... The Beatific Vision, *Sat Chit Ananda*, Being-Awareness-Bliss – for the first time I understood, not on the verbal level, not by inchoate hints or at a distance, but precisely and completely what those prodigious syllables referred to.[4]

Huxley was heavily influenced in his description by Vivekānanda's neo-Vedānta and the idiosyncratic version of Zen exported to the West by D.T. Suzuki. Both of these thinkers expounded their own versions of the perennialist thesis. For Huxley, his experiments with mescaline overwhelmingly demonstrated the enduring validity of monistic experiences as well as the enduring truth and unanimity of mysticism in the various world religions.

In 1957 a direct response to Huxley's *Doors of Perception* was published in the form of R.C. Zaehner's *Mysticism Sacred and Profane*.[5] There are two fundamental aspects of Zaehner's response to Huxley. First, Zaehner's work can be seen as a critique of Huxley's claim that drug-induced mystical experiences are noetic and that they bear some resemblance to the mystical experiences of the major world religions. Second, *Mysticism Sacred and Profane* involves an explicit repudiation of Huxley's perennialist claim that 'mysticism' represents a 'common core' at the centre of all religions. Instead, Zaehner argued, there are three fundamentally different types of 'mysticism': theistic, monistic and panenhenic. For Zaehner, the theistic category (which includes most forms of Christian and Islamic mysticism, Hindu theologians like Rāmānuja the Viśiṣṭādvaitin, texts like the *Bhagavad Gītā*, etc.), is superior to the other two. The monistic category, which Zaehner describes as an experience of the unity of one's own soul, includes Buddhism (despite its rejection of both monism and belief in a soul), Sāṃkhya (which has a dualistic ontology) and the non-dualistic Hindu school, Advaita Vedānta.

For Zaehner, followers of these traditions, whatever they might believe they are experiencing, are in reality having a deeply introvertive realization of the unity of their own souls. A number of scholars, notably Ninian Smart and Frits Staal, have criticized Zaehner for the theological violence his analysis does to a variety of non-theistic religious perspectives, forcing them into a framework defined by Zaehner's own brand of 'liberal Catholicism'.[6] Panenhenic or 'nature' mysticism, Zaehner's third category, seems to be something of a ragbag collection of those mystics not easily classifiable in terms of the 'world-religious traditions'. Thus, this category includes poets such as Wordsworth, the mystical experiences of animistic or so-called 'primitive' religions and drug-induced experiences in general (exemplified for Zaehner by Huxley's experiences with mescaline, which Zaehner takes as normative for all drug-induced mystical experiences).

For Zaehner, these three categories are distinct and mutually exclusive. Indeed theistic mysticism is said to be superior to the other forms, most notably because it is the only type of mysticism that has a firm moral imperative as a fundamental and constitutive aspect of the experience itself. This claim belongs to a much older Christian theological strategy, which is to suggest that non-theistic religions lack a proper moral foundation since they do not believe in the existence of a benevolent deity in which the notion of a moral goodness can be grounded.

In 1960 Zaehner's distinction between theistic and monistic mysticism was challenged by Walter Stace in his book *Mysticism and Philosophy*. Stace criticized Zaehner (as later authors such as Smart and Staal have) for his obvious Catholic bias. Replacing Zaehner's threefold typology, Stace distinguished between two types of mystical experience (cross-culturally) – introvertive and extrovertive mystical experiences. The introvertive mystical experience is a complete merging of everything and constitutes for Stace not only the superior of the two types of experience but also the mystical core of all religions. The extrovertive experience is only a partial realization of introvertive union – and amounts to a sense of harmony between two things. For Stace all mystical experiences have the following characteristics: they provide a sense of objectivity or reality, a sense of blessedness and peace and a feeling of the holy, the sacred or the divine. Mystical experiences are also characterized by paradoxicality and are alleged to be ineffable by mystics. Both extrovertive and introvertive mystical experiences are of an underlying unity (a unifying vision of all things in the case of extrovertive cases and a transcendent unitary consciousness beyond space and time in the case of introvertive mysticism).[7]

Furthermore, Stace argued that Zaehner and his predecessors had failed to make a distinction between mystical experiences *as such* and the interpretations placed upon them. Zaehner's typology, Stace suggested, was based not upon the mystical experiences themselves but rather on the reports and interpretations of those experiences offered by mystics. Following James' emphasis upon mystical experience as ineffable, Stace urged scholars to be much more sceptical of the interpretations offered by mystics of their experiences than had hitherto been the case. In fact, Stace suggests, if one accepts the ineffability thesis (that mystical experiences are really indescribable), then the differences between monistic and theistic may simply reflect the cultural context of the reports. Perhaps the underlying experience is the same but the mystic is reporting it differently according to his or her particular expectations, language and beliefs, etc. For Stace, what we have is an unmediated and ineffable mystical experience that is then understood according to culturally conditioned interpretations. This is a significant feature of all perennialist accounts of mystical experiences. The apparent differences between a revelation of Christ for Teresa of Avila and an awareness of the presence of Kṛṣṇa for a Vaiṣṇava Hindu are undermined by driving a wedge between the 'pure' experience itself and the mystic's interpretation of it. As we saw with Huxley, perennialism supports its position by suppressing (or at least radically underemphasizing) the cultural and historical particularity of mystical experiences. To support this contention, Stace offers the example of a visitor to Madame Tussaud's wax museum who mistakenly approaches a waxwork of a policeman to ask a question.

> If such an incident ever occurred, it must have been because the visitor had a sense experience which he first wrongly interpreted as a live policeman and later interpreted correctly as a wax figure. If the sentence I have just written is intelligible, it proves that an interpretation is distinguishable from an experience; for there could not otherwise be two interpretations of the same experience.[8]

For Stace the actual experience of saying hello to a live policeman and a wax model in this case are the same. It is only *later* when one realizes that one is talking to a waxwork that one then places a different interpretation upon the experience. In this case correct interpretation comes after the experience. This example is then used as a paradigm case for the diversity of accounts of mystical experience across the world. One can have the same type of experience but interpret it differently according to one's own particular socioreligious context. Thus, when a Hindu and a Roman Catholic experience a vision of a young woman walking towards them the Catholic might interpret this as a vision of the Virgin Mary, while the Hindu is more likely to see a Hindu figure like Pārvatī or Kālī.

Stace accepts that one cannot isolate a 'pure' experience from interpretations of it simply because we remain reliant upon reports of the experience in our analysis of it. However, it is possible, he says, to distinguish between levels of interpretation. For example, consider the following statements:

> 'I have a visual sensation of black and white.'
> 'I see a black and white cloth.'
> 'I see a chequered flag.'
> 'I have won the race.'

This is a point that has also been made by Ninian Smart who argues that 'phenomenologically' mystical experiences are everywhere the same but that they differ according to the nature and degree of 'doctrinal ramification' involved in the interpretations of such experiences.[9] Smart wishes us to acknowledge that reports of experience can have more or less 'ramification' – that is, references outside the experience to the context in which it occurs. For both Stace and Smart, therefore, we can set aside doctrinally loaded interpretations in order to get closer to the phenomena of the experience itself. When we do this, Stace argues, we shall see that the various world religions have a pure experience in common which is interpreted differently according to specific cultural norms and expectations of that religion.[10] The problem with this account, however, is that the experiences are bound to appear similar once one dilutes accounts of them to such a degree as to eradicate any specificity to their cultural and religious context. One is entitled to respond that the resulting account bears minimal resemblance to the experience as described by the mystics concerned.

Stace's epistemological position, of course, also undercuts the particularity of any claims that may be made by specific religious traditions. For Stace, mystical experience validates 'Religion' as opposed to 'the religions'.[11] However, as Stace himself admits, this argument from unanimity, based upon the apparent similarity of mystical experiences cross-culturally, will not convince the sceptic. Even if all mystics experienced the same thing and agreed that their accounts were of the same objective reality, they might all be deluded.[12] If I drink too much beer the ceiling appears to spin. If other people have the same experience when they also drink too much beer does that mean that the ceiling really is spinning? How does one distinguish between *delirium tremens* and Otto's *mysterium tremendum*?

The constructivist response to perennialism

In 1978 a collection of influential articles written by contemporary scholars of mysticism was published in a single volume entitled *Mysticism and Philosophical Analysis*. This was followed in 1983 by a companion collection entitled *Mysticism and Religious Traditions*. Together both anthologies provide a sustained critique of the perennialism of authors such as Aldous Huxley and Walter Stace with regard to the phenomena of mysticism in the various world religions. The editor of these two collections, Steven Katz, describes his work as a 'plea for the recognition of differences', involving a much greater sensitivity to the cultural particularity of mystics and their traditions than is to be found in the works of the perennialists. The primary focus of Katz's approach is a consideration of the question 'What is the relationship between a mystical experience and its interpretation?' Katz asks his readership to accept a basic epistemological principle which provides the theoretical foundation for his own position – namely, the impossibility (indeed incoherence) of the idea of a pure or unmediated experience. There is no such thing, Katz argues, as an experience that is free from interpretation, an experience free from any recognisable content.

> [T]he experience itself as well as the form in which it is reported is shaped by concepts which the mystic brings to, and which shape, his experience ... [T]he forms of consciousness which the mystic brings to experience set structured and limiting parameters on what the experience will be ... [T]his process of differentiation of mystical experiences into the patterns and symbols of established religious communities is experiential and does not take place in the post-experiential process of reporting and interpreting the experience itself: it is at work before, during, and after the experience.[13]

Since all experience involves interpretation – including mystical experiences, Katz argues that the perennialist position had failed to take account of the sense in which mystical experiences are conditioned by the socioreligious and cultural context in which they occur. Thus, Jewish mystical experiences are conditioned by the following beliefs:

1   There is more to reality than physical world.
2   This reality is ultimate and is a Personal God.
3   God created the world and humankind.
4   Men have spiritual souls which commune with God.
5   God enters into covenants with humans.
6   Even in covenants God remains distinct.

7   God and humans are ontologically distinct.
8   God entered into special covenants with Abraham and his children.
9   Covenants are expressed in the acts of circumcision and the giving of Torah.
10 The Torah and the Commandments are the most perfect expression of God's will.

In contrast, Buddhist mystics, Katz points out, are conditioned by their acceptance of the four noble truths, the doctrine of *anattā* (no-abiding-self), the notion of *nirvāṇa* as a non-personal liberation from rebirth, the doctrines of *karma* and *saṃsāra*, etc.

Katz, like Robert Gimello,[14] Hans Penner,[15] Wayne Proudfoot[16] and numerous others agree in rejecting attempts to drive a wedge between interpretation and the experience itself. Mystics do not have context-free, 'pure' experiences that they later interpret according to their own particular cultural and theological presuppositions. The very nature of the experience is itself socially constructed according to the culture, beliefs and expectations of the mystics having the experiences. Catholics do not experience a vision of a young woman that they then interpret as the Virgin Mary – they experience the Virgin Mary. This is what their tradition tells them to expect, this is what they hope for, and this is what they end up seeing. On this view, mystical experiences are preconditioned by cultural values, beliefs and expectations and are radically contextual.

Katz offers a pluralistic account that he claims neither overlooks any of the evidence provided by the perennialist nor requires any simplification of the available evidence to fit into cross-cultural categories. Moreover, Katz suggests, his social constructivist analysis is not based upon any a priori assumptions about the nature of ultimate reality.

> As a consequence of these hermeneutical advantages, one is in a position to respect the richness of the experiential and conceptual data involved in this area of concern: 'God' can be 'God', 'Brahman' can be 'Brahman' and *nirvāṇa* can be *nirvāṇa* without any reductionist attempt to equate the concept of 'God' with that of 'Brahman', or 'Brahman' with *nirvāṇa*. This respect for the relevant evidence is an essential element in the study of mysticism.[17]

Upon analysis most mystics can be seen to be rather orthodox in the sense that they tend to see precisely what they have been conditioned and expect to see. It is not just the language of mystical reports that is culturally conditioned but the experience itself. The problem, Katz suggests, is that scholars have tended to emphasize the radical examples in order to suggest that mysticism somehow transcends the particularity of the religious tradition in which it occurs and is evidence of a spiritual 'common core' underlying the religions of the world. As a number of critics have pointed out, however,

Katz's own epistemological position does not provide an adequate account of innovation within religious traditions. If one's experiences are socially constructed, how can one ever come up with anything new?[18]

The social location of social constructivism

The social constructivist position of Steven Katz has now become the mainstream philosophical position within the study of mysticism, and the historicist repudiation of the possibility of a 'pure experience' has become an increasingly popular and dominant trend within Western culture and scholarship. From post-structuralism and postmodernist relativism to contemporary work within 'the sociology of knowledge', one finds an almost universal rejection of the possibility of an unconditioned or unmediated experience of reality. Everything it seems these days is mediated in terms of society and culture.

The intellectual roots of social constructivism, however, have been around for a number of centuries, gaining an initial intellectual impetus from figures such as Giambattista Vico (1668–1744) and Immanuel Kant (1724–1804) before achieving wider circulation and popularity within Europe as a result of the rise of secular and humanistic philosophies from the Enlightenment period onwards. Feuerbach's famous thesis (1841, *The Essence of Christianity*), that religious beliefs, ideals and concepts are in reality projections of human value systems, effectively reversed the traditional Christian belief that God created the world and presaged the arrival of Nietzsche's proclamation of 'the death of God'. In the new era of atheistic humanism, it is human beings and human societies in particular that have created the gods rather than the other way around. From this perspective, Christianity, and by extension all other religions, become socially constructed artefacts.

With the emergence of the hermeneutics of suspicion and systems of thought that remained sceptical of the claims of religion (for example, Marxism, Freudian psychoanalysis), the social constructivist paradigm first began to take root in the study of religion towards the end of the nineteenth century, further bolstered by a growing awareness of the diversity of cultures, religions and social systems. The work of scholars such as Robertson Smith (*The Religion of the Semites*, 1889) and Emile Durkhem (*The Elementary Forms of the Religious Life*, 1912) demonstrates an increasing tendency not only to interpret religious phenomena in terms of their social context but also to explain religion as a product of those sociological conditions and relations. Durkheim, for instance, often revered as a founding father of the sociology of religion, maintained that the religious life was an expression of the collective values and life of the social group. Religion, despite what its adherents might claim, is really the idealization of each given society's image of itself. This trend, of course, provided a useful corrective to the tendency to treat religion as an experiential and private phenomenon in the work of scholars such as E.B. Tylor and William James. As Durkheim maintains, for instance:

> Thus the collective ideal which religion expresses is far from being due to a vague innate power of the individual, but it is rather at the school of collective life that the individual has learned to idealize ... For society has constructed this new world in constructing itself, since it is society itself which this expresses.[19]

The term 'the sociology of knowledge' ('*sociologie des wissens*'), however, was not coined until 1924 when German philosopher Max Scheler (1874–1928) used this phrase to denote an approach to knowledge that emphasized its social location and genesis. More recently, the symbolic interactionism of G.H. Mead (*Mind, Self and Society*, 1934) is premised on the belief that as social beings, humans construct their identities and knowledge of the world through a complex process of social interaction. However, the current vogue for social constructivism, particularly within sociology, first gained attention as a result of Peter Berger and Thomas Luckmann's work, *The Social Construction of Reality* (1966).[20] For Berger and Luckmann, the development of societies is a dialectical process of interaction between society and its constitutive members.[21]

The 'constructivist' paradigm has also gained greater influence in the late twentieth century with the expansion of consumerism in modern industrial societies. The modern Western world (and beyond) is now saturated with a bewildering variety of consumer products with the advent of post-Fordist methods of production. Consequently, the productivist metaphor of 'construction' has taken on ever greater significance and authority among intellectuals in such societies. Since the late 1960s this has led to the emergence of another variant of constructivist thought with the advent of varieties of post-structuralism (for example, Michel Foucault, Hans Georg Gadamer, Jacques Lacan) and postmodernism (for example, Jean Baudrillard, Jean-François Lyotard, Richard Rorty and Jacques Derrida). The constructivist position has also taken pride of place as a firmly established position within contemporary Euro-American feminist theory, undergirding the position of a variety of theorists, most strikingly in the work of French thinkers such as Hélène Cixous, Julia Kristeva and Luce Irigaray.

What characterizes these more recent forms of constructivism is a firm belief in the conditioned nature of human existence. All knowledge is conditioned by and firmly embedded within linguistic and cultural forms. We also see a rejection of universal 'grand narratives' in favour of a multiplicity of localized histories and a repudiation of a variety of essentialisms. Post-structuralist and feminist analysis in particular has also grounded this constructivism in a sharp appreciation of the political dimension of all knowledge-claims.

Steven Katz's work should be understood as developing within this broad context, representing a greater appreciation of social location and cultural context as crucial factors in the development of human conceptions of reality. Katz describes his work as a critique of the 'essentialist reductionism' of the perennialist position,[22] and this might lead one to think that his own version of constructivism has been influenced by the later post-structuralist or postmodernist versions of constructivism, since essentialism is a frequent object of criticism in such accounts. However, Katz's stance displays none of the characteristics that one normally associates with post-structuralist and postmodernist thought. His explicit claim that his work is not based upon any assumptions about the nature of reality illustrates Katz's continuing faith in the Enlightenment ideals of dispassionate and objective scholarship. In so far as Katz takes this stance he is of course open to the criticism that he has failed to acknowledge the social location of his own position. This is in stark contrast to post-structuralist and postmodernist trends of thought, which tend to disavow all attempts to privilege any discourse or theory from the consequences of the constructivist analysis. Nevertheless, it would seem that Katz's theory is proving amenable to scholars of a post-structuralist and feminist persuasion. In her recent critique of the study of Christian mysticism, Grace Jantzen provides explicit support for Katz's position from a feminist and broadly Foucauldian perspective. The view that there could be 'pure experiences' of any kind is, Jantzen argues, 'contrary to *our* basic understanding of what experience is' (my italics). Indeed, she continues:

> Katz's position on this is one that is congenial to feminists, who have long insisted that the ideal of a neutral, objective, universal stance is a fiction which disguised male partiality. There are no views from nowhere, and there are no views from everywhere. There are only views from somewhere, and the particular place will have an inescapable effect on what can be seen. If one assumes the contrary, then what is happening is that one is falsely universalising a particular perspective.[23]

Jantzen's suggests that the idea of 'the mystical' and the category of 'mysticism' are social constructions embedded in a web of conflictual power relations and discursive processes. She argues:

> ... that the idea of 'mysticism' is a social construction and that it has been constructed in different ways at different times. Although ... medieval mystics and ecclesiastics did not work with a concept of 'mysticism', they did have strong views about who should count as a mystic, views which changed over the course of time ... The current philosophical construction of mysticism is therefore only one in a series of social constructions of mysticism; and, like the others, is implicitly bound up with issues of authority and gender.[24]

172 Orientalism and Religion

I agree with Jantzen, not only in acknowledging the sense in which the category of 'the mystical' is socially constructed, but also in her Foucauldian-inspired recognition that as a result 'the mystical' also represents the conceptual site of a historical struggle for power and authority. However, I wish to argue that this position is not, as Jantzen seems to imply in her book, a corollary of the Katzian epistemological stance that there are no 'pure' (that is, unmediated) experiences. One can accept the position that ideas such as 'the mystical' are social constructions, but that does not *in and of itself* require us to accept the view that all dimensions of human experience are socially constructed. Of course, to distinguish between the two positions one would have to entertain the possibility (and nothing more) that there was a realm of human experience that might indeed be devoid of conceptualization, linguistic forms and socially constructed forms of apprehension. Jantzen, like Katz, is not prepared to accept this possibility, not only because it implies that the web of language and cultural conditioning can be transcended, but also because such claims have often been used to support pernicious claims to universal authority and a denial of one's own cultural particularity. As Jantzen points out, such claims have been a common strategy for disguising patriarchal partiality and silencing women.

However, we should note that the social-constructivist stance of scholars like Katz and Jantzen on this issue effectively undermines the authority and truth-claims of many of the mystics and traditions that they are examining. This is particularly the case with regard to Asian traditions such as Advaita Vedānta, Rāja Yoga, most forms of Buddhism, philosophical Taoism and a significant number of Christian mystics (Meister Eckhart, in particular, comes to mind). This may not be an issue for social constructivists such as Katz and Jantzen; it is, however, a very real concern for male and female members of these traditions – many of whom have been subjected to centuries of colonial oppression and the ideological subversion of their traditions by Westerners who have claimed to know better.

We have seen that for Katz, 'respect for the relevant evidence is an essential element in the study of mysticism'. His constructivist stance, however, seriously calls into question the claim that his position allows him 'to respect the richness of the experiential and conceptual data involved in this area of concern'.[25] Indeed, in a response to Sallie King's suggestion that his position 'negates the very foundation of yoga, most of Buddhism, large segments of Hinduism, and philosophical Taoism',[26] Katz has replied:

> True enough. But this is what scholarship, as compared to confessionalism or theological pronouncements from within a tradition, is about ... Surely the study of religion cannot be limited by the view that only believers can discuss their tradition, whatever that tradition be.[27]

Katz is right to reject the idea that religion should only be studied by its own adherents. However, he fails to acknowledge the sense in which all scholarship – including his own – operates from *within* a tradition. Indeed, all of the constructivist trends that we have so far considered display a reliance (whether acknowledged or not) upon the epistemological paradigms of post-Kantian thought. In other words, the way in which this debate has been framed has tended to reflect the presuppositions and concerns of post-Enlightenment Western thought.

Grace Jantzen draws attention to the fact that the perennialist–constructivist debate is peculiarily modern in its exclusively experiential definition of the mystical.[28] She suggests, rightly in my view, that 'the modern conception of mysticism, with the characteristic of ineffability as the key ingredient, is as much a social construction as were all the previous constructions'.[29] However, we should also note that the modern (that is, post-Jamesian) characterization of the mystical as well as the social constructivisms of Katz and Jantzen are also peculiarly Western. The predominance of post-Kantian influences in Western forms of constructivism (whether modern or postmodern in nature) reflects a series of post-Christian and post-Enlightenment presuppositions about the nature of humanity and its inherent limitations.

Immanuel Kant has been an enormously influential figure in the development of modern Western intellectual thought. His own 'Copernican Revolution' involved the realization that our experience of the world is preconditioned by certain a priori categories that provide the framework through which humans experience the world. For Kant, humans experience the world in spatio-temporal terms primarily because 'space' and 'time' are a priori categories through which we construct our picture of the world. What we experience, Kant argued, are not things-in-themselves (*noumena*) but *phenomena* constructed from the 'synthesis of the manifold of appearances' that are organized and rendered intelligible via the conditions provided by the a priori categories of our intellect. For Kant, knowledge of things as they are (*noumena*) remains strictly beyond human apprehension. This recognition of the agency of the human subject in the construction of a world-picture and the impossibility of an unmediated cognition of reality has had such a lasting influence upon Western intellectual thought since the Enlightenment that it is often simply taken for granted.

Katz has made his own allegiance to a neo-Kantian position explicit in his response to criticisms of his position.[30] Indeed, he suggests that 'this "mediated" aspect of our experience seems an inescapable feature of any epistemological inquiry'.[31] However, since the late 1980s a number of critical responses have been made to the constructivist position. Most of this work has involved questioning Katz's 'single epistemological assumption' that all experiences are mediated by cultural, historical and religious factors. Robert Forman, for instance, makes a distinction between two alternatives: *complete constructivism* (the view that the entirety of one's experiences are structured by one's cultural context and mind-set) and *incomplete* or *partial constructivism* (the view that concepts and beliefs are not the only factors involved in experiences, there being other factors such as sensory input, etc.).[32] Forman argues that partial constructivism will not suffice for Katz's analysis to be proven – that is, to demonstrate that there can be no common core to mystical experiences, since perennialists could argue that the common feature is to be found in the non-conceptual or unconstructed aspects of those experiences. Only complete constructivism (with its refusal to distinguish between experience and interpretation at all) can carry the argument forward. A similar point is made by Sallie King,[33] which she illustrates with the example of drinking coffee for the first time.

> Certainly one may be predisposed to like or dislike coffee depending upon what one has heard and witnessed with respect to coffee ... Being told that coffee is bitter would certainly predispose one to find bitterness in the taste. But there, I claim, is where the conditioning power of the 'coffee tradition' ends. It cannot cause the subject to have the total experience s/he has upon drinking coffee. Why? The main reason is that the taste of coffee is ineffable ... The act of drinking coffee in its totality can by no means be said to be an unmediated experience. Nonetheless, before one drinks coffee one really has no idea what it tastes like ... In the end, though drinking coffee is a mediated experience, that mediation is a relatively insignificant element of the experience itself.[34]

Katz has responded to these kinds of criticisms by stating: 'I do not assign percentages to mediation. I only claim the experience is mediated.'[35] However, this move by Katz leaves open the possibility that there is an aspect of mystical experiences that is not conditioned by the mind-set and cultural background of the mystic.

As time has gone by it has become clear that the position one takes with regard to this debate is bound up with the type of epistemology one accepts. Katz, as we have seen, bases his stance upon the presuppositions of neo-Kantian epistemology. On this view all experience involves conceptualization and some form of culturally determined interpretation as a constitutive factor in the arising of the experience itself. It is not possible to have an experience (even a 'mystical' one) that is devoid of cultural baggage. This view, of course, is presumed and is not argued for. Katz's own claim that his account does not 'begin with a priori assumptions about the nature of ultimate reality',[36] is undermined by his admission that his work proceeds from the epistemological assumption that 'there are NO pure (i.e. unmediated) experiences'.[37]

However, once this debate moves beyond Western intellectual horizons and one attempts to make universal claims about human experience one is obliged to reconsider the ethnocentric presuppositions of the neo-Kantian paradigm and consider the political and colonial implications of imposing one's own position on the debate. I suggest that there is a need to problematize the modernist and Eurocentric framework of this debate. For my own part I wish to suggest two trajectories that such a problematization might take. First, one might question whether the way in which Kant and his successors have framed epistemological debates is the only, or even the most fruitful, way of understanding human experience. This approach can be said to characterize interventions in the debate by Sallie King and Robert Forman *et al*. Second, however, one could problematize the modernist construction of 'the mystical' as a predominantly experiential phenomenon, an approach taken by Grace Jantzen but not applied to the comparative study and appraisal of Asian mysticism. The first approach involves a 'plea for the recognition of differences' in the realm of epistemological theory. The second seeks to undermine the false dichotomy between perennialism and constructivism by displacing the psychologically inspired paradigm that has framed the debate in the first place.

Indian constructivisms: the epistemology of enlightenment

According to Katz, mystics are wrong to think that an unconditioned experience of reality is even possible. From his neo-Kantian perspective, mystics recondition themselves (with a new conceptual mind-set) rather than attain a release from cultural and conceptual conditioning as some traditions and texts proclaim.

> For it is in appearance only that such activities as yoga produced the desired state of 'pure' consciousness. Properly understood, yoga, for example, is not an *un*conditioning of consciousness or *de*conditioning of consciousness, but rather it is a *re*conditioning of consciousness, i.e. a substituting of one form of conditioned and/or contextual consciousness for another.[38]

This has led to responses such as the critique of Donald Evans, which focuses on the inappropriateness of scholars casting judgement over issues about which they are not qualified to speak. Evans suggests that academic philosophers are not in a position to prescribe limits on what mystics can or cannot experience. Who is Katz, Evans asks rhetorically, to say whether or not someone can have an experience of pure consciousness?[39] Similarly, Robert Forman contests Katz's position by appealing to autobiographical evidence: 'I, too, have undergone a PCE [Pure Consciousness Event].'[40] The following is Forman's account of his experience:

> In 1972 I was several months into a nine-month meditation retreat on a neo-Advaitan *sadhāna* (path). I had been meditating alone in my room all morning when someone knocked on my door. I heard the knock perfectly clearly, and upon hearing it I knew that, although there was no 'waking up' before hearing the knock, for some indeterminate length of time prior to the knocking I had not been aware of anything in particular. I had been awake but with no content for my consciousness. Had

no one knocked I doubt that I would ever have become aware that I had not been thinking or perceiving. The experience was so unremarkable, as it was utterly without content, that I simply would have begun at some point to recommence thinking and probably would never have taken note of my conscious persistence devoid of mental content.[41]

This is a highly unusual departure for the debate to take since Western academics have generally eschewed autobiographical evidence as 'too subjective' to warrant serious consideration. It reflects, however, the belief that something important is at stake in this debate – that Katz's radical constructivism moves beyond description and analysis to prescription and reductionism. Forman's account is itself problematic and difficult to assess. Crucially, what does Forman mean when he says that he was not aware of 'anything in particular'? The apparent denial of any mental content is suggestive of a trance state rather than an instance of non-conceptual awareness (*nirvikalpa jñāna*), at least according to the criteria outlined in Asaṅga's *Mahāyānasaṃgraha*. However, given the difficulty of explaining the content of such states (and from Asaṅga's point of view non-conceptual awareness *does* have a content, even if it is characterized by ineffability),[42] one could at least give Forman the benefit of the doubt. Katz, however, denies that his position is reductionist – there may indeed be a transcendent reality – but the crucial point, he suggests, is that one cannot have an *unmediated* experience of it.[43]

Scholars such as Huston Smith and Donald Evans have made casual (though no less pointed) references to the cosy compatibility of this stance with Katz's own Jewish tradition. Katz's analysis safeguards Jewish beliefs in a transcendent reality and the inherent limitations of human beings, while at the same time underscoring the exclusivism of Judaism in his emphasis upon a recognition of differences between religions.[44] It is clear that Katz's account creates problems for the non-dualistic and monistic traditions in particular. Mystical experiences of a 'unitive-absorptive nature' (that is, precisely those forms of mysticism that tend to presuppose some kind of unmediated experience of ultimate reality) can be found in Buddhism, 'Hinduism' (Advaita and Yoga), and Islam (Sufism). Testimony to such an experience can even be found, Katz notes, in the Christian mystical tradition but 'is absent from its Jewish counterpart'.[45]

Long before Berger, Luckmann or even Immanuel Kant for that matter, Indian philosophers have propounded and debated constructivist philosophies to explain the way in which human beings make sense of the world in which they live. Referring to the impact of Berger and Luckmann's 1966 work *The Social Construction of Reality*, Klaus Klostermaier remarks that:

The interpretation of *reality* as a *social construction*, mainly through the instrumentality of language and communication, created a minor sensation in Western intellectual circles some ten years ago and is still

considered by many sociologists as a break-through in our understanding of the real world in which people live. It may, in fact, connect
with a fairly universally held view among the major (ancient) traditions
of mankind.[46]

Consider for instance the early Mahāyāna Buddhist text the *Pratyutpanna-
buddha-saṃmukhāvasthita-samādhi Sūtra* (*Pratyutpanna Sūtra* for short).[47]
This text clearly belongs to the emerging Perfection of Wisdom
(*prajñāpāramitā*) strand of early Mahāyāna. The Sūtra, however, constitutes
an attempt to 'bridge the gap' between the Perfection of Wisdom, with its
radically non-realist stance, and the early Pure Land traditions (as outlined
in the larger and smaller *Sukhāvatī Sūtras*), which advocated contemplation
of and devotion to Amitābha Buddha. The *Pratyutpanna Sūtra*, then,
spends a great deal of time discussing the practice of *buddhānusmṛti* or
'mental recollection of the Buddha'. *Buddhānusmṛti* is the prolonged exercise of intense concentration upon the form of the Buddha (sometimes
based upon a particularly splendid iconographical representation). In the
Pure Land traditions this practice was believed to aid the aspirant in
attaining a vision of Amitābha Buddha as well as prepare the practitioner
for a future rebirth in Amitābha's heavenly 'Land of Bliss' (*Sukhāvatī*).
These traditions believed that *Sukhāvatī* was a land that dwelt in the west
and was considered superior to the mixed fortunes of life in *Sahā* – the
world of Gautama Buddha (in which we dwell). Clearly, for the devotional
Pure Land traditions, *Sukhāvatī* – the Land of Bliss – was a *real* place to
which one could be transported in meditative states (*samādhi*) and to which
one could aspire to be reborn in one's next life.

In contrast, the Perfection of Wisdom *Sūtras* expounded a radically non-
realist position. This world is an illusion (*māyā*) – the product of nescience
(*avidyā*) and the tendency of the unenlightened mind to construct a static
picture of the world based upon one's past karmic proclivities. From this
perspective, then, the Pure Land adherence to a realist position was a sign of
inferior spiritual development. How then does the *Pratyutpanna Sūtra*, a
text that adopts the Perfection of Wisdom stance, evaluate the contemplative practices of the Pure Land traditions? The *Sūtra* accepts that the fixing
of one's mind upon this 'image' eventually induces an intense meditative
concentration (named *pratyutpanna-samādhi*, hence the *Sūtra*'s title). It is
also made clear that strict moral purity is a fundamental prerequisite for this
practice, as is the intention to see the Buddha in his fullness. Thus, the *Sūtra*
states that:

In the same way, Bhadrapāla, *bodhisattvas*, whether they be house-
holders or renunciants (*pravrajita*), go alone to a secluded spot and sit
down, and in accordance with what they have learned they concentrate
their thoughts on the *Tathāgata*, *Arhat*, and Perfectly Awakened One
Amitāyus; flawless in the constituent of morality and unwavering in

mindfulness (*smṛti*) they should concentrate their thoughts for one day and one night, for two, or three, or four, or five, or six, or seven days and nights. If they concentrate their thoughts with undistracted minds on the *Tathāgata* Amitāyus for seven days and nights, then, when a full seven days and nights have elapsed, they see the Lord and *Tathāgata* Amitāyus. Should they not see that Lord during the daytime, then the Lord and *Tathāgata* Amitāyus will show his face in a dream while they are sleeping.[48]

This is not all that surprising. Try practising intense meditative concentration upon an image of Amitābha Buddha for seven days in a row and you too are likely to have some kind of 'vision' or experiences of Amitābha – if only in your dreams! The *Sūtra*, therefore, would seem to provide further evidence to support Katz's thesis that mystical experiences are the product of the mystic's own mind-set, expectations and cultural conditioning. What might surprise Katz and his followers, however, is that the *Pratyutpanna Sūtra* itself adopts a constructivist position to explain the nature and status of the visions resulting from *buddhānusmṛti* practice. Where, the text asks, do visions of the Buddha come from and where do they go when they end? The answer is that such visions do not 'come' or 'go' from anywhere, since they are nothing more than constructions (*vikalpitā*) of one's own mind.

> In thinking: 'Did these Tathāgatas come from anywhere? Did I go anywhere?' they understand that the Tathāgatas did not come from anywhere. Having understood that their own bodies did not go anywhere either, they think: 'Whatever belongs to this Triple World is nothing but thought. Why is that? It is because however I imagine things [*vikalpayati*, mentally construct], that is how they appear.[49]

For the *Pratyutpanna Sūtra* and subsequent Mahāyāna philosophy, this is the realization that our experience of the world as unenlightened beings is an illusion (*māyā*) – a conceptual construction based upon an erroneous perception of reality. In Chapter 8 of the *Saṃdhinirmocana Sūtra*, another Mahāyāna Buddhist text, the same question is asked with regard to the visions experienced during meditative practice and then extrapolated from this context and applied to everyday experiences.

A few centuries later we find the Buddhist philosopher Dignāga (*c.* 480–540 CE) arguing that that sense-perception (*pratyakṣa*), although immediate and non-conceptual in itself, is mediated in human experience by conceptual constructions (*kalpanā*). What we apprehend with our senses, in its unmediated givenness, is the particular instant (*svalakṣaṇa*) that characterizes what is really there. However, the picture of reality that we, as unenlightened beings, construct is the product of the association of our 'pure sensations' with linguistic forms – such as names (*nāma*), categories (*jāti*) and concepts in general – acquired from our linguistic and cultural context.[50] These, Dignāga argued, result in a misapprehension of reality since they derive from the construction of universals (*samānyalakṣaṇa*) in a world in which only unique particulars exist. The goal of Dignāga's Buddhist system of thought, of course, is to liberate the Buddhist practitioner from attachment to these linguistic and cultural forms through meditative cultivation of the mind (*citta-bhāvanā*), ethical discipline (*śīla*) and the development of analytical insight (*prajñā*). Dignāga's constructivism, therefore, postulated a way out of the web of cultural and linguistic conditioning through the cultivation of the perfection of wisdom (*prajñāpāramitā*) and the development of a non-dual (*advaya*) and unconstructed or non-conceptual awareness (*nirvikalpa jñāna*) of things as they really are (*yathābhūta, tathatā*). In other words, his constructivism was based upon what one might call an *epistemology of enlightenment*. Sallie King has also explored what she calls a 'Buddhist-phenomenological epistemological model' as an alternative to the Katzian position on the possibility of unmediated awareness. She suggests that the study of mystical experiences does not require us to accept the Yogācāra position that 'true reality' is given in the 'immediately given presence of primitive experience', only that such unmediated experiences do happen (whatever their truth-giving status).

In sum, this means that if we ask 'can there be unmediated experience?' we must reply that there cannot be unembodied experience. But why should we suppose that there cannot be moments of experience free of the influence of ideas, concepts, words, philosophies and religious traditions? We do not constantly have our linguistic functions turned on in every moment. Not only is the turning off of this function the very purpose of many forms of meditation, but we can think of many examples of secular experience in which the individual experiences in the 'primitive' mode without the presence of verbal functions in the noetic correlate. When one gives oneself up completely to the present moment of physical exertion in sports, or the present moment of sound in listening to music, or the present moment of singing, there is no experiential sense of a separate self. There is just the event in which one is 'lost.'[51]

This Buddhistic position, of which Dignāga's Yogācāra version is another variant, is to be sharply contrasted with epistemologies that restrict the potential of human beings to achieve some form of unmediated awareness.[52] As such, the Kantian position and its post-Enlightenment successors can be described as *epistemologies of limitation*. Nevertheless, even in this regard, one should note that there has been a long history of debate within the Indo-Tibetan traditions of Buddhism concerning the precise nature of non-conceptual awareness (*nirvikalpa jñāna*) and the conditioning process that leads up to it. Dharmakīrti, for instance, makes it clear that enlightenment is the result of effort (*yatna*)[53] and the practice of methods (*upāyābhyāsa*).[54]

How one experiences the world is dependent upon one's emotional and mental proclivities and the conditioned nature of one's particular thought patterns, since, for Dharmakīrti, 'experience generates convictions of certainty as a result of the repetition of thoughts'.[55] On this view, even the perception of a yogin includes more than is immediately present since the yogin has learnt (that is, conditioned) his own faculties to see beyond appearances and experience the world according to the liberating truth of the Buddha's *Dharma*.

It is clear that for most Buddhist traditions the non-conceptual nature of enlightenment is the result of a long and often arduous path of disciplined mental activity. The constitutive role of conceptual reasoning in this process is a feature particularly emphasized, for instance, in the Tibetan *dGe lugs pa* tradition of Buddhist scholasticism.[56] Paul Williams notes, in his analysis of the eighth-century 'Great Debate' between Kamalaśīla and the Chinese monk Mahāyāna, that:

> Kamalaśīla may accept a mental state which is in some sense nonconceptual, but the process by which it is brought about implicitly involves the use of conceptual reasoning ... For Kamalaśīla, the process of attainment in some sense determines the eventual state. It may be nonconceptual but it is a nonconceptuality which contains, as it were, all that went before.[57]

The Buddhist examples of Dharmakīrti, Kamalaśīla and the subsequent *dGe lugs pa* illustrate that acceptance of the conditioning role of cultural, mental and behavioural factors in the eventual attainment of enlightenment was not always seen by Buddhists as implying that one cannot have a non-conceptual experience of reality as it is. This position is in agreement with Katz in acknowledging the role of conditioning factors as constitutive of the final experience of enlightenment. Indeed, for Buddhists such as Kamalaśīla and Dharmakīrti, one cannot attain enlightenment unless one first determines what reality is like and cultivates such an awareness through vigilant practice. However, where Buddhist versions of constructivism tend to diverge from Katz is in the recognition that the enlightenment experience that results from such conditioning processes is an event of such transformative proportions that it propels one beyond the wheel of conditioning (*saṃsāra*), thereby resulting in a transcendence of cultural particularity. It seems to me that it is only in this sense that the Buddhist tradition can maintain the view that Buddhas attain a definitive, incontrovertible and direct apprehension of reality that is both ultimately true and universally applicable to all.

There are, of course, other varieties of constructivism within the Indian philosophical traditions. The Hindu grammarian philosopher Bhartṛhari, for instance, like his modern Lacanian and Derridean counterparts, rejected the view that one could escape the web of language in any cognition. All knowledge is mediated through language (*śabda*): 'If this eternal identity between knowledge and the word were to disappear, knowledge would cease to be knowledge; it is this identity which makes identification possible.'[58]

Bhartṛhari did not require the postulation of an innate structure to the human brain, as Chomsky does, for instance, to account for difficult cases such as the experiences of new-born babies because of the Indian belief in rebirth (*saṃsāra*). Thus, even the newly born child carries with it the cultural baggage and linguistic mode of apprehending the world as a result of its experiences in past lives.[59] In some respects, then, Bhartṛhari's version of constructivism is even more rigorous and unyielding than Katz's position. Nevertheless, for Bhartṛhari, the linguistic structure of reality is unitary and cannot be divided into smaller atomic units, except for the heuristic purpose of grammatical analysis. Bhartṛhari's belief in the indivisibility (*akhaṇḍatva*) of language thus enables him to postulate a monistic reality grounded in the notion of the indivisibility of the word-principle (*śabda-brahman*). This form of constructivism, therefore, does not undermine the non-dualistic presuppositions of much Asian mysticism.

In the Sāṃkhya tradition of Indian thought there is the acceptance of two basic and irreducible ontological principles: *prakṛti* – the insentient and dynamic material out of which the world is developed – and the principles of pure consciousness (*puruṣa*, literally 'person'). The latter constitutes the unseen seer – a transcendent and immaterial pure consciousness – our true selves according to the Sāṃkhya school. *Puruṣa* becomes intrigued by *prakṛti* and 'forgets' its true nature, thereby mistakenly identifying itself with embodied existence through a succession of lives (*saṃsāra*). The goal of the Sāṃkhya tradition, as well as the Rāja Yoga tradition, is to realize that one's true nature is that of a pure witness consciousness (*sākṣin*), untouched by the vicissitudes and fluctuations of worldly existence. Thus, in the *Yoga sūtras* of Patañjali, a progressive path is outlined for overcoming the fluctuations of the mind (*citta vṛtti*) and attaining a state of unconstructed and concentrated awareness (*nirvikalpa samādhi*), where one perceives reality as it is and the seer dwells in its own pure form. Again, in the Advaita Vedānta tradition of Śaṅkara, the realization of enlightenment is best exemplified by the *jīvanmukta* – one who is liberated while alive. Such a being is said to pierce the veil of illusions that constitutes our illusory (*māyā/mithyā*) experience of the world and achieve what the dualist Vedāntin Madhva described as an unmediated awareness (*aparokṣa jñāna*) of reality.

All of these Asian traditions accept the role played by concepts and cultural conditioning in everyday states of consciousness. Clearly, they also accept that releasing oneself from these conditioning factors requires cultivation through constant yogic practice (*abhyāsa*) and the overcoming of attachment (*vairāgya*) (as expressed in the *Yoga Sūtra* of Patañjali). In Buddhist traditions this might be described as mental development or culture (*citta-bhāvanā*) and the cultivation of equanimity (*upekṣā*). Where these traditions differ from modern Western intellectuals like Katz (and post-structuralist feminists such as Jantzen) is in the acknowledgement of the possibility of transcending one's own personal and cultural particularity and the attainment of some final state of ultimate understanding, desig-nated by terms such as *bodhi* (enlightenment), *asaṃprajñāta-samādhi*, *jīvanmukta* (liberated while alive), and so on.

The acceptance of the reality (indeed, for these Indian traditions the *centrality*) of an unmediated and unconstructed awareness constitutes a major point of disagreement between mainstream Western intellectual thought and classical Asian traditions of spirituality. This disagreement is highly significant since to accept neo-Kantian versions of constructivism is to reject the possibility of such enlightenment and therefore to subvert the central tenet of these traditions. I find the ease with which the neo-Kantian position has been assumed in Western discussions of mysticism to be disturbing in its own pretensions to universality. Western epistemologies of limitation reflect the sociocultural and political changes that have occurred in the West since the Enlightenment and thus remain peculiarly Eurocentric in orientation.

My intention in drawing attention to Indian alternatives to Western forms of constructivism is to offer my own 'plea for the recognition of differences'. There are other ways of seeing the world than are dreamt of in post-Enlightenment Western philosophy and one should not seek to close one's account on reality too prematurely. To accept modern Western episte-mological theories without highlighting their cultural and social particularity is to remain within a long and well-established tradition of Western arrogance about the superiority of Western ways of understanding the world. The introduction of indigenous forms of Indian constructivism to the debate, therefore, both broadens its parameters and causes a trans-gression or disruption of the hegemonic philosophical trends of modern Western intellectual orthodoxy. As Anne Klein points out, when we examine the claim to an unmediated awareness in Asian traditions:

> ... we confront some of the fundamental issues that divide us, as contemporary Euro-Americans, from the worldview in which it was conceived. How are we to understand a literature whose fundamental theses are anathema to most contemporary Western intellectual tradi-tions? For example, both dGe-lugs-pa and Rnying-ma, and Buddhism generally, claim that one can become a knower or self whose agency is free from the constraints of language (compare Lacan), who gains some form of unmediated knowledge (compare Kant), and – most antithet-ical of all – that this knowledge and its object are unconditioned by particularities of history and thus accessible in the same form, albeit through different means, to all persons regardless of cultural or psycho-logical particularity (compare Foucault).[60]

Such Asian 'mystical' traditions challenge some of the central tenets of Western secular culture and, in my view, should not be so easily dismissed. Asian epistemologies of enlightenment are likely to be viewed with a great deal of scepticism by contemporary Westerners since they conflict with modern, secularist presuppositions about the nature of reality and the possibilities of human experience. Such epistemologies are also likely to be the subject of criticism by postmodern theorists as further examples of a totalizing discourse claiming to possess a 'God's-eye view' of the universe. The impossibility of 'thinking that' for such thinkers points to the Judaeo-Christian roots of contemporary Western debates about the nature and status of mysticism and the limitations of humans in relation to the divine. These presuppositions, of course, are not shared by Asian traditions such as Taoism, Buddhism, Advaita Vedānta, and Rāja Yoga, etc. My point is not that Western scholars should necessarily accept the emic perspectives over which they are claiming the authority to speak, but rather that they at least entertain the possibility that such perspectives are a legitimate stance to adopt and engage them in constructive debate. Note, for instance, that traditional Indian constructivist epistemologies tend to emphasize the role played by the individual mind in the construction process. In contrast, Western constructivisms, sharpened to the realities of cultural diversity as a factor in human difference, tend to emphasize the role played by society (and in the case of post-structuralist versions, power) in the construction of worldviews. Such theories, however, tend to deny agency to the individual in a manner that is strikingly reminiscent of Orientalist representations of the colonial subject. Perhaps engagement in a cross-cultural analysis of these theories might yield interesting new theories and paradigms of knowledge. Such engagement, however, is not possible if one assumes as an a priori assumption that the theoretical ground for a particular form of life is based upon an epistemological error and that Western (or Indian for that matter) theories are superior.

Perennialism is based upon what one might call the 'Myth of the Transcendent Object'. Perennialist philosophers postulate a common core – that is, some kind of transcendent reality or truth that underlies the diversity of mystical accounts. In contrast to this, Katzian constructivism is grounded in a form of cultural isolationism or the 'Myth of the Isolated Context'. On this view all mystical experiences are fundamentally culturally bound, rendering the establishment of cross-cultural similarities inherently problematic. As we have seen, the perennialist or common-core thesis presumes and requires a distinction of some sort between experience and interpretation. On the other hand, the pluralist account offered by constructivists such as Katz presumes and requires that experience is itself constructed by culturally determined interpretations.

This dichotomy, however, does not exhaust the options. Rejecting Katz's version of constructivism does not force one into a perennialist position. The history of Indian philosophical debate demonstrates rather well that none of the Indian traditions discussed above conceived of themselves as in agreement with each other regarding the precise nature of reality, despite their common endorsement of a constructivist epistemology of enlightenment. The Rāja Yoga tradition exemplified in the *Yoga Sūtra* of Patañjali, for instance, is often associated with the ontological dualism of the Saṃkhya school. Within the mainstream traditions of South Asian Buddhism (Vaibhāṣika, Sautrāntika, Theravāda) we find evidence of a pluralistic phenomenalism (of *dharmas*, or momentary events). The Advaita Vedānta of Śaṅkara postulates an immutable and undifferentiated absolute reality underlying all illusory appearances, while the Mahāyāna schools of Madhyamaka and Yogācāra Buddhism reject Advaitic monism in favour of the philosophy of emptiness (*śūnyatā*). Even here the Madhyamaka and Yogācāra schools differed in their interpretation of this basic Mahāyāna notion.[61]

As we have seen, there are alternatives to Katz's neo-Kantian constructivism. One could, for instance, uphold a position of partial constructivism. On this view, experience is produced by pre-experiential conditions such as tradition, mind-set, expectation and so on, and it is these that provide the limits of possibility for one's experience. Nevertheless, there may be dimensions of human experience that are not conditioned by such cultural factors. A constructivism grounded in an epistemology of enlightenment – postulating an unconstructed awareness – provides some light at the end of a very dark tunnel. One might also opt for a more open-ended and agnostic position, refusing to pass judgement on the question of the farthest reaches of human possibility. Further work is also needed in the development of alternatives to the late Capitalist constructivist or productivist metaphor as a paradigm or model for understanding the nature of the interaction between humans and their cultures.

If one accepts an epistemology of limitation, which accords rather well with contemporary secular, historicist and postmodern understandings of human experience, then it seems to me that one must rule out *nirvikalpa jñāna*, enlightenment or some transcultural experience of ultimate reality as a possibility. This, however, would seem to subvert not only the world-view of many traditional Indian systems of thought (such as Yoga, Advaita Vedānta, Buddhism), but also undermine the position of certain Christian mystics such as Meister Eckhart, for whom the realization of an uncreated divine spark in humanity remains the *summum bonum* of the religious path. On the other hand, if one accepts an epistemology that allows for the possibility of experiences that in some sense transcend cultural conditioning (as traditional Indian yogic epistemologies clearly do) this does not necessitate the adoption of a perennialist position, at least as this is usually understood.

The answer to the question 'What is relationship between a mystical experience and its interpretation?' has been represented by scholars as central to debates about the nature and significance of 'mysticism', as well as to the question of the possibilities and limitations of cross-cultural analysis in this area. The privatization of modern notions of 'the mystical' has caused the comparative study of 'mysticism' to be reduced to a debate about which epistemological theory one wishes to hold. Such debates ignore the shifting meanings and contexts of the category of 'the mystical' throughout its history. More specifically, no attention has been paid to the way in which the construction of a number of stereotypical images of the East – D.T. Suzuki's 'Zen Buddhism', Vivekānanda's or Śaṅkara's 'Advaita Vedānta', Patañjali's 'Yoga', Lao Tzu's *Dao De Jing* – have been pressed into service as token representatives of 'the global phenomenon of mysticism'. Whether colonized and homogenized by perennialists or essentialized and segregated by the constructivists, these stereotypes of 'the Mystic East' have been used to make a variety of competing claims about the 'mystical', spiritual or otherworldly nature of Eastern culture and the limitations (or not) of human experience. Such debates also serve to locate certain aspects of Asian and Western culture within a modernist and psychologized framework that misreads the phenomenon of 'mysticism' on a number of levels.[62] From a postcolonial perspective, contemporary debates within the comparative study of mysticism ignore the inequality of power implied when Western scholars pass judgement upon the belief systems and forms of life of cultures that are still coming to terms with centuries of Western colonial hegemony.

As Grace Jantzen has pointed out, the tenor and framing of these debates are modern in nature and reflect neither the concerns nor the agenda of the pre-modern mystics and literature that are the subject of such analysis.[63] However, as I have been arguing, these debates are not only peculiarly modern in their orientation and agenda, they are also Eurocentric in their failure to question the post-Enlightenment assumptions that continue to structure the debate. Moreover, such comparativism fails to engage seriously with the indigenous theories, categories and forms of life of those under analysis. Fundamentally, the problem with this entire debate is that the study of mystics has become skewed by the contemporary (post-Jamesian) construction of 'mysticism' in exclusively experiential terms. This, above all else, does violence to the traditions, literature and lives of those who are described as 'mystical', as well as to those who are subject to the sweeping cultural caricatures that such representations frequently imply.

The study of non-Western cultures by Western scholars necessitates an awareness of the wider power dynamic in which such discursive practices operate and are received, as well as an openness and appreciation of indigenous categories, theories and forms of life in and on their own terms. In taking this position I am not arguing for an uncritical acceptance or endorsement of 'the indigenous' as if this were free from its own set of power relations and oppressive practices. Nor am I unaware of the problems involved in reconstructing 'the indigenous', particularly after the radical reconfiguration of indigenous forms of knowledge precipitated by European colonialism. Rather, my point is that Western scholars should pay far more attention to the nature and operation of the 'fusion of horizons' that occurs in comparative analysis. Engagement with the theories, categories and world-views of the cultures under examination also requires an acknowledgement of the cultural particularity of Western concepts and theories and a recognition of the politics of comparative analysis.

9 Beyond Orientalism?

Religion and comparativism in a postcolonial era

In recent years we have witnessed an increasing tendency to think of colonialism as a period of history that is now behind us. Combined with this contemporary lauding of the 'postcolonial era', the 1990s have brought forth a number of works heralding the move 'beyond Orientalism'.[1] We must remain sceptical of such claims if they are meant to imply that the period of domination of 'the rest' by the West has now come to an end and that scholars who have taken the post-Saidian 'postcolonial turn' can now claim to be free from complicity with regimes of domination. Conversely, one might also ask whether the recent wave of postcolonial studies has itself tended to overvalue or privilege the colonial space at the expense of an awareness of precolonial and (so-called) postcolonial regimes of power.[2]

The broad methodological stance that I have been advocating throughout this book could be described as an attempt to 'anthropologize' the West (Paul Rabinow),[3] in particular to render contemporary Western constructions of reality 'exotic' by drawing attention to the cultural particularity of such knowledge systems and their historical involvement in the systematic and violent suppression of non-Western ways of life, forms of knowledge and constructions of reality. This is a strategic (or perhaps in Certeau's terms a tactical) stance, grounded in my own institutional location as a British scholar of Indian religion and philosophy working within a Western, metropolitan university.

The approach that I am advocating is context-sensitive, in the sense that my own work is to be seen as a response to the colonial past of my particular field of interest (Indology/Orientalism) and an attempt to come to terms with the colonial legacy of the England in which I was born. As a scholar specializing in the study of ancient Indian philosophy and religion I am invested with the authority to 'speak about' or 'represent' such phenomena by virtue of my institutional location within the modern Academy. Problematizing the way in which Indian religion has been represented within Western scholarship, therefore, is an exercise in calling into question the paradigms of knowledge and constellations of power that have continued to divide the world up into 'us' and 'them' – maintaining an asymmetrical relationship between the relatively powerful and the relatively disempowered. This intellectual and ethical 'malaise' exists, of course, in many forms other than the classic Orientalist division between 'East' and 'West' so staunchly attacked by Edward Said, and is by no means a peculiarly European or Occidental 'disease'. Today, rather than a division between 'East' and 'West' one might more accurately speak of a division between 'North' and South' or between 'First' and 'Third' Worlds. Such binary oppositions, however, tend to function in a similar fashion to Orientalist discourses. Difference is perceived in oppositional rather than pluralistic terms, and differences between cultures become fetishized at the same time as internal heterogeneities within each culture are effaced. Moreover, as Urdu poet and Marxist literary theorist Aijaz Ahmed notes in his critique of 'Third World' theory, dividing humanity up into three 'worlds' tends to privilege the category of the 'nation' as the paradigmatic unit of sociopolitical identity (undermining other forms of collectivity) and also segregates what are, in reality, globally interactive networks of human activity and power relations.

> But one could start with a radically different premiss: namely, the proposition that we live not in three worlds but in one; that this world includes the experience of colonialism and imperialism on both sides of [the] global divide.[4]

As a Marxist, Ahmed asks us to conceive of this global unity in terms of the universality of class division. This is not a step many would be willing to take (myself included), though I am fully supportive of Ahmed's call for a recognition of the mutual imbrication of (so-called) 'First' and 'Third' Worlds and a repudiation of the continued involvement of the West (particularly in the form of 'multinational corporations' and direct and indirect forms of political intervention) in a neo-colonialist separation of the two. In this sense, I believe that the 'Three Worlds' theory should be abandoned, not only for the reasons outlined by Ahmed, but also because the agenda of 'modernization' (whether conceived in Capitalistic or Marxist terms) that underlies its usage remains as problematic as it is Eurocentric.

What I have in mind, therefore, is a methodological stance described by the subalternist historian Dipesh Chakrabarty as a project of 'provincializing Europe' – 'the "Europe" that modern imperialism and (third-world) nationalism have, by their collaborative venture and violence, made universal'.[5] For Chakrabarty this project involves the realization that:

> insofar as the academic discourse of history – that is, 'history' as a discourse produced at the institutional site of the university – is concerned, 'Europe' remains the sovereign theoretical subject of all histories, including the ones we call 'Indian', 'Chinese', 'Kenyan', and so on. There is a peculiar way in which all these other histories tend to

become variations on a master narrative that could be called 'the history of Europe.'[6]

To paraphrase one of the characters in Salman Rushdie's *Satanic Verses*, 'the trouble with the English is that their history happened overseas and so they have no idea what it means'.[7] The era of British colonial expansion and the subjugation of foreign lands and peoples – all of which occurred far away from the 'homeland' – nevertheless constituted the most significant factor in the political, economic and cultural power of England and the English language in the nineteenth and early twentieth centuries. Moreover, Rushdie's remark resonates with Chakrabarty's suggestion that Europe cannot be conceived of as an autonomous and self-contained process, 'as if the self-fashioning of the West were something that occurred only within its self-assigned geographical boundaries'.[8] The history of Europe, or more specifically of England, cannot be divorced from the unfolding of events beyond the 'home-land'. The history of the colonizer is bound up with the populations and regions that have been conquered and colonized. Nevertheless, in an increasingly 'internationalized' world, the homogeneity of constructs such as 'Englishness', etc. are increasingly becoming problematized.[9] Consider, for instance, the following account of cultural diversity in the Balsall Heath district of Birmingham offered by a young, white reggae fan:

> [T]here's no such thing as 'England' anymore ... [W]elcome to India brothers! This is the Caribbean! ... Nigeria! ... There is no England, man. This is what is coming. Balsall Heath is the centre of the melting pot, 'cos all I ever see when I go out is half-Arab, half-Pakistani, half-Jamaican, half-Scottish, half-Irish. I know 'cos I am [half-Scottish/half-Irish] ... [W]ho am I? Tell me who I belong to? They criticize me, the good old England. Alright, where do I belong? You know I was brought up with blacks, Pakistanis, Africans, Asians, everything, you name it ... [W]ho do I belong to? I'm just a broad person. The earth is mine ... you know we was not born in Jamaica ... we was not born in 'England'. We were born here man. It's our right. That's the way I see it. That's the way I deal with it.[10]

A major problem with any attempt to 'provincialize Europe', however, is, as Chakrabarty himself concedes, that it is a project that 'must realize within itself its own impossibility'. For Chakrabarty, this reflects the origins of 'history' as an academic practice grounded in the institutional invocation of the 'nation-state' and the tendency to represent 'Europe' as the home of 'the modern'. Such an undertaking, therefore, cannot involve the production of rival histories that merely reproduce the basic explanatory categories and methodological strategies of European accounts of history. The postcolonial appeal to diversity and the heterogeneity of historical accounts is not a call for more of the same. The complicity between European imperialism and Third World nationalism in establishing the 'nation-state' as the primary signifier of political community necessitates a stance that problematizes not only the construction of a hyperreal 'Europe' at the centre of 'History' but also analogous constructs such as 'India', 'Hinduism' and 'the Indian mentality'. For Chakrabarty, therefore, the project of dismantling 'Europe' as the focal point of history should not result in the production of rival accounts in the form of nationalist, nativist or atavistic histories. Rather, such a project should look to displace the tendency to construct a newly established set of relations between a 'centre' and a 'periphery' as the locus of a unified, homogeneous and uncontested history.

> I ask for a history that deliberately makes visible, within the very structure of its narrative forms, its own repressive strategies and practices ... This is a history that will attempt the impossible: to look toward its own death by tracing that which resists and escapes the best human effort at translation across cultural and other semiotic systems, so that the world may once again be imagined as radically heterogeneous.[11]

Postcolonialism and the 'Subaltern Studies' project

Perhaps the boldest attempts to undertake this project have been those of a group of (mainly diaspora) Indian historians, known as the Subaltern Studies Collective. Ranajit Guha, perhaps the primary exponent of this approach, defines the subaltern as *'the demographic difference between the total Indian population and all those whom we have described as the "elite"'*.[12] For Guha, the 'élite' is a heterogeneous category made up of dominant foreign groups (such as British colonial officials, missionaries and industrialists), dominant indigenous groups operating at the all-India level, and dominant indigenous groups acting at regional and local levels. These groupings are to be distinguished from the 'subaltern classes' or 'the people'. The interest of the Subalternist historians, therefore, is in the 'history of the people' – the indigenous voices that do not constitute part of the native élite and have been silenced by 'élite historiography'.

The early work of the subaltern group focused upon moments of insurgency in Indian history when subordinated groups have risen up and offered direct, sometimes violent, and self-conscious resistance to élite power.[13] This masculinist model of resistance, however, has tended to conceive of everyday life as an extended period of subaltern submissiveness punctuated by sudden, violent irruptions and contestations of élite dominance. Such a model of resistance effaces the variety of strategies and modes of resistance undertaken by the 'relatively disempowered' on a day-to-day basis. More nuanced accounts have gradually emerged, therefore, which pay much greater attention to everyday forms of resistance.[14] Much of this work involves an explicit problematization of the conventional separation of 'the political' from other spheres of human activity such as the religious, the cultural and the domestic.[15]

The Subalternist historians have also been criticized for reintroducing the problematized notions of autonomous agency and subjectivity that they repudiated in their assault upon élitist historiography. Guha notes, for instance, that the subaltern 'was an autonomous domain ... it neither originated in élite politics nor did its existence depend upon the latter'.[16] Rosalind O'Hanlon thus argues that:

> At the very moment of this assault upon western historicism the classic figure of western humanism – the self-originating, self-determining individual, who is at once a subject in his possession of a sovereign consciousness whose defining quality is reason, and an agent in his power of freedom – is readmitted through the backdoor in the figure of the subaltern himself, as he is restored to history in the reconstructions of the Subaltern project.[17]

For O'Hanlon, the Subalternist goal of recovering the voice of the silenced subaltern elides too easily with the restoration project of liberal humanism in its attempt to recapture a 'history of the subaltern', free from the constraining influences of élite forces or external leadership.[18] Moreover, as Haynes and Prakash point out, the search for an autonomous subject provides an obstacle to any attempt to understand how 'the subaltern' is constituted within a heterogeneous field of power relations.[19] It is necessary, therefore, to 'counter the notion that the subaltern consciousness is either a completely independent product or that it is a mere reflection of a totalizing hegemony from above'.[20]

> If we assume that 'consciousness' is achieved in most acts of resistance and hold that the 'recovery' gives the subaltern a voice, then the critical edge provided by the notion of subalternity may be lost. For then we may fail to understand the structures that have conditioned the subaltern in the past and which continue to shape our own discourse in the present.[21]

It would be a mistake, however, to represent all the writings of the Collective as uniform in nature, and indeed some critics have suggested that there is a clash of agendas between a romanticized search for the heroic subaltern on the one hand and a deconstructionist/Foucauldian stance that remains sceptical of the existence of anything outside of discursive power relation on the other.[22] Partha Chatterjee, for instance, argues that the reason for claiming that the subaltern is an autonomous realm is not to deny that such groups are dominated but rather to:

conceptualise this domination as a relation of power ... For domination to exist, the subaltern classes must necessarily inhabit a domain that is their own, which gives them their identity, where they exist as a distinct social form ... To deny autonomy in this sense and simply to assert that the subaltern classes are 'deeply subjugated' is to deny that they represent a distinct form of social existence. [23]

The point of subaltern historiography, therefore, 'is to conceptualise a whole aspect of Indian history as a history, i.e. as a movement which flows from the opposition between two distinct social forces'.[24] This point is crucial for an understanding of the importance and the limitations of the subaltern project. In so far as emphasis is placed upon the apparent autonomy or subject-agency of the subaltern (resulting in O'Hanlon's charge of incipient essentialism), the Subalternist historians have prevented a detailed and nuanced examination of the complex operations of power (as dominance and resistance) that Chatterjee suggests is the *raison d'être* of the subalternist enterprise.[25] Recovering subaltern agency and autonomy prevents a detailed analysis of the effects of power upon the colonized subject and can also lead to a dangerous assimilation of 'the subaltern voice' to the position outlined in the Subalternist historical account.[26]

In the work of Gayatri Chakravorty Spivak, the writings of Subaltern Studies Collective are subjected to a reading 'against the grain' in order to highlight both the value and the limitations of the project. Spivak reads the search for the subaltern as a form of *strategic* essentialism that in its boldness reveals both the ethnocentric limitations of Western critiques of humanism and the limitations of its own analysis. While the anti-humanisms of Althusser and Foucault function as an oppositional stance to the dominant, post-Enlightenment emphasis upon a sovereign individual subject at the centre of history, Spivak argues that such a strategy is not viable for colonized groups where the concern must be to displace the structures of Western colonial violence, both epistemic and material, that continue to oppress them. Although the subaltern project is marked by inevitable 'cognitive failure' (the deconstructive *différance*) it remains in Spivak's view complex, highly nuanced and valuable in its transgressive and deconstructive potential.[27]

The subaltern project is characterized not only by its critique of colonialist histories but also by its rejection of the 'nationalist' model of Indian history that is seen to be a product of European colonial influence and another example of 'élite historiography'.[28] Indeed in India the reception of subaltern historiography has most often been in terms of its avowedly anti-nationalist stance.[29] Perhaps because of the comparative 'newness' of the Indian nation and a perception that the period of Indian 'nation-building' remains an ongoing process, there is no doubt a much greater sensitivity within Indian academic circles to the implications of such critiques for the stability of the 'modern Indian nation'.[30] Aijaz Ahmed, however, has criticized this stance among postcolonial theorists such as Edward Said, the Subalternists and Ronald Inden because of their tendency to render the entire colonial archive as a 'realm of pure untruth', conveniently allowing all of modern India's problems (for example, nationalism, communalism, casteism) to be placed at the foot of British colonial rule.[31] The problem with such accounts, of course, is that they deprive indigenous Indians of any recognisable agency, thereby perpetuating the myth of the passive and indolent Oriental. Similarly, such approaches efface the instabilities and ambivalences of colonial power in favour of a Manichean account that simplistically separates the righteous (the colonized) from the malevolent (the colonizer).[32] While there is no doubting the necessity of attempts to redress the balance in historical accounts and emphasize the cultural and material violence carried out in the name of European imperial expansion, it is also important to acknowledge the existence of precolonial forms of oppression within India and the agency of indigenous subjects (both élite and subaltern) during the colonial period itself.

The third target of Subalternist historiography, ironically reflecting the earlier allegiances and interests of many of its practitioners, is the repudiation of Marxist approaches to history.[33] Partha Chatterjee argues, for instance, that Marxist teleology empties subaltern movements of their own intentions, consciousness and ideas. The specificities of subaltern historical struggles are effaced in Marxist accounts by the superimposition of supposedly universal and foundational categories such as 'capital' and 'class-consciousness' in a manner that is profoundly ahistorical. The task of the subaltern approach, therefore, is to resist this tendency to conceive of the subaltern in terms of what it lacks – namely, 'class-consciousness', or to place the subaltern within a sweeping evolutionary history that moves from feudalism to capitalism. The universalism of traditional Marxist teleology, Chatterjee argues, rides roughshod over the historical specificities and interests of subaltern movements, depriving such groups of their own autonomous voices – in effect, denying their own presence within history.

> The problem is that within the theoretical framework of Marx's *Capital*, there is no room for us to talk about the *variable* social forms of capital. In that framework, Capital is the universal category, the most general category that is known to us in the historical evolution of economic categories ... How are we to conceptualise the variable form of capital? Are we to continue to regard Capital as the universal category? ... Are we to explain 'retarded' capitalism simply in terms of a time-lag, or should we treat it as an expression of the historical limits of Capital's universalising mission? ... I feel bold enough, and stupid enough, to attempt to *supersede* the terms of that debate. That for what it is worth is my 'project'.[34]

As we have seen, the tendency to treat the subaltern as a unitary conscious-ness, however, is also apparent in the works of many Subalternists.[35] A central feature of this approach, however, has been its refusal to be confined by the limitations of Marxist historical categories. Much of the work within the Subaltern Collective (and beyond) involves an explicit repudiation of the economic reductionism of dominant strands of Marxist theory.[36] In this regard, one can see further evidence of the influence of Italian Marxist Antonio Gramsci, for whom the economism of Marxist theorists such as Bukharin represented a failure to appreciate the complex reciprocity of structure and superstructure occurring within the dialectic of history. Economism, according to Gramsci, represented a simplistic reading of Marx's writings and failed to recognize the involvement of culture in the power dynamics of society and the role of cultural expression in the process of historical change.

> The claim, presented as an essential postulate of historical materialism, that every fluctuation of politics and ideology can be presented and expounded as an immediate expression of the structure, must be contested in theory as primitive infantilism, and combated in practice with the authentic testimony of Marx, the author of concrete political and historical works.[37]

The representation of Marxist thought as a form of socio-economic reduc-tionism in the work of some Subalternist scholarship, however, has not gone unquestioned and indeed such criticism has also been placed at the foot of the Subalternists themselves. Rosalind O'Hanlon argues, for instance, that the unguarded pursuit of subaltern subjectivity and agency,

> fails adequately to displace familiar classifications of activity – the economic, the political and the cultural – from their familiar and respected roles: roles which, in their insistence on a clear distinction between the material and the ideal, the instrumental and the symbolic, have themselves been a formidable ally in elite historiography's denial of a political significance to a whole range of subaltern activity.[38]

In his clarion call for post-Orientalist and post-foundationalist historiogra-phies of the 'Third World', Gyan Prakash praises the concept of 'the subaltern' as superior to fixed and universalized constructs such as the older Marxist notion of 'class' and its implicit teleology of redemption. In an analysis reminiscent of Chatterjee, Prakash argues that Marxist historiogra-phies frame India and its history as 'preludes to the emergence of full-fledged class consciousness' and thereby represent the 'third-worldliness' of India as incomplete and characterized by absence. This is, of course, a familiar colonialist trope.[39] According to Prakash, the shift in emphasis from the category of 'class' to that of 'the subaltern' allows historians such as Ranajit Guha to view subalternity:

> as an effect of power-relations expressed through a variety of means – linguistic, economic, social and cultural. This perspective, therefore, breaks the undivided entity of India into a multiplicity of changing positions that are then treated as the effects of power-relations. The displacement of foundational subjects and essences allowed by this also enables Guha to treat histories written from those perspectives as documents of counterinsurgency ... Writing subaltern history, from this point of view, becomes an activity that is contestatory because of its insurgent readings.[40]

Nevertheless, Prakash equivocates in his own appraisal of the subaltern project, suggesting at one point that Guha's analysis displaces 'foundational subjects'[41] but arguing on the next page that the subaltern project 'replaces one autonomous subject (the nation) with another (the subaltern)'. All of this seems to be pointing towards the need for a much greater recognition of the status of the category of 'the subaltern' as a shifting signifier, that is as a context-relative category constructed according to the specificities of local power relations as opposed to a static, homogeneous and universal category.[42] Recognition of the polysemic nature of 'the subaltern' remains a strength of a theoretically sophisticated and nuanced use of the category by subalternists, rather than a weakness since it acts as a crucial counterpoint to the dangers of an incipient essentialism often found in the use of the category. It would seem, therefore, that one can be 'subaltern' in one context and a member of an 'élite' group in another.[43] Such a recognition would also obviate the tendency to represent 'the subaltern' as a homogeneous community devoid of internal hierarchies, hegemonies, and gender politics.[44]

Prakash's subtle distancing of his own work, which he describes as the production of 'post-Orientalist' or 'post-foundationalist' historiographies of the 'Third World', from the Subaltern Studies Collective is interesting in this regard since he clearly shares a great deal in common with their general orientation and political objectives.[45] For Prakash, the emphasis of 'post-Orientalist historiography' is upon a 'disfiguring' or disrupting interrogation of the 'master narratives' of colonialism. The object of such study is not the subaltern as such but the 'forms of knowledge, culture and "traditions" canonized by colonial and hegemonic Western discourses of inquiry'.[46] Another difference is that the site of such intellectual activity is invariably 'the first world academy where the power of the hegemonic Western discourses in the knowledge produced about India appears palpable'.[47] Although, as Prakash himself notes, most of the Subaltern Studies historians have received a 'First World' academic training, his point is presumably that the focal point of 'post-Orientalist historiography' is on the displacement of 'Europe' as the centre of history rather than a recovery of the Indian subaltern. Such an orientation, of course, is deeply consonant with the aims of the Subaltern Studies Collective but is primarily concerned with calling into question Western hegemonies and paradigms of knowledge and highlighting the cultural and material violence of Western colonialism. Such work, of course, may also function as a 'space-clearing exercise' for the emergence of subaltern historiographies, but its concerns are with the displacement of European colonial hegemonies from within the Western academy rather than with the displacement of the élitist and nationalist narratives within India. Indeed, one might ask to what extent this project fundamentally differs from Dipesh Chakrabarty's call to 'provincialize Europe'.

What then is a 'post-foundationalist' or 'post-Orientalist' historiography? For Prakash, such an approach means 'riding more than one horse' at the same time.[48] It is an approach to historiography that does not privilege any particular category or mode of analysis as foundational, emphasizing the mutual imbrication of multiple axes of power and the inherent instability of such categories of analysis. Such an approach is avowedly multifocal in orientation and refuses to adopt fixed or static categories of analysis such as 'class', 'gender' or 'race' to explain the past. For Prakash the problem with a 'foundationalist history' is that it homogenizes the histories that remain heterogeneous with it since it is based upon the assumption that history is ultimately founded upon and representable by some principle of fixed identity, whether that be 'individuality', 'class' or 'ethnicity', and that these fundamental categories resists further decomposition into heterogeneity.[49]

> It is one thing to say that the establishment of capitalist relations has been one of the major features in India's recent history but quite another to regard it as the foundation of colonialism. It is one thing to say that class relations affected a range of power relations in India – involving the caste system, patriarchy, ethnic oppression, Hindu–Muslim conflicts – and quite another to oppose the latter as forms assumed by the former. The issue here is not that of one factor versus several; rather, it is that, as class is inevitably articulated with other determinations, power exists in a form of relationality in which the dominance of one is never complete.[50]

I am less confident than Prakash that such an approach could be described as 'post-foundationalist' since this seems to herald a break with previous scholarly practice that is problematic precisely in so far as it fetishizes its own innovativeness and distinctiveness. The explicit pluralism of 'post-foundationalist' approaches is also in danger of causing such accounts to 'die the death of a thousand qualifications', thereby undermining the effectiveness of both analysis and political action.[51] In response to this, some have appealed to the idea of a confluence of marginalized interests or a 'rainbow alliance', an issue to which we shall return later.[52]

Much of the contemporary reflection that has gone on within 'postcolonial studies' has been informed by the popularity of post-structuralist and postmodernist theories within Western intellectual circles since the 1980s. This involvement begs a serious question. To what extent should the postcolonial agenda be aligned with the kind of anti-representationalism characteristic of much post-structuralist and postmodernist thought?[53] Thus, Nicholas Dirks asks us:

> What does it mean that Edward Said, or Ranajit Guha and the Subaltern Studies collective of Indian historians, take the very same texts by Gramsci, Foucault, or Williams as fundamental that are recited elsewhere in the academy. We ignore at our peril the manifestations of the postcolonial predicament in provincial universities in Asia and Africa where these theorists would all signify elitist forms of exclusion, new Western forms of domination.[54]

The postmodernist and post-structuralist interest in dissolving unities into more complex heterogeneities has much in common with similar postcolonial moves but has been seen by some as undermining the legitimacy of the 'search for an identity' by oppressed groups. Similar issues, of course, have come to the fore in feminist theory. To what extent are 'postmodernism' and post-structuralism allies or enemies of a feminist approach? The problem of aligning oneself with an anti-representationalist stance is aptly summed up by Nancy Hartsock, 'Why is it that just at the moment when so many of us who have been silenced begin to demand the right to name ourselves, to act as subjects rather than objects of history, that just then the concept of subjecthood becomes problematic?'[55] Similarly, Donna Haraway in her outline of feminist standpoint epistemology shows a similar concern for the way in which contemporary forms of social constructivism render all appeals to reality problematic:

> The strong programme in the sociology of knowledge joins with the lovely and nasty tools of semiology and deconstruction to insist on the rhetorical nature of truth ... This is a terrifying view of the relationship between the body and language for those of us who would still like to talk about reality with more confidence than we allow the Christian right's discussion of the Second Coming and their being raptured out of the final destruction of the world. We would like to think our appeals to real worlds are more than a desperate lurch away from cynicism and an act of faith like any other cult's.[56]

One response to this problem is of course an appeal to something like Spivak's notion of 'strategic essentialism'. As 'a strategy for our times', such a context-sensitive stance allows for appeals to humanism in the political interest of oppressed groups such as the following instance, taken from a contemporary Dalit protest song:

> Rise, people, rise up now, break the chains of caste
> Throw off the corpse of slavery, smash the obstacles,
> Rise people –
> We may be Maratha, Mahar, Brahman, Hindu, Muslim, Christian,
> Humanity is all one, all are brothers.[57]

There are, of course, problems involved in adopting such strategic stances. Amanda Anderson argues, for instance, that the 'call to embrace the paradox' involves a privileging of the post-structuralist position. 'By associating essentialism with practice and anti-essentialism with an ultimate theoretical truth, the articulation of strategic essentialism generates a theory/practice split.'[58] Moreover, I would argue that the postmodernist rejection of 'identity' as foundational and pernicious in favour of a decentred and fragmentary self has tended to take the free-floating dislocation of the 'postmodern subject' far too seriously. Instead, emphasis should be placed upon 'identity' as *relational* rather than fragmentary and as embedded in historically produced social forms and political structures rather than disengaged from historical location.

Indeed, what is increasingly clear from the dispute between post-structuralism and humanism is the narrowly Eurocentric way in which the debate has progressed. Why are 'the sovereign and universal subject' of humanism and the radically heterogeneous identity of the anti-humanist camp offered as the only possible alternatives? As we saw in Chapter 2, the rise of humanistic philosophies in the Enlightenment was bound up with the rise of anti-clericalism and a confrontational stance with Christian theology. Equally, the rise of anti-humanisms within contemporary post-structuralist thought aims to overturn the notion of an autonomous and sovereign subject at the centre of history. The critique of humanism is also premised upon a rejection of universalism and the positing of a unified human nature during the Enlightenment period. The Indian Dalit is entitled to respond 'What has this got to do with me?'

The problem for postcolonial theory, which makes its relationship with post-structuralist theory somewhat uneasy, has been that of finding a moral platform from which to speak and a recognition of solidarity both among the oppressed and between divergent groups, having excluded the possibility of a humanistic appeal to a common human nature. Edward Said, as we have seen, refused to take this step and therefore parted company with post-structuralists such as Foucault. Yet why should theorists be limited by the Western framing of this debate? Consider, for instance, the example of Buddhist philosophy. In ancient Buddhist thought there has been no postulation of an all-powerful deity nor of an immortal soul constituting our real and essential identity. The spat between the Church and the secular humanists simply did not occur. In contrast, Buddhist philosophy and practice is grounded upon a realization of the impermanent (*anitya*) and fluctuating nature of the self (*anātman*) and a deeply empathetic realization of the inter-connectedness (*pratītyasamutpāda*) of all sentient beings as impermanent, multifaceted and 'relational' processes.

Given the virulently anti-essentialist stance of most Buddhist philosoph-ical traditions, there could be no possibility of an appeal to a universal human nature or essence as a unifying principle in ethical praxis. Similarly, the sheer radicalness of the Buddhist rejection of an abiding or essential self will allow for no postulation of a sovereign or autonomous subject at the centre of history. Nevertheless, ethical praxis within the Buddhist tradition remains firmly grounded in a recognition of the universality of suffering (*duḥkha*) and the fluidity of boundaries dividing the different 'species' (since all beings experience innumerable embodiments in the 'flowing together' of *saṃsāra* – rebirth). Indeed, it is our non-essentiality (*anātman*) – the rela-tional nature of our existence (*pratītyasamutpāda*) – that we all share in common.

Thus Buddhist philosophical culture allows for a recognition of the universality of suffering among all sentient beings (not just humans) and the cessation of this state of affairs as a primary and *universal* objective. Now I am not suggesting that postcolonial theorists should become Buddhists in order to avoid the Scylla and Charybdis of contemporary postcolonial theory. As in the previous chapter, the introduction of the anti-essentialist universalism of ancient Buddhist thought into the debate at this point is deliberately disruptive on my part. My intention is not to argue that the Buddhist position is true or superior to Western world-views, only to induce a recognition that it is significantly *different*. One could just as easily explore traditional Islamic notions of 'brotherhood' as an alternative to the autonomous subject of Enlightenment humanism. Such disruption is moti-vated on my part by a concern to transgress the limits set up by the opposition of humanism and anti-humanism and thereby to highlight the lacunae in much contemporary postcolonial theorizing – as if the European framings of the debate were the only options available to the postcolonial critic. The introduction of a variety of indigenous epistemic traditions is, in my view, the single most important step that postcolonial studies can take if it is to look beyond the Eurocentric foundations of its theories and contest the epistemic violence of the colonial encounter. This challenge requires engagement with the knowledge-forms and histories of those cultures that have been colonized by the West and, somewhat ironically, provides a role for disciplines such as Indology in the questioning of Western hegemonies and regimes of epistemic violence. Notable in this regard have been the recent collaborations between Spivak and scholars such as the late Bimal Krishna Matilal in exploring ancient Indian paradigms and traditions of knowledge, particularly as a means to 'think beyond' Western theory and examine the ethical subject 'outside its histories in the Judaeo-Christian tradition'.[59]

Postmodernism as a specific cultural and intellectual movement within the West has also tended to be rather narcissistic and self-congratulatory in its claim to have unmasked the universalistic pretensions of all meta-narratives. Postcolonial theory, therefore, should remain wary of the rather premature call for the postmodernist 'to dance upon the grave of modernity' and this is best achieved by displacing 'Europe' and the European paradigms of knowledge that inform much postmodernist reflection from the centre of the postcolonial space. This should involve asking why:

> Third World reality is presumed in First World representations to determine postcolonial discourse exhaustively, whereas postmodernity is able to constitute its own groundless ground rules ... If postmodernism prides itself on its alert deconstruction of any and all master narratives, then postcolonialism too can benefit from alertness to deconstructive strategies ... [It] should seek an interventionist mode, should become not more restricted to the local and particular 'reality' but more engaged with the transnational circuits of theoretical debate.[60]

More recently, Ziauddin Sardar has argued, in *Postmodernism and the Other* (1998), that postmodernism is 'simply a new wave of domination riding on the crest of colonialism and modernity'.[61] This work is worth some attention, though the author has a tendency to homogenize and demonize a variety of trends within Western culture that are classified under the catch-all designation of 'postmodernism'. No attempt, for instance, is made to question the homogeneity of 'the postmodern' itself but Sardar does offer a challenging indictment of cultural and intellectual trends within contemporary Western culture that hits the mark at least as often as it misses its target. The danger of Sardar's sweeping analysis is that it will be ignored by some as setting up a straw man and uncritically embraced by others as part of a resurgent Occidentalism. I find much within Sardar's critique with which I agree, but see fissures and heterogeneities where he sees confluence and homogeneity. I am also less willing to dismiss all post-structuralist thought at a stroke or to identify it with the worst excesses of Baudrillard's work, which for Sardar typifies the postmodernist attitude and its denial of material realities.

Mimesis, hybridity and the ambivalence of colonial discourse

Much of the contemporary literature invoking 'colonial discourse analysis' displays a marked indebtedness to the works of Michel Foucault. For Foucault, power is immanent within the social body being 'the multiplicity of force relations' within society. As such, it should not be conceived of as emanating from a centralized authority, but as dispersed throughout the capillaries of the sphere in which it operates.

Power comes from below; that is, there is no binary and all-encompassing opposition between rulers and ruled at the root of power relations, and serving as a general matrix – no such duality extending from the top down and reacting on more and more limited groups to the very depths of the social body. One must suppose rather that the manifold relationships of force that take shape and come into play in the machinery of production ... are the basis for wide-ranging effects of cleavage that run through the social body as a whole.[62]

Some scholars have argued, however, that the Foucauldian analysis of power results in an acute form of political paralysis.[63] Janaki Nair, for instance, suggests that the Foucauldian concern to avoid a replication of universalizing hegemonic positions may lead scholars only to consider 'irreducibly local' issues. For scholars such as Foucault, de Certeau and a plethora of postcolonial theorists, rejecting a conception of power as something that is 'possessed' by some and not by others in favour of 'the relational character of power relationships' leads to an appreciation that where there is power there is also resistance.[64] For Nair, however, such a position is a 'dilution of power/resistance to a relatively weakened concept, far removed from an emancipatory agenda'.[65] Yet, as Gyan Prakash notes:

[I]t is one thing to acknowledge that political practice requires the notion of agency and quite another to assert that the space for agency must be defined in terms of centered, not dispersed power relations. If agency and 'experience' are attributed to the centering and 'founding' force of power relations, then how can resistance be even conceived except in terms given them by the dominant.[66]

Doubts have also been expressed about the usefulness of Foucauldian analysis for exploring the imperial space.[67] Thus, Ann Stoler argues that:

Europe's eighteenth- and nineteenth-century discourses on sexuality, like other cultural, political, or economic assertions, cannot be charted in Europe alone. In short-circuiting empire, Foucault's history of European sexuality misses key sites in the production of that discourse, discounts the practices that racialized bodies, and thus elides a field of knowledge that provides the contrasts for what a 'healthy, vigorous, bourgeois body' was all about.[68]

Stoler offers us the possibility of recapturing Foucault's work by interlacing his analysis of European sexuality with a postcolonial attention to the politics of empire. Nevertheless, despite criticisms to the contrary (e.g. Sumit Sarkar), Foucault's analysis, in acknowledging the polyphonic and unstable nature of discourses, allows not only for cultural resistance but also for the active reversal of dominant discourses.[69] This, of course, is somewhat in spite of his own interests in the effects of dominant regimes of power in the construction of subjects rather than upon modes of resistance to such hegemonies. I have argued in earlier chapters that Foucault's tendency to underplay the possibilities of resistance to dominant discourses suggests that we consider Michel de Certeau's modifications of Foucault's analysis of power in terms of his emphasis upon the micro-politics of resistance.[70]

> The project entailed by de Certeau's concept of *heterology* is to illuminate the discourse of the other. To illustrate that writing's authority is by no means absolute, that always there is a space (a hole) through which the repressed can return, a gap in the blanket of power which enable the repressed to remain, to evade without exit. The return of the repressed means precisely this: shining lights on the fissures within the fabric of power in order to demonstrate that despite appearances to the contrary the exercise of power is never absolute.[71]

In the field of colonial discourse analysis this conception of power as dispersed throughout the capillaries of the social body has been further developed in the works of Homi Bhabha. Bhabha rejects what he sees as an overly simplistic reading of Foucault in Said's insistence upon 'the intentionality and uni-directionality of colonial power' and in the assumption that colonial power and discourse were possessed entirely by the colonizer.[72] In contrast, Bhabha applies the Derridean notion of '*différance*', denoting the endless deferral and differentiation of meaning within texts in order to emphasize the inherent ambivalence of colonial discourse. This feature of colonial enunciation, Bhabha argues, provides an opportunity for contestation on the part of the colonized subject. As we shall see, however, one of the dangers of Bhabha's account of resistance is that it may further reinforce the hegemonic impact of imperialism.[73]

For Bhabha, colonial power is produced in an *agonistic* space. Colonial discourses, therefore, are not the product of a self-contained (and all-powerful) colonial master but are the result of a *hybridization* process caused by the encounter between the colonialist and native traditions. For Bhabha, this 'reveals the ambivalence at the source of traditional discourses of authority and enables a form of subversion, founded on that uncertainty, that turns the discursive conditions of dominance into the grounds for intervention'.[74] On this view, the meanings and implications of colonial discourses can never be fully contained by authorial intentions. Discourses, like texts, can come to mean different things and be appropriated for heterogeneous purposes. An excellent example of the instability of colonial discourses can be seen, for instance, in the case of the *Ezourvedam*, a spurious French 'translation' of a Hindu Veda. Voltaire used this text to demonstrate the subtlety and superiority of Indian thought in comparison to a decadent Christianity. The text, however, was a 'fake' originally composed by Jesuit missionaries in Pondicherry to demonstrate the inferiority of idolatrous Indians in comparison to Christianity.[75] Discourses, therefore, cannot be controlled once they have entered the public arena and become subject to contestation, appropriation and inversion by others.

The key to the subversion of colonial discourses, according to Bhabha, can be found in the subversive mimesis of the colonialist by the colonized native. This is where Bhabha's notion of hybridity is pressed into service as an example of an anti-colonial subversion 'from within'.

> [Hybridity] is the name for the strategic reversal of the process of domination through disavowal (that is, the production of discriminatory identities that secure the 'pure' and original identity of authority). Hybridity is the revaluation of the assumption of colonial identity through the repetition of discriminatory identity effects ... It unsettles the mimetic or narcissistic demands of colonial power but reimplicates its identifications in strategies of subversion that turn the gaze of the discriminated back upon the eye of power.[76]

For Bhabha, hybridity 'reveals the ambivalence at the source of traditional discourses of authority and enables a form of subversion, founded on that uncertainty, that turns the discursive conditions of dominance into the grounds of intervention'.[77] The ambivalent figure of the English-speaking Indian in British India thus remains central to Bhabha's analysis of hybridity precisely in so far as he or she represents the instability of the colonizer–colonized dichotomy.

The problem, however, with the appeal to mimesis as a counterhegemonic strategy for both the colonial subject and for feminists (as advocated by Irigaray) is that it is difficult to distinguish between *re-presentative* mimesis (that is, merely re-presenting or mirroring the hegemonic stereotype) – an act that involves conformity to the cultural stereotype – and *parodic* mimesis (undoing by overdoing). This is especially problematic given the dominant status of such stereotypes; the parody in parodic mimesis can so easily be subjected to the normative (and therefore prima facie) interpretations of the 'master discourse'.[78] One could also call into question the extent to which such an approach is an effective instrument for counteracting oppression and marginalization. Is parody anything more than a toothless grin – a mocking critique that lacks any real bite? The justification of parody as a strategy also allows dominant discursive practices to remain intact, cushioned from criticism on the grounds that they are merely being ironic.

> Politically speaking, the ironist is extremely hard to assail precisely because it is virtually impossible to fix her or his text convincingly. In the ironic discourse, every position undercuts itself, thus leaving the politically engaged writer in a position where her ironic discourse might just come to deconstruct her own politics.[79]

I do not wish to imply that scholars such as Bhabha and Irigaray intend their appeal to mimesis to be viewed as 'merely ironic'. Far from it.[80] However, it is important to bear in mind that there is a strand of postmodernist thought that is quite conservative in its refusal to acknowledge a sociopolitical position from which one might engage in contestation. Postmodernist interests in the aesthetics of *pastiche* lead far too easily into complicity, albeit *ironic*, with the status quo. Undoing by overdoing has a place as a subversive practice but it is a dangerous strategy, particularly if it is seen as the *primary* means of contestation, since overdoing can so easily be misread and subsumed by hegemonic perspectives.

Nevertheless, despite his recognition of the unstable nature of colonial discourses, Bhabha's appeal to mimicry as the primary means of contesting such discourses ends up reinscribing colonialism as a totalizing presence. In Spivak and Bhabha's analysis there is simply no space in which the colonized can respond to their subjugation other than in the terms already defined by their masters. As Benita Parry points out, on this view there is no Archimedian point beyond the totalizing discourse from which an effectively *different* contestatory stance can be taken. The only option available to the colonized subject is 'to place incendiary devices within the dominant structures of representation and not to confront these with another knowledge'.[81] Similarly, Bhabha's notion of 'hybridity' implies that the colonial space involves the interaction of two originally 'pure' cultures (the British/European and the native) that are only rendered ambivalent once they are brought into direct contact with each other.[82]

In this regard, Bhabha's Derridean-influenced approach differs somewhat from the analysis offered by the Subaltern historians, though the nature of their difference is somewhat effaced by Spivak's 'against the grain' reading of the Subaltern Studies project as a kind of deconstructionist historiography. As I have argued, the appeal to the subaltern as an 'autonomous domain' should be seen not as an attempt to reintroduce a sovereign subject but rather as a rejection of the overestimation of the power of Western imperialism at the expense of the agency of indigenous subalterns. By rejecting the totalization of colonial discourse, the Subaltern Studies historians are attempting to create a space for the emergence of a multiplicity of contestatory discourses that are not constrained by the knowledge paradigms and presuppositions of the colonialist master narrative. Spivak and Bhabha's emphasis upon colonial ambivalence does not seem to allow for the possibility of a subject position that is radically heterogeneous with the colonial episteme.[83] Subalternist accounts of resistance, therefore, necessarily involve the contestation of a variety of fields of dominance, including not only the discourses of the Western colonialist but also the mimetic responses of indigenous Indian élites. Although the latter may have been successful in overthrowing *direct* colonial rule of India, in Subalternist terms the achievement of home rule (*swaraj*) has not led to a participation of 'the people' in their own governance. The nationalism of such élite groups, therefore, reproduced many of the oppressive and élitist structures of the foreign colonizer. The hegemony of the indigenous yet colonially educated élite also continued to represent 'India' according to the categories and stereotypes of the colonial era.

Here we encounter one of the central dilemmas of contemporary post-colonial theory. In rejecting monolithic and unidirectional conceptions of power, postcolonial theorists have attempted to recapture the agency of the colonized subject, thereby avoiding both the erasure of the colonized native from history and a reproduction of colonialist tropes such as the myth of the passive Oriental. However, in blurring the power dichotomy between colonizer and colonized, one is in danger of undermining the historicity of colonialism and underplaying the reality of colonial violence and oppression. Such accounts obscure, in Fanon's terms, 'the murderous and decisive struggle between two protagonists'.[84] Thus, Kyung-Won Lee argues that the 'dialogism' of much contemporary postcolonial theory, grounded as it is in the works of European thinkers such as Bakhtin, Foucault, Gramsci and Derrida, remains fundamentally incompatible with the historical reality of colonialism.

> Given the silence of the natives and the relative absence of discursive interactions between metropole and periphery, colonialist discourse was not a dialogue in a Bakhtinian sense ... If there had been a dialogue at all it might have taken place between 'in-groups' themselves, namely, between dominant and dissident voices within the metropolitan boundaries, not between imperial self and colonial Other.[85]

On the other hand, avoiding the pitfalls of dialogism can lead postcolonial theorists to *overplay* the power and negativity of the colonial encounter at the expense of native agency and resistance. Such accounts are also in danger of privileging the colonial space. As Henry Louis Gates Jr. notes:

> The critical double-bind these charges raise is clear enough. You can empower discursively the native, and open yourself to charges of down-playing the epistemic (and literal) violence of colonialism; or play up the absolute nature of colonial domination, and be open to the charges of negating the subjectivity and agency of the colonized, thus textually replicating the repressive operations of colonialism. In agency, so it seems, begins responsibility.[86]

One way to overcome this dilemma is by dissolving the easy polarization of the two options. Accepting a dispersed model of power and the polyphonic nature of discourses for the good reasons highlighted earlier offers a complex and multidimensional analysis of the fluidity of power relations. Nevertheless, this blurring of the Manichean distinction between colonizer and colonized (JanMohamed) must *at the same time* take account of the very real disparity in power relations between the two. Acceptance of a dialogical (and broadly Foucauldian) model of power as dispersed throughout the social body does not *in and of itself* require us to dispense with the distinction between the 'relatively empowered' and the 'relatively disempowered'. As Prakash points out, the postcolonial interest in dialogical theories is grounded not in a postmodernist exaltation of the pleasures of Bakhtinian carnivalesque, but in a highly politicized engagement with the profound imbalance in relations of domination.[87] Nevertheless, such an approach must also point to the complicity between the colonizer and the colonized élite. We must bear in mind that the interaction between colonizer and colonized has often been at the expense of those who have been silenced – namely indigenous, subaltern groups.

As Rosalind O'Hanlon points out, colonialist discourses about India were produced in a power dynamic involving *three* parties: (1) the Orientalist scholar, (2) the native informant and (3) those others among the colonized unable to represent themselves, and, therefore, reliant upon (2) for representation. Consequently, Orientalist discourses remained unstable and ambivalent in their trajectories precisely because:

> the seemingly omnipotent classifications of the Orientalist were vulnerable to purposeful misconstruction and appropriation to uses which he never intended, precisely because they had incorporated into them the readings and the political concerns of his native informants. It is this sense of mutuality – not as common contribution but as struggle and contestation – which is missing from much contemporary discussion of discourse ..., the ever present possibility of reversal, in the play of power itself between agents.[88]

To varying degrees both (2) and (3) might be described as subordinate to the Orientalist scholar and thereby to some degree 'subaltern', though the tendency of the Subaltern historians has been to identify group (2) with indigenous élites such as the nationalists and, therefore, part of the problem rather than the solution. This presents us with a number of questions related to the degrees of confluence between these three groups. To what extent can one read Orientalist discourses 'against the grain' – that is, provide counter-readings in order to highlight those positions that have been silenced or transformed by the Western colonial filter? Equally, to what extent should we problematize Orientalist and native representations of those groups for whom self-representation was an impossibility?

I have suggested in previous chapters that the problematization of Orientalist discourses must also involve a questioning of the authority of those who have claimed to represent India and its people. Highlighting the ways in which the anti-colonial discourses often inverted rather than displaced Orientalist motifs, tropes and stereotypes enables us to see that the focus upon a select group of individuals as representative icons of an essentialized 'India' itself effaces the subaltern voice.[89] Certain indigenous figures have come to function as representatives of a variety of 'imagined communities' (for example, Vivekānanda and Daisetz Suzuki as the spokesmen for 'Hinduism' and 'Zen Buddhism'). The anti-colonial discourses of Vivekānanda, of course, did wonders to invigorate Hindus and restore their sense of self-worth. We can admire the ways in which Vivekānanda, like an expert in judo, used the essentialist classification of India in Western Orientalist discourses to undermine claims of the superiority of the West. The result of this dialogical and mimetic process, however, has not been to displace or overthrow prevailing Orientalist stereotypes about 'India' but to further reinforce them. As Seyla Benhabib argues:

> The traditional politics of the subject assumes that there is one group of humans whose strategic position uniquely entitles them to represent the plurality. The philosophy of the subject always searches for a particular group – be it the proletariat, women, the avant-garde, Third World revolutionaries, or the Party – whose particularity represents universality as such. The politics of empowerment, by contrast, proceeds from the assumption that there is no single spot in the social structure that privileges those who occupy it with a vision of the social totality. This is so not only because late-capitalist societies and their grievances generate a pluralization of social victims, their objectives, and their modes of struggle, but also because the experience of difference that cannot be co-opted in imposed identity is liberatory.[90]

The mutual imbrication of religion, culture and power

Readers will no doubt have noticed the Foucauldian imprint upon this work, modified though it is by Michel de Certeau's emphasis upon the micropolitics of resistance. Foucauldian analysis provides us with a useful pair of spectacles for drawing attention to the power relations involved in truth/knowledge-claims.[91] The Foucauldian emphasis upon a network of 'force relations' might seem to provide rather a negative and conflictual account of the operations of power. Foucault's conception of power, however, is complex and multifaceted and his work can be seen as an attempt to subvert notions of 'power' as necessarily 'destructive', repressive or based upon a dichotomy between those who possess power and those who do not. As Amit Rai notes, an acknowledgement of the polyvalence of discourse replaces a politics of *negation* (the view that colonial discourse silences or negates the colonized) with a politics of *negotiation*. This ambivalent and contested space, therefore, is not concerned so much with recapturing the silenced voices of history as interrogating the multiple strategies that lead to hybrid identities and the mutual imbrication of colonizer and colonized.[92]

Nevertheless, the reception of Foucault's works and the subversive tenor of his writing has tended to inculcate a 'hermeneutics of suspicion' with regard to all knowledge/truth-claims. For Dorothy Figueira, for instance, 'the present-day desire to subsume everything under a hegemonic agenda ignores the rich history of extra-political motivations'. Figueira argues that the totalization of discourse has ignored the role of individual intentions and therefore prefers a more Gadamerian and psychologically nuanced approach to the study of Orientalist literature. The problem with an exclusive emphasis upon the politics of knowledge, she argues, is that:

> Nothing much exists beyond Foucault's epistemic power, Derrida's logocentric thought and Said's Orientalist discourse. All is viewed as repetition with *Différence* (*sic*) ... By halting the discussion at the concept of power, interweaving, imbricating, and embedding all discussions in multiple reveries concerning the variations of domination/dominated relationships, the critic's fantasies all too often promiscuously displace the consciously fictionalized object of inquiry.[93]

When approached as a totalistic system of explanation, Foucault's approach is in danger of becoming a form of political reductionism. As anthropologist Steven Parrish remarks:

> Where we pursued symbols yesterday, today we reduce all to what Foucault termed 'the monotony of power', and detach 'culture' from lived worlds, reifying self, life, and action into the arid and seamless one-dimensionality of 'discourse' – while waiting for tomorrow's concept to slouch onto the scene ... However, I do not think we can reduce human life to power, to discourse, even to culture. Life is bigger, more tangled, more nuanced and multi-dimensional than even the best of our theories allows for.[94]

It is necessary, therefore, to appreciate Foucault's mode of analysis for what it is: namely, a lens for examining a particular dimension of the sociocultural dynamic and in no sense to be taken as a definitive or all-encompassing position that *reduces* everything to power relations. The latter attempt to 'discipline' Foucault's work is a move that is not easily rendered compatible with his own Nietzschean-style perspectivism. Indeed, one might even argue that in Foucault's later work he was looking to go beyond 'power' as the definitive category of analysis.[95] It is important to remember that Foucault was explicit in his acknowledgement of the limitations of his own work and in the refusal to tell others how to think. As an explicitly *strategic* writer he remarked that:

> All my books ... are little tool boxes ... [I]f people want to open them, to use this sentence or that idea as a screwdriver or spanner to short-circuit, discredit or smash systems of power, including eventually those from which my books have emerged ... so much the better.[96]

This challenge has been taken up by Lisa Lowe who uses Foucault's notion of *heterotopia* – 'the spaces of otherness' – to provide a challenge to the totalization of Orientalist discourses in Edward Said's work. Lowe displaces the emphasis upon Orientalism as a self-contained set of power relations by drawing attention to the mutual imbrication of a variety of discursive sites as they are mediated through culture.

> I want to render more complex Foucault's sense of oppositional spatial heterogeneities by taking it out of its ultimately binary frame of opposi-tions to recast spatial difference in terms of multiple sites. That is, on discursive terrains, such as the one in which orientalism is one forma-tion, articulations and rearticulations emerge from a variety of positions and sites, as well as from other sets of representational relations, including those that figure class, race, nation, gender and sexuality.[97]

How might one classify the project that I have undertaken? I remain supportive of the general aims of the Subaltern Studies Collective, though the focus of this study can hardly be described as Subalternist, particularly in so far as it has focused not upon the subaltern but upon the élitist discourses of Western Orientalism. However, I see this work as occupying a place within the growing field of 'Colonial Discourse Analysis' that has been precipitated by the influence of Edward Said's *Orientalism* and the develop-ment of postcolonial theory/studies since the 1980s. Locating the discussion within the disciplinary fields of 'religious studies' and 'Indology', my aim has been to displace the Orientalist dichotomy between 'East' and 'West' through a critical examination of the way in which a hyperreal (Christian/secular) 'Europe' has been defined in opposition to a hyperreal (Hindu/religious) 'India'. In stating my position in the language of 'hyperre-ality', I am not arguing that 'there is nothing out there to which these terms refer' – a kind of postmodernist, linguistic idealism that ignores the material realities of colonial violence.[98] Rather, I wish to highlight the sense in which the existence of such constructs as 'Europe' and 'India' are relational, inter-dependent, unstable and crucially *unrepresentative*. The instability of binary oppositions – and the slippage between them – consistently draws attention to their failure to contain the heterogeneities they are claimed to represent. This indeed is the highly nuanced stance taken by Edward Said in *Orientalism*. By refusing to offer an alternative account of an 'authentic' or 'real' Orient, Said argued for a displacement of the 'East–West' dichotomy itself as well as the tendency to speak of the 'Orient' as if it were a unitary and homogeneous entity. This does not leave one dealing with an 'endless play of representations' with no recourse to material realities. Crucially, and this is where I agree with Said's rejection of a radically anti-representational epistemology, it is the *unrepresentative* nature of the 'East–West' dichotomy – its failure to relate to the complexities of material reality – which necessi-tates its active displacement by a 'discourse of heterogeneity'.

What is required of the study of Indian culture and 'religion' in a post-colonial context is an attempt to think across or beyond traditional Orientalist representations – to 'transgress the boundaries' imposed by normative Western models of 'religion'. This must involve an interrogation and displacement of Western (Judaeo-Christian/secular) paradigms of what 'religion' is, a problem that continues to dog the discipline of 'religious studies', despite appeals to its apparently non-confessional and non-theological orientation. Such an approach should resist the temptation to redefine 'religion', if by that one means to treat it as an isolated cultural phenomenon, divorced from social, political and economic relations of power. As Talal Asad has pointed out, this is an invitation to separate religion from the realm of politics. One can abstract 'the religious' from the wider cultural dynamic in which it operates but this remains a purely intellectual abstraction. 'Religion', therefore, is a theoretical construction useful for the purposes of examining one particular aspect of the human experience but should not be reified, as if it could exist apart from that context. Increasing academic specialization, appeals to the *sui generis* and privileged status of religion, and the legitimation and preservation of the institutional 'expert on religion' in the secular Academy, have all led to a tendency to treat 'religion' as if it were more than an explanatory construct with a particular cultural and ideological genealogy of its own.

To reiterate a point made in Chapter 3, problematizing the 'textualization' of religion does not mean ignoring textual manifestations of 'religion' nor abandoning close textual analysis. However, it can no longer be claimed that a careful study of, say, Vedāntic texts will provide us with privileged access to some essentialized 'Hindu mind'. Similarly, scholars must acknowledge that the way in which one approaches the study of religion (indeed the way in which one defines or constructs such a study) reflects ideological positioning. Scholars may not always be aware of the political ramifications or ideological underpinning of their approaches but this does not make such approaches any less *political*.

Ivan Strenski has argued that:

> Surely the reason people designate some portion of their experience as 'religious' is not because of the powerhouse of western intellectual life, modern Religious Studies. It is frankly ludicrous to imply that the academic study of religion, so meager in its resources, has hegemonically imposed a concept of 'religion' on the wretched of the earth, as some of our comrades believe.[99]

Strenski is right to question the power fantasies of the contemporary academic in this regard and points to the Waco tragedy as an example of how powerless scholars of religion are in practice when it comes to influencing public discussion and understanding of such events. Nevertheless, it is misleading to divorce academics from the wider cultural context in which they work and from the network of power relations that locates the scholar as both an institutionally inscribed 'expert' as well as a privileged commentator upon certain cultural and political events. To refuse the opportunity to examine and criticize the power dynamic implied in the use of taken-for-granted categories (such as 'religion', 'Hinduism' and 'mysticism') on the grounds that one is relatively impotent as an initiator of popular cultural change is to misunderstand the fluid and diversified nature of power and to abdicate the responsibility that accompanies one's role as a commentator upon and a conduit of wider cultural trends. As Edward Said has noted:

> [C]ultural forms like the novel or the opera do not cause people to go out and imperialize – Carlyle did not drive Rhodes directly, and he certainly cannot be 'blamed' for the problems in today's southern Africa – but ... [w]e are entitled to ask how this body of humanistic ideas co-existed so comfortably with imperialism, and why – until the resistance to imperialism in the imperial domain, among Africans, Asians, Latin Americans, developed – there was little significant opposition or deference to empire at home.[100]

Throughout this work I have argued that the central normative concepts of the discipline of 'religious studies' – terms such as 'religion' and 'mysticism', as well as constructs such as 'Hinduism' and 'Buddhism' – have a discursive history that is bound up with the power struggles and theological issues of Western Christianity. What is required for the comparative study of 'religion' to move into a postcolonial space, therefore, is a conscious attempt to develop new conceptual models and methodological frameworks for the comparative study of cultures. Michael Pye has recently called for a proliferation of 'ethno-critical' perspectives within the study of religion to counteract the Christian theological factors that have conditioned the history of the discipline.

> If there is need for a gender-critical approach to the study of religion, there is also a need for an Afro-critical approach and a Sino-critical approach – that is, for approaches that allow African and Chinese perceptions of religion to influence our view of its shape.[101]

This is vital for the comparative study of religion, not only in avoiding a reinforcement (however unintentional) of the Europeanization of other cultures but also in order to take account of the religious pluralism that is now the norm rather than the exception, especially within the major metropolitan centres and urban settlements of Europe and North America. However, it is important that the proliferation of such perspectives does not lead to fragmentation, and scholars wishing to explore alternative cultural models for understanding religion must be prepared to consider this to be a truly *comparative* exercise. Replacing Western Christian models of religion with Indian, African or Chinese conceptual frameworks not only creates the danger of falling into the trap of cultural isolationism and a chauvinistic indigenism but may also ignore the heterogeneity of these cultures themselves. There is no single 'Indian', 'Chinese' or 'African' way of looking at the world, just as there is no definitive 'gender-critical stance' from which to approach the study of religion. A lesson to learn from the explosion of feminist approaches to the study of religion, I think, is not to fear a heterogeneity of perspectives, so long as the goals of such approaches remain reasonably consonant with each other (that is, the critique of patriarchy and the end of masculinist oppression of women and men), however differently conceived.

Moreover, such approaches, in my view, should not base themselves upon the nationalist mode of classification, which, as the Subalternist historians have aptly demonstrated, is itself a 'derivative discourse'. Thus the exploration of an 'Indo-critical' perspective within religious studies and Indology should not be seen as an exploration of *the* Indian response to a given situation. The '-critical' aspect of the enterprise must remain as vigilantly self-reflexive as it is critical of Western epistemic hegemony. Nevertheless, such an approach must involve itself in the development of critical perspectives that are grounded in (though not subsumed by) Indian cultural and epistemic forms.

In his call for an indigenous 'ethnosociology' of India, McKim Marriott has argued that:

> All social sciences develop from thought about what is known to particular cultures and are thus 'cultural' or 'ethno-' social sciences in their origins ... The assertion that all social sciences are cultural (and therefore '-emic') amounts to denying the privileged position claimed for an imaginary '-etic' social science, which is really derived from the investigator's emics.[102]

Marriott's stance reflects a concern to show a much greater sensitivity to indigenous categories and approaches in the study of Indian culture. At first glance, Marriott's project sounds rather like the project of 'provincializing Europe', but his stance pays no attention to problems of reconstructing the indigenous after British imperialism, nor does he seem particularly concerned with the epistemological problems and political dangers of his call for indigenism.[103]

It is important to demonstrate that the colonization of the past by contemporary Hindu nationalist movements is itself a power construction that marginalizes certain groups (such as Indian Muslims) at the same time as it subsumes others (such as Buddhists, Jains, and Sikhs) through the elision of 'Indian' with 'Hindu'.[104] Moreover, nationalist discourses have tended to subordinate subaltern groups and perspectives that are asked to rally together 'for the good of the nation'.[105] Nevertheless, the Hindu nationalism of the Bharatiya Janata Party has developed a strong ground-swell of support among middle-class women and has offered a unique opportunity for women to become involved in public life in India, in some cases inciting men to violence in the name of Hindutva.[106] This demon-strates precisely what is at issue here – a critique of patriarchy and a chauvinistic masculinism or militarism, whether expressed by men or women.

Critics of the Western colonial legacy should not allow themselves to be 'blackmailed' into thinking that there are only two alternatives – Western colonialism or Hindu nationalism – and that to repudiate the former is to align with the latter.[107] For this reason, Brian K. Smith is incorrect to think that the only alternative to secularism in India is Hindu nationalism, for, as he himself admits, 'There are other indigenous voices besides those of the Hindutva faction that can and should be heard; their representations also must be thrown into the mix.' I am in full agreement with Smith's conclusion that 'after Ayodhya, Western observers must choose which of the multi-plicity of Indian insiders they wish to support with their representations',[108] but I remain unwilling to accept that a critique of imperialism and secu-larism (on the grounds that they are 'Western' or that they constitute another form of 'religion') necessarily leads to complicity with the forces of religious conservatism. By 'anthropologizing' (rendering exotic) Western secular forms of nationalism and contemporary Hindu nationalisms, one calls into question such either/or dichotomies and creates a space for alter-native models to emerge in a post-nationalist world. Equally, by calling into question constructs such as the 'world religions' (see Chapters 2 and 3), one is also questioning the homogenizing function of constructs such as 'Hinduism' and 'Hindu nationalism' and creating a space for heterogeneity and (non-oppositional) differences to be heard.

As we have seen, for postcolonial critics such as Gayatri Spivak, there can be no return to a pure nativism 'after the planned epistemic violence of the imperialist project'.[109] Nevertheless, the paralysis that this totalization of the imperial space might seem to induce should not prevent us from a dogged refusal to be limited by the horizons of recent history, from taking that 'impossible step' – to think 'beyond the epistemic violence of colo-nialism'.[110] Spivak is right in her refusal to endorse a nativist or atavistic nostalgia for lost origins. Colonialism may have inextricably transformed non-Western forms of knowledge. I refuse to believe, however, that it has wholeheartedly eradicated them. Moving forward, then, must also involve looking back with renewed vigour at the legacy of precolonial forms of indigenous knowledge. To fail to do so is to concede defeat to colonialism and to accept as unproblematic Western-derived notions of 'modernity', thereby cutting ourselves off from our disparate pasts. Questioning the seductive allure of modernity need not involve a nativist appropriation of 'tradition' if one is prepared to displace the binary opposition between tradi-tion and modernity that has characterized post-Enlightenment thought in its modernist and postmodernist variations. Accepting that the modern world is rooted in a variety of historical tributaries and that these traditions remain alive *within* and *in spite of* modernity is a first step in the displacement of this central post-Enlightenment dichotomy. Similarly, going 'beyond Orientalism' should not be seen as the end of 'Indology' as an academic practice within Western academia, as this would be to give up any hope of mutuality in the intellectual encounter between India and 'the West'. Nevertheless, taking 'the postcolonial turn' must necessarily involve the transformation of Indology as a discipline and regime of knowledge.

'Postcolonial criticism', of course can mean different things to different people, ranging from a challenge to Eurocentrism (both from outside or within the metropolitan centre) to resistance to the totalizing conceptualization of the nation.[111] Bearing this in mind, postcolonial approaches must remain sensitive to context. It is important to pay attention not only to what is said and by whom (the social location of the speaker) but also where such speech goes and how it is received. If the work of Mikhail Bakhtin has taught us anything it is that we should be mindful of the diverse ways in which our words can be appropriated and reinterpreted by others. Much of the concern that Aijaz Ahmed expresses with Ronald Inden's attempt to 'recapture authentic Indian agency' reflects anxieties not only about the social location of the author but also about the dangers involved in the reception and appropriation of his work by right-wing reactionary forces within contemporary India.[112] Although one can never be held responsible for the way in which one's words are understood and applied by others, it is important to remain mindful of the ways in which they *might* be applied.

Similarly, Linda Alcoff challenges postcolonial writers to consider the material effects of their statements by asking the crucial question – does your narrative enable the empowerment of oppressed groups?[113] In this sense, intellectuals involved in 'the postcolonial turn' should avoid the tendency to indulge in theoretical hair-splitting (a useful exercise in gaining tenure but distracting from the political aims of 'postcolonialism'),[114] and become, as Stephen Slemon argues, more tolerant of methodological difference, especially when the common goal is an anti-colonial emancipation of the oppressed.[115]

Indeed it is in this context that the debate between 'universalism' and 'cultural relativism' is shown to be something of an intellectual 'red herring' so long as it ignores the power relations that produce differences both within and between cultures.[116] As Dipesh Chakrabarty remarks:

> For the point is not that Enlightenment rationalism is always unreasonable in itself but rather a matter of documenting how – through what historical process – its 'reason', which was not always self-evident to everyone, has been made to look 'obvious' far beyond the ground where it originated. If a language, as has been said, is but a dialect backed up by an army, the same could be said of the narratives of 'modernity' that,

almost universally today, point to a certain 'Europe' as the primary habitus of the modern.[117]

As we noted in Chapter 3, this involves a rejection of the monadic essentialism that characterizes much of what passes for 'cultural relativism', aligned with a displacement of the myth of the autonomous sovereign agent or culture.[118] However, as Gupta and Ferguson suggest, 'if one begins with the premise that spaces have always been hierarchically interconnected, instead of naturally disconnected, then cultural and social change becomes not a matter of cultural contact and articulation but one of rethinking difference *through* connection'.[119] This opens up the possibility of a new comparativism grounded in an awareness and investigation of heterogeneities and cross-cultural parallels and the destabilization of fixed, oppositional and homogenized entities such as 'India' and 'Europe'.[120] Such an approach avoids the essentializing of differences that has characterized most forms of cultural relativism (isolationism) but does not thereby fall back into a universalist discourse of homogeneity. Simply speaking, this represents a recognition that there are differences and similarities to be noted within as well as between cultures. The comparativism of the postcolonial space, however, must develop a keen awareness of the *multiple* axes of power relations. As Anne McClintock argues:

> [I]mperialism cannot be understood without a theory of gender power. Gender power was not the superficial patina of empire, an ephemeral gloss over the more decisive mechanisms of class and race. Rather, gender dynamics were, from the outset, fundamental to the securing and maintenance of the imperial enterprise.[121]

Similarly, works such as Mrinalini Sinha's *Colonial Masculinity* (1995) highlight the mutual imbrication of British and Bengali conceptions of gender, race and sexuality during the nineteenth century in order to highlight 'the multiple axes of domination and subordination in colonial Indian society as a whole'.[122] In this regard, Sinha's work is part of a wider trend within recent feminist scholarship that has questioned analysis of the 'sex–gender system' that is conceived narrowly as the history of women and sexuality. The category of gender, on this view, is a 'useful category of analysis' for examining the heterogeneity of power relations within society. For Sinha this means that 'since the experience of gender itself is deeply implicated in other categories such as class/caste, race, nation, and sexuality, an exclusive focus on gender can never be adequate for a feminist historiography'.[123] Thus it is important to bear in mind that patriarchy and gender issues in the modern era cannot be divorced from a theory of colonial power. As my colleague Jeremy Carrette and I have argued elsewhere:

When entering a cross-cultural space it is important to realize the sense in which western feminist debates can become implicated with issues of colonial authority and the might (as opposed to the right) of certain cultures to classify, locate and manipulate others. As Sinha reminds us, the critique of patriarchy within non-western religions and cultures must remain mindful of the sense in which a merely gendered perspective will not suffice so long as it ignores the broader network of issues and tensions caused by the disparity in power-relations between the cultures of the west and 'the rest'. In other words, gender studies within the comparative study of religion must maintain a vigilant awareness not only of the impact of race, class and sexuality upon constructions of gender identity but of the dangers of complicity with colonial agendas when involved in the enterprise of cross-cultural comparison and evaluation.[124]

Primary to this emerging style of comparativism is a recognition of the mutual imbrication of a variety of axes of domination as well as a concern for the mutuality of cross-cultural interaction and influence, thereby opening up a space for comparative dialogue and preventing isolationist appeals to indigenism.[125] In this sense, both universalist and ethno-specific accounts of history are rendered inadequate. Such an approach also involves a shift in emphasis away from the epistemological concern with 'how is translation and cross-cultural engagement possible?' towards a consideration of the material realities underlying the politics of difference. In the words of Gupta and Ferguson:

> [W]e want to problematize the unity of 'us' and the otherness of the 'other', and question the radical separation between the two that makes the opposition possible in the first place. We are interested less in establishing a dialogic relation between geographically distinct societies than in exploring the processes of production of difference in a world of culturally, socially, and economically interconnected and interdependent spaces.[126]

The development of 'Indo-critical' approaches, therefore, should be grounded in a commitment to a comparative dialogism both between and within cultures. McKim Marriott's search for an authentic Indian 'ethnosociology' displays a tendency to homogenize India at a number of levels and cannot succeed so long as it is conceived as a unified enterprise.[127] Whose India are we talking about here? Such a project must also already be a *comparative* one – one cannot construct an Indian ethnosociology without recognizing both the heterogeneity of Indian culture and the role that Western imperialism has played in reconfiguring Indian forms of knowledge.[128] Rabindra Ray in fact argues that the search for an ethnosociology of India is itself a Western enterprise. Why, he asks, if it is so important, are

Indians not doing it themselves?[129] In response, one could point to the work of the Subalternist historians and anthropologists such as Arjun Appadurai (though crucially these are all *diaspora* intellectuals). However, native Indians (particularly those educated according to the standards of the modern metropolitan university) cannot themselves claim to be free from Western influence. This is the problem highlighted by Spivak's rejection of a return to the indigenous. The sheer violence of Western imperialism has transformed everything that it has come into contact with, though not, I would argue, to such an extent that we can find no evidence of influence in the other direction. As Gyan Prakash points out in his analysis of the transformation that occurred when 'science went native' in nineteenth-century India:

> [T]he imbalance of power between the white and the black does not disappear but acquires a different balance after the two have been imbricated ... [T]he subject of representation (the West, science, the 'native') is always different from, and can never contain and control, the act of its signification.[130]

Prakash's analysis shows how Western rhetoric about the 'universality of science' was pressed into service by native Indians in a way that limited the power of Western scientific narratives. If science is truly universal, it cannot be limited to Western approaches, thereby legitimating indigenous forms of knowledge such as āyurvedic medical practices. Moreover, if science is truly universal then there can be no scientific grounds for excluding Indians from the practice of science. As Prakash points out, the European appeal to universalism tended to undermine colonial discourses, based as they were upon the separation of the colonizer from the colonized.

Similarly, this position also led to a questioning of the use of English as the linguistic medium for scientific teaching and practice. Why could one not have Bengali science? This final example is a wonderful demonstration of the way in which the global authority of science as a cultural phenomenon is bound up with the might of Western imperialism. English became the international language of science and was thereby further legitimated as the international language of scientific discourse and objectivity at the same time as science gained some of its cultural authority through the medium of English as the language of the colonial master.[131]

What, then, is the role of the academic in this new situation? Bryan Turner has suggested four intellectual responses to the problem of 'orientalism'.[132] First, there should be a commitment to self-reflexivity – that is, an awareness of the way in which one's own prejudices (in a Gadamerian sense) impinge upon the representation of that which one is examining. This involves the adoption of a firmly anti-essentialist stance, avoiding easy dichotomies and stereotypical formulations of complex heterogeneities. Second, Turner suggests that the 'discourse of difference' that has characterized the Orientalist problematic in the past should be replaced by a 'discourse of sameness', which examines diverse cultures 'within a global context of interpenetration with the world-system'.[133] Third, scholarship should work to displace the 'nationalistic' mode of analysis and the cultural parochialism that such approaches encourage. Finally, Turner argues, 'the anthropological gaze should also be directed towards the otherness of Western culture in order to dislodge the privileged position of dominant Western cultures'.[134] A mere half a century after the establishment of Independence from colonial rule in India, such a task has barely begun. Within the emerging postcolonial framework there must be a willingness to transgress, or think beyond traditional intellectual, disciplinary and cultural boundaries – to consider 'the stark impossibility of thinking *that*'.[135] To some degree, Turner is right to suggest that this is consonant with traditional, critical scholarship at its best. For Turner, 'feminist methodology is just good sociology'.[136] However, such a characterization ignores the overtly political nature of feminist and 'post-Orientalist' scholarship that stands in stark contrast to traditional notions of the academic as a 'detached observer'. Postcolonial scholarship must continue to work within the creative space between a utopian idealism and the pragmatic requirements of politics at the local level. As Gayatri Spivak states:

> [I]f we engage ourselves not only in the end of exploitation of our own community, but for the distant and impossible but necessary horizon of the end of exploitation, then we will not be confined within fantasmic and divisive cultural boundaries.[137]

Notes

Introduction

1 Nicholas B. Dirks, 'The original caste', in McKim Marriott (ed.), *India Through Hindu Categories*, London, Sage Publications, 1990, p. 61.
2 Ashis Nandy, *The Intimate Enemy: Loss and Recovery of Self under Colonialism*, Delhi, Oxford University Press, 1983, pp. 71–2.
3 Paul Rabinow, 'Representations are social facts: modernity and post-modernity in anthropology', in James Clifford and George E. Marcus (eds), *Writing Culture: The Poetics and Politics of Ethnography*, Berkeley, University of California Press, 1986, p. 241.
4 Bernard McGrane, *Beyond Anthropology: Society and the Other*, New York, Columbia University Press, 1989, p. 5.
5 Julius Lipner, *The Face of Truth: A Study of Meaning and Metaphysics in the Vedāntic Theology of Rāmānuja*, Albany, State University of New York Press, 1986, p. x.

1 The power of definitions

1 Michel de Certeau, *The Practice of Everyday Life*, translated by Steven Rendall, Berkeley, University of California Press, 1984, p. 50.
2 Bernard McGill, *The Foundations of Mysticism*, Vol. 1, London, SCM Press, 1991, p. 267.
3 Michel de Certeau, ' "Mystique" au XVIIe siècle: Le problème du langage "mystique" ', in *L'Homme devant Dieu: Mélanges offerts au Père Henri du Lubac*, Vol. 2, Paris, Aubier, 1964, pp. 267–91.
4 See Margaret Smith, 'The nature and meaning of mysticism', in Richard Woods (ed.), *Understanding Mysticism*, London, Athlone Press, 1980, p. 20.
5 Evelyn Underhill, 'The essentials of mysticism', in Woods, *Understanding Mysticism*, pp. 29–30.
6 Ibid., p. 28.
7 Grace Jantzen, 'Mysticism and experience', in *Religious Studies* 25, 1989, pp. 295–315.
8 Hans Penner has argued that ' "mysticism" is an illusion, unreal, a false category that has distorted an important aspect of religion. This is not to imply that the assertions made by yogis, Śaṃkara, St John of the Cross, or Eckhart are unreal or illusory. It is precisely such puzzling data that have led scholars to construct so-called mystical systems and, in turn, to see "mysticism" as the essence of religion.' Hans H. Penner, 'The mystical illusion', in Steven Katz (ed.), *Mysticism and Religious Traditions*, New York, Oxford University Press, 1983, p. 89.

9 Grace Jantzen, *Power, Gender and Christian Mysticism*, Cambridge, Cambridge Studies in Ideology and Religion 8, Cambridge University Press, 1995, p. 12.

10 Talal Asad, *Genealogies of Religion: Discipline and Reasons of Power in Christianity and Islam*, London, Johns Hopkins University Press, 1993, p. 29.

11 Jantzen, *Power, Gender and Christian Mysticism*, p. 14.

12 For an insightful and pertinent critique of this stance, I refer the reader to Russell McCutcheon, *Manufacturing Religion: The Discourse on Sui Generis Religion and the Politics of Nostalgia*, New York and Oxford, Oxford University Press, 1997.

13 Jonathan Z. Smith, *Imagining Religion: From Babylon to Jonestown*, Chicago, University of Chicago Press, 1982, p. xi.

14 Asad, *Genealogies of Religion*, p. 28.

15 Bryan Wilson, *Contemporary Transformations of Religion*, Oxford, Oxford University Press, 1976, p. 277.

16 This is a thesis propounded in numerous publications by Ninian Smart. More recently see the discussion in John E. Smith, *Quasi-Religions: Humanism, Marxism and Nationalism*, London, Macmillan, 1994.

17 See Peter Moore, 'Mystical experience, mystical doctrine, mystical technique', in Steven Katz (ed.), *Mysticism and Philosophical Analysis*, New York, Oxford University Press, 1978, p. 119.

18 Louis Bouyer, *The Christian Mystery: From Pagan Myth to Christian Mysticism*, Edinburgh, T. and T. Clark, 1990. See also Bouyer, 'Mysticism: an essay on the history of the word', in Woods (ed.), *Understanding Mysticism*, pp. 42–55.

19 Thus, members of the Church collective represent the *Corpus Mysticum* or 'mystical body' of Christ (see 1 Corinthians 12.12–28) as linked to the liturgy – the Eucharistic sacrament. Similarly, understanding the biblical message requires a contemplative knowledge of God and that contemplative knowledge is itself dependent upon a correct understanding of scripture, and so on.

20 Augustine distinguished between what he called *signa propria* – when linguistic signs are used to refer to something else, what became known as *allegoria in verbis* (allegory in words) and *signa naturalia* – when really existent things (*res*) – that is objects, persons, events created by God, have subtle meanings beyond the human, everyday level.

21 Justin Martyr, I *Apology* 55, quoted in Robert Doran, *Birth of a Worldview: Early Christianity in its Jewish and Pagan Context*, Boulder and Oxford, Westview Press, 1995, p. 75.

22 *Luther's Works*, Vol. 39, p. 178, quoted in Gerald L. Bruns, *Hermeneutics, Ancient and Modern*, New Haven and London, Yale University Press, 1992, p. 143.

23 *Luther's Works*, Vol. 6, pp. 561–2, quoted in Michel de Certeau, *The Mystic Fable*, Vol. 1. *The Sixteenth and Seventeenth Centuries*, translated by Michael B. Smith, Chicago, University of Chicago Press, 1992, p. 95.

24 Certeau, *The Mystic Fable*, pp. 95–101.

25 As Pascal noted there are two types of meaning, 'the literal' and 'the mystical'. Pascal, *Works*, Vol. 6, p. 89, quoted in Certeau, *The Mystic Fable*, p. 95.

26 Sandra Schneiders, 'Scripture and spirituality', in Bernard McGinn, John Meyendorff and Jean Leclerq (eds), *Christian Spirituality: Origins to the Twelfth Century*, New York, Crossroads Publishing Co., 1985, pp. 16–17.

27 Certeau, 'Mystic speech', ch. 6 of *Heterologies: Discourses on the Other*, Manchester, Manchester University Press, 1986, p. 82.

28 Luce Irigaray, *Speculum of the Other Woman*, translation by Gillian C. Gill, Ithaca, NY, Cornell University Press, 1985, p. 191.

29 Elizabeth A. Petroff (ed.), *Medieval Women's Visionary Literature*, Oxford, Oxford University Press, 1986, p. 7.
30 Julian of Norwich, *A Book of Showings*, short text, ch. 6, 1:222. Note that this is not found in the Long version.
31 According to Hildegard, Adam was made of clay while Eve was subsequently made from flesh. For this reason, Hildegard argues, Eve was weaker and this caused her to sin first. If Adam had caused the Fall there would have been no possibility of redemption since his sin would have been much stronger. See Gerda Lerner, *The Creation of Feminist Consciousness: From the Middle Ages to Eighteen-seventy*, Oxford, Oxford University Press, 1993, p. 60.
32 There are for two reasons why it is not accurate to dichotomize the visionary and apophatic strands of Christian mysticism in terms of gender. Firstly, one should not underestimate the sense in which the apophatic orientation of Neoplatonism and Christian scholasticism permeated the Christian world-view in general and, secondly, there are a number of women mystics who clearly have both a knowledge of and are deeply influenced by the apophatic and abstract strands of Christian mysticism (e.g. Marguerite Porete).
33 *The Cloud of Unknowing*, chapter 53, edited by Clifton Wolters, Harmondsworth, Penguin, 1961, p. 116.
34 See Jantzen, *Power, Gender and Christian Mysticism*, p. 191.
35 *Ascent of Mount Carmel*, II.11. 2, 3, 5, 7.
36 Pseudo-Dionysius, *Mystical Theology* I (997B–1000A), see Paul Rorem, *Pseudo-Dionysius: A Commentary on the Texts and an Introduction to their Influence*, Oxford, Oxford University Press, 1993, pp. 185–6.
37 Teresa of Avila, *The Fourth Mansion, The Interior Castle*, edited by Halcyon Backhouse, London, Hodder & Stoughton, 1988, p. 52.
38 Ninian Smart, 'Interpretation and mystical experience', in *Religious Studies* 1.1, 1975, reprinted in Woods (ed.), *Understanding Mysticism*, p. 78.
39 Grace Jantzen, 'Where two are to become one: mysticism and monism', in Godfrey Vesey (ed.), *The Philosophy of Christianity*, Cambridge, Cambridge University Press, 1990, p. 166.
40 Jantzen, *Power, Gender and Christian Mysticism*, pp. 321, 345–6.
41 See Denys Turner, *The Darkness of God: Negativity in Christian Mysticism*, Cambridge, Cambridge University Press, 1995.
42 John E. Smith, 'William James's account of mysticism: a critical appraisal', in Steven Katz (ed.), *Mysticism and Religious Traditions*, New York, Oxford University Press, 1983, p. 247.
43 Grace Jantzen, 'Mysticism and experience', in *Religious Studies* 25, 1989, pp. 299–300. See also Jantzen, *Power, Gender and Christian Mysticism*, pp. 304–21, 342–6.
44 See Jeremy R. Carrette, 'The psychology of religion: re-examining the psychological "subject"', in *Journal of Psychology of Religion* 2.3, 1993–4, pp. 171–99.
45 William James, *The Varieties of Religious Experience*, The Gifford Lectures 1901–2, Glasgow, Collins, 1977, p. 374.
46 See José Casanova, 'Private and public religions', in *Social Research* 59, 1992, pp. 17–57.
47 Paul Tillich, *Dynamics of Faith*, New York, Harper & Row, 1957, p. 60.
48 Certeau, *Heterologies*, p. 80
49 William James, *The Varieties of Religious Experience*, p. 414.
50 Ibid., pp. 414–15.
51 See Richard King, *Indian Philosophy. An Introduction to Hindu and Buddhist Thought*, Edinburgh, Edinburgh University Press, 1999, chapters 1, 2 and 10.

52 Innocent Onyewuenyi, 'Is there an African philosophy', in T. Serequeberhan (ed.), *African Philosophy: The Essential Readings*, New York, Paragon, 1991, p. 36.
53 Kevin Hart, *The Trespass of the Sign: Deconstruction, Theology and Philosophy*, Cambridge, Cambridge University Press, 1989, p. 210.
54 Jorge J.E. Gracia, *Philosophy and Its History: Issues in Philosophical Historiography*, Albany, State University of New York Press, 1992, p. 2.
55 Ibid., p. 5.
56 Ibid., p. 6.
57 Ibid., p. 7.
58 Ibid., p. 9.
59 Ibid., p. 7.
60 Ibid., p. 11.
61 Bertrand Russell, *Mysticism and Logic*, Melbourne, London and Baltimore, Pelican Books, 1953, originally published in 1914, p. 25.

2 Disciplining religion

1 Peter Harrison, *'Religion' and the religions in the English Enlightenment*, Cambridge, Cambridge University Press, 1990, p. 1.
2 Cicero, *De Natura Deorum* II.72. See S.N. Balagangadhara, *'The Heathen in His Blindness': Asia, the West and the Dynamic of Religion*, Leiden, E.J. Brill, 1994, p. 241.
3 Balagangadhara, *'The Heathen in His Blindness'*, p. 46.
4 Lactantius, *Institutiones Divinae* IV.28, translated by Sister McDonald, 1964, pp. 318–20, quoted in Balagangadhara, *'The Heathen in His Blindness'*, p. 242.
5 Balagangadhara, *'The Heathen in His Blindness'*, p. 62.
6 Peter Bichsel, *Der Leser, Das Erzählen: Frankfurter Poetik-Vorlesungen*, Darmstadt und Neuwied: Hermann Luchterhand Verlag, 1982, pp. 13–14, translation in Balagangadhara, *'The Heathen in His Blindness'*, pp. 409–10.
7 Frits Staal, for instance, argues that in Asia grouping people into 'religions' is 'not only uninteresting and uninformative, but tinged with the unreal. What counts instead are ancestors and teachers – hence lineages, traditions, affiliations, cults, eligibility, and initiation – concepts with ritual rather than truth-functional overtones.' Frits Staal, *Rules Without Meaning: Rituals, Mantras and the Human Sciences*, New York, Toronto Studies in Religion, Vol. 4, Peter Lang, 1989, p. 393.
8 See Balagangadhara, *'The Heathen in His Blindness'*, ch. 8, especially p. 307. See also Talal Asad, *Genealogies of Religion: Disciplines and Reasons of Power in Christianity and Islam*, London, Johns Hopkins University Press, 1993, ch. 1.
9 For Balagangadhara this is a question not just of where one chooses to locate 'religion' (in texts or rituals, etc.), but more fundamentally of whether 'religion' is an appropriate category to use when discussing non-Western cultures. See Balagangadhara, *'The Heathen in His Blindness'*, p. 314.
10 Ibid., pp. 284–5.
11 Peter Gay, *The Enlightenment: An Interpretation*, 2 vols, London, Wildwood House, 1973, p. xii. See also Roy Porter, *The Enlightenment*, London, Macmillan, 1990.
12 Peter Hamilton, 'The Enlightenment and the Birth of Social Science', in Stuart Hall and Bram Gieben (eds), *Formations of Modernity*, Oxford, Open University and Polity Press, 1992, pp. 21–2.

13 Walter H. Capps, 'The interpenetration of new religion and religious studies', in Jacob Needleman and George Baker (eds), *Understanding the New Religions*, New York, Seabury Press, 1978, p. 104.

14 Robert N. Bellah, 'Religious studies as "new religion"', in Needleman and Baker, *Understanding the New Religions*, pp. 108–9. See also Bellah, *Beyond Belief*, New York, Harper & Row, 1970. For a similar analysis see David Lyons, *The Steeple's Shadow: On the Myths and Realities of Secularization*, London, SPCK, 1985, pp. 34–5.

15 Peter Berger, *The Social Reality of Religion*, London, Faber & Faber, 1969, pp. 106 and 182.

16 For an outline of the debate see Robin Gill, *The Social Context of Theology*, Oxford, Mowbrays, 1975, pp. 31–4.

17 See Christina Larner, *Witchcraft and Religion: The Politics of Popular Belief*, Oxford and New York, Basil Blackwell, 1984, p. 111.

18 Bellah, 'Religious studies as "new religion"', p. 109.

19 Bellah, *Beyond Belief*, p. 253.

20 See Malcolm Hamilton, *The Sociology of Religion: Theoretical and Comparative Perspectives*, London, Routledge, 1995, p. 5.

21 That Bellah's position amounts to agnosticism can be gleaned from the following statement: 'It is of course impossible to prove Christianity or any religion, but it is impossible to prove cognitively or scientifically any ultimate perspective on human life, including Marxism, rationalism, or any kind of scientism.' Bellah, *Beyond Belief*, p. 245.

22 Bellah, 'Religious studies as "new religion"', pp. 111–12.

23 Asad, *Genealogies of Religion*, pp. 198–9.

24 Of course, two questions (at least!) remain here. First, do reductionist accounts always involve the undermining of religious truth claims, and second, even if they do, should that be a reason for academics to abandon such accounts? I suspect that the answer one gives to these questions, particularly the latter, also reflects personal attitudes towards religion and religious truth claims in general. My own view is that while reductionist accounts can be adopted heuristically in order to provide explanations and insights from social or psychological or economic or political angles, they are more often than not adopted by scholars as definitive explanations of religious phenomena. In so far as this is the case, reductionist accounts do appear to undermine religious truth claims in a significant number of instances. With regard to the second question, I refer the reader to the ensuing discussion in this chapter.

25 For critical discussions of Bellah's 'symbolic realism' see Dick Anthony, Thomas E. Curtis and Thomas Robbins, 'The limits of symbolic realism: problems of empathic field observation in a sectarian context,' *Journal for the Scientific Study of Religion* 12.3, 1973, pp. 259–71. See also the continuation of this debate between Bellah and these authors in *Journal for the Scientific Study of Religion* 13.4, pp. 487–95 and 14.4, 1975, pp. 395–414.

26 John Milbank, *Theology and Social Theory: Beyond Secular Reason*, Oxford, Basil Blackwell, 1990, p. 1.

27 Ibid., p. 2.

28 Ibid., p. 3.

29 See Bellah, *Beyond Belief*, p. 253, quoted above.

30 Prakash Chandra Upadhyaya, 'The politics of Indian secularism', in *Modern Asian Studies* 26.4, 1992, pp. 815–53. See also Mark Tully, *No Full Stops in India*, London, Penguin, 1991, passim.

31 Bryan S. Turner, *Religion and Social Theory*, London, Sage Publications, 2nd edn, 1991, pp. 56–8.

32 Bryan Turner, *Orientalism, Postmodernism and Globalism*, London and New York, Routledge, 1994, p. 61.
33 Asad, *Genealogies of Religion*, p. 9.
34 Russell T. McCutcheon, *Manufacturing Religion: The Discourse on Sui Generis Religion and the Politics of Nostalgia*, New York and Oxford, Oxford University Press, 1997, p. 193.
35 Gavin D'Costa, 'The end of systematic theology', in *Theology* XCV, No. 767, 1992, p. 332.
36 McCutcheon, *Manufacturing Religion*, p. 210.
37 Ibid., pp. 210–11.
38 Timothy Fitzgerald, 'Religious studies as cultural studies: a philosophical and anthropological critique of the concept of religion', in *Diskus* (Web Edition) 3.1, 1995, pp. 35, 47.
39 McCutcheon, *Manufacturing Religion*, p. 19.
40 Ivan Strenski, 'Religion, power and final Foucault', in *Journal of the American Academy of Religion* 66.2, Summer 1998, p. 365.

3   Sacred texts, hermeneutics and world religions

1 Jack Goody, *The Logic of Writing and the Organization of Society*, Cambridge, Cambridge University Press, 1986, p. 3.
2 See Walter Ong, *Orality and Literacy: The Technologizing of the Word*, London and New York, Methuen, 1982, p. 7.
3 Carl A. Keller, 'Mystical literature', in Steven Katz (ed.), *Mysticism and Philosophical Analysis*, New York, Oxford University Press, 1978, p. 97.
4 Ong, *Orality and Literacy*, pp. 8–9.
5 Ibid., p. 12.
6 The terms 'non-literate', 'pre-literate' and, worst of all, 'illiterate' are all inherently problematic since they imply a linear evolution from non-literacy/illiteracy to literacy, suggesting that orality lacks something that the prevailing ('normative') paradigm of literacy attains.
7 Accurate estimates of the degree of literacy within India at various points in its history are difficult to find. Kathleen Gough suggests that Gupta India of the fifth and sixth century CE may have had a literacy rate as high as that of classical Greece (once one takes into account the fact that non-citizens, women and foreigners were generally excluded from literate culture in Greece). She also estimates that possibly half the men and perhaps as many as one-fifth or one-sixth of women were literate during the most prosperous periods of Indian history. However, it is difficult to see how such estimates could be reliably verified. See Kathleen Gough, 'The implications of literacy in traditional China and India', in Jack Goody (ed.), *Literacy in Traditional Societies*, Cambridge, Cambridge University Press, 1968, pp. 70–1.
8 Thus, in discussing the claim that the voluminous collection of Pāli texts represents an undistorted account of the Buddha's teaching, Richard Gombrich notes that, 'as hard-headed historians we cannot think that over 45 years the Buddha could have been entirely consistent – and especially when we take into account that he could not read over or play back what he had said. If the texts have any valid claim to be the record of so long a preaching career, they cannot be wholly consistent. Indeed … the texts are too consistent to be a wholly credible record.' See Richard Gombrich, 'Recovering the Buddha's message', in T. Skorupski (ed.), *The Buddhist Forum*, Vol. I, New Delhi, Heritage Publishers, School of Oriental and African Studies, University of London, 1990, p. 9.

9 For a critique of the 'myth of the isolated reader', see Elizabeth Long, 'Textual interpretation as collective action', in J. Boyarin (ed.), *The Ethnography of Reading*, Berkeley, University of California Press, 1992, pp. 180–211.

10 Silent reading, though rare, did occur for instance in ancient Greece. See Jesper Svenbro, 'The "voice" of letters in Ancient Greece: on silent reading and the representation of speech', in *Culture and History* 2, 1987, pp. 31–47.

11 Ong, *Orality and Literacy*, p. 131.

12 Ibid., pp. 130, 132.

13 Jack Goody, *The Domestification of the Savage Mind*, Cambridge, Cambridge University Press, 1977, pp. 49–50.

14 Ong, *Orality and Literacy*, p. 103.

15 See Goody (ed.), *Literacy in Traditional Societies*, p. 2; Goody, *The Logic of Writing and the Organization of Society*, pp. 3–12. It has even been suggested that ancient Greek supremacy over its neighbours and the ability of the Graeco-Roman (and eventually Western) world to control and assimilate the cultures and languages of others is related to the development of an alphabetical script. See Ong, *Orality and Literacy*, pp. 90–1, and Jack Goody and Ian Watt, 'The consequences of literacy', in Goody (ed.), *Literacy in Traditional Societies*, p. 44.

16 Ong, *Orality and Literacy*, p. 105.

17 Gregory Schopen suggests that 'Epigraphical evidence, at least, does not support the idea that Buddhist literature was widely known in actual Buddhist communities, but in fact points in the opposite direction.' See Schopen, 'Archaeology and Protestant presuppositions in the study of Indian Buddhism', in *History of Religions* 31.1, 1991, p. 5, note 12. Schopen suggests that more attention should be placed upon archaeological evidence rather than a narrowly textual focus in Buddhist studies. While this is undoubtedly a valid point to make, one should also acknowledge the extent to which archaeology 'does not function independently of the societies in which it is practised. The questions that are asked and the answers which appear reasonable reflect the position that societies occupy within the modern world-system and change as the positions of countries alter within that system.' See Bruce G. Trigger, 'Alternative archaeologies: nationalist, colonialist, imperialist', in *Man* (N.S.) 19.3, 1984, p. 368.

18 S.J. Tambiah, 'Literacy in a Buddhist village in north-east Thailand', in Goody (ed.), *Literacy in Traditional Societies*, p. 105.

19 This, however, is not necessarily against the spirit of the founder of Buddhism, since Gautama appears to have encouraged his disciples to teach the Dharma in vernacular languages.

20 Goody, *The Logic of Writing and the Organization of Society*, pp. 3, 15, 21.

21 Timothy Fitzgerald, 'Hinduism and the "world religion" fallacy', in *Religion* 20, 1990, pp. 101–18.

22 Ibid., p. 104.

23 Michel Foucault, *Discipline and Punish: the Birth of the Prison*, Harmondsworth, Penguin, 1977, pp. 218–20.

24 Goody, *The Logic of Writing and the Organization of Society*, p. 21.

25 See Fitzgerald, 'Hinduism and the "world religion" fallacy', p. 110.

26 Emmanuel Le Roy Ladurie, *Montaillou, village occitan, de 1294 à 1324*, Paris, 1975; English version, *Montaillou: The Promised Land of Error*, translated by Barbara Bray, New York, G. Braziller, 1978.

27 See M. Goodridge, 'Ages of faith: romance or reality?', in *Sociological Review* 23.2, 1975, pp. 381–96, quoted in David Lyons, *The Steeple's Shadow: On the Myths and Realities of Secularization*, London, SPCK, 1985, p. 18.

28 Mircea Eliade, *The Sacred and the Profane: The Nature of Religion*, translated by Willard R. Trask, New York, Harcourt Brace Jovanovich, 1959, p. 164, quoted in

Schopen, 'Archaeology and Protestant presuppositions in the study of Indian Buddhism', p. 18. As Gregory Schopen notes in commenting on Eliade's view, 'What European peasants do or do not believe is excluded from the history of their own religion and is assigned to something called "ahistorical Christianity".'

29 Martin Southwold, *Buddhism in Life: The Anthropological Study of Religion and the Sinhalese Practice of Buddhism*, Manchester, Manchester University Press, 1983, p. 6.

30 Charles Neumann, for instance, notes that 'we must carefully separate Buddhism *as it is* and Buddhism *as it ought to be*, according to the scriptures' (original emphasis; Neumann, *Catechism of the Shamans: On the Laws and Regulations of the Priesthood of Buddha in China*, London, Oriental Text Fund, 1831, p. 67, note 4).

31 S. Hardy, *A Manual of Buddhism in its Modern Development*, 1st edn, London, Partridge & Oakey, 1860, p. 397. This is also quoted in Schopen, 'Archaeology and Protestant presuppositions in the study of Indian Buddhism', p. 22, note 56 (though Schopen's page numbering refers to the second edition).

32 Richard F. Gombrich, *Precept and Practice: Traditional Buddhism in the Rural Highlands of Ceylon*, Oxford, Oxford University Press, 1971, p. 243.

33 For an interesting if somewhat cursory discussion of the limitations of textualist approaches to the study of Hinduism, see Milton Singer, *When a Great Tradition Modernizes*, London, Pall Mall Press, 1972, pp. 39–52. Singer argues convincingly that studies of religion should involve both textual analysis and anthropological fieldwork, but his analysis fails to engage with the deeper issues relating to the epistemological and culturally specific presuppositions of modern Western academic studies of religion.

34 Jack Goody (ed.), *Literacy in Traditional Societies*, p. 5.

35 Richard Palmer has outlined six ways in which hermeneutics may be understood: (1) a theory of biblical exegesis; (2) a general methodology for the philological analysis of all texts; (3) a science of linguistic understanding (Schleiermacher); (4) the methodological foundation of the *Geisteswissenschaften*, i.e. the humanities and social sciences (Wilhelm Dilthey); (5) the phenomenology of existence and of existential analysis (Heidegger); and finally, (6) systems of interpretation used by humans to grasp the meaning of symbols and myths (Paul Ricoeur). See Richard Palmer, *Hermeneutics: Interpretation Theory in Schleiermacher, Dilthey, Heidegger and Gadamer*, Evanston, Northwestern University Press, 1969, p. 33. Palmer also describes Gadamer's work as a 'well-developed form [of] the Heideggerian critique in the older style of Dilthey' (p. 42).

36 As Lawson and McCauley have recently suggested, 'The problem in short is that religious systems are not texts. The hermeneutical method must be force-fitted to those features of religious systems (or any symbolic-cultural system) which are not literary. Obvious examples include ritual, a wide array of non-ritual religious practices, and nearly all iconography. The insistence on construing all cultural phenomena along textual lines inevitably blinds inquirers to many of their non-linguistic features.' See E. Thomas Lawson and Robert N. McCauley, 'Crisis of conscience, riddle of identity: making space for a cognitive approach to religious phenomena', in *Journal of the American Academy of Religion* 41.2, Summer 1993, p. 214.

37 Georgia Warnke argues that 'the association of Gadamer's hermeneutics with a Rortian neo-pragmatism or anti-Enlightenment view is misguided. Against the Enlightenment ... Gadamer does emphasize the historical character of our beliefs and practices ... None the less ... it does not mean that we must give up a concern with reason, with the validity of our knowledge.' Georgia Warnke, *Gadamer: Hermeneutics, Tradition and Reason*, Cambridge, Polity Press, 1987, p.

168. Warnke's analysis provides a highly readable and sympathetic yet critical study of Gadamer's thought and follows Habermas in questioning the conservativism inherent in Gadamer's emphasis upon the predominance of tradition (see pp. 87, 106, 111ff., 135ff.), as well as the subjectivist elements that seem to be entailed by some of Gadamer's argumentation.

38 Gadamer, 'Wahrheit in den Geisteswissenschaften', in *Kleine Schriften*, Vol. 1, 1967, p. 42, quoted in Warnke, *Gadamer*, p. 66.

39 Hans Georg Gadamer, *Truth and Method*, English translation, New York, Seabury Press, 1975, p. 267.

40 See Andrew P. Tuck, *Comparative Philosophy and the Philosophy of Scholarship: On the Western Interpretation of Nāgārjuna*, New York and Oxford, Oxford University Press, 1990, p. 15.

41 Susan J. Hekman, *Gender and Knowledge: Elements of a Postmodern Feminism*, Cambridge, Polity Press, 1990, p. 66.

42 See, for instance, E.D. Hirsch, *Validity in Interpretation*, New Haven, Yale University Press, 1967; P.D. Juhl, *Interpretation*, Princeton, Princeton University Press, 1980. For an endorsement of the subjectivism often attributed to Gadamer, see Harold Bloom, *The Anxiety of Influence: A Theory of Poetry*, Oxford, Oxford University Press, 1973.

43 Warnke, *Gadamer*, p. 78.

44 'The naive belief in the objectivity of historical method was a delusion. But what replaces it is not a simple relativism. Indeed, it is not chance and not arbitrary who we ourselves are and what we can hear from the past.' See Gadamer, 'Wahrheit in den Geisteswissenschaften', quoted in Warnke, *Gadamer*, p. 81. Yet Gadamer does acknowledge at certain points the relativistic implications of his work, though he refuses to see these as problematic. Thus, he states that 'In this domain of historical science one must see the "result" of the happening of interpretation not as much in progress, which exists only in partial aspects, as in a process opposed to the decline and fall of knowledge; in the revival of language and the re-acquisition of the meaning that is spoken in and through tradition. This is a dangerous relativism only from the standard of an absolute knowledge that is not ours.' Gadamer, 'Replik', in *Hermeneutik und Ideologiekritik*, see Warnke, *Gadamer*, p. 130 and p. 193, note 37.

45 Gadamer, *Truth and Method*, p. 238.

46 Clifford Geertz, *The Interpretation of Cultures*, New York, Basic Books, 1973, ch. 1.

47 Charles Taylor, *Sources of the Self: The Making of the Modern Identity*, Cambridge, Cambridge University Press, 1989, p. 80.

48 Gadamer, Preface to W. Dilthey, *Grundriss der allgemeinen Geschichte der Philosophie* (Frankfurt, 1949), p. 18, quoted in Wilhelm Halbfass, *India and Europe: An Essay in Understanding*, Albany, State University of New York Press, 1988, p. 164.

49 Wilhelm Halbfass, *India and Europe*, p. 165.

50 On the 'imagined' nature of nationalism see Benedict Anderson, *Imagined Communities: Reflections on the Origin and Spread of Nationalism*, London, Verso, 1983.

51 For a critique of the concept of 'culture', see James Clifford, *The Predicament of Culture: Twentieth Century Ethnography, Literature and Art*, Cambridge, Cambridge University Press, 1988, pp. 273–4.

52 Akhil Gupta and James Ferguson, 'Beyond "culture": space, identity, and the politics of difference', in *Cultural Anthropology* 7.1, 1992, p. 13.

53 Anthony Giddens, *New Rules of Sociological Method*, Cambridge, Polity Press, 1993, p. 58.

54 Rorty argues that Gadamer's rejection of the 'myth of objectivity' has implications for all forms of knowledge, including the natural sciences. Whereas
Gadamer attempts to differentiate the human and social sciences from the positivism of the natural science paradigm, Rorty's neo-pragmatism reduces all
claims to knowledge (including the natural sciences) to a purely pragmatic level.
In Rorty's work, Gadamer's hermeneutics signals the end of epistemology. Thus,
the purpose of revising interpretations is not to find some neutral, transcultural
understanding of the world but rather to keep the conversation going.

55 Jurgen Habermas, 'A review of Gadamer's *Truth and Method*', in Fred Dallmayr
and Thomas McCarthy (eds), *Understanding and Social Inquiry*, Notre Dame,
Indiana, University of Notre Dame Press, 1977, pp. 337ff.

56 Karl-Otto Apel, 'Scientistics, hermeneutics and the critique of ideology: outline
of a theory of science from a cognitive-anthropological standpoint', in Glyn
Adey and David Frisby (eds), *Towards a Transformation of Philosophy*, London,
Routledge & Kegan Paul, 1980, pp. 64ff.

57 Gadamer maintains that 'It is a grave misunderstanding to assume that emphasis
on the essential factor of tradition which enters into all understanding implies an
uncritical acceptance of tradition and sociopolitical conservativism. In truth the
confrontation of our historic tradition is always a critical challenge of this tradition.' See Hans Georg Gadamer, 'The problem of historical consciousness', in
Paul Rabinow and William Sullivan (eds), *Interpretive Social Science*, Berkeley,
University of California Press, 1979, p. 108.

58 Warnke, *Gadamer*, p. 170.

4 Orientalism and Indian religions

1 Talal Asad, *Genealogies of Religion: Disciplines and Reasons of Power in
Christianity and Islam*, London, Johns Hopkins University Press, 1993, p. 1.

2 Said's work is clearly indebted to earlier works that have focused upon the
Western construction of images of Asian culture and its people. Important
works here are Raymond Schwab's 1950 study, *The Oriental Renaissance:
Europe's Discovery of India and the East, 1680–1880*, English translation, New
York, Columbia University Press, 1984; and John M. Steadman, *The Myth of
Asia*, London, Macmillan, 1970. However, the first work that appears to focus
upon the way in which Orientalism functions ideologically as a support for colonial hegemony is Anwar Abdel-Malek's, 'Orientalism in crisis', in *Diogenes*, Vol.
44, 1963.

3 See Chapters 2, 3 and 5 of this volume. For a recent critique of the world-religions approach and its inapplicability in the particular case of Hinduism, see
Timothy Fitzgerald, 'Hinduism and the "world religion" fallacy', in *Religion* 20,
1990, pp. 101–18.

4 Edward Said, *Orientalism: Western Conceptions of the Orient*, London, Penguin,
1991, pp. 2–3.

5 Said, in fact, criticizes Foucault's historical approach for ignoring the role played
by the individual in the construction of discourses (Said, *Orientalism*, p. 23).
However, Said's own structural analysis of the relationship between colonial
power and Orientalist constructions of knowledge can also be said to
marginalize the authors of such discourses as well as those it purports to explain.
See for instance, Jayant Lele, 'Orientalism and the social sciences', in Carol A.
Breckenridge and Peter van der Veer (eds), *Orientalism and the Postcolonial
Predicament*, Philadelphia, University of Pennsylvania Press, 1993, p. 46. See
also David Ludden, 'Orientalist empiricism: transformations of colonial knowledge', in Breckenridge and van der Veer (eds), p. 250.

6 Said, *Orientalism*, p. 272. For a clearer example of such an anti-representation-alist stance see David Ludden, 'Orientalist empiricism: transformations of colonial knowledge', pp. 250–78.

7 Said, *Orientalism*, p. 5. David Ludden has suggested that Said's own work remains bound to the Orientalist tradition, 'For to imply as he does, that orien-talism sustains a body of false, colonial images of the East and its peoples leaves us with the implicit promise that a true image would be constructed if these peoples were free to render images of themselves ... By presuming that there is to be found in the East a real truth about its self-existent peoples, Said employs the very positivist logic that gives orientalism life.' See Ludden (1993), 'Orientalist empiricism', p. 271. However, to be fair to Said, his reticence in providing an alternative conception of the Orient is grounded in the twin realizations that (1) the division between 'Occident' and 'Orient' is an imaginary one, and (2) concep-tions of the 'Orient' are powerful misrepresentations of real peoples and cultures.

8 James Clifford, 'On Orientalism', in *The Predicament of Culture: Twentieth Century Ethnography, Literature and Art*, Cambridge, Cambridge University Press, 1988, p. 260.

9 Some analysts have argued that Foucault's position is not incompatible with a humanistic moral concern for others. See, for instance, Charles Lemert, *Sociology and the Twilight of Man: Homocentrism and Discourse in Sociological Theory*, Carbondale, Southern Illinois University Press, 1979, pp. 230–1; Alexander Hooke, 'The order of others: is Foucault's antihumanism against human action', in *Political Theory* 15, 1987, pp. 38–60.

10 See Clifford, 'On Orientalism', pp. 258–9, 260, 262–6, 269. See also Aijaz Ahmed, 'Between Orientalism and historicism: anthropological knowledge of India', in *Studies in History* 7.1, 1991, pp. 135–63. Rosalind O'Hanlon suggests that 'central and inescapable tensions' present in Said's work stem from the conflict between his historicist use of post-structuralist analysis to undermine hegemonic discourses on the one hand and the fact that his project remains 'firmly rooted within a humanist discourse of freedom' on the other. Rosalind O'Hanlon, 'Cultures of rule, communities of resistance: gender, discourse and tradition in recent South Asian historiographies', in *Social Analysis* 25, 1989, p. 109.

11 Bruce Robbins, 'The East is a career: Edward Said and the logics of profession-alism', in Michael Sprinker (ed.), *Edward Said: A Critical Reader*, Oxford, Basil Blackwell, 1992, p. 54.

12 See the interview with Said in Imre Salusinzsky, *Criticism in Society*, London, Methuen, 1987, p. 137, cited in Rosalind O'Hanlon and David Washbrook, 'After Orientalism: culture, criticism, and politics in the Third World', in *Comparative Studies in Society and History* 34.1, January 1992, p. 156.

13 Michel Foucault, 'Is it useless to revolt?', in *Philosophy and Social Criticism* 8, 1981, p. 9.

14 Lawrence Kritzman (ed.), *Michel Foucault: Politics, Philosophy, Culture*, New York, Routledge, 1988, p. 265.

15 Clifford, 'On Orientalism', p. 263.

16 Ahmed, 'Between Orientalism and historicism', pp. 146–7. See Said, *Orientalism*, p. 325.

17 See, for instance, Gyan Prakash, 'Orientalism now: a review of reviews', in *History and Theory* 34, 1995, pp. 199–212.

18 Sheldon Pollock, 'Deep Orientalism? Notes on Sanskrit and power beyond the Raj', in Breckenridge and van der Veer (eds), *Orientalism and the Postcolonial Predicament*, pp. 76–133.

19 One should note here that in so far as Said ignores the effect of Orientalist narratives upon the colonizer he does not follow Foucault's approach, which focuses upon the sense in which discourses construct both the subject and the object of their analysis.

20 Richard H. Minear, 'Orientalism and the study of Japan', in *Journal of Asian Studies* 39.3, 1980, pp. 507–17. See also Stefan Tanaka, *Japan's Orient: Rendering Pasts into History*, Berkeley, University of California Press, 1993, for a discussion of the ways in which Orientalism functioned to supplant the emerging nationalist discourses of Japan.

21 Lele, 'Orientalism and the social sciences', p. 59.

22 Ashis Nandy, *The Intimate Enemy: Loss and Recovery of Self under Colonialism*, Delhi, Oxford University Press, 1983, pp. 71–4. Nandy, by way of a broadly psychoanalytic account of cultural interchange, suggests that the Orientalist projection of the East as the West's inverse double or 'other' is a reflection of the suppressed 'shadow' side of Western culture. It is in this sense that we can see how the Enlightenment subordinated the poetic, the mystical and the feminine elements within European culture and projected such qualities onto the Orient.

23 See, for instance, Benita Parry, 'Overlapping territories and intertwined histories: Edward Said's postcolonial cosmopolitanism', in Sprinker (ed.), *Edward Said: A Critical Reader*, p. 34. See also Peter van der Veer, 'The foreign hand: Orientalist discourse in sociology and communalism', in Breckenridge and van der Veer (eds), *Orientalism and the Postcolonial Predicament*, p. 23; and Rosalind O'Hanlon, 'Cultures of rule, communities of resistance', p. 109.

24 See for instance Homi Bhabha, 'Signs taken for wonders: questions of ambivalence and authority under a tree outside Delhi, May 1817', in *Critical Inquiry* 12, 1985, pp. 144–65.

25 Richard G. Fox, 'East of Said', in Sprinker (ed.), *Edward Said: A Critical Reader*, p. 146. But see Peter van der Veer, *Religious Nationalism: Hindus and Muslims in India*, Berkeley, University of California Press, 1994, pp. 53–6, where he argues that Sikh identity was utilized but not constructed by the British.

26 Clifford, 'On Orientalism', p. 261.

27 Fox, 'East of Said', p. 152.

28 David Kopf, 'Hermeneutics versus history', in *Journal of Asian Studies* 39.3, May 1980, p. 499. Rosane Rocher also argues that Said's approach 'does to orientalist scholarship what it accuses orientalist scholarship of having done to the countries East of Europe: it creates a single discourse, undifferentiated in space and time and across political, social and intellectual identities'. Rosane Rocher, 'British Orientalism in the eighteenth century: the dialectic of knowledge and government', in Breckenridge and van der Veer (eds), *Orientalism and the Postcolonial Predicament*, p. 215.

29 Kopf, 'Hermeneutics versus history', p. 498.

30 Ibid., p. 501.

31 Ibid., p. 502.

32 Macauley's *Minute of Education* (1835), quoted in Kopf, 'Hermeneutics versus history', p. 504, but originally quoted in David Kopf, *British Orientalism and the Bengal Renaissance: The Dynamics of Indian Modernization, 1773–1835*, Berkeley, University of California Press, 1969, p. 248.

33 Kopf, 'Hermeneutics versus history', p. 503.

34 Kopf, *British Orientalism and the Bengal Renaissance*, p. 275.

35 Ibid., pp. 275–6.

36 Ibid., pp. 277–8. For Kopf then it is merely a historical accident that the social process of modernization began in Europe (p. 276). However, even if this were

the case, it is still naïve to believe that one can export the results of this process without also exporting those features that are peculiarly European in nature.

37 Kopf, 'Hermeneutics versus history', p. 505.
38 Kopf, *British Orientalism and the Bengal Renaissance*, p. 250.
39 Gayatri Chakravorty Spivak, 'The burden of English', in Breckenridge and van der Veer (eds), *Orientalism and the Postcolonial Predicament*, p. 151.
40 Prakash, 'Orientalism now', p. 203.
41 O.P. Kejariwal, 'William Jones: the Copernicus of history', in Garland Cannon and Kevin R. Brine (eds), *Objects of Enquiry: The Life, Contributions and Influences of Sir William Jones (1746–1794)*, New York and London, New York University Press, 1995, p. 109.
42 Tejaswini Niranjana, 'Translation, colonialism and rise of English', in *Economic and Political Weekly* 25.15, 14 April 1990, p. 774.
43 Ibid., p. 775.
44 See Romila Thapar, *Interpreting Early India*, Delhi, Oxford University Press, 1992, pp. 5–6; 89. See also van der Veer, 'The foreign hand', p. 31.
45 As Carol Breckenridge and Peter van der Veer argue, 'While denying the absoluteness and uni-directionality of colonial hegemony and while ascribing agency to both colonizers and colonized, there is no doubting the larger evolving picture of colonial domination that goes far beyond the individual intentions or aspirations of any of its principal actors.' See Breckenridge and van der Veer (eds), *Orientalism and the Postcolonial Predicament*, p. 15.
46 Kopf, 'Hermeneutics versus history', p. 505.
47 Thomas Babington Macauley (1835), 'Minute on Indian education', in Bill Ashcroft, Gareth Griffiths and Helen Tiffin (eds), *The Post-colonial Studies Reader*, London and New York, Routledge, 1995, p. 430.
48 Ranajit Guha, 'On some aspects of the historiography of colonial India', *Subaltern Studies* 1, Delhi, Oxford University Press, 1982, p. 1.
49 Ronald Inden, 'Orientalist constructions of India', in *Modern Asian Studies* 20.3, 1986, p. 411.
50 Ibid., pp. 415; 441.
51 Richard G. Fox criticizes Inden for his condemnation of 'all South Asian scholarship as Orientalist'. According to Fox, Inden's work displays precisely the stereotyping tendencies in his approach to Orientalist scholarship that he attacks in the scholarship itself, though this may reflect a lack of appreciation on Fox's part of the extent to which even 'affirmative Orientalism' contributes to European hegemony over the East. See Fox, 'East of Said', pp. 144–5.
52 Inden, 'Orientalist constructions of India', p. 440.
53 Ibid., pp. 444–5. As with Edward Said, we can clearly see the influence of Foucault on Inden's work.
54 For a critique of Inden's work see Ahmed, 'Between Orientalism and historicism', pp. 152ff.
55 Peter Marshall, *The British Discovery of Hinduism in the Eighteenth Century*, Cambridge, Cambridge University Press, 1970, pp. 43–4, quoted in Inden, 'Orientalist constructions of India', p. 430.
56 Niranjana, 'Translation, colonialism and rise of English', p. 778.
57 Mohandas Gandhi, too, was influenced by Western, Orientalist conceptions of India, only really discovering the fruits of India's religious traditions through the romanticist works of the Theosophical Society. For a discussion of this and its relevance to the Orientalist debate see Fox, 'East of Said', pp. 152ff.
58 *The Complete Works of Swāmi Vivekānananda*, Calcutta, Advaita Ashrama, 13th edn, 1970, Vol. III, p. 275; Vol. II, p. 139.
59 Robbins, 'The East is a career', p. 50.

5 The modern myth of 'Hinduism'

1 Friedhelm Hardy, 'A radical reassessment of the Vedic heritage: the *Ācāryahṛdayam* and its wider implications', in Vasudha Dalmia and H. von Stietencron (eds), *Representing Hinduism: The Construction of Religious Traditions and National Identity*, New Delhi, Sage Publications, 1995, p. 48.

2 Peter Harrison, *'Religion' and the religions in the English Enlightenment*, Cambridge, Cambridge University Press, 1990, p. 3.

3 See Mark Juergensmeyer, 'What the Bhikkhu said: reflections on the rise of militant religious nationalism', in *Religion* 20, 1990, pp. 53–76.

4 With regard to our current discussion, Cantwell Smith states that, 'The term "Hinduism" is, in my judgement, a particularly false conceptualization, one that is conspicuously incompatible with any adequate understanding of the religious outlook of Hindus.' See Wilfred Cantwell Smith, *The Meaning and End of Religion*, Minneapolis, Fortress Press, 1991 (original. 1964), p. 61. As McCutcheon notes, however, Cantwell Smith privileges private faith over cumulative tradition, which is then viewed as 'free, homogenous and original'. See Russell McCutcheon, *Manufacturing Religion: The Discourse of Sui generis Religion and the Politics of Nostalgia*, New York and Oxford, Oxford University Press, 1997, p. 15. More recently, Friedhelm Hardy has suggested: 'That the global title of "Hinduism" has been given to [this variety of religions] must be regarded as an act of pure despair.' *The Religions of Asia*, London, Routledge, 1990, p. 72.

5 H. von Stietencron argues that this usage of the term is attested to in Old Persian cuneiform inscriptions from the time of Darius I, who expanded his empire as far as the Indus in 517 BCE. See H. von Stietencron, 'Hinduism: on the proper use of a deceptive term', in Günter D. Sontheimer and Hermann Kulke (eds), *Hinduism Reconsidered*, New Delhi, Manohar Publications, 1991, p. 12.

6 Romila Thapar, 'Imagined religious communities? Ancient history and the modern search for a Hindu identity', in *Modern Asian Studies* 23.2, 1989, p. 224 (reprinted in Thapar, *Interpreting Early India*, Delhi, Oxford University Press, 1992). See also Narendra K. Wagle, 'Hindu–Muslim interactions in medieval Maharashtra', in Sontheimer and Kulke (eds), *Hinduism Reconsidered*, pp. 51–66, and Joseph T. O'Connell, 'Gauḍiya Vaiṣṇava symbolism of deliverance from evil', in *Journal of the American Oriental Society* 93.3, 1973, pp. 340–3.

7 Thierry Verhelst, *Cultures, Religions and Development in India: Interviews Conducted and recorded by Thierry Verhelst, 14 to 23-1-1985*, a PhD working group on Religions and Cultures, Brussels, Broederliyk Delen, Mimeo, p. 9, quoted in S.N. Balagangadhara, *'The Heathen in His Blindness': Asia, the West and the Dynamic of Religion*, Leiden, E.J. Brill, 1994, p. 16.

8 Partha Chatterjee, in fact, argues that the notion of 'Hindu-ness' has no specifically religious connotation to it and that 'The idea that "Indian nationalism" is synonymous with "Hindu nationalism" is not the vestige of some premodern religious conception. It is an entirely modern, rationalist, and historicist idea. Like other modern ideologies, it allows for a central role of the state in the modernization of society and strongly defends the state's unity and sovereignty. Its appeal is not religious but political. In this sense the framework of its reasoning is entirely secular.' See Partha Chatterjee, 'History and the nationalization of Hinduism', in *Social Research* 59.1, 1992, p. 147.

9 R.E. Frykenberg, 'The emergence of modern "Hinduism" as a concept and an institution: a reappraisal with special reference to South India', in Sontheimer and Kulke (eds), *Hinduism Reconsidered*, p. 31.

10 Romila Thapar, 'Imagined religious communities?', p. 223.

11 This has led Frits Staal, for instance, to argue that 'Hinduism does not merely fail to be a religion; it is not even a meaningful unit of discourse. There is no way to abstract a meaningful unitary notion of Hinduism from the Indian phenomena, unless it is done by exclusion.' See Frits Staal, *Rules Without Meaning: Rituals, Mantras and the Human Sciences*, New York, Toronto Studies in Religion, Vol. 4, Peter Lang, 1989, p. 397.

12 David Kopf, 'Hermeneutics versus history', in *Journal of Asian Studies* 39.3, May 1980, p. 502.

13 See Max Müller, *Chips from a German Workshop*, II, xxvii, 1880, p. 304. See Frykenberg, 'The emergence of modern "Hinduism"', p. 43, note 7. Clearly the term is in provenance by this time since we find Charles Neumann using the term 'Hindooism' in 1831, while explaining the sense in which Buddhism is to be understood as 'a reform of the old Hindoo orthodox Church' (Neumann, *Catechism of the Shamans: On the Laws and Regulations of the Priesthood of Buddha in China*, London, Oriental Text Fund, 1831, p. xxvi).

14 Dermot Killingley, *Rammohun Roy in Hindu and Christian Tradition: The Teape Lectures 1990*, Newcastle upon Tyne, Grevatt & Grevatt, 1993, p. 60.

15 In fact one could argue that in focusing one's critical attention upon Orientalist texts the textualist paradigm which underlies them remains largely unchallenged. See for instance, Carol A. Breckenridge and Peter van der Veer (eds), *Orientalism and the Postcolonial Predicament*, Philadelphia, University of Pennsylvania Press, 1993, p. 5, where this point is made in passing but never properly addressed.

16 Frykenberg even goes as far as to suggest that Christian missionary activity was probably the largest single factor in the development of a 'corporate' and 'revivalist' Hinduism in India. See Frykenberg, 'The emergence of modern "Hinduism"', p. 39. See also Vinay Dharwadker, 'Orientalism and the study of Indian literatures', in Breckenridge and van der Veer (eds), *Orientalism and the Postcolonial Predicament*, pp. 158–85 for an insightful discussion of the ways in which the various forms of 'Indian literature' were studied according to the European literary standards of the time. Dharwadker discusses the nature of nineteenth-century European philology and its presuppositions (e.g. pp. 175, 181). Dharwadker also draws attention to the Sanskritic bias of the Western Orientalists. See also Rosane Rocher, 'British Orientalism in the eighteenth century: the dialectic of knowledge and government', in Breckenridge and van der Veer (eds), pp. 220–5 (especially p. 221), and Peter van der Veer, 'The foreign hand: Orientalist discourse in sociology and communalism', in Breckenridge and van der Veer (eds), p. 40.

17 Rosalind O'Hanlon, 'Cultures of rule, communities of resistance: gender, discourse and tradition in recent South Asian historiographies', in *Social Analysis* 25, 1989, p. 105.

18 See Breckenridge and van der Veer (eds), *Orientalism and the Postcolonial Predicament*, p. 7.

19 See Romila Thapar, 'Imagined religious communities?', pp. 220–1. See also Balagangadhara, *'The Heathen in His Blindness'*, pp. 16–17 and chapters 3 and 4 in general.

20 Rocher, 'British Orientalism in the eighteenth century', p. 242.

21 H. von Stietencron, 'Hinduism', pp. 14–15.

22 Christopher A. Bayly, *Indian Society and the Making of the British Empire*, Cambridge, Cambridge University Press, 1988, pp. 155–8.

23 Brahmanization, or the general process whereby non-brahmanical forms of Indian religion are colonized and transformed by hegemonic brahmanical discourses, can be distinguished from the more general process of Sanskritization. The confutation of the two stems from a mistaken association of

Sanskritic culture exclusively with the *brāhmaṇa* castes. As Milton Singer has suggested Sanskritization may follow the *kṣatriya*, *vaiśya* or even the *śūdra* models. See Milton Singer, 'The social organization of Indian civilization', in *Diogenes* 45, 1964, pp. 84–119. Srinivas, in his later reflections upon Sanskritization, also points to the Sanādh brahmins of Western Uttar Pradesh as evidence that the culture of the brahmins is not always highly Sanskritic in nature. See M.N. Srinivas, *Social Change in Modern India*, Berkeley, University of California Press, 1966, p. 20. While brahmanization in the widest sense, then, cannot be universally equated with Sanskritization, throughout this chapter I shall use the term 'brahmanization' as a short-hand term for Sanskritic brahmanization – that is, to denote a particular species of Sanskritization.

24 The ideological constructs and colonial nature of brahmanical discourses, as represented in distinctions between *vaidik* (i.e. derived from the Vedas), *shastrik* (derived from the *śāstras*), and *laukik* (worldly) forms of knowledge, clearly demonstrate the sense in which the imperialist thrust of Orientalism is not an isolated historical or even an exclusively Western phenomenon. For a discussion of this, see Sheldon Pollock, 'Deep Orientalism? Notes on Sanskrit and power beyond the Raj', in Breckenridge and van der Veer (eds), *Orientalism and the Postcolonial Predicament*, pp. 78; 96ff.; 107; 117, note 1.

25 For a discussion of this in relation to the politics of translation, see Richard Burghart, 'Something lost, something gained: translations of Hinduism', in Sontheimer and Kulke (eds), *Hinduism Reconsidered*, pp. 213–25. See also Peter van der Veer, 'The foreign hand', p. 23, 26–7, 40; Bernard Cohn, 'Notes on the history of the study of Indian society and culture', in Milton Singer and Bernard Cohn (eds), *Structure and Change in Indian Society*, Chicago, Aldine, 1968, pp. 3–28; Jonathan Parry, 'The brahmanical tradition and the technology of the intellect', in Joanna Overing (ed.), *Reason and Morality*, London, Tavistock, 1985, pp. 200–25. Talal Asad, *Genealogies of Religion: Discipline and Reasons of Power in Christianity and Islam*, London, Johns Hopkins University Press, 1993, provides a cogent discussion of the political implications of linguistic and cultural translation in the light of inequalities of power between the contexts of the translator and the translated (pp. 189–99). Asad notes that, 'To put it crudely, because the languages of third world societies ... are seen as weaker in relation to Western languages (and today, especially to English), they are more likely to submit to forcible transformation in the translation process than the other way around' (p. 190).

26 See Khushwant Singh in *Sunday*, 23–29 December 1990, p. 19, quoted in Gerald Larson, 'Discourse about "religion" in colonial and postcolonial India', in Ninian Smart and Shivesh Thakur (eds), *Ethical and Political Dilemmas of Modern India*, New York and Basingstoke, St Martin's Press and Macmillan, 1993, pp. 189–90.

27 Frykenberg, 'The emergence of modern "Hinduism"', p. 34. For discussions of the active part that native Indians played in the construction of Orientalist discourses, see Nicholas B. Dirks, 'Colonial histories and native informants: biography of an archive', and David Lelyveld, 'The fate of Hindustani: colonial knowledge and the project of a national language', both in Breckenridge and van der Veer (eds), *Orientalism and the Postcolonial Predicament*, pp. 279–313 and 189–214.

28 Romila Thapar, 'Syndicated Moksha', in *Seminar* 313, September 1985, p. 21.

29 Ibid., p. 228.

30 See Daniel Gold, 'Organized Hinduism: from Vedic truth to Hindu nation', in Martin E. Marty and R. Scott Appleby (eds), *Fundamentalisms Observed*,

Chicago, University of Chicago Press, 1991, pp. 531–93, for an outline of contemporary 'fundamentalist' and 'nationalist' trends in India.

31 See Hans Bakker, 'Ayodhyā, a Hindu Jerusalem: an investigation of "holy war" as a religious idea in the light of communal unrest in India', in *Numen* 38.1, 1991, pp. 80–109.

32 I am using *epistēme* here in a broadly Foucauldian sense to denote that which 'defines the conditions of possibility of all knowledge, whether expressed in a theory or silently invested in practice'. See Michel Foucault, *The Order of Things*, New York, Pantheon, 1973, p. 168.

33 H. von Stietencron, 'Hinduism', pp. 20–1.

34 Van der Veer, 'The foreign hand', pp. 42–3.

35 See Partha Chatterjee, 'History and the nationalization of Hinduism', pp. 111–49 and *Nationalist Thought and the Colonial World: A Derivative Discourse*, London, Zed Books Ltd, 1986; Mark Juergensmeyer, *The New Cold War? Religious Nationalism Confronts the Secular State*, Berkeley, University of California Press, 1993. Of relevance here also is the work of David Lelyveld on the role that Hindustani and Hindi played in the failed colonial project of constructing a national language in India; see Lelyveld, 'The fate of Hindustani'. See also Arjun Appadurai's discussion of the way in which the quantification process initiated by gathering of statistical information for the Census, etc., functions as a means of constructing homogeneity; see Appadurai, 'Number in the colonial imagination', in Breckenridge and van der Veer (eds), *Orientalism and the Postcolonial Predicament*, especially pp. 330–4.

36 For a comprehensive discussion of the colonial roots of Indian nationalist consciousness, see Chatterjee, *Nationalist Thought and the Colonial World*, and 'History and the nationalization of Hinduism'. See also the work of other members of the Subaltern Studies Group. For further discussion see Chapter 9 of this volume.

37 David Ludden, 'Orientalist empiricism: transformations of colonial knowledge', in Breckenridge and van der Veer (eds), *Orientalism and the Postcolonial Predicament*, p. 274. In relation to this a number of commentators have suggested that the problems associated with 'communalism' are legacies of British imperial rule. Thus Aditya Mukherjee argues that 'Indian society was not split since "time immemorial" into religious communal categories. Nor is it so divided today in areas where communal ideology has not yet penetrated ... However, communalism as it is understood today ... is a modern phenomenon, which took root halfway through the British colonial presence in India – in the second half of the nineteenth century.' See A. Mukherjee, 'Colonialism and communalism', in Sarvepalli Gopal (ed.), *Anatomy of a Confrontation: The Babri Masjid-Ramjanmabhumi Issue*, New Delhi and Calcutta, Penguin, 1990, p. 165. See also Romila Thapar, 'Imagined religious communities?', p. 209, and Gyanendra Pandey, *The Construction of Communalism in Colonial North India*, Delhi, Oxford University Press, 1990. See also Appadurai, 'Number in the colonial imagination', pp. 314–40; Ludden, 'Orientalist empiricism', pp. 266–7; van der Veer (1993), 'The foreign hand', p. 39; Sheldon Pollock, 'Deep Orientalism?', p. 107; 123, note 42. From a Western secular perspective 'the problem of communalism' is understood as evidence of the existence of old religious allegiances that are in conflict with the secular perspective of modern nationalism. However, for a critique of the hegemony of the secular nationalist model of the West, see Juergensmeyer, *The New Cold War*.

38 Romila Thapar, 'Imagined religious communities?', p. 230. Daniel Gold suggests that 'Postcolonial Hindu fundamentalism can thus appear as a new colonialism of the victors. In representing an emergence of Indic group consciousness in new

forms shaped by the colonial experience, it can easily lead to a tyranny of the majority. For it keeps the Western idea of religious community as an ideally homogenous group, but abandons the ideas of equality among communities and protections for minorities introduced with secular British administration.' See Gold, 'Organized Hinduism', p. 580.

39 Julius J. Lipner, 'Ancient Banyan: an inquiry in to the meaning of "Hinduness"', in *Religious Studies* 32, 1996, pp. 109–26. Lipner's use of '*Hindutā*' reflects his explicit avoidance of the term '*Hindutva*' which has been appropriated in the political arena by Hindu nationalists (see pp. 112–13).

40 Ibid., p. 110.

41 Wilhelm Halbfass, *India and Europe: An Essay in Understanding*, Albany, State University of New York Press, 1988, p. 333.

42 Wilhelm Halbfass, 'The Veda and the identity of Hinduism', in Halbfass, *Tradition and Reflection: Explorations in Indian Thought*, Albany, State University of New York Press, 1991, p. 15.

43 See Halbfass, *India and Europe*, ch. 18.

44 G. Eichinger Ferro-Luzzi, 'The polythetic-prototype approach to Hinduism', in Sontheimer and Kulke (eds), *Hinduism Reconsidered*, p. 192.

45 Kalpana Ram, 'Modernist anthropology and the construction of Indian identity', in *Meanjin* 51, 1992, pp. 589–90. See also Ashis Nandy, *The Intimate Enemy: Loss and Recovery of Self under Colonialism*, Delhi, Oxford University Press, 1983, pp. 71–4.

46 See Ram, 'Modernist anthropology and the construction of Indian identity', pp. 594–8; Gyan Prakash, 'Writing post-Orientalist histories of the Third World: perspectives from Indian historiography', in *Comparative Studies in Society and History* 32.2, 1990, p. 393; Ronald Inden, 'Orientalist constructions of India', in *Modern Asian Studies* 20.3, 1986, p. 440; Ronald Inden, *Imagining India*, Oxford, Basil Blackwell, 1990, especially p. 154, but see also pp. 201–4; Veena Das, *Critical Events: An Anthropological Perspective on Contemporary India*, Oxford, Oxford University Press, 1995, pp. 24–54; Declan Quigley, *The Interpretation of Caste*, Oxford, Clarendon Press, Oxford, 1994, ch. 3; Mary Searle-Chatterjee and Ursula Sharma (eds), *Contextualising Caste: Post-Dumontian Approaches*, Sociological Review monograph, Oxford, Blackwell, 1994. While it is true that Dumont's account of the centrality of caste in Indian culture does function as a means of contrasting Indian culture with modern Western conceptions of itself as socially fluid and egalitarian, it is important to bear in mind that the emphasis upon caste as a defining feature of Indian culture did not begin with the Western Orientalists and was a major preoccupation of earlier accounts of India, such as that provided by the Muslim scholar al-Bīrunī.

47 See Edward Said, *Orientalism: Western Conceptions of the Orient*, London, Penguin, 1991, p. 188; 'Orientalism and after: an interview with Edward Said', in *Radical Philosophy* 63, Spring 1993, pp. 26–7.

48 O'Hanlon, 'Cultures of rule, communities of resistance', pp. 105–106.

49 Jane Miller, *Seductions: Studies in Reading and Culture*, London, Virago, 1990, pp. 118–22. See also Reina Lewis, *Gendering Orientalism: Race, Femininity and Representation*, New York and London, Routledge, 1996.

50 John Mitchell, *An Essay on the Best Means of Civilising the Subjects of the British Empire in India and of Diffusing the Light of the Christian Religion Throughout the Eastern World*, Edinburgh, W. Blackwood, and London, T. Cadell & W. Davies, 1805, pp. 79–80. This work received an award from the University of Glasgow, bequeathed by the Rev. Claudius Buchanan, Vice-Provost of the College of Fort-William in Bengal.

51 Ibid., pp. 88–9.

52 Tejaswini Niranjana, 'Translation, colonialism and rise of English', in *Economic and Political Weekly* 25.15, 14 April 1990, p. 774. See, for instance, Jones' approval of Henry Lord's (1630) description of the Banians as 'maidenly and well-nigh effeminate, of a countenance shy and somewhat estranged, yet smiling out a glazed and bashful familiarity'. See also Peter Marshall, *The British Discovery of Hinduism in the Eighteenth Century*, Cambridge, Cambridge University Press, 1970, p. 250.

53 John Strachey, *India*, 1888, cited in Claude Alvares, *Decolonizing History: Technology and Culture in India, China and the West, 1492 to the Present Day*, Goa, India, The Other India Press, and New York, Apex Press, 1991, p. 187. See Inden, *Imagining India*, pp. 86–7, 123 for a brief mention of the feminization of India in the Western imagination.

54 Mrinalini Sinha, *Colonial Masculinity: The 'Manly Englishman' and the 'Effeminate Bengali' in the Late Nineteenth Century*, Manchester, Manchester University Press, 1995. See also Nandy, *The Intimate Enemy*, 1983, ch. 1; Ann Laura Stoler, *Race and the Education of Desire: Foucault's History of Sexuality and the Colonial Order of Things*, London, Duke University Press, 1995.

55 Ram, 'Modernist anthropology and the construction of Indian identity', p. 590. See O'Hanlon, 'Cultures of rule, communities of resistance', p. 111.

56 See, for instance, Simone de Beauvoir, *The Second Sex*, Harmondsworth, Penguin, 1972; Dale Spender, *Man-Made Language*, London, Routledge & Kegan Paul, 1980, e.g., p. 23.

57 Hélène Cixous and Catherine Clement, *The Newly Born Woman*, translated by Betsy Wing, Minneapolis, University of Minnesota Press, 1986, p. 68.

58 Veena Das, 'Gender studies, cross-cultural comparison and the colonial organization of knowledge', in *Berkshire Review* 21, 1986, p. 73. For a psychoanalytically inspired account of the West's projection of a the 'feminine' onto India, see Nandy, *The Intimate Enemy*, ch. 1.

59 For a critique of notions of 'modernization' and 'development' and the ideology of progress underlying them, see Mark Hobart (ed.), *An Anthropological Critique of Development: The Growth of Ignorance*, London, Routledge, 1993. See also Aijaz Ahmed, *In Theory: Classes, Nations, Literature*, London, Verso, 1992.

60 Alvares, *Decolonizing History*, pp. 55–64.

61 Ibid., p. 67.

62 Susan J. Hekman, *Gender and Knowledge: Elements of a Postmodern Feminism*, Cambridge, Polity Press, 1990, p. 94.

6 'Mystic Hinduism'

1 Diderot' s article on 'Bramines', in *Encylopédie*. This is a literal paraphrase of Bayle's 1738 article 'Brachmanes', in his *Dictionaire historique et critique*, with Diderot's own addition of the reference to opium, cited in Wilhelm Halbfass, *India and Europe: An Essay in Understanding*, Albany, State University of New York Press, 1988, pp. 59–60.

2 S.N. Balagangadhara, *'The Heathen in His Blindness': Asia, the West and the Dynamic of Religion*, Leiden, E.J. Brill, 1994, pp. 133–6.

3 In 1815, Friedrich Schlegel, for instance, describes Anquetil's work as a 'bungling work' and 'one of the most turbid sources of information on ancient India', contrasting it with the authenticity of H.T. Colebrooke's translations from the original Sanskrit (see F. Schlegel, *Werke* VI, 131–2). Similarly, Schlegel's Sanskrit teacher, British Orientalist Alexander Hamilton, suggests that the quality of Anquetil's work is 'greatly diminished, by coming through the medium of a Persic translation'. See Rosane Rocher, *Alexander Hamilton (1762–1824): A*

Chapter in the Early History of Sanskrit Philology, American Oriental Series 51, New Haven, American Oriental Society, 1968, pp. 24ff.

4 *Oupnek'hat* I, p. 792.

5 Ibid., p. 711. Translation in Halbfass, *India and Europe*, p. 67.

6 A. Schopenhauer, *Parerga und Paralipomena*, Vol. II, section 184, from the edition of Schopenhauer's works begun by Paul Deussen, 1911–42, quoted in Halbfass, *India and Europe*, p. 106.

7 *Oupnek'hat* I, p. viii. In this respect, Anquetil was no doubt further convinced of the remarkable correspondences between Christianity and the ancient Vedas, by his continued acceptance of the authenticity of the spurious *Ezourvedam*, a text purporting to be a French 'translation' of an ancient Hindu Veda. Anquetil remained a staunch advocate of the authenticity of the text despite its exposure as a Jesuit missionary composition by Pierre Sonnerat in 1782.

8 A similar approach can be found in the romantic and Christianized conception of the *Upaniṣads* provided in Jean Mascaro's hugely popular Penguin Classic edition of the *Upaniṣads* (an anthology of texts in English translation, published in 1965 and reprinted consistently since then).

9 Charles Wilkins, *The Bhagvat-Geeta or Dialogues of Kreeshna and Arjoon in 18 Lectures with Notes*, London, C. Nowse, 1785, pp. 23–4.

10 *The Works of William Jones*, Vol. 1, 1799, p. 363.

11 Note, for instance, that Mohandas Gandhi's own interest in the *Gītā* was inspired by Western interest from groups such as the Theosophists, for whom the *Gītā* represented a central example of the perennial philosophy in India.

12 See, for instance, *Bhagavad Gītā* VII. 21; IX. 23; X. 20–1. See also the frequently quoted verse from the *Ṛg Veda*, which states that 'Him, who is the One existent, sages name variously' (I. 164.46). For a discussion of inclusivism in early Advaita Vedānta see Richard King, *Early Advaita Vedānta and Buddhism: The Mahāyāna Context of the Gauḍapādīya-kārikā*, Albany, State University of New York Press, 1995, pp. 194–203.

13 Wilkins, *The Bhagvat-Geeta*, p. 24. See also p. 143, note 44, where Wilkins argues that the *Gītā's* rendering of *sannyās* as one who forsakes the hope of reward is motivated by an attempt to 'unite the various religious opinions which prevailed in those days'.

14 Ibid., p. 25.

15 Ibid., p. 139, note 6.

16 Anquetil-Duperron himself rendered the term *'upaniṣad'* as the Latin *'secretum tegendum'*, meaning 'a secret to be kept'.

17 It is generally accepted that the earliest stratum contains the *Bṛhadāraṇyaka* and *Chāndogya Upaniṣads*. These are said to contain material that is pre-Buddhist, placing them at some time before the sixth to fourth century BCE (depending upon the dates of the Buddha). The *Taittirīya*, *Aitareya* and *Kauṣītaki* are probably next in chronological composition and these too seem to contain some pre-Buddhist material, dating from around the fifth or fourth centuries BCE. These are followed by the verse *Upaniṣads*, including the *Kena* (probably the oldest of the verse *Upaniṣads*), the *Kaṭha*, *Īśa*, *Śvetāśvatara* and *Muṇḍaka Upaniṣad*, all of which were probably composed in the last few centuries BCE. Finally, we have the prose *Upaniṣads* – the *Māṇḍūkya* and the *Praśna* dating from the first two centuries CE. There are also other texts such as the *Mahānārāyaṇa Upaniṣad*, a composite text constituting part of the *Taittirīya Āraṇyaka* and the *Maitrayānīya* (or *Maitrī*) *Upaniṣad*.

18 See Halbfass, *India and Europe*, p. 134.

19 Quoted in Halbfass, *India and Europe*, p. 51.

20 Note that by 'brahmanical élite' I am not proposing that the *Upaniṣads* were the product of brahmins alone. Much has been made of the *kṣatriya* contribution to Upaniṣadic thought. See Patrick Olivelle, *Upaniṣads*, Oxford World's Classics, Oxford University Press, 1996, p. xxxiv.

21 Indira Chowdury-Sengupta, 'Reconstructing spiritual heroism: the evolution of the Swadeshi Sannyasi in Bengal', in Julia Leslie (ed.), *Myth and Mythmaking*, Collected Papers on South Asia No.12, School of Oriental and African Studies, London, 1996, pp. 124–42. On British conceptions of the Bengali male as effeminate, see Chapter 5 of this volume.

22 Swami Nikhilananda, *Vivekananda: A Biography*, New York, Ramakrishna Centre, 1953, p. 167.

23 Paul J. Will, 'Swami Vivekananda and cultural stereotyping', in N. Smart and B. Srinivasa Murthy (eds), *East–West Encounters in Philosophy and Religion*, Mumbai, Popular Prakashan, Long Beach Publications, 1996, pp. 384–5.

24 See Halbfass, *India and Europe*, pp. 70–1.

25 Ibid., pp. 77–8.

26 See, for instance, Schelling's 1809 work, 'Philosophical investigations on the essence of human freedom' ('*Philosophische Untersuchungen über das Wesen der menschlichen Freiheit*').

27 F.W.J. Schelling, *Sämmlichte Werke* I. 6, 38, quoted in Halbfass, *India and Europe*, p. 102.

28 Quoted in Halbfass, *India and Europe*, p. 60. This is of course, the source of Marx's famous assertion that religion is the opiate of the masses.

29 See Ignatius Viyagappa, *G.W.F. Hegel's Concept of Indian Philosophy*, Rome, Università Gregoriana, 1980, p. 224.

30 See Dorothy M. Figueira, *The Exotic: A Decadent Quest*, Albany, State University of New York Press, 1994, pp. 72–80; Viyagappa, *G.W.F. Hegel's Concept of Indian Philosophy*, ch. 1.

31 G.W.F. Hegel, *Sämmlichte Werke* (Kritische Ausgabe, Bd XVa), p. 290. English translation in Ignatius Viyagappa, *G.W.F. Hegel's Concept of Indian Philosophy*, p. 192.

32 Wilhelm Halbfass, *India and Europe*, p. 95. See also Figueira, *The Exotic*, pp. 72–3.

33 A. Schopenhauer, *Senilia*, 1858, quoted in Halbfass, *India and Europe*, p. 111.

34 Rudolf Otto, *Mysticism East and West: A Comparative Analysis of the Nature of Mysticism*, 1932, London, Quest English edition, 1987, p. 167.

35 Ibid., pp. 168–70.

36 Ibid., p. 173.

37 Ibid., p. 175.

38 Ibid., p. 177.

39 Ibid., p. 182.

40 Ibid., p. 185.

41 Ibid., p. 205.

42 Ibid., passim, but see also especially pp. 129, 193 and Appendix IV.

43 Ibid., p. 213.

44 See, for instance, Otto's explicit reference to Eckhart's German '*Gemuts-mystik*' on p. 204.

45 See Herman Tull, F. Max Müller and A.B. Keith, ' "Twaddle", the "stupid" myth, and the disease of indology', in *Numen* 38.1, pp. 42–3.

46 Paul Hacker, 'On Śaṅkara and Advaitism', 1964, reprinted in Wilhelm Halbfass (ed.), *Philology and Confrontation: Paul Hacker on Traditional and Modern Vedānta*, Albany, State University of New York Press, 1995, p. 30.

47 T.M.P. Mahadevan, *Ramaṇa Mahārshi: The Sage of Aruṇācala*, London, Allen & Unwin, 1977, p. 126.
48 See Śaṅkara's commentary on *Bṛhadāraṇyaka Upaniṣad* 3.5.1 and 4.5.15. Note that even Śaṅkara's immediate disciples are less rigid in their adherence to the exclusivity of the *brāhmaṇa* castes. See Sureśvara's *Vārttika* (verse 1,651) to *Bṛhadāraṇyaka Upaniṣad* 3.5.1 and Ānandajñāna's commentary upon this, where both accept that *kṣatriyas* are able to take up a renunciate lifestyle.
49 Hacker, 'On Śaṅkara and Advaitism', p. 31.
50 William Cenkner, *A Tradition of Teachers: Śaṅkara and the Jagadgurus Today*, Delhi, South Asia Books, 1983, p. 110.
51 Dhar, Niranjan, *Vedānta and the Bengal Renaissance*, Calcutta, Minerva Associates, 1977. Dhar, described on the dust cover of his book as a 'rational humanist', argues that Vedānta has been an historic obstacle to the development of 'rationalism' in India. Although not a Marxist, Dhar argues that Vedānta is the 'opium of the people', and is constituted by 'a metaphysical-mystical potion concocted by princes, landlords and priests to hold the masses down'. The secular rationalism of the author is prevalent throughout the work, as is Dhar's anti-Vedāntic polemic, but is especially evident in Chapter 6 which contains a particularly virulent and scientistic attempt to pathologize the religious experiences of Ramakrishna.
52 See H.T. Colebrooke, 'Essays on the Vedas or sacred writings of the Hindus', in *Asiatic Researches*, 1805, pp. 31–2.
53 David Kopf, *British Orientalism and the Bengal Renaissance: The Dynamics of Indian Modernization, 1773–1835*, Berkeley and Los Angeles, University of California Press, 1969, pp. 58–9. William Jones, however, read Vedāntic texts with '*Brahmen* of the *Vedānti* school'. Rosane Rocher suggests that this may refer to Rādhākānta, the brahmin responsible for transforming Jones' negative appraisal of Bengali pundits. See Rosane Rocher, 'Weaving knowledge: Sir William Jones and Indian pundits', in Garland Cannon and Kevin R. Brine (eds), *Objects of Enquiry: The Life, Contributions, and Influences of Sir William Jones (1746–1794)*, New York and London, New York University Press, 1995, p. 79, note 52.
54 Kopf, *British Orientalism and the Bengal Renaissance*, pp. 46–7.
55 Letter from Henry Dundas to Marquis Wellesley, 4 September 1800, Cheltenham, in Edward Ingram (ed.), *Two Views of British India: The Private Correspondence of Mr Dundas and Lord Wellesley: 1798–1801*, Bath, Adams & Dart, 1970, p. 287.
56 See Wellesley's letter to Dundas, 7 March 1801, in Ingram (ed.), *Two Views of British India*, p. 326. See also letter dated 18 August 1800 from Wellesley to Dundas (Ingram (ed.), *Two Views of British India*, p. 282–3).
57 Lord Wellesley, *Minute on the Foundation of a College at Fort William*, 10 July 1800, reprinted in M. Martin, *The Despatches: Minutes and Correspondence of the Marquess Wellesley, K.G.; during his Administration in India*, Vol. II, W.H. Allen, 1837, p. 346. Quoted in Kopf, *British Orientalism and the Bengal Renaissance*, p. 47 and in Dhar, *Vedānta and the Bengal Renaissance*, p. 36, note 2.
58 David Kopf, 'The historiography of British Orientalism, 1772–1992', in Cannon and Brine (eds), *Objects of Enquiry*, 1995, p. 156.
59 Jyotsna G. Singh, *Colonial Narratives, Cultural Dialogues: 'Discoveries' of India in the Language of Colonialism*, London and New York, Routledge, 1996, pp. 68–9.
60 Halbfass pinpoints the *Informatio de quibusdam moribus mationis indicae* (1613), composed by Italian Jesuit Robert Nobili (1577–1656) as the first clear reference

to Śaṅkarācārya ('Ciancaraciarien') as the founder of the Advaita tradition of Vedānta (*māyāvāda*, rendered '*maiavadae*') in European literature. See Halbfass, *India and Europe*, p. 40.

61 Kopf, *British Orientalism and the Bengal Renaissance*, pp. 168–9; 176–7.

62 Ibid., pp. 199–200.

63 Mikhail Bakhtin, *The Dialogical Imagination*, edited by Michael Holquist, translation by Caryl Emerson and Michael Holquist, Austin, University of Texas Press, 1981, pp. 293–4, quoted in Stefan Tanaka, *Japan's Orient: Rendering Pasts into History*, Berkeley, University of California Press, 1993, p. 8.

64 Michel Foucault, *History of Sexuality*, Vol. 1, Harmondsworth, Penguin, 1978, p. 94.

65 Ibid., p. 93.

66 Kopf, *British Orientalism and the Bengal Renaissance*, p. 114.

67 Ketu H. Katrak, 'Indian nationalism, Gandhian 'Satyagraha,' and representations of female sexuality', in A. Parker, M. Russo, D. Sommer and P. Yaeger (eds) *Nationalisms and Sexualities*, New York and London, Routledge, 1992, p. 395. Katrak, in fact, argues that Gandhi's non-violent philosophy evolved from 'his personal observations of passive resistance from his mother and wife' (p. 396), but that his 'uses of female sexuality were channelled through his evocations of woman's obedience and nurturance as wife and mother', and that he failed to recognise the extent of women's struggle against patriarchal oppression (p. 397).

68 Ibid., p. 397.

69 For a generally positive appraisal of Gandhian protest as an authentic subversion of British colonial discourse, see Partha Chatterjee, *Nationalist Thought and the Colonial World: A Derivative Discourse*, London, Zed Books, 1986. For a critical review of this see Sumit Sarkar, 'Orientalism revisited: Saidian frameworks in the writing of modern Indian history', in *Oxford Literary Review* 16, 1994, pp. 205–24. Ashis Nandy is less laudatory in his appraisal of the extent to which Gandhi effectively represented the subaltern groups of India, but agrees nevertheless that he 'successfully articulated in politics the consciousness which had remained untamed by British rule in India'. See Ashis Nandy, *The Intimate Enemy: Loss and Recovery of Self under Colonialism*, Delhi, Oxford University Press, 1983, p. 100.

70 Richard G. Fox, 'East of Said', in Michael Sprinker (ed.), *Edward Said: A Critical Reader*, Oxford, Basil Blackwell, 1992, pp. 151–2.

71 Sarvepalli Radhakrishnan, *The Hindu View of Life*, London, 1927, Unwin Paperback, 1988, p. 18.

72 Ibid., p. 25.

73 Sarvepalli Radhakrishnan (speech delivered 20 January 1963, Calcutta) and reprinted in Radhakrishnan, *Our Heritage*, Delhi, Hind Pocket Books, 1973, p. 97.

74 Gauḍapāda is understood by the Advaita traditions to be Śaṅkara's *paramaguru* – the teacher of his teacher. For a detailed analysis of this text, its philosophical position, questions of authorship and its relationship to the prevailing Mahāyāna Buddhist schools of the day, see King, *Early Advaita Vedānta and Buddhism*.

75 *Māṇḍūkya-Kārikā* III.17–18 and IV.4–5.

76 Inclusivism akin to that of the *Māṇḍūkya-Kārikā* can be found in the *Paramārtha-sāra* (for a brief discussion of the date of the *Paramārtha-sāra* see King, *Early Advaita Vedānta and Buddhism*, p. 260n). This theme re-emerges strongly in the post-Śaṅkarite *Yogavāsiṣṭha* (final version *c.*tenth to eleventh century CE; see, for instance, the translation in Swami Venkatesananda, *The*

Concise Yogavasistha, Albany, State University of New York Press, 1984, p. 178), and provides a systematic basis for an inclusivist account of rival perspectives in later Advaita thought, with the notion of the different levels of attainment (*adhikāri-bheda*) among humans. On this view, different levels of knowledge require the acceptance of a diversity of approaches (usually classified, following the *Gītā*, in terms of *karma*, *bhakti* and *jñāna*, and resulting in the production of a variety of conceptions of the ultimate reality).

77 Vivekānanda, 'Unity', in *The Complete Works of Swami Vivekānanda*, Vol. VIII, Calcutta, Advaita Ashrama, pp. 250–1.

78 Theos Bernard, *Hindu Philosophy*, Delhi, Motilal Banarsidass, 1947, Reprint 1985, p. 5.

79 Swāmi Vivekānanda, *Complete Works*, Vol. I, pp. 21–4. See also VIII.103, 287; III.528–9; III.526; II. 478; IV. 135–6.

80 Vivekānanda, 'Vedic religious ideals', in *Complete Works*, Vol. I, p. 347. Compare this with IV.135 – 'Buddhism is one of our sects'. In V.309 the Buddha is described as a *saṁnyāsin* of the Vedanta. He started a sect but the ideas now called Buddhism were not his, for they were ancient (i.e. deriving from Vedas). See also V.82 – the practical 'yoga-perception' form of Vedanta, Vivekānanda says, is called Buddhism.

81 'True Buddhism' (report in *Brooklyn Standard Union*, 4 February 1895) in Vivekānanda, *Complete Works*, Vol. II, p. 509. See also V.225, 227; III.230.

82 Vivekānanda, *Brooklyn Standard Union*, 27 February 1895, *Complete Works*, Vol. II, pp. 510–11.

83 Ibid., III.275

84 For a detailed analysis of the philosophical differences between Buddhism and Vedānta traditions, see King, *Early Advaita Vedānta and Buddhism*, passim.

85 'The Real and the Apparent Man' (lecture delivered in New York), *Complete Works*, Vol. II, pp. 272–5. In fact according to the letter that Vivekānanda wrote to Swarup(ānanda), dated 9 February 1902 (Vol. V, pp. 172–3), Vivekānanda claims that Mahāyāna Buddhism, as well as being a form of Advaita, is also the oldest school of Buddhism. He states that 'A total revolution has occurred in my mind about the relation of Buddhism and neo-Hinduism. I may not live to work out the glimpses, but I shall leave the lines of work indicated, and you and your brethren will have to work it out.' (p. 173).

86 Vivekānanda, 'The Essence of Religion' (report of a lecture given in America), *Complete Works*, Vol. VIII, pp. 254–8.

87 'The Way to the Realisation of a Universal Religion' (lecture delivered in Universalist church, Pasadena, California, 28 January 1900), *Complete Works*, Vol. II, p.374.

88 Ibid., Vol. II, p. 367.

89 For Vivekānanda, each 'world religion' is said to have cultivated particular qualities of the Universal Religion. Thus Islam fosters an appreciation of the equality of brotherhood, Christianity is praised for its pure spirit of anticipation (awaiting the coming of the kingdom of God), while Hinduism is to be lauded for its great spirituality. *Complete Works*, Vol. II, pp. 371–2.

90 'The Absolute and Manifestation' (lecture delivered in London, 1896), in *Complete Works*, Vol. II, p. 139.

91 Ibid.

92 Hans Torwesten, *Vedanta, Heart of Hinduism*, 1985, English translation, Grove Press, 1991, pp. 12–13.

93 Ibid., p. 14.

94 Ibid., pp. 14–15.

7 Orientalism and the discovery of 'Buddhism'

1 Stephen Batchelor, *The Awakening of the West: The Encounter of Buddhism and Western Culture*, London, Aquarian Press, 1994, p. 231.

2 Donald Lopez Jr., 'Introduction', in Lopez (ed.), *Curators of the Buddha: The Study of Buddhism Under Colonialism*, Chicago, Chicago University Press, 1995, p. 7.

3 Philip Almond seems to pinpoint the earliest reference to a recognisable group known as 'Boodhists' in an 1827 account by Michael Symes, which documents an embassy to the Kingdom of Ava in 1795. (See Philip Almond, *The British Discovery of Buddhism*, Cambridge, Cambridge University Press, 1988, p. 10.) Almond also states that Edward Upham's 1829 work *The History and Doctrine of Budhism* was the first book in English to use the word 'Budhism' in its title (p. 14).

4 Peter Bishop, *Dreams of Power: Tibetan Buddhism and the Western Imagination*, London, Athlone Press, 1992, p. 17.

5 John Ross Carter, *On Understanding Buddhists: Essays on the Theravāda Tradition in Sri Lanka*, Albany, State University of New York Press, 1992, ch. 1.

6 Kristofer Schipper, *The Taoist Body*, translated by Karen C. Duval, Berkeley, University of California Press, 1993, p. 3.

7 Frits Staal, *Rules Without Meaning: Rituals, Mantras and the Human Sciences*, New York, Toronto Studies in Religion, Vol. 4, Peter Lang, 1989, p. 393.

8 For detailed and insightful accounts of the various stages in the Western discovery of Buddhism, see Almond, *The British Discovery of Buddhism*, and Batchelor, *The Awakening of the West*.

9 Lopez, 'Introduction', in *Curators of the Buddha*, p. 11.

10 Almond, *The British Discovery of Buddhism*, pp. 17–24.

11 See Richard King, *Early Advaita Vedānta and Buddhism: The Mahāyāna Context of the Gaudapādīya-kārikā*, Albany, State University of New York Press, 1995.

12 Charles F. Neumann, *Catechism of the Shamans: On the Laws and Regulations of the Priesthood of Buddha in China*, London, Oriental Text Fund, 1831, pp. xxvi–xxviii. Overall, Neumann notes that the Hindu 'clergy' of brahmins remain tolerant of 'every sect and every worship which would not deprive them of their worldly privileges' (p. xxviii).

13 Quoted in Almond, *The British Discovery of Buddhism*, p. 73

14 Ibid., p. 75.

15 Bishop, *Dreams of Power*, p. 91.

16 Ibid., p. 37.

17 Quoted in Lopez, 'Introduction', in *Curators of the Buddha*, p. 2.

18 Bishop, *Dreams of Power*, p. 34.

19 Batchelor, *The Awakening of the West*, pp. 239–40.

20 Lopez, 'Introduction', in *Curators of the Buddha*, p. 7.

21 Charles Hallisey, 'Roads taken and not taken in the study of Theravāda Buddhism', in Lopez (ed.), *Curators of the Buddha*, p. 32.

22 Edward Said, *Orientalism: Western Conceptions of the Orient*, London, Penguin, 1991, p. 5.

23 Hallisey, 'Roads taken and not taken', p. 50.

24 Max Müller, *Chips from a German Workshop* 1, 1862, pp. 115–16, quoted in Lopez, 'Introduction', in *Curators of the Buddha*, pp. 24–5. Despite this commendation of the native, William Jones seems to have experienced a certain amount of disdain, or at least ambivalence, towards his native informants, noting that for scholars 'it was found highly dangerous to employ natives as interpreters, upon whose fidelity they could not depend' (Sir William Jones, *A Grammar of the*

Persian Language, 1771, London, W. Nicol, London, 8th edn, 1823, p. vii, quoted in Lopez, 'Introduction', p. 5).

25 Hallisey, 'Roads taken and not taken', p. 43. See S.N. Balagangadhara, *'The Heathen in His Blindness': Asia, The West and the Dynamic of Religion*, Leiden, E.J. Brill, 1994, pp. 120–4, for a discussion of the complicity and overlapping interests of the native informant in India and the Christian missionary, particularly in terms of the repudiation of 'popular' religious practices.

26 This appeal to authorial transparency, of course, is also to be found in the Asian texts and commentaries that the Orientalists were examining and should also not be seen as an exclusively Western or 'Orientalist' phenomenon. See Hallisey, 'Roads taken and not taken', pp. 41–3.

27 Gananath Obeyesekere, 'Religious symbolism and political change in Ceylon', in *Modern Ceylon Studies* 1.1, 1970, pp. 46–7.

28 Bishop, *Dreams of Power*, p. 83.

29 Michel de Certeau, *The Practice of Everyday Life*, translated by Steven Rendall, Berkeley, University of California Press, 1984, pp. xiv–xv.

30 Lopez, 'Introduction', in *Curators of the Buddha*, pp. 11–12.

31 Charles F. Neumann, *Catechism of the Shamans*, 1831, pp. xxix–xxxi.

32 Charles Wilkins, *The Bhagvat-Geeta or Dialogues of Kreeshna and Arjoon in 18 Lectures with Notes*, London, C. Nowse, 1785, p. 13.

33 David Kopf, 'Hermeneutics versus history', in *Journal of Asian Studies* 39.3, May 1980, p. 503.

34 See A.J. Arberry, *British Orientalists*, London, William Collins & Company, 1943, p. 32, cited in David Kopf, *British Orientalism and the Bengal Renaissance: The Dynamics of Indian Modernization, 1773–1835*, Berkeley and Los Angeles, University of California Press, p. 28.

35 Nicholas B. Dirks, 'Introduction', in Dirks (ed.), *Colonialism and Culture*, Ann Arbor, University of Michigan Press, 1992, p. 7.

36 Hallisey, 'Roads taken and not taken', pp. 32–3.

37 Robert Sharf, 'The Zen of Japanese nationalism', in Donald Lopez Jr (ed.), *Curators of the Buddha*, 1995, p. 140.

38 Ibid.

39 See William James, *The Varieties of Religious Experience*, The Gifford Lectures 1901–2, Glasgow, Collins, 1977, p. 386, note 1.

40 *His Eastern and Western Disciples: The Life of Swāmi Vivekānanda*, Calcutta, Advaita Ashrama, 1960, p. 405, quoted in Paul J. Will, 'Swami Vivekananda and cultural stereotyping', in N. Smart and B. Srinivasa Murthy (eds), *East–West Encounters in Philosophy and Religion*, Mumbai, Popular Prakashan, Long Beach Publications, 1996, p. 385.

41 Paul Hacker, 'Aspects of neo-Hinduism as contrasted with surviving traditional Hinduism', 1970, reprinted in Wilhelm Halbfass (ed.), *Philology and Confrontation: Paul Hacker on Traditional and Modern Vedānta*, Albany, State University of New York Press, 1995, p. 246.

42 Sarvepalli Radhakrishnan, *An Idealist View of Life*, London, Unwin Books, 2nd edn, 1937, pp. 66–78.

43 Daisetz T. Suzuki, *Mysticism, Christian and Buddhist*, London, George Allen & Unwin, 1957; Unwin Paperback, 1979, p. 4.

44 Ibid., p. 10.

45 Ibid., p. 16.

46 Ibid., p. 18.

47 Daisetz Suzuki, *Outlines of Mahāyāna Buddhism*, 1907, Schocken Books Inc., 1963, pp. 144–5. For a discussion of the differences between Advaita Vedānta and Buddhism in this regard see King, *Early Advaita Vedānta and Buddhism*.

48 Robert Sharf, 'The Zen of Japanese nationalism', in Lopez (ed.), *Curators of the Buddha*, 1995, p. 140.
49 Paul J. Will, 'Swami Vivekananda and cultural stereotyping', p. 385.
50 See Robert Sharf, 'Whose Zen? Zen nationalism revisited', in James W. Heisig and John C. Maraldo (eds), *Rude Awakenings: Zen, the Kyoto School, and the Question of Nationalism*, Honolulu, University of Hawaii Press, 1994, pp. 40–51.

8 The politics of privatization

1 F.C. Happold, *Mysticism: A Study and an Anthology*, Harmondsworth, Pelican Books, 1963, p. 20.
2 Aldous Huxley, 'Introduction', in *The Perennial Philosophy*, London, Harper & Row, 1944, p. vii.
3 Aldous Huxley, *The Doors of Perception*, London, Chatto & Windus, 1954, reprinted in *The Doors of Perception and Heaven and Hell*, London, Grafton Books (Collins), 1977, p. 19.
4 Ibid., p. 16.
5 R.C. Zaehner, *Mysticism Sacred and Profane*, New York, Clarendon Press, 1957.
6 See Ninian Smart, 'Interpretation and mystical experience', in Richard Woods (ed.), *Understanding Mysticism*, London, Athlone Press, 1980, pp. 78–91 (originally published in *Religious Studies* 1.1, 1975), and Frits Staal, *Exploring Mysticism*, Harmondsworth, Penguin, 1975, pp. 73–5.
7 Walter Stace, *Mysticism and Philosophy*, London, Jeremy P. Tarcher Inc., 1960, pp. 131–2.
8 Ibid., p. 31.
9 See Smart, 'Interpretation and mystical experience', pp. 78–91.
10 Ninian Smart does not quite take this step, though it is unclear how his position differs significantly from the perennialist position on this issue.
11 Stace, *Mysticism and Philosophy*, pp. 341–3.
12 Ibid., p. 136.
13 Steven Katz, 'Language, epistemology and mysticism', in Katz (ed.), *Mysticism and Philosophical Analysis*, New York, Oxford University Press, 1978, pp. 26–7.
14 Robert Gimello, 'Mysticism and meditation', in Katz (ed.), *Mysticism and Philosophical Analysis*, pp. 170–99.
15 Hans H. Penner, 'The mystical illusion', in Katz (ed.), *Mysticism and Religious Traditions*, New York, Oxford University Press, 1983, pp. 89–116.
16 Wayne Proudfoot, *Religious Experience*, Berkeley, California University Press, 1985.
17 Katz, 'Language, epistemology and mysticism', p. 66.
18 See Robert Forman 'Introduction: mysticism, constructivism and forgetting', in Forman (ed.), *The Problem of Pure Consciousness: Mysticism and Philosophy*, New York, Oxford University Press, 1990, pp. 19–21; Michael Stoeber, 'Constructivist epistemologies of mysticism: a critique and a revision', in *Religious Studies* 28, 1992, p. 108. See also Michael Stoeber, *Theo-Monistic Mysticism: A Hindu–Christian Comparison*, London, St Martins Press, 1994, ch. 1.
19 Emile Durkheim, *The Elementary Forms of the Religious Life*, 1st edn, 1912, London, Allen & Unwin, 1976, p. 423.
20 Peter Berger and Thomas Luckmann, *The Social Construction of Reality*, New York, Doubleday & Co., 1966.
21 To illustrate this point, Berger and Luckmann isolate three aspects of the construction process. First, there is externalization. Human beings act in the world, expressing themselves in a variety of forms. In so doing they produce

material and non-material artefacts or practices. Society itself represents part of this human expression. This is followed by objectification. These artefacts and practices become a part of one's cultural environment and confront members of that society as objective realities. Finally, we have internalization. This denotes the processes of socialization – the absorption of such artefacts and practices as constitutive of the 'way things are'.

22 Katz, 'Language, epistemology and mysticism', p. 24.
23 Grace Jantzen, *Power, Gender and Christian Mysticism*, Cambridge, Cambridge Studies in Ideology and Religion 8, Cambridge University Press, 1995, pp. 336–7; 12–25.
24 Ibid., p. 12.
25 Katz, 'Language, epistemology and mysticism', p. 66.
26 Sallie B. King, 'Two epistemological models for the interpretation of mysticism', in *Journal of American Academy of Religion* 56.2, 1988, p. 263.
27 Steven Katz, 'Responses and rejoinders: on mysticism', in *Journal of American Academy of Religion* 56.4, 1988, p. 756.
28 See Jantzen, *Power, Gender and Christian Mysticism*, ch. 8.
29 Ibid., p. 320.
30 Katz explicitly acknowledges his own debt to Kantian epistemology in his response to Sallie King's critique of his work. See Katz, 'Responses and rejoinders', p. 757. It would be fair to say that Katz's position is more accurately deemed neo-Kantian rather than strictly Kantian, since Immanuel Kant made no reference to acquired or social conditioning as a priori factors in the construction of one's experience of the world.
31 Katz, 'Language, epistemology and mysticism', p. 26.
32 Forman, 'Introduction: mysticism, constructivism and forgetting', p. 13.
33 King, 'Two epistemological models', pp. 262–3.
34 Ibid., pp. 264–5.
35 Katz, 'Responses and rejoinders', p. 756.
36 Ibid., p. 66.
37 Ibid., p. 26. For a critique of Katz's argumentation (though not his thesis) see Nelson Pike, *Mystic Union: An Essay in the Phenomenology of Mysticism*, Ithaca and London, Cornell University Press, 1992, pp. 194–207.
38 Katz, 'Language, epistemology and mysticism', p. 57.
39 Donald Evans, 'Can philosophers limit what mystics can do? A critique of Steven Katz', in *Religious Studies* 25, 1989, p. 54.
40 Forman, 'Introduction: mysticism, constructivism and forgetting', p. 28.
41 Ibid.
42 Specifically the ineffability of *dharmas* (*dharma-nirabhilāpyatā*). See *Mahāyānasaṃgraha* 8.2.
43 Katz, 'Responses and rejoinders', p. 754.
44 Huston Smith, 'Is there a perennial philosophy?', in *Journal of American Academy of Religion* 55.3, 1987, p. 558. Evans, 'Can philosophers limit what mystics can do?', p. 55.
45 Katz, 'Language, epistemology and mysticism', p. 41.
46 Klaus Klostermaier, 'The creative function of the word', in Harold Coward (ed.), *Language in Indian Philosophy and Religion*, Quebec, Canadian Studies in Religion, Supplement 5, 1976, p. 5.
47 This *Sūtra* derives from the early period of Mahāyāna development in India, being translated into Chinese by Lokakṣema in 179 CE, and is the earliest known literary reference to the cult of Amitābha (Amitāyus) Buddha and his Buddha-field (*buddha-kṣetra*) in the West (Sukhāvatī – 'Land of Bliss'). See Paul

Harrison, '*Buddhānusmṛti* in the *Pratyutpanna-Buddha-Saṃmukhāvasthita-Samādhi-Sūtra,*' in *Journal of Indian Philosophy* 6, 1978, pp. 35–57.

48 *Pratyutpanna Sūtra* [3B]. Translation in Paul Harrison, *The Samādhi of Direct Encounter with the Buddhas of the Present: An Annotated Translation of the Tibetan Version of the Pratyutpanna-Buddha-Saṃmukhāvasthita-Samādhi-Sūtra,* Tokyo, International Institute for Buddhist Studies, Studia Philologica Buddhica Monograph Series V, 1990, p. 32.

49 *Pratyutpanna Sūtra* [3L]. Translation in Harrison, *The Samādhi of Direct Encounter with the Buddhas of the Present,* p. 42.

50 See Dignāga, *Pramāṇasammuccaya* I.3.

51 King, 'Two epistemological models', p. 277. See also Paul J. Griffith, 'Pure consciousness and Indian Buddhism', in Forman (ed.), *The Problem of Pure Consciousness,* 1990, pp. 77–8.

52 As Ian Harris notes, 'What becomes apparent is that Buddhism, since it accepts the possibility of a revolution in the way we actually see the world, may not be easily defined in terms abstracted from Western philosophical discourse. This is because Western systems, both secular and religious, generally fail to accept the notion of the perfectibility of man to the extent that it is employed in the East. Buddhism, in consequence, may only be apprehended by Western thought forms when small portions of it are examined *in vacuo.*' See Ian Harris, *The Continuity of Madhyamaka and Yogācāra in Indian Mahāyāna Buddhism,* Leiden, E.J. Brill, 1991, p. 153.

53 *Pramāṇavārtika* I. 194.

54 *Pramāṇavārtika* I. 140.

55 See Richard P. Hayes, 'Whose experience validates what for Dharmakīrti', in P. Bilimoria and J.N. Mohanty (eds), *Relativism, Suffering and Beyond: Essays in Memory of Bimal K. Matilal,* Delhi, Oxford University Press, 1997, p. 113.

56 See Anne Klein, *Knowledge and Liberation: Tibetan Buddhist Epistemology in Support of Transformative Religious Experience,* Ithaca, Snow Lion, 1986.

57 Paul Williams, 'Non-conceptuality, critical reasoning and religious experience: some Tibetan Buddhist discussions', in Michael McGhee (ed.), *Philosophy, Religion and the Spiritual Life,* Cambridge, Cambridge University Press, 1992, pp. 195–6.

58 Bhartṛhari, *Vākyapadīya,* 1.124, translation in K.A. Subramania Iyer, *The Vākyapadīya of Bhartṛhari and its Vṛtti,* Deccan College Monograph, 1965, pp. 110–11.

59 Bhartṛhari, *Vākyapadīya,* 1.121.

60 Anne C. Klein, 'Mental concentration and the unconditioned: a Buddhist case of unmediated experience', in Robert E. Buswell Jr. and Robert M. Gimello (eds), *Paths to Liberation: The Mārga and Its Transformations in Buddhist Thought,* Honolulu, Kuroda Institute Studies in East Asian Buddhism 7, University of Hawaii Press, 1992, p. 270.

61 For an interesting discussion of these Asian systems of thought in relation to wider debates about the nature of non-duality and the comparative study of 'mysticism', see David Loy, *Non-Duality: A Study in Comparative Philosophy,* New Haven and London, Yale University Press, 1988.

62 For a critique of the tendency to conceive of 'Buddhism' as peculiarly concerned with the cultivation of 'mystical experiences' and therefore as an archetypally 'mystical' religion, see Robert Sharf, 'Buddhist modernism and the rhetoric of meditative experience', in *Numen* 42.3, 1995, pp. 228–83. Sharf questions, 'The tendency to approach the compendious Buddhist *mārga* treatises (texts delineating the stages on the Buddhist path) as if they presented a phenomenological analysis of the experiences of seasoned meditators' (p. 232). Rather, he argues,

traditional references to meditation or mental development (*bhāvanā*) should be seen not in terms of the cultivation of extraordinary and private states of consciousness but as primarily liturgical and propadeutical in orientation. Such practice 'consisted largely of the recitation of Pāli texts pertaining to meditation ..., chanting verses enumerating the qualities of the Buddha, reciting formulaic lists of the thirty-two parts of the body, and so on' (p. 242). Moreover, in the modern period the 'rhetoric of experience' functions as an empty category in which a variety of Buddhist ideological positions can be placed and 'Buddhism' as a spiritual phenomenon can be assigned a 'trans-cultural, trans-historical reality'. Moreover, the privatization of Buddhism in terms of 'the rhetoric of experience' resulted in the construction of a 'world religion' amenable to both perennialist and secular interpretations and successfully divorced the understanding and interpretation of traditional Buddhist meditation from the ethical, doctrinal, liturgical and sociopolitical context in which such practices occur.

63 Jantzen, *Power, Gender and Christian Mysticism*, ch. 8.

9 Beyond Orientalism?

1 See, for instance, Eli Franco and Karin Preisendanz (eds), *Beyond Orientalism: The Work of Wilhelm Halbfass and Its Impact on Indian and Cross-cultural Studies*, Amsterdam, Atlanta GA, Rodopi, Poznań: Studies in the Philosophy of the Sciences and the Humanities, Vol. 59, 1997; Fred Dallmayr, *Beyond Orientalism: Essays on Cross-cultural Encounter*, Albany, State University of New York, 1996.

2 Ali Rattansi, 'Postcolonialism and its discontents', in *Economy and Society* 26.4, 1997, p. 491. See also Aijaz Ahmed, *In Theory: Classes, Nations, Literature*, London, Verso, 1992, p. 172.

3 Paul Rabinow, 'Representations are social facts: modernity and post-modernity in anthropology', in James Clifford and George E. Marcus (eds), *Writing Culture: The Poetics and Politics of Ethnography*, Berkeley, University of California Press, 1986, p. 241. See also Amrita Srinivasan, 'Reform or conformity? Temple "prostitution" and the community in the Madras presidency', in Bina Agarwal (ed.), *Structures of Patriarchy: State, Community and Household in Modernizing Asia*, Delhi, Kali for Women, 1988, for an example of 'anthropologizing' the colonial discourse of reform through an analysis of the transformation of the precolonial *devadāsī* in terms of the notion of 'temple prostitute'. As Spivak notes in her discussion of Srinivasan's work, the most striking feature of her analysis is the displacement of conventional notions of sexuality through the postulation of an Indocentric redefinition of celibacy in terms of the temple practices of the *devadāsī*. Gayatri Spivak, 'How to teach a "culturally different" book', in *differences* 3.3, 1991, pp. 139–70, revised version reprinted in Donna Landry and Gerald Maclean (eds), *The Spivak Reader*, London, Routledge, 1996, pp. 237–66.

4 Aijaz Ahmed, 'Jameson's rhetoric of otherness and the national allegory', in *Social Text* 17, 1987; abridged version in Bill Ashcroft, Gareth Griffiths and Helen Tiffin (eds), *The Post-colonial Studies Reader*, London, Routledge, 1995, p. 80. See also Ella Shohat, 'Post-Third-Worldist culture: gender, nation, and the cinema', in M. Jacqui Alexander and Chandra Talpade Mohanty (eds), *Feminist Genealogies, Colonial Legacies, Democratic Futures*, London, Routledge, 1997, especially pp. 188–91.

5 Dipesh Chakrabarty, 'Postcoloniality and the artifice of history: who speaks for "Indian pasts"?', in *Representations* 37, Winter 1992, p. 20.

6 Ibid., p. 1.
7 The exact words of the character concerned (Mr 'Whisky' Sisodia) are: 'The trouble with the Engenglish is that their hiss hiss history happened overseas, so they dodo don't know what it means.' Salman Rushdie, *The Satanic Verses*, London, Viking Press, Penguin, 1988, p. 343.
8 Chakrabarty, 'Postcoloniality and the artifice of history', p. 22.
9 See Talal Asad, *Genealogies of Religion: Discipline and Reasons of Power in Christianity and Islam*, London, Johns Hopkins University Press, 1993, ch. 7.
10 Dick Hebdige, *Cut 'n Mix: Culture, Identity and Carribean Music*, London, Methuen Press, 1987, pp. 158–9, quoted in Akhil Gupta and James Ferguson, 'Beyond "culture": space, identity and the politics of difference', in *Cultural Anthropology* 7.1, 1992, p. 10.
11 Chakrabarty, 'Postcoloniality and the artifice of history', p. 23. This is reminiscent of Gayatri Spivak's deconstructionist reading of the Subalternist project. She argues that the Subalternist Group 'tracks failures in attempts to displace discursive fields. A deconstructive approach would bring into focus the fact that they are themselves engaged in an attempt at displacing discursive fields, that they themselves "fail" (in the general sense) for reasons as "historical" as those they adduce for the heterogenous agents they study; and it would attempt to forge a practice that would take this into account.' See Spivak, 'Subaltern Studies: deconstructing historiography', in Ranajit Guha and Gayatri Spivak (eds), *Selected Subaltern Studies*, Delhi, Oxford University Press, 1988, p. 9, reprinted in Landry and Maclean, *The Spivak Reader*, p. 210.
12 Ranajit Guha, 'On some aspects of the historiography of colonial India', in *Subaltern Studies* 1, Delhi, Oxford University Press, 1982, p. 8.
13 See Sumit Sarkar, 'The conditions and nature of subaltern militancy: Bengal from swadeshi to noncooperation', in *Subaltern Studies* 3, Delhi, Oxford University Press, 1984.
14 See Douglas Haynes and Gyan Prakash (eds), *Contesting Power: Resistance and Everyday Social Relations in South Asia*, Berkeley, University of California Press, 1991. The shift in more recent work on the subaltern has been towards an analysis of the everyday life of the subaltern as a form of resistance. This approach resonates well with Nancy Hartsock's call for a feminist approach to questions of power and knowledge: 'we need a theory of power that recognizes that our practical daily activity contains an understanding of the world – subjugated perhaps, but present. Here I am reaffirming Gramsci's argument that everyone is an intellectual and that each of us has an epistemology. The point, then, for "minority" theories is to "read out" the epistemologies in our various practices.' Nancy Hartsock, 'Foucault on power: a theory for women?', in Linda J. Nicholson (ed.), *Feminism/Postmodernism*, London, Routledge, 1990, p. 172. Janaki Nair, however, has criticized the emphasis upon 'everyday non-confrontational resistance' as a dilution of the concept of resistance and a return of the 'victim as heroine' scenario. The notion of 'everyday life' as a form of resistance, she argues, remains a minor consideration so long as it fails to transform the nature of larger, systemic power structures. Janaki Nair, 'On the question of agency in Indian feminist historiography', in *Gender and History* 6.1, April 1994, pp. 90–4.
15 See Rosalind O'Hanlon, 'Recovering the subject: Subaltern Studies and histories of resistance in colonial South Asia', in *Modern Asian Studies* 22.1, 1988, pp. 216 and 223.
16 Ibid., p. 4.
17 Ibid., p. 191.
18 Ibid., p. 196.

250   *Notes*

19 Douglas Haynes and Gyan Prakash, 'Introduction: the entanglement of power and resistance', in Haynes and Prakash (eds), *Contesting Power*, p. 9.
20 Ibid., p. 19. In a similar vein, Rosalind O'Hanlon suggests that the presence of the subaltern might be recovered in history without slipping into an essentialist position, 'by revealing that presence to be one constructed and refracted through practice, but no less "real" for our having said that it does not contain its own origins within itself.' See O'Hanlon, 'Recovering the subject', p. 202.
21 Haynes and Prakash, 'Introduction', in *Contesting Power*, p. 20.
22 Christopher A. Bayly, 'Modern Indian historiography', in Michael Bentley (ed.), *Companion to Historiography*, London, Routledge, 1997, p. 688.
23 Partha Chatterjee, 'Peasants, politics and historiography: a response', in *Social Scientist* 120, May 1983, p. 59.
24 Ibid.
25 As O'Hanlon notes, such an approach to the study of colonial discourse must avoid the assumption (which she mistakenly associates with a Foucauldian position) 'that one can capture a discursive formation before it is markedly affected by those over whom it exerts power'. O'Hanlon, 'Recovering the subject', p. 217.
26 Ibid., p. 211. See also p. 215.
27 Spivak, 'Subaltern Studies'.
28 For examples of this see Guha, 'On some aspects of the historiography of colonial India'; Partha Chatterjee, *Nationalist Thought and the Colonial World: A Derivative Discourse*, London, Zed Books, 1986; Gyanendra Pandey, *The Construction of Communalism in Colonial North India*, Delhi, Oxford University Press, 1990.
29 Nicholas B. Dirks, 'Introduction', in Dirks (ed.), *Colonialism and Culture*, Ann Arbor, University of Michigan Press, 1992, p. 14.
30 In this regard Gyan Prakash argues that 'in India itself, the power of Western discourses is concealed and operates through its authorization and deployment by the nation-state; deeply sedimented in the national body politic, the knowledge generated and bequeathed by colonialism neither manifests itself nor functions exclusively as a form of imperial power'. See Gyan Prakash, 'Writing post-Orientalist histories of the Third World: Indian historiography is good to think', in Nicholas B. Dirks (ed.), *Colonalism and Culture*, Ann Arbor, University of Michigan Press, 1992, p. 374. Note that this is a revised version of an article originally published in *Comparative Studies in Society and History* 32.2, 1990, pp. 383–408.
31 See Aijaz Ahmed, 'Between Orientalism and historicism: anthropological knowledge of India', in *Studies in History* 7.1, 1991, pp. 135–63, especially pp. 150–8. See also Sumit Sarkar, 'Orientalism revisited: Saidian frameworks in the writing of modern Indian history', in *Oxford Literary Review* 16, 1994, pp. 210–17; Jayant Lele, 'The two faces of nationalism: on the revolutionary potential of tradition', in Jacques Dofmy and Akinsola Akiwowo (eds), *National and Ethnic Movements*, Sage Publications, 1980, pp. 201–16.
32 Abdul R. JanMohamed, 'The economy of Manichean allegory: the function of racial difference in colonialist literature', in *Critical Inquiry* 12.1, 1985, pp. 59–87, abridged version in Ashcroft *et al.* (eds), *The Post-colonial Studies Reader*, pp. 18–23.
33 See Prakash, 'Writing post-Orientalist histories', pp. 365–9.
34 Partha Chatterjee, 'Peasants, politics and historiography', pp. 63; 64–5.
35 See Dipankar Gupta, 'On altering the ego in peasant history: paradoxes of the ethnic option', in *Peasant Studies* 13.1, 1985, pp. 15–16, cited in O'Hanlon, 'Recovering the subject', p. 207.

36 For evidence of Marx's acceptance of the interpenetration of base and super-structure see Karl Marx, *Collected Works*, Vol. III, London, pp. 926–7.
37 Antonio Gramsci, *Selections from the Prison Notebooks*, edited and translated by Quintin Hoare and Geoffrey Nowell Smith, London, Lawrence & Wishart, 1971, p. 407.
38 O'Hanlon, 'Recovering the subject', p. 213–14. See also pp. 216; 223–4.
39 Note, however, the critique of Aijaz Ahmed in this regard. He is critical of what he sees as the simplistic rejection of Marx as 'another Orientalist' in the works of Edward Said and his followers and criticizes the representation of Marxist philosophy as just another neo-colonial master-narrative on the grounds that this radically ignores the role played by Marxism as an anti-colonial force in the modern world. See Ahmed, *In Theory*, p. 178. For a brief but critical response to Ahmed, see Rattansi, 'Postcolonialism and its discontents', pp. 496–7.
40 Prakash, 'Writing post-Orientalist histories', p. 371. See also pp. 367 and 369.
41 Ibid., p. 371.
42 In a limited fashion this point is noted by Ranajit Guha in his early clarification of the subaltern–élite distinction: 'Some of these classes and groups such as the lesser rural gentry, impoverished landlords, rich peasants and upper-middle peasants who "naturally" ranked among the "people" and the "subaltern", could under certain circumstances act for the "elite" ... and therefore be classified as such in some local or regional situations – an ambiguity which it is left up to the historian to sort out on the basis of choice and judicious reading of his evidence.' See Guha, 'On some aspects of the historiography of colonial India', p. 8. Gramsci himself was clear that 'The subaltern classes, by definition, are not unified' and that 'the history of the parties of the subaltern groups is very complex too'. This necessitated careful study of the factors involved in the forma-tion of subaltern groupings, 'their active and passive affiliation to the dominant political formations', the birth of new parties aiming to gain the assent of and control of such groups, and 'new formations which assert the autonomy of the subaltern groups'. See Gramsci, *Selections from the Prison Notebooks*, p. 52.
43 As Florencia Mallon points out, 'no subaltern identity can be pure and trans-parent, most subalterns are both dominated and dominating subjects'. See Florencia Mallon, 'The promise and dilemmas of Subaltern Studies: perspectives from Latin American history', in *American Historical Review* 99.5, 1994, p. 1511.
44 Janaki Nair argues, for instance, that 'the "subaltern studies" project remains singularly inattentive to questions of gender in historical analysis'. See Nair, 'On the question of agency in Indian feminist historiography', p. 84. Nair does acknowledge that there are exceptions to this appraisal, citing Ranajit Guha's (1987) study 'Chandra's death'. One might also mention Partha Chatterjee, 'Colonialism, nationalism and colonialized women: the context in India', in *American Ethnologist* 16, 1989, pp. 622–33.
45 Prakash tends to fetishize the difference and innovativeness of his own 'post-Orientalist' approach at the expense of the Subalternists, while at the same time equivocating and making connections with both the subaltern project and earlier historical work such as that of Bernard Cohn and Romila Thapar. See Prakash, 'Writing post-Orientalist histories', p. 375. Rosalind O'Hanlon and David Washbrook criticize Prakash for misrepresenting the 'foundationalist histori-ographies' of Marxist and social historians of India (e.g. p. 145 and note 13), making it difficult to determine what is distinctive about his 'post-foundationalist' approach (p. 148). They further argue that Prakash is committed to an emancipatory politics for the dispossessed that is opposed to his 'extreme Foucauldian view of the inescapability of relations of power and domination'. Consequently, Prakash's refusal to define the structures and trajectories of

struggle and the categories of analysis for understanding them 'push the burden of representing such a politics ... onto those who are in struggle themselves' (p. 150). See Rosalind O'Hanlon and David Washbrook, 'After Orientalism: culture, criticism, and politics in the Third World', in *Comparative Studies in Society and History* 34.1, January 1994, pp. 141–67. In reply to this Prakash has argued that his stance does not require 'abandoning Marxism altogether', only the 'mode of production story as a normative universal' characteristic of 'unexamined Eurocentric Marxism'. In his view, Marx can be 'recaptured' by 'writing about histories that remained heterogenous with the logic of capital' (p. 178). See Gyan Prakash, 'Can the "subaltern" ride? A reply to O'Hanlon and Washbrook', in *Comparative Studies in Society and History* 34.1, January 1994, pp. 168–84. On the possibility of a 'post-structuralist' Marxism see Barbara Foley, 'Marxism in the post-structuralist moment: some notes on the problem of revising Marx', in *Cultural Critique* 15, Spring 1990, pp. 5–37. See also Prakash, 'Writing post-Orientalist histories', pp. 370ff.

46 Prakash, 'Writing post-Orientalist histories', p. 373.
47 Ibid., p. 374.
48 This phrase is used by Prakash in response to a critique of his work by O'Hanlon and Washbrook, which argued that in his equivocation between Marxist and post-structuralist–deconstructionist methodologies, Prakash was attempting to ride two horses at once. His response was to argue that this indeed was the case and that the ambiguities and 'heuristic' nature of such an enterprise did not prevent political engagement but enabled the critic 'to mark the space of the subaltern as aporetic' and prevents a 'paternalistic recovery of the subaltern's voice' and the 'imperialist attempt to speak for the colonized subaltern woman. Basically, an attempt to ride two horses at once.' See Prakash, 'Can the "subaltern" ride?', 1994, p. 175.
49 Prakash, 'Writing post-Orientalist histories', p. 368
50 Prakash, 'Can the "subaltern" ride?', p. 176.
51 For a discussion of the problems of pluralist versus reductionist accounts with regard to Marxist thought, see S.H. Rigby, 'Marxist historiography', in Bentley (ed.), *Companion to Historiography*, pp. 913–15.
52 For an insightful discussion of the politics of location of the diaspora intellectual with specific reference to the 'Rainbow Coalition' of Reverend Jesse Jackson in the 1988 US Presidential campaign, see Rajagopalan Radhakrishnan, *Diasporic Mediations: Between Home and Location*, Ann Arbor, University of Minnesota Press, 1996.
53 There has been a plethora of material discussing the issue of the relationship between 'postcolonialism', post-structuralism and postmodernism. For a useful bibliography of such works, see Bart Moore-Gilbert, *Postcolonial Theory: Contexts, Practices, Politics*, London, Verso, 1997, p. 223, note 27.
54 Dirks, 'Introduction', in *Colonialism and Culture*, p. 12.
55 Hartsock, 'Foucault on power', p. 163.
56 Donna Haraway, 'Situated knowledges: the science question in feminism and the privilege of partial perspective', in *Feminist Studies* 14.3, 1988, p. 585.
57 Translated by Gail Omvedt and quoted in Barbara R. Joshi (ed.), *Untouchable! Voices of the Dalit Liberation Movement*, London, Zed Books, 1986, p. 97; see also Steven M. Parrish, *Hierarchy and Its Discontents: Culture and the Politics of Consciousness in Caste Society*, Philadelphia, University of Pennsylvania Press, 1996, p. 82.
58 Amanda Anderson, 'Cryptonormativism and double gestures: the politics of post-structuralism', in *Cultural Critique* 21, Spring 1992, p. 73.

59 Bimal Krishna Matilal and Gayatri Spivak, *Epic and Ethic*, New York, Routledge, forthcoming. See Moore-Gilbert, *Postcolonial Theory*, p. 98.
60 Samir Dayal, 'Postcolonialism's possibilities: subcontinental diasporic intervention', in *Cultural Critique* 33, Spring 1996, pp. 129–30.
61 Ziauddin Sardar, *Postmodernism and the Other: The New Imperialism of Western Culture*, London, Pluto Press, 1998, p. 13.
62 Michel Foucault, *History of Sexuality*, Vol. 1, Harmondsworth, Penguin, 1978, p. 94.
63 Nancy Hartsock ('Foucault on power', p. 167) argues, for instance, that Foucault's rather pessimistic world is one 'in which things move, rather than people, a world in which subjects become obliterated or, rather, recreated as passive objects, a world in which passivity or refusal represent the only possible choices'.
64 Foucault, *History of Sexuality*, Vol. 1, p. 95.
65 Nair, 'On the question of agency in Indian feminist historiography', pp. 90–1.
66 Prakash, 'Can the "Subaltern" ride?', p. 183.
67 See, for instance, Rashmi Bhatnagar, 'Uses and limits of Foucault: a study of the theme of origins in Edward Said's *Orientalism*', in *Social Scientist* 16.7, 1986, pp. 3–22; Sarkar, 'Orientalism revisited', pp. 205–24.
68 Ann Laura Stoler, *Race and the Education of Desire: Foucault's History of Sexuality and the Colonial Order of Things*, London, Duke University Press, 1995, p. 7.
69 See Joseph Bristow, *Sexuality*, The New Critical Idiom Series, London, Routledge, 1997, pp. 176–9.
70 For a critique of Michel de Certeau's conception of power relations, see John Frow, 'Michel de Certeau and the practice of representation', in *Cultural Studies* 5.1, 1991, pp. 56–7. Frow's description of Certeau as offering a monolithic and polar model of domination, however, is a misreading of his stance. For a response in relation to the question of postcolonialism, see the critique of Frow in Ian Buchanan, 'Writing the wrongs of history: De Certeau and post-colonialism', in *SPAN* (Journal of the South Pacific Association for Commonwealth Literature and Language Studies), no. 33, May 1992, p. 41.
71 Buchanan, 'Writing the wrongs of history', p. 42.
72 Homi Bhabha, 'The other question: difference, discrimination, and the discourse of colonialism', in Francis Barker (ed.), *Literature, Politics and Theory*, London, Methuen, 1986, p. 158. Originally published in Francis Barker (ed.), *The Politics of Theory*, Colchester, University of Essex, 1983. Reprinted in Padmini Mongia (ed.), *Contemporary Postcolonial Theory: A Reader*, London, Hodder Headline Press, 1996, p. 42.
73 'Bhabha's conception of postcolonial agency and resistance in fact depends upon the continuing authority of the dominant for its operation and consequently risks reconstituting the dominant.' Moore-Gilbert, *Postcolonial Theory*, p. 138.
74 Homi Bhabha, 'Signs taken for wonders: questions of ambivalence and authority under a tree in Delhi, May 1817', in *Critical Inquiry* 12.1, 1985, pp. 144–65, abridged version in Ashcroft *et al.* (eds), *The Post-colonial Studies Reader*, see p. 35. Said's appeal to individual intention (e.g. *Orientalism: Western Conceptions of the Orient*, London, Penguin, 1991, p. 23) reflects the limitations of his approach to power, restricting his suggestions of a response to Orientalism in terms of a narrowly oppositional stance. According to Young, however, the emphasis upon ambivalence in the Derridean deconstructionism of Bhabha and Spivak allow the postcolonial critic to 'exploit the ambivalence of the discourse of Orientalism and position himself or herself in an equally ambivalent relation to the theoretical method that is being employed, so as to disconcert and

disorient the reader from the familar politico-theoretical structures which it seems to promise'. Robert Young, *White Mythologies*, London, Routledge, 1990, p. 173.

75 Ludo Rocher, *Ezourvedam: A French Veda of the Eighteenth Century*, Amsterdam and Philadelphia, John Benjamins Publishing Company, University of Pennsylvania, Studies on South Asia, Vol. 1, 1984. See also Wilhelm Halbfass, *India and Europe: An Essay in Understanding*, Albany, State University of New York Press, 1988, pp. 46; 57–8.

76 Bhabha, 'Signs taken for wonders'. See Ashcroft *et al.* (eds), *The Post-colonial Studies Reader*, pp. 35–6.

77 Bhabha, 'Signs taken for wonders', p. 36.

78 Moore-Gilbert, *Postcolonial Theory*, pp. 134–5.

79 Toril Moi, *Sexual/Textual Politics: Feminist Literary Theory*, New York, Routledge, 1985, p. 40.

80 In a move clearly indebted to Spivak, Diane Fuss reads Irigaray's use of essentialist language as an intentional and transgressive strategy: 'In the hands of a hegemonic group, essentialism can be employed as a powerful tool of ideological domination; in the hands of the subaltern, the use of humanism to mime (in the Irigarayian sense of "to undo by overdoing") humanism can represent a powerful displacing repetition. The question of the permissibility, if you will, of engaging in essentialism is therefore framed and determined by the subject-positions from which one speaks.' Diana Fuss, 'Reading like a feminist', in Naomi Schor and Elizabeth Weed (eds), *The Essential Difference*, Indiana University Press, essays from *differences. A Journal of Feminist Cultural Studies*, 1994, p. 108. See also Naomi Schor, 'This essentialism which is not one: coming to grips with Irigaray', in *The Essential Difference*, pp. 40–62.

81 Benita Parry, 'Problems in current theories of colonial discourse', in *Oxford Literary Review* 9, 1987, p. 43; abridged version in Ashcroft *et al.* (eds), *The Post-colonial Studies Reader*, p. 43. See also Young, *White Mythologies*, ch. 8; Nicholas Thomas, *Colonialism's Culture: Anthropology, Travel and Government*, Cambridge, Polity Press, 1994, pp. 40; 51–9, for critiques of Bhabha's approach. In 'Difference, discrimination and the discourse of colonialism' (originally published in 1983), Bhabha acknowledges that anti-colonial struggle has to be more than simply 'the under/other side of "colonial discourse"', and that it requires 'an alternative set of questions, techniques and strategies in order to construct it' (p. 198). However, by the time of 'Signs taken as wonders' (1985), Bhabha sees mimicry as an active disruption of colonial pretensions rather than as a disquieting reminder of colonial ambivalences. See Young, *White Mythologies*, pp. 145–51. For a sympathetic but critical account, see Moore-Gilbert, *Postcolonial Theory*, ch. 4. Similarly, for Spivak there is no space from which the subaltern can speak. See Gayatri Spivak, 'The Rani of Sirmur', in Francis Barker *et al.* (eds), *Europe and Its Others*, Vol. I, Colchester, University of Essex, 1985, pp. 128–32; and 'Three women's texts and a critique of imperialism', in *Critical Inquiry* 12.1, 1985, p. 254.

82 Young, *White Mythologies*, p. 150.

83 See Thomas, *Colonialism's Culture*, p. 57.

84 Frantz Fanon, *Les Damnés de la terre*, 1961, English title: *The Wretched of the Earth*, translated by Constance Farrington, London, MacGibbon & Kee, 1965, p. 30, cited in Parry, 'Problems in current theories of colonial discourse', p. 43; also in Ashcroft *et al.* (eds), *The Post-colonial Studies Reader*, p. 43.

85 Kyung-Won Lee, 'Is the glass half-empty or half-full? Rethinking the problems of postcolonial revisionism', in *Cultural Critique* 36, Spring 1997, pp. 103–4.

86 Henry Louis Gates Jr., 'Critical Fanonism', in *Critical Inquiry* 17.3, 1991, p. 462, cited in Kyung-Won Lee, 'Is the glass half-empty or half-full', p. 104.

87 Prakash, 'Writing post-Orientalist histories', p. 382.

88 O'Hanlon, 'Recovering the subject', p. 217.

89 As Gayatri Spivak suggests: 'Quite often what happens also is that remarkable organic intellectuals ... who become spokespersons for subalternity are taken as token subalterns. This reception is a feature of our desire to fixate on intellectuals ... The effort required for the subaltern to enter into organic intellectuality is ignored by our desire to have our cake and eat it too: that we can continue to be as we are, and yet be in touch with the speaking subaltern.' See 'Subaltern talk: an interview', in Landry and Maclean (eds), *The Spivak Reader*, p. 292.

90 Seyla Benhabib, *Critique Norm and Utopia: A Study of the Foundations of Critical Theory*, New York, Columbia University Press, 1986, p. 352.

91 For a detailed discussion of Foucault and religion, see Jeremy Carrette, *Foucault and Religion*, London, Routledge, forthcoming.

92 Amit Rai, 'The King is dead: a review of Breckenridge and van der Veer (1993), *Orientalism and the Post-colonial Predicament*', in *Oxford Literary Review* 16, 1994, pp. 295–301.

93 Dorothy M. Figueira, *The Exotic: A Decadent Quest*, Albany, State University of New York Press, 1994, p. 7. See also pp. 11 and 17. As Sara Mills argues, there is a need 'to reinscribe individual agency at some level' in colonial discourse analysis 'after Foucault'. See Sara Mills, *Discourse*, New Critical Idiom Series, London, Routledge, 1997, p. 122. This is particularly important as a means of highlighting the fissures and heterogeneities of Orientalist discourses and to be able to make distinctions between individuals with regard to their complicity with imperialism (as David Kopf wishes to in the case of the Orientalists and Anglicists). This is necessary if one wishes to provide a more subtle, nuanced and contextual analysis that avoids the Manichean dualism that JanMohammed correctly ascribes to much contemporary postcolonial analysis. For a critique of Foucault as undermining individual agency, see Mark Philp, 'Foucault', in Quentin Skinner (ed.), *The Return of Grand Theory in the Human Sciences*, Cambridge, Cambridge University Press, 1985, p. 79 and O'Hanlon, 'Recovering the subject', p. 215.

94 Parrish, *Hierarchy and Its Discontents*, pp. x–xi.

95 See Michel Foucault, *The Archaeology of Knowledge and the Discourse on Language*, translated by Alan Sheridan, New York, Pantheon Books, 1972, p. 17. In 'A portrait of Foucault', Gilles Deleuze suggests that the later Foucault was looking to move beyond 'power' as the central explanatory category of his work: 'I think that he must have come up against the question of whether there was anything "beyond" power – whether he was getting trapped in a sort of impasse within power relations ... The first volume [of the *The History of Sexuality*] did of course identify points of resistance to power; it's just that their character, their origin, their production were still vague. Perhaps Foucault had the feeling that he must at all costs cross that line, get to the other side, go still further than knowledge and power. Even if it meant reconsidering the whole project of the *History of Sexuality*.' Gilles Deleuze, *Negotiations*, New York, Columbia University Press, 1995, p. 109. (I would like to thank my colleague Dr Jeremy Carrette for drawing my attention to this reference.)

96 Cited in Paul Patton, 'Of power and prisons', in Meaghan Morris and Paul Patton (eds), *Michel Foucault: Power/Truth/Strategy*, Sydney, Feral Publications, 1979, p. 115, and again in Mills, *Discourse*, p. 17.

97 Lisa Lowe, *Critical Terrains: French and British Orientalism*, Ithaca and London, Cornell University Press, 1991, p. 15.

98 See Abdul R. JanMohamed and David Lloyd, 'Introduction: minority discourse – what is to be done?', in *Cultural Critique*, Fall 1987, p. 12. See also O'Hanlon and Washbrook, 'After Orientalism', p. 155 and K. Sivaramakrishnan, 'Situating the subaltern: history and anthropology in the Subaltern Studies project', in *Journal of Historical Sociology* 8.4, December 1995, p. 418.

99 Ivan Strenski, 'Religion, power and final Foucault', in *Journal of American Academy of Religion* 66.2, Summer 1998, p. 358.

100 Edward Said, *Culture and Imperialism*, London, Chatto & Windus, 1993, p. 97. See also Russell McCutcheon, *Manufacturing Religion: The Discourse of Sui Generis Religion and the Politics of Nostalgia*, New York and Oxford, Oxford University Press, 1997, p. 22; ch. 6.

101 Michael Pye, 'Religion: shape and shadow', in *Numen* 41, 1994, p. 56.

102 McKim Marriott, 'Constructing an Indian ethnosociology', in *Contributions to Indian Sociology* 23.1, 1989, p. 1.

103 For critiques of Marriott's position see R.S. Khare, 'Indian sociology and the cultural other', and Michael Moffatt, 'Deconstructing McKim Marriott's ethnosociology: an outcaste's critique', both in *Contributions to Indian Sociology* 24.2, 1990, pp. 186–96 and pp. 223–9 respectively; Ákos Östör and Lina Fruzzetti, 'For an ethnosociology of India?', in *Contributions to Indian Sociology* 25.2, 1991, pp. 309–20.

104 As I have argued, the displacement of 'Europe' and European epistemes also involves the displacement of constructions of 'India' that are based upon such epistemes. My position is that the chauvinism of the contemporary form of Hindu nationalism can be problematized by demonstrating Western colonial influence in the construction of modern notions of Hindutva on the one hand and by highlighting the hegemonies and indigenous power struggles (internal colonialism!) involved in such movements. My intention in doing so is not to undermine Indian attempts at self-representation but rather to create a space for subaltern alternatives to such hegemonic discourses to emerge.

105 A. Parker, M. Russo, D. Sommer and P. Yaeger (eds), *Nationalism and Sexualities*, New York and London, Routledge, 1992.

106 Tanika Sarkar, 'The woman as communal subject: Rashtrasevika Samiti and Ram Janmabhoomi Movement', in *Economic and Political Weekly* 26, 31 August 1991, pp. 2057–62.

107 See Radhakrishnan, *Diasporic Mediations*, 1996, p. 212.

108 Brian K. Smith, 'After Said, after Ayodhya: new challenges for the study of Indian religions', in *Religion* 26, 1996, p. 370. See also 371–2, note 17.

109 Spivak, 'The Rani of Sirmur', p. 131.

110 Ibid.

111 Dayal, 'Postcolonialism's possibilities', pp. 133–4.

112 Ahmed, 'Between Orientalism and historicism'. For a critique of Inden and other 'post-Orientalists' from an Indological perspective see Wilhelm Halbfass, 'Beyond Orientalism? Reflections on a Current Theme', in Franco and Preisendanz (eds), *Beyond Orientalism*, pp. 1–25.

113 Linda Alcoff, 'The problem of speaking for others', in *Cultural Critique* 20, 1991, pp. 5–32.

114 For a perceptive discussion of the explosion of theories in 'postcolonial studies', see Barbara Christian, 'The race for theory', in *Cultural Critique* 6, 1987, pp. 51–63.

115 Stephen Slemon, 'The scramble for post-colonialism', in Chris Tiffin and Alan Lawson (eds), *De-scribing Empire: Post-colonialism and Textuality*, London, Routledge, 1994, p. 30; abridged version in Ashcroft *et al.* (eds), *The Post-colonial Studies Reader*, p. 51.

116 Asad, *Genealogies of Religion*, p. 198; Gupta and Ferguson, 'Beyond "culture"',
pp. 13–20.
117 Chakrabarty, 'Postcoloniality and the artifice of history', pp. 20–1.
118 See Chapter 3 of this volume, pp. 78–80.
119 Gupta and Ferguson, 'Beyond "culture"', p. 8.
120 See Prakash, 'Writing post-Orientalist histories', pp. 365; 380.
121 Anne McClintock, *Imperial Leather: Race, Gender and Sexuality in the Imperial
Contest*, London, Routledge, 1995, pp. 6–7, quoted in Mills, *Discourse*, p. 79.
122 Mrinalini Sinha, *Colonial Masculinity: The 'Manly Englishman' and the
'Effeminate Bengali' in the Late Nineteenth Century*, Manchester, Manchester
University Press, 1995, p. 11.
123 Ibid. See also the work of feminist historians Kumkum Sangari and Sudesh Vaid
as a example of the view that all of reality is gendered and therefore that gender
should not be treated in isolation from other aspects of human cultural identity
such as race, nationality and social class. See Sangari and Vaid, *Recasting
Women: Essays in Indian Colonial History*, New Brunswick, Rutgers University
Press, 1990, pp. 1–27, also cited as an influence in Sinha, *Colonial Masculinity*,
see p. 29, note 37.
124 Jeremy Carrette and Richard King, 'Giving "birth" to theory: critical perspectives on religion and the body', in *Scottish Journal of Religious Studies* 19.1,
Summer 1998, p. 136.
125 See Sinha, *Colonial Masculinity*; Rattansi, 'Postcolonialism and its discontents',
pp. 482–3; Gupta and Ferguson, 'Beyond "culture"'.
126 Gupta and Ferguson, 'Beyond "culture"', p. 14.
127 Marriott tends to elide India with Hindu, Hindu with brahminical and brahminical with Vedāntic monism (or latterly, Sāṃkhya philosophy).
128 Östör and Fruzzetti, 'For an ethnosociology of India?', pp. 309–20.
129 Rabindra Ray, 'And why an Indian sociology?' in *Contributions to Indian
Sociology* 24.2, 1990, pp. 265–75.
130 Gyan Prakash, 'Science "gone native" in colonial India', in *Representations* 40,
1992, p. 154.
131 See also Partha Chatterjee, 'The disciplines in colonial Bengal', in Chatterjee
(ed.), *Texts of Power: Emerging Disciplines in Colonial Bengal*, Minneapolis,
University of Minnesota Press, 1995, pp. 18–29.
132 Bryan Turner, *Orientalism, Postmodernism and Globalism*, London and New
York, Routledge, 1994, pp. 101–4. See also Bryan Turner, *Religion and Social
Theory*, London, Sage, 2nd edn, 1991, pp. 15–37.
133 Turner, *Orientalism, Postmodernism and Globalism*, p. 104. I remain sceptical,
however, about the role of a 'discourse of sameness' and the 'new form of secular
ecumenicalism' that Turner advocates, particularly the extent to which this dovetails with the global commodification of culture and the threat to cultural
heterogeneity.
134 Ibid. Shame, then, that Turner seems unwilling to acknowledge that the conceptual and theoretical roots of the discipline of sociology are themselves
ethnocentric and culturally specific in their provenance. For Turner, 'It would not
be possible to develop something called Islamic social science, for the same
reason that you cannot have Christian social science or Jewish social science or
any other type of ethnic social science. There is a basic logic and theory to the
social sciences which cannot be subsumed under a particular ethnic or cultural
or historical label' (p. 8). In contrast to this, as we have seen, McKim Marriott
has argued that 'all social sciences are culturally specific in their provenance and
origin' (Marriott, 'Constructing an Indian ethnosociology', p. 1, note 2. See also
this volume p. 212 and note 103.). Of the two positions, my instincts are to side

with Marriott in calling into question the privileged status of Western categories within contemporary social science.

135 I am here alluding to a phrase used by Foucault in the introduction to *The Order of Things* (New York, Pantheon, 1973). In a discussion of the fictional Chinese encyclopaedia occurring in a short story by the Argentine writer Jorge Luis Borges, Foucault marvels at the incomprehensibleness of cultural difference: 'In the wonderment of this taxonomy, the things we apprehend in one great leap, the thing that, by means of the fable, is demonstrated as the exotic charm of another system of thought, is the limitations of our own, the stark impossibility of thinking that' (p. xv).

136 Turner, *Orientalism, Postmodernism and Globalism*, p. 8.

137 Spivak, 'Subaltern talk: an interview', p. 296.

Bibliography

Abdel-Malek, Anwar, 'Orientalism in crisis', in *Diogenes*, Vol. 44, 1963.

Ahmed, Aijaz, 'Between Orientalism and historicism: anthropological knowledge of India', in *Studies in History* 7.1, 1991, pp. 135–63.

—— 'Jameson's rhetoric of otherness and the national allegory', in *Social Text* 17, Fall 1987, pp. 3–25; abridged version in Bill Ashcroft, Gareth Griffiths and Helen Tiffin (eds), *The Post-colonial Studies Reader*, London, Routledge, 1995.

—— *In Theory: Classes, Nations, Literature*, London, Verso, 1992.

Alcoff, Linda, 'The problem of speaking for others', in *Cultural Critique* 20, 1991, pp. 5–32.

Almond, Philip, *The British Discovery of Buddhism*, Cambridge, Cambridge University Press, 1988.

Alvares, Claude, *Decolonizing History: Technology and Culture in India, China and the West, 1492 to the Present Day*, Goa, India, The Other India Press, and New York, Apex Press, 1991.

Anderson, Amanda, 'Cryptonormativism and double gestures: the politics of post-structuralism', in *Cultural Critique* 21, Spring 1992.

Anderson, Benedict, *Imagined Communities: Reflections on the Origin and Spread of Nationalism*, London, Verso, 1983.

Anonymous, *The Cloud of Unknowing*, edited by Clifton Wolters, Harmondsworth, Penguin, 1961.

Anthony, Dick, Curtis, Thomas E. and Robbins, Thomas, 'The limits of symbolic realism: problems of empathic field observation in a sectarian context,' *Journal for the Scientific Study of Religion* 12.3, 1973, pp. 259–71.

Apel, Karl-Otto, 'Scientistics, hermeneutics and the critique of ideology: outline of a theory of science from a cognitive-anthropological standpoint', in *Towards a Transformation of Philosophy*, translated by Glyn Adey and David Frisby, London, Routledge & Kegan Paul, 1980, pp. 46–76 (originally published in 1972–3).

Appadurai, Arjun, 'Number in the colonial imagination', in Carol A. Breckenridge and Peter van der Veer (eds), *Orientalism and the Postcolonial Predicament*, Philadelphia, University of Pennsylvania Press, 1993, pp. 314–40.

Arberry, A.J., *British Orientalists*, London, William Collins & Company, 1943.

Asad, Talal, *Genealogies of Religion: Discipline and Reasons of Power in Christianity and Islam*, London, Johns Hopkins University Press, 1993.

Ashcroft, Bill, Griffiths, Gareth, and Tiffin, Helen (eds), *The Post-colonial Studies Reader*, London, Routledge, 1995.

Bakhtin, Mikhail, *The Dialogical Imagination*, edited by Michael Holquist, translation by Caryl Emerson and Michael Holquist, Austin, University of Texas Press, 1981.

Bakker, Hans, 'Ayodhyā, a Hindu Jerusalem: an investigation of "holy war" as a religious idea in the light of communal unrest in India', in *Numen* 38.1, 1991, pp. 80–109.

Balagangadhara, S.N., *'The Heathen in His Blindness': Asia, the West and the Dynamic of Religion*, Leiden, E.J. Brill, 1994.

Batchelor, Stephen, *The Awakening of the West: The Encounter of Buddhism and Western Culture*, London, Aquarian Press, 1994.

Bayly, Christopher A., *Indian Society and the Making of the British Empire*, Cambridge, Cambridge University Press, 1988.

—— 'Modern Indian historiography', in Michael Bentley (ed.), *Companion to Historiography*, London, Routledge, 1997, pp. 677–91.

Beauvoir, Simone de, *The Second Sex*, Harmondsworth, Penguin, 1972.

Bellah, Robert N., 'Religious studies as "new religion"', in Jacob Needleman and George Baker (eds), *Understanding the New Religions*, New York, Seabury Press, 1978, pp. 106–12.

—— *Beyond Belief*, New York, Harper & Row, 1970.

Benhabib, Seyla, *Critique Norm and Utopia: A Study of the Foundations of Critical Theory*, New York, Columbia University Press, 1986.

Berger, Peter, *The Social Reality of Religion*, London, Faber & Faber, 1969.

Berger, Peter, and Luckmann, Thomas, *The Social Construction of Reality*, New York, Doubleday & Co., 1966.

Bernard, Theos, *Hindu Philosophy*, Delhi, Motilal Banarsidass, 1947, reprint 1985.

Bhabha, Homi, 'The other question: difference, discrimination and the discourse of colonialism', in Francis Barker, Peter Hulme, Margaret Iversen and Diana Loxley (eds), *Literature, Politics and Theory: Papers from the Essex Conference 1976–84*, London, Methuen, 1986, pp. 148–73. Originally published in Francis Barker (ed.), *The Politics of Theory*, Colchester, University of Essex, 1983. Reprinted in Padmini Mongia (ed.), *Contemporary Postcolonial Theory: A Reader*, London, Hodder Headline Press, 1996.

—— 'Signs taken for wonders: questions of ambivalence and authority under a tree outside Delhi, May 1817', in *Critical Inquiry* 12, 1985, pp. 144–65.

Bhatnagar, Rashmi, 'Uses and limits of Foucault: a study of the theme of origins in Edward Said's *Orientalism*', in *Social Scientist* 16.7, 1986, pp. 3–22.

Bishop, Peter, *Dreams of Power: Tibetan Buddhism and the Western Imagination*, London, Athlone Press, 1992.

Bouyer, Louis, 'Mysticism: an essay on the history of the word', in Richard Woods (ed.), *Understanding Mysticism*, London, Athlone Press, 1980, pp. 42–55.

—— *The Christian Mystery: From Pagan Myth to Christian Mysticism*, Edinburgh, T. and T. Clark, 1990.

Breckenridge, Carol A., and van der Veer, Peter (eds), *Orientalism and the Postcolonial Predicament*, Philadelphia, University of Pennsylvania Press, 1993.

Bristow, Joseph, *Sexuality*, The New Critical Idiom Series, London, Routledge, 1997.

Buchanan, Ian, 'Writing the wrongs of history: De Certeau and post-colonialism', in *SPAN* (Journal of the South Pacific Association for Commonwealth Literature and Language Studies), no. 33, May 1992, pp. 39–46.

Burghart, Richard, 'Something lost, something gained: translations of Hinduism', in Günter D. Sontheimer and Hermann Kulke (eds), *Hinduism Reconsidered*, New Delhi, Manohar Publications, 1991, pp. 213–25.

Capps, Walter H., 'The interpenetration of new religion and religious studies', in Jacob Needleman and George Baker (eds), *Understanding the New Religions*, New York, Seabury Press, 1978, pp. 101–50.

Carrette, Jeremy R. 'The psychology of religion: re-examining the psychological "subject" ', in *Journal of Psychology of Religion* 2.3, 1993–4, pp. 171–99.

—— *Foucault and Religion*, London, Routledge, forthcoming.

Carrette, Jeremy, and King, Richard, 'Giving "birth" to theory: critical perspectives on religion and the body', in *Scottish Journal of Religious Studies* 19.1, Summer 1998, pp. 123–43.

Carter, John Ross, *On Understanding Buddhists: Essays on the Theravāda Tradition in Sri Lanka*, Albany, State University of New York Press, 1992.

Casanova, José, 'Private and public religions', in *Social Research* 59, 1992, pp. 17–57.

Cenkner, William, *A Tradition of Teachers: Śaṅkara and the Jagadgurus Today*, Delhi, South Asia Books, 1983.

Certeau, Michel de, ' "Mystique' au XVIIe siècle: Le problème du langage "mystique" ', in *L'Homme devant Dieu: Mélanges offerts au Pere Henri du Lubac*, Vol. 2, Paris, Aubier, 1964, pp. 267–91.

—— *The Practice of Everyday Life*, translated by Steven Rendall, Berkeley, University of California Press, 1984.

—— 'Mystic speech', in *Heterologies: Discourses on the Other*, Manchester, Manchester University Press, 1986, ch. 6.

—— *The Mystic Fable*, Vol. 1. *The Sixteenth and Seventeenth Centuries*, translated by Michael B. Smith, Chicago, University of Chicago Press, 1992.

Chakrabarty, Dipesh, 'Postcoloniality and the artifice of history: who speaks for "Indian pasts"?', in *Representations* 37, Winter 1992, pp. 1–26.

Chatterjee, Partha, 'Peasants, politics and historiography: a response', in *Social Scientist* 120, May 1983, pp. 58–65.

—— *Nationalist Thought and the Colonial World: A Derivative Discourse*, London, Zed Books, 1986.

—— 'Colonialism, nationalism and colonialized women: the context in India', in *American Ethnologist* 16, 1989, pp. 622–33.

—— 'History and the nationalization of Hinduism', in *Social Research* 59.1, 1992, pp. 114–49.

—— 'The disciplines in colonial Bengal', in Partha Chatterjee (ed.), *Texts of Power: Emerging Disciplines in Colonial Bengal*, Minneapolis, University of Minnesota Press, 1995, pp. 18–29.

Chowdury-Sengupta, Indira, 'Reconstructing spiritual heroism: the evolution of the Swadeshi Sannyasi in Bengal', in Julia Leslie (ed.), *Myth and Mythmaking*, Collected Papers on South Asia No.12, School of Oriental and African Studies, London, 1996, pp. 124–42.

Christian, Barbara, 'The race for theory', in *Cultural Critique* 6, 1987, pp. 51–63.

Cixous, Hélène, and Clement, Catherine, *The Newly Born Woman*, translated by Betsy Wing, Minneapolis, University of Minnesota Press, 1986.

Clifford, James, *The Predicament of Culture: Twentieth Century Ethnography, Literature and Art*, Cambridge, Cambridge University Press, 1988.

Clifford, James, and Marcus, George E. (eds), *Writing Culture: The Poetics and Politics of Ethnography*, Berkeley, University of California Press, 1986.

Cohn, Bernard, 'Notes on the history of the study of Indian society and culture', in Milton Singer and Bernard Cohn (eds), *Structure and Change in Indian Society*, Chicago, Aldine, 1968, pp. 3–28.

Colebrooke, H.T., 'Essays on the Vedas or sacred writings of the Hindus', in *Asiatic Researches*, 1805, pp. 369–476.

Dallmayr, Fred, *Beyond Orientalism: Essays on Cross-cultural Encounter*, Albany, State University of New York, 1996.

Das, Veena, 'Gender studies, cross-cultural comparison and the colonial organization of knowledge', in *Berkshire Review* 21, 1986, pp. 58–76.

—— *Critical Events: An Anthropological Perspective on Contemporary India*, Oxford, Oxford University Press, 1995.

Dayal, Samir, 'Postcolonialism's possibilities: subcontinental diasporic intervention', in *Cultural Critique* 33, Spring 1996, pp. 113–49.

D'Costa, Gavin, 'The end of systematic theology', in *Theology* XCV, No. 767, 1992, pp. 324–34.

Deleuze, Gilles, *Negotiations*, New York, Columbia University Press, 1995.

Dhar, Niranjan, *Vedānta and the Bengal Renaissance*, Calcutta, Minerva Associates, 1977.

Dharwadker, Vinay, 'Orientalism and the study of Indian literatures', in Carol A. Breckenridge and Peter van der Veer (eds), *Orientalism and the Postcolonial Predicament*, Philadelphia, University of Pennsylvania Press, 1993, pp. 158–85.

Dirks, Nicholas B., 'The original caste', in McKim Marriott (ed.), *India Through Hindu Categories*, London, Sage Publications, 1990.

—— (ed.), *Colonialism and Culture*, Ann Arbor, University of Michigan Press, 1992.

—— 'Colonial histories and native informants: biography of an archive', in Carol A. Breckenridge and Peter van der Veer (eds), *Orientalism and the Postcolonial Predicament*, Philadelphia, University of Pennsylvania Press, 1993, pp. 279–313.

Doran, Robert, *Birth of a Worldview: Early Christianity in its Jewish and Pagan Context*, Boulder and Oxford, Westview Press, 1995.

Durkheim, Emile, *The Elementary Forms of the Religious Life*, 1st edn, 1912, London, Allen & Unwin, 1976.

Eliade, Mircea, *The Sacred and the Profane: The Nature of Religion*, translated by Willard R. Trask, New York, Harcourt Brace Jovanovich, 1959.

Evans, Donald, 'Can philosophers limit what mystics can do? A critique of Steven Katz', in *Religious Studies* 25.1, 1989, pp. 53–60.

Fanon, Frantz, *Les Damnés de la terre*, 1961, English title: *The Wretched of the Earth*, translated by Constance Farrington, London, MacGibbon & Kee, 1965.

Ferro-Luzzi, G. Eichinger, 'The polythetic-prototype approach to Hinduism', in Günter D. Sontheimer and Hermann Kulke (eds), *Hinduism Reconsidered*, New Delhi, Manohar Publications, 1991, pp. 187–96.

Figueira, Dorothy M., *The Exotic: A Decadent Quest*, Albany, State University of New York Press, 1994.

Fitzgerald, Timothy, 'Hinduism and the "world religion" fallacy', in *Religion* 20, 1990, pp. 101–18.

—— 'Religious studies as cultural studies: a philosophical and anthropological critique of the concept of religion,' in *Diskus* (Web Edition) 3.1, 1995, pp. 101–18.

Foley, Barbara, 'Marxism in the post-structuralist moment: some notes on the problem of revising Marx', in *Cultural Critique* 15, Spring 1990, pp. 5–37.

Forman, Robert (ed.), *The Problem of Pure Consciousness: Mysticism and Philosophy*, New York, Oxford University Press, 1990.

Foucault, Michel, *The Archaeology of Knowledge and the Discourse on Language*, translated by Alan Sheridan, New York, Pantheon Books, 1972.

—— *The Order of Things*, New York, Pantheon, 1973.

—— *Discipline and Punish: the Birth of the Prison*, Harmondsworth, Penguin, 1977.

—— *History of Sexuality*, Vol. 1, Harmondsworth, Penguin, 1978.

—— 'Is it useless to revolt?', in *Philosophy and Social Criticism* 8.1, 1981, pp. 1–9.

—— *Religion and Culture*, selected and edited by Jeremy Carrette, Manchester, Manchester University Press, 1999.

Fox, Richard G., 'East of Said', in Michael Sprinker (ed.), *Edward Said: A Critical Reader*, Oxford, Blackwell, 1992, pp. 144–56.

Franco, Eli, and Preisendanz, Karin (eds), *Beyond Orientalism: The Work of Wilhelm Halbfass and Its Impact on Indian and Cross-cultural Studies*, Amsterdam, Atlanta GA, Rodopi, Poznań: Studies in the Philosophy of the Sciences and the Humanities, Vol. 59, 1997.

Frow, John, 'Michel de Certeau and the practice of representation', in *Cultural Studies* 5.1, 1991, pp. 52–60.

Frykenberg, R.E., 'The emergence of modern "Hinduism" as a concept and an institution: a reappraisal with special reference to South India', in Günter D. Sontheimer and Hermann Kulke (eds), *Hinduism Reconsidered*, New Delhi, Manohar Publications, 1991, pp. 29–60.

Fuss, Diana, 'Reading like a feminist', in Naomi Schor and Elizabeth Weed (eds), *The Essential Difference*, Indiana University Press, essays from *differences. A Journal of Feminist Cultural Studies*, 1994, pp. 98–115. Also in Diana Fuss *Essentially Speaking: Feminism, Nature, and Difference*, London, Routledge, 1989, pp. 23–37.

Gadamer, Hans Georg, 'Wahrheit in den Geisteswissenschaften', in *Kleine Schriften*, Vol. 1, 1967.

—— *Truth and Method*, English translation, New York, Seabury Press, 1975 (originally published 1960, *Wahrheit und Methode*).

—— 'The problem of historical consciousness', in Paul Rabinow and William Sullivan (eds), *Interpretive Social Science*, Berkeley, University of California Press, 1979, pp. 82–140.

Gates, Henry Louis Jr., 'Critical Fanonism', in *Critical Inquiry* 17.3, 1991, pp. 457–70.

Gay, Peter, *The Enlightenment: An Interpretation*, 2 vols, London, Wildwood House, 1973.

Geertz, Clifford, *The Interpretation of Cultures*, New York, Basic Books, 1973.

Giddens, Anthony, *New Rules of Sociological Method*, Cambridge, Polity, 1993.

Gill, Robin, *The Social Context of Theology*, Oxford, Mowbrays, 1975.

Gimello, Robert, 'Mysticism and meditation', in Steven Katz (ed.), *Mysticism and Philosophical Analysis*, New York, Oxford University Press, 1978, pp. 170–99.

Gold, Daniel, 'Organized Hinduism: from Vedic truth to Hindu nation', in Martin E. Marty and R. Scott Appleby (eds), *Fundamentalisms Observed*, Chicago, University of Chicago Press, 1991, pp. 531–93.

Gombrich, Richard F., *Precept and Practice: Traditional Buddhism in the Rural High-lands of Ceylon*, Oxford, Oxford University Press, 1971.

—— 'Recovering the Buddha's message', in T. Skorupski (ed.), *The Buddhist Forum*, Vol. I, New Delhi, Heritage Publishers, School of Oriental and African Studies, University of London, 1990.

Goody, Jack (ed.), *Literacy in Traditional Societies*, Cambridge, Cambridge University Press, 1968.

—— *The Domestification of the Savage Mind*, Cambridge, Cambridge University Press, 1977.

—— *The Logic of Writing and the Organization of Society*, Cambridge, Cambridge University Press, 1986.

Goody, Jack, and Watt, Ian, 'The consequences of literacy', in Jack Goody (ed.), *Literacy in Traditional Societies*, Cambridge, Cambridge University Press, 1968, pp. 27–84.

Gopal, Sarvepalli (ed.), *Anatomy of a Confrontation: The Babri Masjid-Ramjanmab-humi Issue*, New Delhi and Calcutta, Penguin, 1990.

Gough, Kathleen, 'The implications of literacy in traditional China and India', in Jack Goody (ed.), *Literacy in Traditional Societies*, Cambridge, Cambridge University Press, 1968.

Gracia, Jorge J.E., *Philosophy and Its History: Issues in Philosophical Historiography*, Albany, State University of New York Press, 1992.

Gramsci, Antonio, *Selections from the Prison Notebooks*, edited and translated by Quintin Hoare and Geoffrey Nowell Smith, London, Lawrence & Wishart, 1971.

Griffith, Paul J., 'Pure consciousness and Indian Buddhism', in Robert Forman (ed.), *The Problem of Pure Consciousness: Mysticism and Philosophy*, New York, Oxford University Press, 1990, pp. 71–97.

Guha, Ranajit, 'On some aspects of the historiography of colonial India', in *Subaltern Studies* 1, Delhi, Oxford University Press, 1988.

Gupta, Akhil, and Ferguson, James, 'Beyond "culture": space, identity and the politics of difference', in *Cultural Anthropology* 7.1, 1992, pp. 6–23.

Gupta, Dipankar, 'On altering the ego in peasant history: paradoxes of the ethnic option', in *Peasant Studies* 13.1, Fall 1985, pp. 5–24.

Habermas, Jurgen, 'A review of Gadamer's *Truth and Method*', in Fred Dallmayr and Thomas McCarthy (eds), *Understanding and Social Inquiry*, Notre Dame, Indiana, Notre Dame Press, 1977, pp. 335–63.

Hacker, Paul, 'On Śaṅkara and Advaitism', 1964, reprinted in Wilhelm Halbfass (ed.), *Philosophy and Confrontation: Paul Hacker on Traditional and Modern Vedānta*, Albany, State University of New York Press, 1995, ch. 1.

—— 'Aspects of neo-Hinduism as contrasted with surviving traditional Hinduism', 1970, reprinted in Wilhelm Halbfass (ed.), *Philology and Confrontation: Paul Hacker on Traditional and Modern Vedānta*, Albany, State University of New York Press, 1995, ch. 11.

Halbfass, Wilhelm, *India and Europe: An Essay in Understanding*, Albany, State University of New York Press, 1988.

—— 'The Veda and the identity of Hinduism', in Wilhelm Halbfass, *Tradition and Reflection: Explorations in Indian Thought*, Albany, State University of New York Press, 1991, pp. 1–22.

—— (ed.), *Philology and Confrontation: Paul Hacker on Traditional and Modern Vedānta*, Albany, State University of New York Press, 1995.

Hallisey, Charles, 'Roads taken and not taken in the study of Theravāda Buddhism', in Donald Lopez Jr. (ed.), *Curators of the Buddha: The Study of Buddhism Under Colonialism*, Chicago, Chicago University Press, 1995, pp. 31–62.

Hamilton, Malcolm, *The Sociology of Religion: Theoretical and Comparative Perspectives*, London, Routledge, 1995.

Hamilton, Peter, 'The enlightenment and the birth of social science', in Stuart Hall and Bram Gieben (eds), *Formations of Modernity*, Oxford, Open University and Polity Press, 1992, pp. 17–70.

Happold, F.C., *Mysticism: A Study and an Anthology*, Harmondsworth, Pelican Books, 1963.

Haraway, Donna, 'Situated knowledges: the science question in feminism and the privilege of partial perspective', in *Feminist Studies* 14.3, Fall 1988, 575–99.

Hardy, Friedhelm, *The Religions of Asia*, London, Routledge, 1990.

—— 'A radical reassessment of the Vedic heritage: the *Ācāryahṛdayam* and its wider implications', in Vasudha Dalmia and H. von Stietencron (eds), *Representing Hinduism: The Construction of Religious Traditions and National Identity*, New Delhi, Sage Publications, 1995, ch. 1.

Hardy, S., *A Manual of Buddhism in its Modern Development*, 1st edn, London, Partridge & Oakey, 1860.

Harris, Ian, *The Continuity of Madhyamaka and Yogācāra in Indian Mahāyāna Buddhism*, Leiden, E.J. Brill, 1991.

Harrison, Paul, '*Buddhānusmṛti* in the *Pratyutpanna-Buddha-Saṃmukhāvasthita-Samādhi-Sūtra*,' in *Journal of Indian Philosophy* 6, 1978, pp. 35–57.

—— *The Samādhi of Direct Encounter with the Buddhas of the Present: An Annotated Translation of the Tibetan Version of the Pratyutpanna-Buddha-Saṃmukhāvasthita-Samādhi-Sūtra*, Tokyo, International Institute for Buddhist Studies, Studia Philologica Buddhica Monograph Series V, 1990.

Harrison, Peter, *'Religion' and the religions in the English Enlightenment*, Cambridge, Cambridge University Press, 1990.

Hart, Kevin, *The Trespass of the Sign: Deconstruction, Theology and Philosophy*, Cambridge, Cambridge University Press, 1989.

Hartsock, Nancy, 'Foucault on power: a theory for women?', in Linda J. Nicholson (ed.), *Feminism/Postmodernism*, London, Routledge, 1990, pp. 157–75.

Hayes, Richard P., 'Whose experience validates what for Dharmakīrti', in P. Bilimoria and J.N. Mohanty (eds), *Relativism, Suffering and Beyond: Essays in Memory of Bimal K. Matilal*, Delhi, Oxford University Press, 1997, pp. 105–18.

Haynes, Douglas, and Prakash, Gyan (eds), *Contesting Power: Resistance and Everyday Social Relations in South Asia*, Berkeley, University of California Press, 1991.

Hebdige, Dick, *Cut 'n Mix: Culture, Identity and Carribean Music*, London, Methuen Press, 1987.

Hekman, Susan J., *Gender and Knowledge: Elements of a Postmodern Feminism*, Cambridge, Polity Press, 1990.

Hobart, Mark (ed.), *An Anthropological Critique of Development: The Growth of Ignorance*, London, Routledge, 1993.

Hooke, Alexander, 'The order of others: is Foucault's antihumanism against human action', in *Political Theory* 15, 1987, pp. 38–60.

Huxley, Aldous, *The Perennial Philosophy*, London, Harper & Row, 1944.

—— *The Doors of Perception*, London, Chatto & Windus, 1954, reprinted in *The Doors of Perception and Heaven and Hell*, London, Grafton Books (Collins) 1977.

Inden, Ronald, 'Orientalist constructions of India', in *Modern Asian Studies* 20.3, 1986, pp. 401–46.

—— *Imagining India*, Oxford, Basil Blackwell, 1990.

Ingram, Edward (ed.), *Two Views of British India: The Private Correspondence of Mr Dundas and Lord Wellesley: 1798–1801*, Bath, Adams & Dart, 1970.

Irigaray, Luce, *Speculum of the Other Woman*, translation Gillian C. Gill, Ithaca, NY, Cornell University Press, 1985.

Iyer, K.A. Subramania, *The Vākyapadīya of Bhartṛhari and its Vṛtti*, Deccan College Monograph, 1965.

James, William, *The Varieties of Religious Experience*, The Gifford Lectures 1901–2, Glasgow, Collins, 1977.

JanMohamed, Abdul R., 'The economy of Manichean allegory: the function of racial difference in colonialist literature', in *Critical Inquiry* 12.1, 1985, pp. 59–87; abridged version in Bill Ashcroft, Gareth Griffiths and Helen Tiffin (eds), *The Post-colonial Studies Reader*, London, Routledge, 1995, pp. 18–23.

JanMohamed, Abdul R., and Lloyd, David, 'Introduction: minority discourse – what is to be done?', in *Cultural Critique*, Fall 1987.

Jantzen, Grace, 'Mysticism and experience', in *Religious Studies* 25.3, 1989, pp. 295–315.

—— 'Where two are to become one: mysticism and monism', in Godfrey Vesey (ed.), *The Philosophy of Christianity*, Cambridge, Cambridge University Press, 1990.

—— *Power, Gender and Christian Mysticism*, Cambridge, Cambridge Studies in Ideology and Religion 8, Cambridge University Press, 1995.

Joshi, Barbara R. (ed.), *Untouchable! Voices of the Dalit Liberation Movement*, London, Zed Books, 1986.

Juergensmeyer, Mark, 'What the Bhikkhu said: reflections on the rise of militant religious nationalism', in *Religion* 20, 1990, pp. 53–76.

—— *The New Cold War? Religious Nationalism Confronts the Secular State*, Berkeley, University of California Press, 1993.

Katrak, Ketu H., 'Indian nationalism, Gandhian "Satyagraha", and representations of female sexuality', in A. Parker, M. Russo, D. Sommer and P. Yaeger (eds) *Nationalisms and Sexualities*, New York and London, Routledge, 1992, pp. 395–406.

Katz, Steven, 'Language, epistemology and mysticism', in Steven Katz (ed.), *Mysticism and Philosophical Analysis*, New York, Oxford University Press, 1978, pp. 24–66.

—— (ed.), *Mysticism and Philosophical Analysis*, New York, Oxford University Press, 1978.

—— (ed.), *Mysticism and Religious Traditions*, New York, Oxford University Press, 1983.

—— 'Responses and rejoinders: on mysticism', in *Journal of American Academy of Religion* 56.4, 1988, pp. 751–7.

Kejariwal, O.P., *The Asiatic Society of Bengal and the Discovery of India's Past, 1784–1838*, Delhi, Oxford University Press, 1988.

—— 'William Jones: the Copernicus of history', in Garland Cannon and Kevin R. Brine (eds), *Objects of Enquiry: The Life, Contributions and Influences of Sir William Jones (1746–1794)*, New York and London, New York University Press, 1995.

Keller, Carl A., 'Mystical literature', in Steven Katz (ed.), *Mysticism and Philosophical Analysis*, New York, Oxford University Press, 1978, pp. 75–100.

Khare, R.S., 'Indian sociology and the cultural other', in *Contributions to Indian Sociology* 24.2, 1990, pp. 186–96.

Killingley, Dermot, *Rammohun Roy in Hindu and Christian Tradition: The Teape Lectures 1990*, Newcastle upon Tyne, Grevatt & Grevatt, 1993.

King, Richard, *Early Advaita Vedānta and Buddhism: The Mahāyāna Context of the Gauḍapādīya-kārikā*, Albany, State University of New York Press, 1995.

—— *Indian Philosophy: An Introduction to Hindu and Buddhist Thought*, Edinburgh, Edinburgh University Press, 1999.

King, Sallie B., 'Two epistemological models for the interpretation of mysticism', in *Journal of American Academy of Religion* 61.2, 1988, pp. 275–79.

Klein, Anne C., *Knowledge and Liberation: Tibetan Buddhist Epistemology in Support of Transformative Religious Experience*, Ithaca, Snow Lion, 1986.

—— 'Mental concentration and the unconditioned: a Buddhist case of unmediated experience', in Robert E. Buswell Jr. and Robert M. Gimello (eds), *Paths to Liberation: The Mārga and Its Transformations in Buddhist Thought*, Honolulu, Kuroda Institute Studies in East Asian Buddhism 7, University of Hawaii Press, 1992, pp. 269–308.

Klostermaier, Klaus, 'The creative function of the word', in Harold Coward (ed.), *Language in Indian Philosophy and Religion*, Quebec, Canadian Studies in Religion, Supplement 5, 1976, pp. 5–18.

Kopf, David, *British Orientalism and the Bengal Renaissance: The Dynamics of Indian Modernization, 1773–1835*, Berkeley and Los Angeles, University of California Press, 1969.

—— 'Hermeneutics versus history', in *Journal of Asian Studies* 39.3, May 1980, pp. 495–506.

—— 'The historiography of British Orientalism, 1772–1992', in Garland Cannon and Kevin R. Brine (eds), *Objects of Enquiry: The Life, Contributions and Influences of Sir William Jones (1746–1794)*, New York and London, New York University Press, 1995, pp. 141–60.

Kritzman, Lawrence (ed.), *Michel Foucault: Politics, Philosophy, Culture*, New York, Routledge, 1988.

Ladurie, Emmanuel Le Roy, *Montaillou, village occitan, de 1294 à 1324*, Paris, 1975; English version, *Montaillou: The Promised Land of Error*, translated by Barbara Bray, New York, G. Braziller, 1978.

Landry, Donna, and Maclean, Gerald (eds), *The Spivak Reader*, London, Routledge, 1996.

Larner, Christina, *Witchcraft and Religion: The Politics of Popular Belief*, Oxford and New York, Basil Blackwell, 1984.

Larson, Gerald, 'Discourse about "religion" in colonial and postcolonial India', in Ninian Smart and Shivesh Thakur (eds), *Ethical and Political Dilemmas of*

Modern India, New York and Basingstoke, St Martin's Press and Macmillan, 1993, pp. 181–93.

Lawson, E. Thomas, and McCauley, Robert N., 'Crisis of conscience, riddle of identity: making space for a cognitive approach to religious phenomena', in *Journal of the American Academy of Religion* 61.2, Summer 1993, pp. 201–24.

Lee, Kyung-Won, 'Is the glass half-empty or half-full? Rethinking the problems of postcolonial revisionism', in *Cultural Critique* 36, Spring 1997, pp. 89–117.

Lele, Jayant, 'The two faces of nationalism: on the revolutionary potential of tradition', in Jacques Dofmy and Akinsola Akiwowo (eds), *National and Ethnic Movements*, Sage Publications, 1980, pp. 201–16.

—— 'Orientalism and the social sciences', in Carol A. Breckenridge and Peter van der Veer (eds), *Orientalism and the Postcolonial Predicament*, Philadelphia, University of Pennsylvania Press, 1993, pp. 45–75.

Lelyveld, David, 'The fate of Hindustani: colonial knowledge and the project of a national language', in Carol A. Breckenridge and Peter van der Veer (eds), *Orientalism and the Postcolonial Predicament*, Philadelphia, University of Pennsylvania Press, 1993, pp. 189–214.

Lemert, Charles, *Sociology and the Twilight of Man: Homocentrism and Discourse in Sociological Theory*, Carbondale, Southern Illinois University Press, 1979.

Lerner, Gerda, *The Creation of Feminist Consciousness: From the Middle Ages to Eighteen-seventy*, Oxford, Oxford University Press, 1993.

Lewis, Reina, *Gendering Orientalism: Race, Femininity and Representation*, New York and London, Routledge, 1996.

Lipner, Julius J., *The Face of Truth: A Study of Meaning and Metaphysics in the Vedāntic Theology of Rāmānuja*, Albany, State University of New York Press, 1986.

—— 'Ancient Banyan: an inquiry in to the meaning of 'Hinduness''', in *Religious Studies* 32.1, 1996, pp. 109–26.

Long, Elizabeth, 'Textual interpretation as collective action', in J. Boyarin (ed.), *The Ethnography of Reading*, Berkeley, University of California Press, 1992, pp. 180–211.

Lopez, Donald Jr. (ed.), *Curators of the Buddha: The Study of Buddhism Under Colonialism*, Chicago, Chicago University Press, 1995.

Lowe, Lisa, *Critical Terrains: French and British Orientalism*, Ithaca and London, Cornell University Press, 1991.

Loy, David, *Non-Duality: A Study in Comparative Philosophy*, New Haven and London, Yale University Press, 1988.

Ludden, David, 'Orientalist empiricism: transformations of colonial knowledge', in Carol A. Breckenridge and Peter van der Veer (eds), *Orientalism and the Postcolonial Predicament*, Philadelphia, University of Pennsylvania Press, 1993, pp. 250–78.

Lyons, David, *The Steeple's Shadow: On the Myths and Realities of Secularization*, London, SPCK, 1985.

McClintock, Anne, *Imperial Leather: Race, Gender and Sexuality in the Imperial Contest*, London, Routledge, 1995.

McCutcheon, Russell, *Manufacturing Religion: The Discourse on Sui Generis Religion and the Politics of Nostalgia*, New York and Oxford, Oxford University Press, 1997.

McGill, Bernard, *The Foundations of Mysticism*, Vol. 1, London, SCM Press, 1991.

McGrane, Bernard, *Beyond Anthropology: Society and the Other*, New York, Columbia University Press, 1989.

Mahadevan, T.M.P., *Ramaṇa Mahārshi: The Sage of Aruṇācala*, London, Allen & Unwin, 1977.

Mallon, Florencia, 'The promise and dilemmas of Subaltern Studies: perspectives from Latin American history', in *American Historical Review* 99.5, 1994, pp. 1491–1515.

Marriott, McKim, 'Constructing an Indian ethnosociology', in *Contributions to Indian Sociology* 23.1, 1989, pp. 1–39.

Marshall, Peter, *The British Discovery of Hinduism in the Eighteenth Century*, Cambridge, Cambridge University Press, 1970.

Matilal, Bimal Krishna, and Spivak, Gayatri, *Epic and Ethic*, New York, Routledge, forthcoming.

Milbank, John, *Theology and Social Theory: Beyond Secular Reason*, Oxford, Basil Blackwell, 1990.

Miller, Jane, *Seductions: Studies in Reading and Culture*, London, Virago, 1990.

Mills, Sara, *Discourse*, New Critical Idiom Series, London, Routledge, 1997.

Minear, Richard H., 'Orientalism and the study of Japan', in *Journal of Asian Studies* 39.3, 1980, pp. 507–17.

Mitchell, John, *An Essay on the Best Means of Civilising the Subjects of the British Empire in India and of Diffusing the Light of the Christian Religion Throughout the Eastern World*, Edinburgh, W. Blackwood, and London, T. Cadell & W. Davies, 1805.

Moffatt, Michael, 'Deconstructing McKim Marriott's ethnosociology: an outcaste's critique', in *Contributions to Indian Sociology* 24.2, 1990, pp. 223–9.

Moi, Toril, *Sexual/Textual Politics: Feminist Literary Theory*, New York, Routledge, 1985.

Moore, Peter, 'Mystical experience, mystical doctrine, mystical technique', in Steven Katz (ed.), *Mysticism and Philosophical Analysis*, New York, Oxford University Press, 1978, pp. 101–31.

Moore-Gilbert, Bart, *Postcolonial Theory: Contexts, Practices, Politics*, London, Verso, 1997.

Mukherjee, Aditya, 'Colonialism and communalism', in Sarvepalli Gopal (ed.), *Anatomy of a Confrontation: The Babri Masjid-Ramjanmabhumi Issue*, New Delhi and Calcutta, Penguin, 1990, pp. 164–78.

Nair, Janaki, 'On the question of agency in Indian feminist historiography', in *Gender and History* 6.1, April 1994, pp. 82–100.

Nandy, Ashis, *The Intimate Enemy: Loss and Recovery of Self under Colonialism*, Delhi, Oxford University Press, 1983.

Neumann, Charles F., *Catechism of the Shamans: On the Laws and Regulations of the Priesthood of Buddha in China*, London, Oriental Text Fund, 1831.

Nikhilananda, Swami, *Vivekananda: A Biography*, New York, Ramakrishna Centre, 1953.

Niranjana, Tejaswini, 'Translation, colonialism and rise of English', in *Economic and Political Weekly* 25.15, 14 April 1990, pp. 773–9.

Obeyesekere, Gananath, 'Religious symbolism and political change in Ceylon', in *Modern Ceylon Studies* 1.1, 1970, pp. 43–63.

O'Connell, Joseph T., 'Gauḍiya Vaiṣṇava symbolism of deliverance from evil', in *Journal of the American Oriental Society* 93.3, 1973.

O'Hanlon, Rosalind, 'Recovering the subject: Subaltern Studies and histories of resistance in colonial South Asia', in *Modern Asian Studies* 22.1, 1988, pp. 189–224.

—— 'Cultures of rule, communities of resistance: gender, discourse and tradition in recent South Asian historiographies', in *Social Analysis* 25, 1989, pp. 94–114.

O'Hanlon, Rosalind, and Washbrook, David, 'After Orientalism: culture, criticism, and politics in the Third World', in *Comparative Studies in Society and History* 34.1, January 1994, pp. 141–67.

Olivelle, Patrick, *Upaniṣads*, Oxford World's Classics, Oxford University Press, 1996.

Ong, Walter, *Orality and Literacy: The Technologizing of the Word*, London and New York, Methuen, 1982.

Onyewuenyi, Innocent, 'Is there an African philosophy', in T. Serequeberhan (ed.), *African Philosophy: The Essential Readings*, New York, Paragon, 1991.

Östör, Ákos, and Fruzzetti, Lina, 'For an ethnosociology of India?', in *Contributions to Indian Sociology* 25.2, 1991, pp. 309–20.

Otto, Rudolf, *Mysticism East and West: A Comparative Analysis of the Nature of Mysticism*, 1932, London, Quest English edition, 1987.

Palmer, Richard, *Hermeneutics: Interpretation Theory in Schleiermacher, Dilthey, Heidegger and Gadamer*, Evanston, Northwestern University Press, 1969.

Pandey, Gyanendra, *The Construction of Communalism in Colonial North India*, Delhi, Oxford University Press, 1990.

Parrish, Steven M., *Hierarchy and Its Discontents: Culture and the Politics of Consciousness in Caste Society*, Philadelphia, University of Pennsylvania Press, 1996.

Parry, Benita, 'Problems in current theories of colonial discourse', in *Oxford Literary Review* 9, 1987, pp. 27–58; abridged version in Bill Ashcroft, Gareth Griffiths and Helen Tiffin (eds), *The Post-colonial Studies Reader*, London, Routledge, 1995, pp. 27–58.

—— 'Overlapping territories and intertwined histories: Edward Said's postcolonial cosmopolitanism', in Michael Sprinker (ed.), *Edward Said: A Critical Reader*, Oxford, Blackwell, 1992.

Parry, Jonathan, 'The brahmanical tradition and the technology of the intellect', in Joanna Overing (ed.), *Reason and Morality*, London, Tavistock, 1985, pp. 200–25.

Patton, Paul, 'Of power and prisons', in Meaghan Morris and Paul Patton (eds), *Michel Foucault: Power/Truth/Strategy*, Sydney, Feral Publications, 1979, pp. 109–47.

Penner, Hans H., 'The mystical illusion', in Steven Katz (ed.), *Mysticism and Religious Traditions*, New York, Oxford University Press, 1983, pp. 89–116.

Petroff, Elizabeth A. (ed.), *Medieval Women's Visionary Literature*, Oxford, Oxford University Press, 1986.

Philp, Mark, 'Foucault', in Quentin Skinner (ed.), *The Return of Grand Theory in the Human Sciences*, Cambridge, Cambridge University Press, 1985, pp. 65–82.

Pike, Nelson, *Mystic Union: An Essay in the Phenomenology of Mysticism*, Ithaca and London, Cornell University Press, 1992.

Pollock, Sheldon, 'Deep Orientalism? Notes on Sanskrit and power beyond the Raj', in Carol A. Breckenridge and Peter van der Veer (eds), *Orientalism and the Post-*

colonial Predicament, Philadelphia, University of Pennsylvania Press, 1993, pp. 76–133.

Porter, Roy, *The Enlightenment*, London, Macmillan, 1990.

Prakash, Gyan, 'Writing post-Orientalist histories of the Third World: perspectives from Indian historiography', in *Comparative Studies in Society and History* 32.2, 1990, pp. 383–408; revised version: 'Writing post-Orientalist histories of the Third World: Indian historiography is good to think', in Nicholas B. Dirk (ed.), *Colonialism and Culture*, Ann Arbor, University of Michigan Press, 1992, pp. 353–88.

—— 'Science "gone native" in colonial India', in *Representations* 40, 1992, pp. 153–78.

—— 'Can the "subaltern" ride? A reply to O'Hanlon and Washbrook', in *Comparative Studies in Society and History* 34.1, January 1994, pp. 168–84.

—— 'Orientalism now: a review of reviews', in *History and Theory* 34, 1995, pp. 199–212.

Proudfoot, Wayne, *Religious Experience*, Berkeley, California University Press, 1985.

Pye, Michael, 'Religion: shape and shadow', in *Numen* 41, 1994, pp. 51–75.

Quigley, Declan, *The Interpretation of Caste*, Oxford, Clarendon Press, Oxford, 1994.

Rabinow, Paul 'Representations are social facts: modernity and post-modernity in anthropology', in James Clifford and George E. Marcus (eds), *Writing Culture: The Poetics and Politics of Ethnography*, Berkeley, University of California Press, 1986, pp. 234–61.

Radhakrishnan, Rajagopalan, *Diasporic Mediations: Between Home and Location*, Ann Arbor, University of Minnesota Press, 1996.

Radhakrishnan, Sarvepalli, *The Hindu View of Life*, London, 1927, Unwin Paperback, 1988.

—— *An Idealist View of Life*, London, Unwin Books, 2nd edn, 1937.

—— *Our Heritage*, Delhi, Hind Pocket Books, 1973.

Rai, Amit, 'The King is dead: a review of Breckenridge and van der Veer (1993), *Orientalism and the Post-colonial Predicament*', in *Oxford Literary Review* 16, 1994, pp. 295–301.

Ram, Kalpana, 'Modernist anthropology and the construction of Indian identity', in *Meanjin* 51, 1992, pp. 589–614.

Rattansi, Ali, 'Postcolonialism and its discontents', in *Economy and Society* 26.4, 1997, pp. 480–500.

Ray, Rabindra, 'And why an Indian sociology?' in *Contributions to Indian Sociology* 24.2, 1990, pp. 265–75.

Rigby, S.H., 'Marxist historiography', in Michael Bentley (ed.), *Companion to Historiography*, London, Routledge, 1997, pp. 889–928.

Robbins, Bruce, 'The East is a career: Edward Said and the logics of professionalism', in Michael Sprinker (ed.), *Edward Said: A Critical Reader*, Oxford, Basil Blackwell, 1992, pp. 48–73.

Rocher, Ludo, *Ezourvedam: A French Veda of the Eighteenth Century*, Amsterdam and Philadelphia, John Benjamins Publishing Company, University of Pennsylvania, Studies on South Asia, Vol. 1, 1984.

Rocher, Rosane, *Alexander Hamilton (1762–1824): A Chapter in the Early History of Sanskrit Philology*, American Oriental Series 51, New Haven, American Oriental Society, 1968.

—— 'British Orientalism in the eighteenth century: the dialectic of knowledge and government', in Carol A. Breckenridge and Peter van der Veer (eds), *Orientalism and the Postcolonial Predicament*, Philadelphia, University of Pennsylvania Press, 1993, pp. 215–49.

—— 'Weaving knowledge: Sir William Jones and Indian pundits', in Garland Cannon and Kevin R. Brine (eds), *Objects of Enquiry: The Life, Contributions, and Influences of Sir William Jones (1746–1794)*, New York and London, New York University Press, 1995, pp. 51–79.

Rorem, Paul, *Pseudo-Dionysius: A Commentary on the Texts and an Introduction to their Influence*, Oxford, Oxford University Press, 1993.

Rushdie, Salman, *The Satanic Verses*, London, Viking Press, Penguin, 1988.

Russell, Bertrand, *Mysticism and Logic*, Melbourne, London and Baltimore, Pelican Books, 1953, originally published in 1914.

Said, Edward, *Orientalism: Western Conceptions of the Orient*, London, Penguin, 1991.

—— 'Orientalism and after: an interview with Edward Said', in *Radical Philosophy* 63, Spring 1993, pp. 22–32.

—— *Culture and Imperialism*, London, Chatto & Windus, 1993.

Salusinzsky, Imre, *Criticism in Society*, London, Methuen, 1987.

Sangari, Kumkum, and Vaid, Sudesh, *Recasting Women: Essays in Indian Colonial History*, New Brunswick, Rutgers University Press, 1990.

Sardar, Ziauddin, *Postmodernism and the Other: The New Imperialism of Western Culture*, London, Pluto Press, 1998.

Sarkar, Sumit, 'The conditions and nature of subaltern militancy: Bengal from swadeshi to noncooperation', in *Subaltern Studies* 3, Delhi, Oxford University Press, 1984.

—— 'Orientalism revisited: Saidian frameworks in the writing of modern Indian history', in *Oxford Literary Review* 16, 1994, pp. 205–24.

Sarkar, Tanika, 'The woman as communal subject: Rashtrasevika Samiti and Ram Janmabhoomi Movement', in *Economic and Political Weekly* 26, 31 August 1991, pp. 2057–62.

Schipper, Kristofer, *The Taoist Body*, translated by Karen C. Duval, Berkeley, University of California Press, 1993.

Schneiders, Sandra, 'Scripture and spirituality', in Bernard McGinn, John Meyendorff and Jean Leclerq (eds), *Christian Spirituality: Origins to the Twelfth Century*, New York, Crossroads Publishing Co., 1985, pp. 1–22.

Schopen, Gregory, 'Archaeology and Protestant presuppositions in the study of Indian Buddhism', in *History of Religions* 31.1, 1991, pp. 1–23.

Schor, Naomi, 'This essentialism which is not one: coming to grips with Irigaray', in Naomi Schor and Elizabeth Weed (eds), *The Essential Difference*, Indiana University Press, essays from *differences. A Journal of Feminist Cultural Studies*, 1994, pp. 40–62.

Schwab, Raymond, *The Oriental Renaissance: Europe's Discovery of India and the East, 1680–1880* (1950), English translation, New York, Columbia University Press, 1984.

Searle-Chatterjee, Mary, and Sharma, Ursula (eds), *Contextualising Caste: Post-Dumontian Approaches*, Sociological Review monograph, Oxford, Blackwell, 1994.

Sharf, Robert, 'Whose Zen? Zen nationalism revisited', in James W. Heisig and John C. Maraldo (eds), *Rude Awakenings: Zen, the Kyoto School, and the Question of Nationalism*, Honolulu, University of Hawaii Press, 1994, pp. 40–51.

—— 'Buddhist modernism and the rhetoric of meditative experience', in *Numen* 42.3, 1995, pp.228–83.

—— 'The Zen of Japanese nationalism', in Donald Lopez Jr (ed.), *Curators of the Buddha*, 1995, p. 140.

Shohat, Ella, 'Post-Third-Worldist culture: gender, nation, and the cinema', in M. Jacqui Alexander and Chandra Talpade Mohanty (eds), *Feminist Genealogies, Colonial Legacies, Democratic Futures*, London, Routledge, 1997, pp. 183–209.

Singer, Milton, 'The social organization of Indian civilization', in *Diogenes* 45, 1964, pp. 84–119.

—— *When a Great Tradition Modernizes*, London, Pall Mall Press, 1972.

Singh, Jyotsna G., *Colonial Narratives, Cultural Dialogues: 'Discoveries' of India in the Language of Colonialism*, London and New York, Routledge, 1996.

Sinha, Mrinalini, *Colonial Masculinity: The 'Manly Englishman' and the 'Effeminate Bengali' in the Late Nineteenth Century*, Manchester, Manchester University Press, 1995.

Sivaramakrishnan, K., 'Situating the subaltern: history and anthropology in the Subaltern Studies project', in *Journal of Historical Sociology* 8.4, December 1995, pp. 395–429.

Slemon, Stephen, 'The scramble for post-colonialism', in Chris Tiffin and Alan Lawson (eds), *De-scribing Empire: Post-colonialism and Textuality*, London, Routledge, 1994; abridged version in Bill Ashcroft, Gareth Griffiths and Helen Tiffin (eds), *The Post-colonial Studies Reader*, London, Routledge, 1995, pp. 45–52.

Smart, Ninian, 'Interpretation and mystical experience', in *Religious Studies* 1.1, 1965, pp. 75-87, reprinted in Richard Woods (ed.), *Understanding Mysticism*, London, Athlone Press, 1980, pp. 78–91.

Smith, Brian K., 'After Said, after Ayodhya: new challenges for the study of Indian religions', in *Religion* 26, 1996, pp. 365–72.

Smith, Huston, 'Is there a perennial philosophy?', in *Journal of American Academy of Religion* 55.3, 1987, pp. 553–66.

Smith, John E., 'William James's account of mysticism: a critical appraisal', in Steven Katz (ed.), *Mysticism and Religious Traditions*, New York, Oxford University Press, 1983, pp. 247–79.

—— *Quasi-Religions: Humanism, Marxism and Nationalism*, London, Macmillan, 1994.

Smith, Jonathan Z., *Imagining Religion: From Babylon to Jonestown*, Chicago, University of Chicago Press, 1982.

Smith, Margaret, 'The nature and meaning of mysticism', in Richard Woods (ed.), *Understanding Mysticism*, London, Athlone Press, 1980.

Smith, Wilfred Cantwell, *The Meaning and End of Religion*, Minneapolis, Fortress Press, 1991 (original 1964).

Sontheimer, Günter D., and Kulke, Hermann (eds), *Hinduism Reconsidered*, New Delhi, Manohar Publications, 1991.

Southwold, Martin, *Buddhism in Life: The Anthropological Study of Religion and the Sinhalese Practice of Buddhism*, Manchester, Manchester University Press, 1983.

Spender, Dale, *Man-Made Language*, London, Routledge & Kegan Paul, 1980.

Spivak, Gayatri Chakravorty, 'The Rani of Sirmur', in Francis Barker *et al.* (eds), *Europe and Its Others*, Vol. I, Colchester, University of Essex, 1985. pp. 128–51. Also published in *History and Theory* 24.3, 1985, pp. 247–72.

—— 'Three women's texts and a critique of imperialism', in *Critical Inquiry* 12.1, 1985, pp. 243–59.

—— 'Subaltern Studies: deconstructing historiography', in Ranajit Guha and Gayatri Spivak (eds), *Selected Subaltern Studies*, Delhi, Oxford University Press, 1988, pp. 3–32; reprinted in Donna Landry and Gerald Maclean (eds), *The Spivak Reader*, London, Routledge, 1996, pp. 287–308.

—— 'How to teach a "culturally different" book', in *differences* 3.3, 1991, pp. 139–70, revised version reprinted in Landry and Maclean (eds), *The Spivak Reader*, 1996, pp. 237–66.

—— 'The burden of English', in Carol A. Breckenridge and Peter van der Veer (eds), *Orientalism and the Postcolonial Predicament*, Philadelphia, University of Pennsylvania Press, 1993, pp. 134–57.

Sprinker, Michael (ed.), *Edward Said: A Critical Reader*, Oxford, Basil Blackwell, 1992.

Srinivas, M.N., *Social Change in Modern India*, Berkeley, University of California Press, 1966.

Srinivasan, Amrita, 'Reform or conformity? Temple "prostitution" and the community in the Madras presidency', in Bina Agarwal (ed.), *Structures of Patriarchy: State, Community and Household in Modernizing Asia*, Delhi, Kali for Women, 1988.

Staal, Frits, *Exploring Mysticism*, Harmondsworth, Penguin, 1975.

—— *Rules Without Meaning: Rituals, Mantras and the Human Sciences*, New York, Toronto Studies in Religion, Vol. 4, Peter Lang, 1989.

Stace, Walter, *Mysticism and Philosophy*, London, Jeremy P. Tarcher Inc., 1960.

Steadman, John M., *The Myth of Asia*, London, Macmillan, 1970.

Stietencron, H. von, 'Hinduism: on the proper use of a deceptive term', in Günter D. Sontheimer and Hermann Kulke (eds), *Hinduism Reconsidered*, New Delhi, Manohar Publications, 1991, pp. 11–28.

Stoeber, Michael, 'Constructivist epistemologies of mysticism: a critique and a revision', in *Religious Studies* 28.1, 1992, pp. 107–16.

—— *Theo-Monistic Mysticism: A Hindu–Christian Comparison*, London, St Martins Press, 1994.

Stoler, Ann Laura, *Race and the Education of Desire: Foucault's History of Sexuality and the Colonial Order of Things*, London, Duke University Press, 1995.

Strenski, Ivan, 'Religion, power and final Foucault', in *Journal of the American Academy of Religion* 66.2, Summer 1998, pp. 345–67.

Suzuki, Daisetz T., *Outlines of Mahāyāna Buddhism*, 1907, Schocken Books Inc., 1963.

—— *Mysticism, Christian and Buddhist*, London, George Allen & Unwin, 1957; Unwin Paperback, 1979.

Svenbro, Jesper, 'The "voice" of letters in Ancient Greece: on silent reading and the representation of speech', in *Culture and History* 2, 1987, pp. 31–47.

Tambiah, S. J., 'Literacy in a Buddhist village in north-east Thailand', in Jack Goody (ed.), *Literacy in Traditional Societies*, Cambridge, Cambridge University Press, 1968.

Tanaka, Stefan, *Japan's Orient: Rendering Pasts into History*, Berkeley, University of California Press, 1993.

Taylor, Charles, *Sources of the Self: The Making of the Modern Identity*, Cambridge, Cambridge University Press, 1989.

Teresa of Avila, *The Interior Castle*, edited by Halcyon Backhouse, London, Hodder & Stoughton, 1988.

Thapar, Romila, 'Syndicated Moksha', in *Seminar* 313, September 1985.

—— 'Imagined religious communities? Ancient history and the modern search for a Hindu identity', in *Modern Asian Studies* 23.2, 1989, pp. 209–31; reprinted in Thapar, *Interpreting Early India*, Delhi, Oxford University Press, 1992, pp. 60–88.

—— *Interpreting Early India*, Delhi, Oxford University Press, 1992.

Thomas, Nicholas, *Colonialism's Culture: Anthropology, Travel and Government*, Cambridge, Polity Press, 1994.

Tillich, Paul, *Dynamics of Faith*, New York, Harper & Row, 1957.

Torwesten, Hans, *Vedanta, Heart of Hinduism*, 1985, English translation, Grove Press, 1991.

Trigger, Bruce G., 'Alternative archaeologies: nationalist, colonialist, imperialist', in *Man* (N.S.) 19.3, 1984, pp. 355–70.

Tuck, Andrew P., *Comparative Philosophy and the Philosophy of Scholarship: On the Western Interpretation of Nāgārjuna*, New York and Oxford, Oxford University Press, 1990.

Tull, Herman, Müller, F. Max, and Keith, A.B., ' "Twaddle", the "stupid" myth, and the disease of indology', in *Numen* 38.1, 1991, pp. 27–58

Tully, Mark, *No Full Stops in India*, London, Penguin, 1991.

Turner, Bryan S., *Religion and Social Theory*, London, Sage Publications, 2nd edn, 1991.

—— *Orientalism, Postmodernism and Globalism*, London and New York, Routledge, 1994.

Turner, Denys, *The Darkness of God: Negativity in Christian Mysticism*, Cambridge, Cambridge University Press, 1995.

Underhill, Evelyn, 'The essentials of mysticism', in Richard Woods (ed.), *Understanding Mysticism*, London, Athlone Press, 1980, pp. 26–41.

Upadhyaya, Prakash Chandra, 'The politics of Indian secularism', in *Modern Asian Studies* 26.4, 1992, pp. 815–53.

van der Veer, Peter, 'The foreign hand: Orientalist discourse in sociology and communalism', in Carol A. Breckenridge and Peter van der Veer (eds), *Orientalism and the Postcolonial Predicament*, Philadelphia, University of Pennsylvania Press, 1993, pp. 23–44.

—— *Religious Nationalism: Hindus and Muslims in India*, Berkeley, University of California Press, 1994.

Venkatesananda, Swami, *The Concise Yogavasistha*, Albany, State University of New York Press, 1984.

Vesey, Godfrey, *The Philosophy of Christianity*, Cambridge, Cambridge University Press, 1990.

Vivekānanda, Swāmi, *The Complete Works of Swāmi Vivekānananda*, 8 Vols, Calcutta, Advaita Ashrama, 1970–2.

Viyagappa, Ignatius, *G.W.F. Hegel's Concept of Indian Philosophy*, Rome, Università Gregoriana, 1980.

Wagle, Narendra K., 'Hindu–Muslim interactions in medieval Maharashtra', in Sontheimer and Kulke (eds), *Hinduism Reconsidered*, pp. 51–66.

Warnke, Georgia, *Gadamer: Hermeneutics, Tradition and Reason*, Cambridge, Polity Press, 1987.

Wellesley, Lord, *Minute on the Foundation of a College at Fort William*, 10 July 1800, reprinted in M. Martin, *The Despatches: Minutes and Correspondence of the Marquess Wellesley, K.G.; during his Administration in India*, Vol. II, W.H. Allen, 1837.

Wilkins, Charles, *The Bhagvat-Geeta or Dialogues of Kreeshna and Arjoon in 18 Lectures with Notes*, London, C. Nowse, 1785.

Will, Paul J., 'Swami Vivekananda and cultural stereotyping', in N. Smart and B. Srinivasa Murthy (eds), *East–West Encounters in Philosophy and Religion*, Mumbai, Popular Prakashan, Long Beach Publications, 1996, pp. 377–87.

Williams, Paul, 'Non-conceptuality, critical reasoning and religious experience: some Tibetan Buddhist discussions', in Michael McGhee (ed.), *Philosophy, Religion and the Spiritual Life*, Cambridge, Cambridge University Press, 1992, pp. 189–210.

Wilson, Bryan, *Contemporary Transformations of Religion*, Oxford, Oxford University Press, 1976.

Woods, Richard (ed.), *Understanding Mysticism*, London, Athlone Press, 1980.

Young, Robert, *White Mythologies*, London, Routledge, 1990.

Zaehner, R.C. *Mysticism Sacred and Profane*, Oxford, Clarendon Press, 1957.

Index

Abhidharma (Buddhist philosophy)
    151–2
Advaita Vedānta 5, 21, 93, 102–3, 108,
    110, 121, 124–30, 132, 135–42, 144,
    157, 162, 164, 172, 175, 176, 181, 183,
    184, 185, 238n, 240–1n, 242n, 244n
Africa 29, 114, 189, 197, 211, 212
Ahmed, Aijaz 85, 188, 192–3, 214, 229n,
    251n
Alcoff, Linda 214
Almond, Philip 145, 146–7, 148–9, 155,
    243n
Althusser, Louis 192
Alvares, Claude 115
Amitābha Buddha 177–8, 246n
anattāa (Pāli: 'no-abiding-self') 70–1,
    163, 168, 199
Anaxagoras 29
Anderson, Amanda 198
Anglicists 87–8, 89, 102, 133, 154, 255n
Anquetil-Duperron 119–20, 125, 238n
anthropology 5, 6, 47, 54, 187, 213, 217,
    218
Apel, Karl Otto 80
apophatic theology 19, 25; tension
    between visionary mysticism and
    19–21, 221n
Appadurai, Arjun 217, 235n
Aquinas, Thomas 30, 64
Aristotle 29, 30
Ārya Samaj 106, 119, 123
Asad, Talal 10, 12, 49, 57, 61, 82, 210,
    234n
Asaînga 139, 176
Asiatic Society of Bengal 87
Augustine, 15, 25, 29, 30, 64–5, 69, 220n
Aurobindo 69
autonomous individual: myth of 4, 23,
    45, 191–2, 215

Averroës 30
Ayodhyā 98, 213
āyurveda 217

Bacon, Francis 31, 115
Baha'ism 55
Bakhtin, Mikhail 133, 205, 206, 214
Balagangadhara, S. N. 36, 40–1, 222n
Barthes, Roland 65, 73
Baudrillard, Jean 170, 200
Bayly, Christopher A. 103
Bechert, Heinz 71
Bellah, Robert 12, 22, 44, 47–9, 50–2, 54,
    56, 57, 223n
Bengal Renaissance 87, 123, 130
Bengali male: British belief in
    effeminacy of 113–14, 123, 134, 215,
    237n
Benhabib, Seyla 207
Berger, Peter 48–9, 170, 176, 245–6n
Bernard, Theos 137–8
Besant, Annie 86
Bhabha, Homi 4, 86, 152, 202–4, 253n,
    254n
Bhagavad Gītā 105, 120–1, 123, 137,
    154–5, 238n
Bharatiya Janata Party (BJP) 213; *see
    also* nationalism, Hindu
Bhartṛhari 180–1
Bischel, Peter 39
Bishop, Peter 147, 152
Bouyer, Louis 15, 23
Brahma Sūtra 6, 64, 121; *see also*
    Vedānta
brahmanical ideology 98, 101, 102–4,
    123, 143, 144, 158–9, 233–4n, 239n
Brahmanism 108
brahmins 13, 104, 119, 120, 129, 134,
    239n

Brahmo Samaj 106, 123
Bras, Gabriel Le 69
Bṛhadāraṇyaka Upaniṣad 122, 238n,
    240n
Bruno, Giordano 31
Buddha 125, 136, 138, 139, 140, 143,
    144–5, 148, 151, 159, 177–8, 180,
    224n, 225n
Buddhaghosa 23
buddhānusmṛti (mental recollection of
    the Buddha) 177–8
Buddhism 8, 21, 22, 24, 53, 54, 55, 58,
    64, 66, 69, 70–2, 143–60, 172, 181,
    182, 183, 198–9, 211, 225n, 242n,
    243n, 244n, 247n; as mystical 28, 33,
    119, 164, 168, 176, 247–8n;
    colonialism and 3, 143–60;
    Mahāyāna 5, 138, 139, 152, 177–80,
    241n, 242n; Neo-Vedāntic
    interpretation of 93, 108–9, 136,
    138–42, 144, 156–60, 162, 212;
    Protestant 150–3; Sautrāntika 184;
    Theravāda 159, 184; Tibetan 147,
    179–80; Vaibhāṣika 184
Burnouf, Eugene 146, 147–8

Capps, Walter 47
Carrette, Jeremy R. 215–16, 221n, 255n
Certeau, Michel de 7, 16–18, 26, 96, 152,
    187, 201, 202, 207, 253n
Chakrabarty, Dipesh 188–90, 196,
    214–15
Chatterjee, Partha 191–2, 193, 194,
    232n, 235n, 241n, 251n
China 153, 211, 212
Chomsky, Noam 181
Chowdury-Sengupta, Indira 123
Christian, Barbara 256n
Cicero 35, 36, 37
Cixous, Hélène 114, 170
Clarke, Peter 24
Clifford, James 83–5, 86, 227n, 229n
Cloud of Unknowing, The 19–20, 21
Cohn, Bernard 251n
Colebrooke, Henry Thomas 120, 124,
    128, 130, 131, 132, 154, 237n
College of Fort William 130–4, 236n
common-core: mysticism as 8, 156–7,
    162–7, 174, 183; *see also* perennialism
constructivism: Indian forms of 175–84;
    see also social constructivism
cultural isolationism 3, 75, 76–80, 95,
    183, 212, 215, 227n

cultural relativism 3, 75, 81, 94, 169,
    214–15, 227n; *see also* cultural
    isolationism
cultural studies 2, 60; *see also* religious
    studies

D'Costa, Gavin 58
darśana (Sanskrit: 'school of
    philosophy') 137–8
Darwin, Charles 151
Das, Veena 104, 114
Davidson, Donald 95
Deleuze, Gilles 255n
Derrida, Jacques 170, 180, 202, 204, 205,
    207, 253n
Deussen, Paul 128
dGe lugs pa 180, 182
Dhar, Niranjan 130–3, 240n
Dharma: as teachings of the Buddha
    143, 146, 180; Hindu notion of 26,
    109–10
Dharmakīrti 179–80
Dharmapāla 151
Dharmaśāstras 102
Diderot, Denis 118
Dignāga 178–9
Dirks, Nicholas 1, 155, 197, 234n
Dumont, Louis 112, 236n
Dundas, Henry 130
Durkheim, Emile 169–70

Eckhart, Meister 18, 21, 23, 25, 30,
    125–8, 142, 157–8, 162, 172, 184,
    219n
Eliade, Mircea 14, 57, 226n
emic and etic perspectives 1, 183, 212;
    see also reductionism
enlightenment (Sanskrit: *bodhi*) 139,
    179–83
Enlightenment, the 2, 3, 4, 21, 41, 43,
    44–8, 51, 87, 91, 111, 169, 173, 179,
    182, 185, 198–9, 213–14, 214–15,
    226n; opposition of intuition and
    reason 32, 33; public–private
    dichotomy in 12–14, 22–3, 31, 34,
    161; prejudice against prejudice in
    72–3, 171
essentialism 3, 8, 10–12, 68–70, 92, 94,
    110–11, 116, 140, 145–6, 148, 154–5,
    162, 170, 171, 185, 195, 206–7, 210,
    215, 217, 250n; strategic 192, 197–9,
    254n, 219n
Evans, Donald 175, 176

Ezourvedam 121, 202–3, 238n

Fanon, Frantz 205
feminism 2, 4, 170, 212, 213, 218, 254n;
   and Orientalism *see* Orientalism; and
   postmodernism 197–8; and the study
   of mysticism 18–22, 171–2, 182
Ferguson, James 79, 216
Ferro-Luzzi, G. E. 110–11
Feuerbach, Ludwig 169
Feyerband, Paul 91
Figueira, Dorothy 208
Fitzgerald, Timothy 57, 59–60, 67
Forman, Robert 173–4, 175–6
Foucault, Michel 68, 83, 84, 85, 94–5,
   133, 152, 170, 171, 182, 191, 192, 197,
   198, 200–2, 205, 206, 207–9, 228n,
   229n, 230n, 231n, 234n, 250n,
   251–2n, 253n, 255n, 258n
Fox, Richard 86, 134–5, 231n
Frykenberg, R. E. 104, 233n

Gadamer, Hans Georg 2, 43, 72–81, 94,
   95, 116, 170, 208, 217, 226n, 227n,
   228n
Gandhi, Mohandas 51, 69, 86, 93, 98,
   116, 134–5, 213n, 241n
Ganeṣa 110
Gates, Henry Louis Jr. 205
Gauḍapāda 137, 241n
Geertz, Clifford 77, 80
Giddens, Anthony 79
Gimello, Robert 168
Gombrich, Richard 71, 150, 224n
Goody, Jack 43, 65–7, 68–9, 71–2, 225n
Gracia, Jorge 30–1
Gramsci, Antonio 108, 194, 197, 205,
   249n, 251n
Guénon, René 162
Guha, Ranajit 90, 190, 191, 195, 197,
   251n
Gupta, Akhil 79, 216

Habermas, Jürgen 80
Hacker, Paul 129
Halbfass, Wilhelm 77–8, 90, 109–10,
   124, 125, 240–1n
Halhead, Nathaniel Brassey 100
Hallisey, Charles 148–50, 152, 155
Hamilton, Peter 44, 45
Happold, F. C. 162
Haraway, Donna 197
Hardy, Friedhelm 77, 96, 226n

Harris, Ian 247n
Harrison, Peter 97
Hart, Kevin 29–30
Hartsock, Nancy 197, 249n, 253n
Hastings, Warren 132–3, 154
Haynes, Douglas 191
Hegel, G. W. F. 124–5
Heidegger, Martin 72, 226n
Hekman, Susan 115
Herder, J. G. 118, 124
hermeneutics: of Gadamer 2, 43, 72–81,
   226n; mystical 15, 16–17, 23, 38, 122,
   161
Herodotus 26, 29
Hildegard of Bingen 19, 221n
Hindu Marriage Act 99
Hindu nationalism *see* nationalism
Hindu revivalism *see* nationalism
Hinduism 3, 4, 6, 7, 28, 33, 40, 41, 58,
   68–9, 89, 90, 92, 93–4, 96, 98–111,
   116–17, 118–42, 143, 145, 149, 159,
   172, 176, 190, 207, 211, 213, 226n,
   233n, 242n; *see also* mysticism *and*
   Vedānta
Hippocrates 29
history of ideas 1, 6, 8
Hodgson, Brian 146
homogeneity: myth of 3, 68–72, 79, 82,
   89, 98, 100, 103, 106–11, 129–30,
   154–5, 162–3, 185, 188, 189, 195, 196,
   200, 209, 213, 215, 217–8, 257n
humanism 43, 45, 131, 136, 147–8, 169,
   191–2, 197–9, 211, 229n, 254n
Humbert of Romans 70
Huxley, Aldous 162–4, 165, 167
hybridity: notion of *see* Bhabha, Homi
Hypatia 29

Inden, Ronald 44, 90–2, 94–5, 112, 116,
   131, 193, 214, 231n
India 1, 5, 77, 88, 93, 98, 100, 102, 107,
   108, 110, 123, 129, 133, 144, 148,
   154–5, 159, 160, 161, 192, 203, 205,
   206–7, 209, 214, 216, 218; as the
   childhood of humanity 118, 124–5,
   147–8; as the West's other 31–2, 90–1,
   96–7, 99, 111–17, 147, 188–90
Indology 6, 71, 80, 90–2, 120, 124, 144,
   154–5, 187, 209–18
intercultural mimesis 148–53, 156; *see
   also* Orientalism: the role of
   indigenous élites in
Irigaray, Luce 19, 170, 203–4, 254n

International Society for Krishna
Consciousness (ISKCON) 117
Islam 29, 40, 41, 53, 55, 58, 66, 68, 82,
    99, 100, 104, 105, 106, 108, 110, 136,
    140, 146, 164, 176, 196, 199, 212,
    242n, 257n

Jainism 41, 108–9, 140, 145, 212, 257n
JanMohamed, Abdul R. 205, 255n
Jantzen, Grace 9–10, 20, 21, 22, 171–2,
    173, 175, 182, 185
James, William 21–3, 24, 27–8, 33, 157,
    161, 170, 185
Japan 85, 156–7, 158, 159, 160, 230n
John of the Cross 18, 20, 21, 219n
Jones, William 88–9, 102, 113, 119, 120,
    131, 132, 133, 150, 237n, 240n,
    243–4n
Judaism 36, 40, 41, 66, 106, 110, 140,
    167–8, 176
Julian of Norwich 19, 23, 221n
Justin Martyr 15–16, 37

Kālī 166
Kamalaśīla 180
Kant, Immanuel 4, 22, 25, 27, 29–30,
    119, 128, 169, 173–6, 179, 182, 184,
    246n
Katz, Steven 167–9, 171–84, 246n
Kejariwal, O. P. 88
Killingley, Dermot 100
King, Richard 215–16, 221n, 238n,
    241n, 242n, 243n, 244n
King, Sallie 172, 174, 175, 179, 246n
Klein, Anne 182
Klostermaier, Klaus 176–7
Kopf, David 86–9, 92–3, 100, 130, 131,
    154, 230–1n, 255n
Kristeva, Julia 170
Kṛṣṇa 40, 105, 110, 165

Lacan, Jacques 170, 180, 182
Lactantius 36, 37–8
Ladurie, Le Roy 69–70
Larner, Christina 48
Lee, Kyung-Won 205
Leibniz, Gottfried Wilhelm 30
Lele, Jayant 85–6
Lewis, Reina 113
Lipner, Julius 6, 108–9, 110
Locke, John 30
Lopez, Donald Jr. 143, 153–4
Lowe, Lisa 209

Luckmann, Thomas 48, 170, 176,
    245–6n
Ludden, David 95, 107–8, 229n
Luther, Martin 16, 145
Lyotard, Jean-François 170

Macauley, Thomas B. 87, 89–90, 101
McClintock, Anne 215
McCutcheon, Russell T. 57–8, 59, 60,
    220n, 232n
MacNaughten, W. H. 88
Madhyamaka ('Middle Way' school of
    Buddhism) 5, 139, 184
Mahābhārata 120
Mahadevan, T. M. P. 129
Mahāyāna, *see* Buddhism
Mallon, Florencia 251n
Maṇḍana Miśra 128
Māṇḍūkya Kārikā 137, 241n
Marriott, McKim 212, 216–17, 256n,
    257n, 258n
Marshall, Peter 92
Marxism 13, 14, 41, 169, 188, 193–5,
    223n, 240n, 251n
Matilal, Bimal Krishna 199
Mead, G. H. 170
methodological agnosticism 49–50, 52,
    75
methodological atheism 48–9, 52
Milbank, John 42, 44, 50–2, 54
Mill, James 29, 88, 89, 106
Miller, Jane 113
Mitchell, John 113
Moses 37, 118
Müller, Max 100, 122, 128, 150
mutual imbrication: of gender, race,
    class, nationality, etc. 113–16, 123,
    196, 208, 209, 215–6, 257n; of
    religion, culture and power 1, 60–1,
    190–1, 207
Mystic East, the 1–6, 62, 96–8, 123–4,
    125, 127, 141–2, 147, 156, 160, 161–2,
    185
mystical: idea of 2–34, 38, 230n; India as
    93, 96–8; origins of 14–15;
    privatization of 4, 21–8, 30–4, 157,
    161–2, 175, 185–6, 247–8n
mysticism 2–34, 62, 72, 127, 161–86, 211;
    as a Christian category 8, 143–4, 161;
    as a social construction 9–12, 14, 28,
    31–2, 40, 161–2, 171–3, 174, 219n;
    Buddhism as a type of 28, 33, 161;

Hinduism as a type of 3, 4, 24, 28, 33, 92, 118–42, 161, 176
Mysticism East and West (1932) 125–8

Nair, Janaki 201, 249n, 251n
Nandy, Ashis 3, 112, 116, 230n, 241n
nationalism 14, 41, 45, 78–9, 90, 107, 134, 158, 190, 192–3, 206, 212, 218, 227n; Hindu 86, 90, 98, 104–5, 108, 112, 116, 119, 133, 135, 212–13, 232n
Neoplatonism 7, 29, 221n
Neo-Vedānta 69, 103, 105, 108–9, 135–42, 144, 156–7, 162, 163
Neumann, Charles F. 153, 226n, 233n, 243n
new age philosophies 27, 142
Nietzsche, Friedrich 17, 50, 169, 207
Niranjana, Tejaswini 89, 113
Nivedita, Sister 86
non-dualism 152, 179, 181, 247n; *see also* Advaita Vedānta
nostalgia for origins 61, 118, 147–8, 213

Obeyesekere, Gananath 150–1
O'Hanlon, Rosalind 102, 112–13, 114, 191, 194, 206, 229n, 250n, 252n
Ong, Walter 43, 62–3, 65–6, 225n
Onyewuenyi, Innocent 29
Orientalism 3–4, 82–95, 117, 187–218, 229n; affirmative 86, 92, 97, 116, 154, 231n; and feminism 111–16, 215–16, 248n, 249n, 251n, 252n; and Occidentalism 5, 159, 188, 200, 230n; concerned with the West 33, 85, 97, 125, 126–8, 147, 155, 211; heterogeneous and polyphonic nature of 86, 97, 116, 133–5, 155–6, 158–60, 202–3, 205, 206, 231n, 254n, 255n; role of indigenous élites in the development of 98, 102–4, 120, 129, 131, 148–53, 159–60, 206, 234n, 243–4n
Origen 23, 29, 161
Otto, Rudolf 25, 30, 125–8, 156, 167
Oupnek'hat 119–20, 125, 238n

pantheism 37, 124–8, 126
Parmenides 30, 31
Parrish, Steven 207
Parry, Benita 204
Pārvatī 166
Penner, Hans 168, 219n

perennialism 26, 120, 121, 125, 135–42, 156–60, 162–9, 171, 174, 183, 185, 238n, 241–2n, 245n, 248n
Perfection of Wisdom 177–8, 179
Petroff, Elizabeth 18
phenomenology of religion 11, 61, 179
philosophy 1, 12, 54, 124; and the silencing of the mystical 26–34; the mystical and Greek 29
Plato 29, 30, 31, 37, 64
Platonism 16, 31, 92
Plotinus 25, 29, 30, 162
politics of knowledge 1, 10, 88–9, 94, 131, 154–5, 207–9
Pollock, Sheldon 85
Porete, Marguerite 23, 221n
postmodernism 46, 50, 55, 58, 72, 91, 169–71, 197–200, 204, 206, 209, 214, 252n
poststructuralism 4, 6, 92, 149, 169–72, 182, 197–200, 229n, 252n
power/knowledge *see* politics of knowledge
prajñāpāramitā see Perfection of Wisdom
Prakash, Gyan 4, 88, 191, 194–6, 201, 206, 217, 250n, 251n, 252n
Pratyutpanna Sūtra, The 177–8, 246–7n
Protagoras 31
Protestant Buddhism *see* Buddhism
Protestantism 16, 23, 43, 62, 70, 92, 96, 97, 101, 126, 145, 146, 148, 151
Proudfoot, Wayne 168
Pseudo-Dionysius 15, 19, 20, 30, 38
Pye, Michael 211
Pythagoras 29, 30

Rabinow, Paul 5, 187
Radhakrishnan, Sarvepalli 69, 98, 134, 135–6, 139, 141, 144, 156, 157, 162
Radical Orthodoxy 50; *see also* Milbank, John
Rai, Amit 207
Rajneesh, Bhagwan Shree 105
Ram, Kalpana 111–12, 114
Rāma 39, 40, 57, 105
Rāmakṛṣṇa 240n
Rāmakṛṣṇa Mission 106, 117, 141
Rāmānuja 121, 164
Rashtriya Svayamsevak Sangh (RSS) 117
Rastafarianism 55, 58
Ray, Rabindra 216

Redfield, Robert 66
reductionism 13–14, 90–1, 168, 207,
    223n; culturalist 1, 61; materialist 1,
    194–5; secular 13, 45–52, 56
religion: concept of 10, 35–41, 53, 56,
    62, 64–72, 82, 104–7, 111, 143–4,
    145–6, 210–12, 233n; as *sui generis*
    11, 13–14, 57–8, 59–61, 210–11;
    relationship to culture and power 1,
    60–1
religious studies 5, 6, 11, 35, 71–2, 94,
    169, 209–18; and secularism 41–52,
    80; and theology 41–2, 46–7, 53–61;
    as a form of cultural studies 2, 57,
    59–61; Enlightenment roots of 2, 43,
    44–53, 68, 72; iatrogenic effect of
    41–4
Ricoeur, Paul 49
rNying-ma 182
Robbins, Bruce 84, 94
Rocher, Rosane 230n, 233n, 237n, 240n
Romanticism 26–7, 89, 92, 97, 118,
    124–6, 128, 147
Rorty, Richard 80, 91, 170, 226n, 228n
Roy, Rammohun 69, 86, 100, 123, 132,
    134
Rushdie, Salman 189
Russell, Bertrand 32–3
Ryle, Gilbert 77, 80

Said, Edward 3, 4, 33, 44, 82–7, 89, 90,
    94–5, 104, 112–13, 131, 153, 155, 156,
    187, 188, 193, 197, 198, 208–9, 211,
    228n, 229n, 230n, 231n, 250n
Śaivism 109
Saṃdhinirmocana Sūtra 178
Sāṃkhya 164, 181
Sangari, Kumkum 257n
Śaṅkara 6, 23, 25, 121, 124–9, 136–7,
    140, 141, 181, 184, 185, 240n, 241n,
    219n; *see also* Advaita Vedānta
Saraswati Dayānanda 86, 119, 123, 134
Sardar, Ziauddin 200
Sarkar, Sumit 201
Sathya Sai Baba 105
Scheler, Max 170
Schelling, F. W. J. 124, 125, 239n
Schlegel, Friedrich von 118, 124, 125,
    147, 128
Schleiermacher, Friedrich 22, 27
Schneiders, Sandra 17
Schopen, Gregory 43, 71, 225n, 226n
Schopenhauer, Arthur 119–20, 125, 128

Scientology 55
secular rationalism 4, 25, 32, 43, 73, 76,
    80, 91, 169, 214–15, 240n
secularism 4, 13–14, 35, 41–61, 182–3,
    213, 247n, 248n, 257n; Indian 51
Sharf, Robert 156–7, 158, 159–60,
    247–8n
Sheilaism 12, 22
Singh, Jyotsna 131
Sinha, Mrinalini 113–14, 215–16
Śiva 110, 144
Slemon, Stephen 214
Smart, Ninian 20–1, 54, 164, 166, 220n,
    245n
Smith, Bryan K. 213
Smith, Huston 176
Smith, Jonathan Z. 11
Smith, Margaret 7
Smith, Robertson 169
Smith, Wilfred Cantwell 98, 232n
social constructivism 58, 91–2, 167–77,
    197, 245–6n
sociology 2, 13, 35, 47, 48–52, 54, 73, 76,
    169–70, 177, 197, 212, 216–18, 228n,
    257–8n
Socrates 29, 37
Sonnerat, Pierre 121, 238n
Southwold, Martin 70
Spinoza, Baruch 124
Spivak, Gayatri C. 4, 88, 192, 197, 199,
    204, 213, 217, 218, 248n, 249n, 253n,
    254n, 255n
Staal, Frits 144, 164, 222n, 233n
Stace, Walter 164–7
Stietencron, H. von 106, 232n
Stoler, Ann 201
Strachey, John 113
strategic essentialism *see* essentialism
Strenski, Ivan 60, 210–11
Suàrez, Francisco 30
subaltern: notion of 206, 250n, 251n,
    252n, 254n, 255n; responses to élite
    dominance 111, 134–5, 160, 190–6,
    204–5, 209, 241n
Subaltern Studies 4, 190–6, 204–5, 206,
    209, 212, 217, 249n, 251n, 252n
subalternist perspective 120, 135, 152,
    256n
Sufism 142, 176
Sukhāvatī (Pure Land) Sūtras 177,
    246–7n
śūnyatā (Sanskrit: emptiness) 157–8, 184
Suzuki, Daisetz T. 156–60, 163, 185, 207

symbolic realism 48–9, 51, 56, 57, 223n

Tambiah, Stanley 66
Taoism 41, 140, 172, 183, 185
Tauler, Johannes 142
Taylor, Charles 77
Teresa of Avila 20, 23, 165
Tertullian 29, 30
textualism 2, 3, 5–6, 43, 61–72, 82, 88–9, 93, 94, 101–3, 107, 121, 145–7, 148, 150–1, 154–5, 210, 224n, 225n, 226n, 233n
Thapar, Romila 99, 104, 108, 251n
theology 2, 35, 38, 46–7, 50, 53–61, 67, 162, 164, 172, 198, 211; *see also* religious studies
Theosophical Society 120, 137, 141, 156, 162, 231n, 238n
Third World 114–15, 188, 190, 194, 195, 200, 207, 234n
Tibet 147
Tibetan Buddhism *see* Buddhism
Tillich, Paul 25
Tolstoy, Leo 86
Torwesten, Hans 141–2
tradition 172–3, 195; contrasted with modernity 46, 118, 147, 213–14; Gadamer on 73–81, 228n
Transcendental Meditation 105
Tuck, Andrew 74
Turner, Bryan 51, 217–18, 257n, 257–8n
Turner, Denys 221n
Tylor, E. B. 170

Underhill, Evelyn 7
Unificationism 55
Unitarianism 100, 121
Upaniṣads 105, 119–23, 128, 142, 238n, 239n

Vācaspati Miśra 128
Vaid, Sudesh 257n
Vaiṣṇavism 109, 165
Vasubandhu 139
Vedas 105, 106, 109, 118–19, 120, 121, 123, 128, 202, 238n

Vedānta: as Hindu mysticism 3, 4, 6, 69, 102–3, 118–42, 157, 210, 240n; *see also* Advaita Vedānta
Veer, Peter van der 230n, 231n, 233n
Verhelst, Thierry 99
Vico, Giambattista 169
Vidyāraúnya 129
Virgil 37
Viśiṣṭādvaita (Sanskrit: 'non-dualism of the qualified') 121, 164
Vishwa Hindu Parishad (VHP) 40, 117; *see also* nationalism, Hindu
Viṣṇu 144
Vivekānanda, Swāmi 69, 86, 93–4, 98, 123, 134, 144, 185, 207, 242n; perennialism of 51, 135–42, 156–7, 162, 163; *see also* Neo-Vedānta
Voltaire, 121, 202

Warnke, Georgia 73, 74, 226–7n
Washbrook, David 252n
Wellesley, Lord 130–1, 132
Wilkins, Charles 120–1, 132, 133, 136, 154, 238n
Will, Paul J. 159–60
Williams, Paul 180
Williams, Raymond 180
Wilson, Bryan 12–13
Wilson, H. H. 88, 131, 150
Wordsworth 164
world religion 2, 64–72, 82, 94, 98, 159, 162, 163, 213, 228n, 242n; Buddhism as a 143–60, 248n; Hinduism as a 3, 93, 100, 106–8, 117, 135–42, 242n

Yoga 5, 21, 22, 64, 172, 175, 176, 181, 183
Yogācāra ('Practice of Yoga' School of Buddhism) 5, 139, 178–80, 184
Young, Robert 253n, 254n

Zaehner, Richard C. 164–5
Zen Buddhism 142, 156–8, 159, 160, 163, 185, 207